Economics for Business

Economics for Business

Andrew Gillespie

OXFORD

UNIVERSITY PRESS

OXFORD

UNIVERSITY PRESS

Great Clarendon Street, Oxford, OX2 6DP,
United Kingdom

Oxford University Press is a department of the University of Oxford.
It furthers the University's objective of excellence in research, scholarship,
and education by publishing worldwide. Oxford is a registered trade mark of
Oxford University Press in the UK and in certain other countries

Published in the United States of America by Oxford University Press
198 Madison Avenue, New York, NY 10016, United States of America

British Library Cataloguing in Publication Data

Data available

Library of Congress Control Number: 2018954271

ISBN 978–0–19–878603–0

Printed in Great Britain by
Bell & Bain Ltd., Glasgow

Preface

Welcome to what is essentially the third edition of *Business Economics*. We were delighted with the response to the first two editions, but rather than simply refresh the case studies for this edition we decided to look again at what you really needed. We talked extensively to lecturers about their courses and what students wanted, and it was clear that what was needed was an even greater focus on how economic theory is of value to people in business. Rather than having an economics book adapted for business, you wanted a book written *about* business using relevant economic concepts and theory. The result is that we decided not just to update the second edition but to develop the book significantly so that it can meet your needs more effectively. We have looked at economics through the eyes of someone in business and considered how economic thought might affect business decisions. We have restructured the book and rewritten it significantly so that it is fully tailored to your needs. We think you will find it even more relevant and engaging than the earlier editions.

Two key aims of this book have always been to show why understanding economics is important in business, and to make studying economics accessible. We have continued with this approach and hope that when reading this book you will see why economics is relevant to you, even if you don't want to be an economist, and how economic theory would be important to managers.

A variety of learning features, many of them new to this edition, are supplied in each chapter to help you master the material.

- **Why do I need to know about . . .?**: at the start of every chapter we have created a scenario to help you appreciate why this topic is important in business.

- **Business case**: these cases are real-life business situations that raise a number of issues related to the topic in the chapter. We put the case at the start of the chapter, with some questions so that you can appreciate what it is you are trying to understand in this chapter. As the chapter progresses you gain the knowledge and skills to answer the questions given at the start. We also have extension questions at the end of the chapter to take your understanding of this issue even further, now you have studied it.

- **Management task**: in this feature we give you examples of the decisions that managers might have to make using the theory we have covered, and we ask for your view of what should be done in the given situation. This feature helps you to relate what you are studying to the types of decision you might make in business.

- **Business insight**: this feature includes insights into real business situations and gives you the opportunity to analyse this using the theory you have been learning.

- **Analysing the business data**: provides you with economic data in a variety of forms, such as tables and charts, and allows you to analyse these with the skills you have developed.

- **Key concepts**: the key issues covered in the chapter are clearly defined and flagged for you throughout the chapter.

- **Doing the business maths**: allows you to apply your quantitative skills. Answers to the problems are supplied at the end of the book.

- **Quick check**: questions allow you to review what you have been reading and quickly test your understanding—for example, through multiple choice or true/false questions. The answers are supplied at the end of the book.

- **Read more**: gives you details of sources you might find interesting to take your learning further.

- **Key learning points**: at the end of the chapter summarize what you have learned.

- **Quick questions**: give you an opportunity to review the whole chapter through some short questions.

Contents

Detailed contents

How to use this book

Why do I need to know about...?

Each chapter opens with a typical scenario you might face in the world of work which demonstrates why this topic is important and relevant to your future career.

Learning objectives

A bulleted list of the learning outcomes contextualises the chapter's main objectives. This feature can help you plan your revision to ensure you identify and cover all of the key concepts.

Business case

A topical, real-life business situation which raises a number of key issues relevant to the chapter is included at the beginning of each chapter, with accompanying questions so that you can identify what it is you are trying to understand in the chapter, and see how it applies in practice.

Key concepts

Are flagged and clearly defined where they first appear in the text, providing a practical way for you to check your understanding.

Business insight

Frequent insights into real business situations are included throughout the book to illustrate how theory works in practice. Accompanying questions encourage you to develop your analytical skills.

Management task

In this feature we give you examples of the decisions that managers might have to make using the theory we have covered, and we ask for your view of what should be done in the given situation. This feature helps you to relate what you are studying to the types of decisions you might make in business.

BUSINESS CASE QUESTIONS: CAN YOU NOW ANS

1. Why do you think Amazon has set an objective of growth?
2. How might this objective affect its decisions within the busine

Business case questions: can you now answer...

As the chapter progresses, you gain the knowledge and skills you need to confidently answer the business case questions included throughout the chapter. These questions refer back to the opening case to consistently reinforce the main concepts.

Year	Return on capita
2017	0.55%
2016	0.67%
2015	−26.13%
2014	7.85%

Analysing the business data

We provide you with the type of data you will come across in your business career, and this supports you in analysing this information with the skills you have developed.

2.2 DOING THE BUSINESS MATHS

To an accountant, the 'costs' incurred by a business means the v
up in a given period. Often this requires assumptions to be made
have been used. These assumptions are stated in the company a
assumptions will affect the profits declared for any given period.

Doing the business maths

Each chapter provides opportunities for you to practice and apply your quantitative skills to common business situations. Answers to the problems are supplied at the end of the book.

READ MORE

Milton Friedman was a very well known writer about the benefit
famously wrote that 'the business of business is business'. You c
benefits of the free market here:

Read more

This feature points you to sources of further information which allow you to take your learning further.

6.4 QUICK CHECK

For each of the following statements, say whether it is true or fal

a. If men get paid more than women this means there must be
b. Labour productivity will affect the demand for labour.

Quick check

These multiple choice and true / false questions allow you to review what you have been reading and quickly test your understanding as you go along.

KEY LEARNING POINTS

- Competitive markets can lead to efficiency and innovation.
- Markets can lead to many failures and imperfections.
- Some products may be over- or under-produced in a free ma
- Governments may intervene in several ways, such as legis

Key learning points

A bulleted list at the end of each chapter enables you to check your progress against the learning outcomes for each chapter.

BUSINESS CASE EXTENSION QUESTIONS

1. Visit the Amazon website, find Amazon's annual report and re
   the company's activities by the chief executive. What does sh
   issues in the business environment that have influenced Ama

Business case extension questions

Each chapter ends with extension questions to the opening business case; allowing you to take your understanding of the topic even further, now you have studied it.

QUICK QUESTIONS

1. What is meant by a public good?
2. How does a negative production externality affect a market?
3. How does information asymmetry distort a market?
4. How might monopoly power distort a market?

Quick questions

Give you an opportunity to review and quickly assess your understanding of the whole chapter

Online Resources

This book is accompanied by a wealth of online resources, providing students and registered lecturers with ready-to-use teaching and learning resources.
www.oup.com/uk/gillespie-busecon/

For students

Additional short cases

> **Additional case study: Government intervention**
>
> The price of raw sugar recently reached its highest level since 1981 due to problems with supply. Historically, raw sugar has traded at between 10 and 12 US cents per pound on the New York Board of Trade. But the price increased to over 18 cents last month.
>
> Growing demand in Brazil for sugar to be turned into ethanol for fuel, coupled with a sharp fall in Indian production have both been factors in the price increase.
>
> Sugar production in India for 2008-09 fell 45% year-on-year due to less rain in the monsoon season damaging a number of agricultural crops.

Extra case studies help highlight how economic concepts can be applied to real business situations.

Sample essays

> 1. To what extent is the economy likely to be the key external factor determining the success of businesses?
>
> *Answer may include:*
>
> The external environment of business includes the macro environment and the competitive environment. The macro environment includes: Political, Economic, Social, Technological, Environmental and Legal factors, The competitive environment includes suppliers, distributors, buyers, competitors and substitutes.

Essay questions and suggested answers provide you with guidance on how to tackle essay-writing.

Self-test questions

> What is meant by opportunity cost?
> ○ The cost of producing
> ○ The cost of producing and marketing
> ○ The cost of the next best alternative
> ○ The cost of borrowing money
>
> Which of the following statements about resources in an economy is true?
> ○ Resources in an economy are unlimited

Provide a quick and easy way to test your understanding, with instant feedback.

Library of video and podcast links

> Demand
> UC Berkeley
> http://www.youtube.com/watch?v=ZR22S6CEbwk
>
> Deriving demand curves
> http://ocw.mit.edu/courses/economics/14-01sc-principles-of-microeconomics-fall-2011/unit-2-consumer-theory/deriving-demand-curves/
>
> Consumer choice
> http://www.youtube.com/watch?v=VNhqKlOWh9U

A curated list of links to topical videos and podcasts from key academics and practitioners.

Visual walkthroughs

Mini tutorials by Andrew Gillespie on some of the trickier concepts discussed in the book.

Jobwatch

Annotated job adverts which identify the key skills you will require for a particular job, and how to demonstrate them.

For registered lecturers

PowerPoint slides

A suite of customizable PowerPoint slides which can be used in lectures or printed as handouts, and can be easily adapted to suit your teaching style.

Case study teaching notes

Notes and guide answers for each chapter's opening case.

Group exercises

A range of more detailed, workshop-based activities that students can complete prior to and during tutorials.

Test bank

A wealth of additional multiple choice questions that can be customised to meet your teaching needs.

Acknowledgements

Many thanks to everyone at OUP, especially Kat Rylance and Joe Matthews, and to Lucy Metzger (copy-editor) for all their support, tolerance, and help in developing this latest edition.

Seth, Romily, Clemency. You shine.

Business insight features

What is a business?

WHY DO I NEED TO KNOW WHAT A BUSINESS IS?

You have been asked to invest in a business. You would become a shareholder. The current share price is £2.50. You are not sure whether to invest at all or, if you do go ahead, how much to spend. Can you take the risk? Is it worth getting involved in the first place? Will you able to influence anything anyway?

The company is a social media business. It is only a few years old and is already going public and opening up to outside investors. It has been very high-profile, and some have called it the new Snapchat. This is what caught your eye, plus the fact one of your friends' relations is a manager in the business, although you have no idea what she actually does. You are not quite sure why the company has gone public or what differences it might make—is it a good sign or a bad one?

There are several different forms of business, including public limited companies. These have different forms of legal structure and ownership. In this chapter we examine these different forms and also consider the role of managers within these organizations.

BY THE END OF THIS CHAPTER YOU WILL BE ABLE TO . . .

- explain the role of a manager
- distinguish between different business legal forms
- distinguish between a private limited company (ltd) and a public limited company (plc)

BUSINESS CASE

The priorities and targets of a business, and the way that things are done within it (which is its culture), can depend on who owns it. Changes in ownership can affect the way that decisions are made and what managers and employees value. Bringing outside investors to a business may raise finance, but the objectives and values of these investors may be different from those of the original owners of the business.

Facebook, the social media company, is known for its 'hacker' culture; build things, try them, and if they don't work just start again. One of the company's favourite sayings is 'If you're not breaking things, you're probably not moving fast enough.'

The founder, Mark Zuckerberg, created the company 'to make the world more open and connected'. Its headquarters in Menlo Park, California, looks and feels like a large university campus. On site there you will find small team-based projects, frequent hackathons, open bars, and free food. The idea is to create an environment where employees are more likely to collaborate and come up with innovative ideas.

In 2012 Facebook became a public limited company, bringing in outside investors. Some analysts worried that Facebook would not be able to retain its hacker culture. However, Zuckerberg retained 57 per cent of the votes, which meant he kept a tight control on the development of the business.

BUSINESS CASE QUESTIONS

This chapter will help you answer the following questions.

1. What is the difference between a company and other forms of business?
2. What is the difference between a private and a public limited company?
3. Why would a business want to become a public limited company?
4. How does Facebook create value for its customers?
5. What do you think the managers of Facebook do?

Managing a business

You have just been appointed as the managing director of a business. So, what does your new job actually involve? The answer is that you are managing a collection of individuals that you hope to direct towards a shared goal—the goal you were appointed to achieve. Typically, the overall goal of a business is linked to profit. You want the people who work for you to work together and help the business to achieve this. This means you want the revenue from your business to be greater than the costs. You need to control the employees' efforts and performance to ensure that goal that has been set is achieved. According to Rosemary Stewart, management is about 'getting things done through others'.

READ MORE

Stewart, R. (2012), *The Reality of Management*, Hoboken, NJ: Taylor and Francis.

KEY CONCEPT

Profit is measured by revenue minus costs.

The features of a business are therefore that it involves:

- a group of individuals working together
- shared goals
- managed performance

What are your employees busy doing?

Although the precise shapes and forms of businesses can be very different, as can the precise nature of the work that employees do, there are certain activities that occur within any form of business (see Figure 1.1).

- Marketing activities: the marketing function forms the link between the business and customers. It enables the business to understand the needs and wants of the market, to decide which customers to target, and to develop an offering that is competitive. Marketing will also involve decisions about the communication of information about the product, its pricing, and its distribution.

- Operations activities: these involve managing the actual process of providing the goods and services. For example, operations might involve ordering stock, managing the production process, maintaining quality, and investing in research and development of new products.

- Financial activities: these will be monitoring and recording the value of all transactions. They will be helping managers assess the financial implications of any decision made and decide on which investments to make in the future.

- Human resource activities: these will involve recruiting and training staff, rewarding them appropriately, and managing their role in the operations process.

These different functions may be separate specialist departments in some organizations, or in the case of a one-person business they may all be undertaken by the owner.

Figure 1.1 The functions of a business

MANAGEMENT TASK

You have organized your staff into specialist departments. Explain why you think this is a good idea.

One danger of having specialist functions is that they may operate in 'silos'. What do you think this means? What actions would you take to avoid this?

Legal forms of business

There are several different legal forms that a business might have. The principal ones are a sole proprietor, a partnership, and a company.

Sole proprietor

This is where an individual runs a business for themselves. The sole proprietor, also called a sole trader, owns the business and is legally responsible for its activities. This is an attractive form of business in that it does not need to be registered in order to be established and does not require specific legal documents to create the business. As a sole proprietor, you are the owner and the manager.

Partnership

This is where two or more people share ownership and profits of a business; they generally have unlimited liability (although limited liability partnerships do exist). The value of this form of business over a sole trader arrangement is that the partners can share ideas, finance, and workload. In some cases, different partners will special-ize in different parts of the business (for example, legal partners who are experts in different areas of the law). The disadvantage is that you are relying on others and are legally responsible for their actions.

Both sole proprietors and standard partnerships have unlimited liability. This means there is no difference in law between your personal assets and those of the business; if used, for example, all your own assets are at risk. By comparison, the owners of a company have limited liability.

Company

A company has its own legal identity. Individuals set up a company and are its shareholders (investors). Typically, there is one vote per share held, but the precise rights and powers attached to each share may be defined in the company's rules. The appeal of setting up a company is that shareholders have limited liability; this means that there is a limit to their risk. If, for example, you invest £100 into a company, this money could be lost but all the rest of your personal assets are safe. The company's funds are at risk, but these are different from the personal assets of the investors. Limited liability is essential to business. It enables businesses to raise funds from selling shares. Investors are willing to put money into a company, even if they are not entirely sure about every aspect of its operations, because they know there is a limit to the risk. To be registered and to operate as company the owners must produce annual accounts that are audited by independent accountants. This, in theory, provides some protection for investors. There are different forms of companies. Some are private, which means that their shares are not traded to the general public. In a public limited company the shares are widely available and bought and sold each day.

Private limited companies in the UK have 'ltd' after their name. Restrictions can be made on who owns these shares and who they are sold to. Family companies, for example, might be private limited companies, and the rules of the company might ensure that shares stay within the family. By comparison, restrictions cannot be placed on the sale of shares of public limited companies. These shares can be advertised and sold easily to others. They are often traded on a stock exchange.

By creating a company it is possible to have specialist managers who run the business, financed by investors who do not necessarily get involved day to day. This allows great managers to raise the finance to run an organization, while those with money who might not be great managers let others control the business on their behalf. This has many benefits—without limited liability investors would not dare to invest because they would be risking all their personal assets, and without limited liability we would need people with money to also be great managers for businesses to be successful. With limited liability people can specialize in the area that plays to their strengths.

However, it may create problems that those running the business are not the same people as the owners. This is known as the principal–agent problem. The principal is the owners and the managers are their agents. The danger arises from the fact that the managers know far more about the day-to-day business than the owners. The managers may therefore keep some information from the owners that they do not want them to know and/or may pursue their own objectives rather than the objectives of the owners. For example, managers may argue that a particular acquisition of a competitor is critical to the business when in fact it is driven by their own ego. Owners must therefore set in place systems to oversee the management of what is their business. The process of managing the managers is known as 'corporate governance'. There are often thousands of investors in a public limited company. They elect the board of directors to represent them (typically 10 or 12 people) and oversee the senior managers. This is part of the process of corporate governance, and the board of directors are responsible for managers' actions.

1. What is the difference between a company and other forms of business?
2. What is the difference between a private and a public limited company?
3. Why would a business want to become a public limited company?
4. Why, and how, might the culture of Facebook have changed with more outside investors?

MANAGEMENT TASK

You have been running your own cleaning business from home for the last few years. It has gone well, and you are now about to rent storage units and office space. You want to expand your business. Is now the time to set up a company, do you think?

1.1 QUICK CHECK

For each of the following statements, say whether it is true or false.

a. The owners of a private and a public company have limited liability.
b. A sole trader has unlimited liability.
c. The owners of a company must be the managers.

KEY CONCEPTS

Corporate governance refers to the systems by which companies are directed and controlled. Boards of directors are ultimately responsible for the governance of their companies.

Limited liability means that the risk for investors is limited to the amount invested; their personal assets are separate from the assets of the business.

ANALYSING THE BUSINESS DATA

Sole proprietorships are the most common legal form in the UK. Companies account for around a third of private sector businesses. Figure 1.2 shows the proportions of businesses with and without employees at the start of 2017.

Figure 1.2 Number of businesses in the UK private sector with and without employees, by legal status, start of 2017

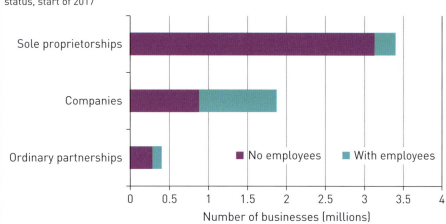

Number of businesses (millions)

Source: www.ons.gov.uk/businessindustryandtrade/business/activitysizeandlocation/bulletins/ukbusinessactivitysizeandlocation/2017.

1. Approximately what proportion of businesses in the UK at the start of 2017 were sole proprietorships?

2. Why do you think such a large proportion of businesses are sole proprietors?

RESEARCH TASK

Research a business that is going public (this is sometimes called an 'initial public offering'—an IPO). Analyse the reasons for this IPO.

MANAGEMENT TASK

You have been running your own management consultancy business as a sole proprietor for the last few years. You are considering creating a private limited company. What factors might you take into account before deciding whether this is the right decision?

Managing the transformation process

As a manager you are overseeing the transformation of inputs into outputs. Your aim is to create value while doing this: that is, to ensure the value of the final products is greater than the value of the inputs used up. The transformation can take many different forms. For example, you may be:

- moving items or people from A to B, e.g. a haulage business or airline
- creating beauty, e.g. a hairdresser or cosmetic surgeon
- producing entertainment, e.g. for TV, a theatre company, or a music label
- helping others do what they do better, e.g. a consultant or financial advisor

If the transformation is in the extractive industries, such as farming and oil extraction, you are operating in the primary sector. If the process produces manufactured items, you are in the secondary sector. If you produce services (intangibles), you are in the tertiary sector. Most of UK business is in the tertiary sector, such as financial services and education.

KEY CONCEPTS

The **primary sector** refers to extractive industries, the **secondary sector** turns raw materials into finished products, and the **tertiary sector** refers to services.

Managing the transformation process involves management of the supply chain as well as the actual process.

- Controlling the supply chain means, for example, choosing whether to produce items yourself or buy them in, where to source supplies from, which suppliers to use, and what terms and conditions to negotiate for payment. These types of decisions will determine whether you get the supplies you need when you need them.
- Managing the process itself means, for example, deciding where to produce, what systems and processes to use, and how to organize what is done when.

MANAGEMENT TASK

You are the chancellor of a university. You are being interviewed tomorrow and have to justify your government funding.

a. Explain how your organization creates value and how you might measure this.

b. Explain the benefits your university brings to the economy.

BUSINESS CASE QUESTIONS: CAN YOU NOW ANSWER . . .

How does Facebook create value for its customers?

What do managers do?

The role of a manager has many aspects to it, summed up in Figure 1.3. She should be scanning the environment now and, more importantly, anticipating possible future changes, in order to plan what is to be done next. Planning is key to provide a focus for people on what they should be doing. Getting the right plan is vital to the success of the business. Turn left when you should have turned right and you have a problem. This is particularly true with major decisions, because they can be difficult to reverse once implemented.

Figure 1.3 What does a manager do?

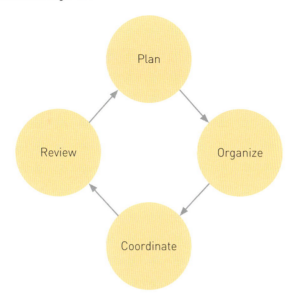

Part of this scanning should cover the business environment. This can be divided into two components.

- The micro or immediate environment includes individuals and organizations that a business has direct and regular interaction with, such as rivals, suppliers, and distributors.

- The macro environment includes factors which affect a business but which it cannot easily influence, such as government legislation, social changes, and developments in technology. One important set of factors in the macro environment is economic. Economic factors that influence the success of a business include the value of the country's currency (exchange rate), the cost of borrowing money (interest rate), and the average income of citizens in the country. Changes in these economic factors will influence the costs and availability of resources, the likely target markets and the prices that can be charged.

Managers must analyse the business environment to determine the strategy or direction the organization is heading in and how it would best compete.

As well as setting the overall direction, business managers need to organize the resources required such as the staff, physical space, equipment, and supplies. This process is not necessarily sequential, in that the resources available will clearly influence the plan in the first place.

Once the resources are organized—such as the right people employed and trained, the right equipment and systems in place—managers need to coordinate the implementation of the plan.

As work continues, managers need to review the progress of the plan. They will have set key indicators of performance and will need to assess whether everything is on target, and what actions to take next. They will review whether what has happened was what was intended, and what targets to set next time around. Future plans will be affected by past experiences.

1.2 QUICK CHECK

Which of the following would you say are in the micro environment of a business, and which in the macro environment?

a. Suppliers

b. Demographic factors

c. Customers

d. New legislation

e. Changes in the exchange rate

f. Competitors

The precise activities of a manager will depend on which area of the business they are focused on and the level they are at. For example, junior managers may concentrate on supervising and controlling subordinates and getting a job done; more senior managers may be more concerned with strategic planning.

The economy and the transformation process

As a business, you are one part of the economy as a whole. The chances are that you are a global business buying materials from abroad and trading overseas; this means you are a small part of the global economy. The decisions you make will have a ripple effect—throughout your local economy, the national economy, and the global economy. For example, your decision to use one supplier rather than another will affect the supplier's business, the staff who work for them, and the businesses who in turn supply them. Your decisions to locate in one area rather than another will affect the regions involved, their economies, and the businesses linked to them. At the same time you will be affected by the decisions of other businesses. Their decisions will affect the demand in your markets, the costs of your resources, and the availability of supplies. You will also be affected by decisions of the government, which will influence factors such as the ease of trade, the conditions of trade, and market conditions.

As a manager you need to understand the economy because it will affect the market for your inputs and the market for your outputs. The economy may be analysed in terms of what is happening locally, nationally, and globally.

- Locally—for example, in your city or region—there may be specific issues such as labour shortages or high land prices.

- Nationally, there are factors that affect the UK as a whole, such as the government's policy on taxation.

- Globally, there are factors affecting the world economy, such as trading agreements between countries.

YOU, THE MANAGER

You have scheduled a meeting with your senior managers later this week to discuss the position of your business and the opportunities and threats it faces. Explain the three key issues that businesses are facing at the moment in (a) the local economy, (b) the UK economy, and (c) the global economy.

1.1 BUSINESS INSIGHT: LOCATING IN FRANKFURT

Political and economic conditions will affect business decisions. For example, in recent years the UK has been negotiating to leave the European Union (EU). Trade between the UK and EU member countries could become more difficult as a result. This possibility has led to some businesses considering where they want to be based. A number of firms have moved offices, or are threatening to move from the UK, to be based in countries that are staying in the EU.

Frankfurt has been home to around 1 million citizens for many years, but the number is now growing as several UK banks have announced they are relocating there from the City of London. These banks, concerned about what would happen if the UK left the EU, decided they needed to plan for an unfavourable outcome and relocate some of their operations to within the EU.

According to a BBC report from August 2017:

> Morgan Stanley, Citigroup and Standard Chartered are among those who have chosen Frankfurt as their new European base, while others such as Goldman Sachs and UBS have promised to move thousands of jobs to the German hub.
>
> Predictions for the number of bankers set to descend on Frankfurt vary wildly, from tens of thousands, up to 100,000.

This has led to significant building of office space in Frankfurt, with plans to build 20 more skyscrapers.

Frankfurt is appealing for many reasons. It has a large English-speaking population. It has good transport connections and is a safe and attractive city for those looking to move. Its time zone is favourable to bankers, allowing contact with Asian markets in the morning and the US in the evening. And the appeal also lies in the price. Office space in Frankfurt costs about 38.50 euros (£35) per square metre per month, roughly half the cost of London office space. A final factor is convenience—many banks already have a presence in Frankfurt and can simply expand.

Source: www.bbc.co.uk/news/business-41026575

Question

What factors do you think might prevent businesses from relocating from London to Frankfurt?

ANALYSING THE BUSINESS DATA

Figure 1.4 Number of businesses in the UK private sector per 10,000 adults, UK region and country, start of 2017

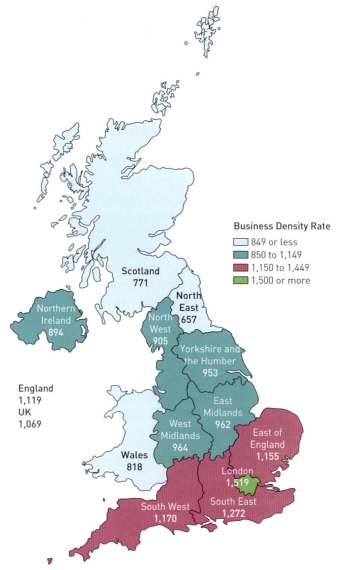

Business Density Rate

- 849 or less
- 850 to 1,149
- 1,150 to 1,449
- 1,500 or more

Scotland
771

North East 657

Northern Ireland
894

North West
905

Yorkshire and the Humber
953

England
1,119
UK
1,069

East Midlands
962

West Midlands
964

East of England
1,155

Wales
818

London
1,519

South West
1,170

South East
1,272

Source: Business Population Estimates www.gov.uk/government/uploads/system/uploads/attachment_data/file/663235/bpe_2017_statistical_release.pdf. Contains public sector information licensed under the Open Government Licence v3.0.

What factors do you think might affect the density of businesses in different parts of the UK (shown in Figure 1.4)?

ANALYSING THE BUSINESS DATA

Table 1.1 Number of business enterprises per country, total and by number of employees

Country	Total no. of enterprises	Breakdown by no. of employees				
		0–9	10–19	20–49	50–249	Over 250
Germany	205,028	131,323	36,624	16,281	16,464	4,336
Greece	63,890	59,886	2,150	1,180	563	111
Italy	389,317	321,837	39,159	18,771	8,338	1,212
Luxembourg	786	481	99	99	83	24
Norway	17,141	13,915	1,354	1,089	663	120
Poland	187,374	164,535	7,768	7,289	6,193	1,589
Turkey	335,311	305,768	0	18,037	9,665	1,841
USA	341,912	229,045	46,635	37,495	23,065	5,672
Romania	48,405	34,974	5,014	4,495	3,147	775

Source: data.oecd.org/entrepreneur/enterprises-by-business-size.htm#indicator-chart

Table 1.1 shows the total number of business enterprises in nine countries in 2015, analysed by number of employees.

Question

1. Why do you think the total number of businesses varies between countries?
2. Discuss the significance of the data in terms of numbers of employees (a) within countries and (b) between countries.

RESEARCH TASK

Research the number of recent startups in your economy. Produce a report on the factors that are likely to influence the number of startups and their chances of survival.

The roles of a manager

Although each individual management job may have its specific demands, objectives, and areas of control, there are some aspects that management jobs may have in common to some degree. According to the management writer Henry Mintzberg, a manager has several roles (Figure 1.5).

- **A manager is a source of information.** For example, she will gather information on the work being done, she will communicate information to those within the organization, and she will act as a spokesperson representing the business.

Figure 1.5 Mintzberg's model

- **A manager works with others: this is an interpersonal role.** She will be regarded as the figurehead of the business, she will be the leader setting out the vision and strategy, and she will liaise between different groups within the organization.
- **A manager is a decision maker.** She will solve disputes, identify new opportunities, allocate resources, and negotiate to defend the interests of the business.

The relative importance of these roles will vary from time to time, and according to the level of management and the precise job of the manager being considered.

READ MORE

If you would like to learn more about the role of a manager, you can read

Mintzberg, H. (1973), *The Nature of Managerial Work*, New York: Harper & Row.

MANAGEMENT TASK

You have worked your way up from being the team manager of a particular shift in a retail outlet to regional sales manager and now chief executive. Although you have always been a manager, your role has changed as you have been promoted. Explain how you think the relative balance of your different roles, as named in Mintzberg's model, have changed as you have been promoted.

Why managers and economists have a lot in common

Problem solving

Managers have to assess the best way of solving problems. For example, in order to boost profits, should the focus be on increasing revenue? Or cutting costs? Managers will have to weigh up the alternatives and make a judgement on what is 'right' for the business. Economists also have to make decisions. If we think people are drinking too much alcohol, should we tax alcohol? Subsidize non-alcoholic drinks? Or invest more in education? Economists will consider how best to resolve an issue given the resources they have. Economic policy involves developing ways of solving economic problems. Politicians who decide on what economic policy to pursue will be judged via the ballot box. Managers will be judged on the performance of their company, which will affect their rewards and whether they keep their jobs.

Data analysis

In terms of how managers make decisions there are again similarities with economists. To make decisions managers will need data. They will gather information to understand the possible causes of any problem and ways in which it might be solved. Economists also analyse data to understand how different elements of the economy work and are related to each in order to come up with better policy decisions.

Limited resources

Economics is about analysing how the limited resources in an economy (such as land, labour, capital, and entrepreneurship) are allocated given the unlimited demands of consumers. Given the scarcity of resources but the unlimited wants, choices have to be made. For example, an economy cannot produce more of everything given the resources available. The government, on behalf of the people, must decide how best to use these resources—for example, how much resource to direct to health, education, or defence. Even within an area such as health care, decisions have to be made about how to use scarce resources. Should the focus be on mental health? Cancer? Our resources are limited. Managers also have limited resources (for example, limited time, limited staff, and limited equipment) and have to decide how best to allocate these. What is the priority? In what order should tasks be completed? Managers, like economists, have to understand that choices must be made and have to consider how best to make those choices.

KEY CONCEPT

Resources are factors of production such as land, labour, capital, and entrepreneurship that are used in the transformation process.

Short- and long-term demands

Managers will be juggling short- and long-term demands. A common issue in the UK is that business owners often push for short-term rewards and this means there are insufficient funds for the long term. However, managers themselves may be guilty of a short-termist view. This is because they may be looking to advance their own careers. Given that managers may change their jobs fairly frequently, this means they are particularly interested in projects that generate fairly quick returns. Longer investments may be less appealing because the returns may arrive after the manager has moved on to a new role.

Model-building

Managers have to anticipate demand and costs. To do this, they build models in which they make various assumptions, notably about relationships such as the link between income changes and demand. Economists also build models—of the economy. These models also make a variety of assumptions: for example, about the ease of entry and exit into a market and the impact of price on quantity demanded and supplied. Using these models, economists can predict the effect of changes in the economy: for example, they can predict the effect on price and quantity of a change in demand. The model may not exactly reflect reality but may help to anticipate the outcomes that occur. Of course, economists will argue about the nature of their models and the assumptions made. If the outcomes that occur do not match those predicted by the model, economists will review and debate why the model was wrong and try and adjust it accordingly. Models provide useful simplications of the real world; however, they do need to be reviewed because there may be changes in behaviour or in the environment that mean the model needs to be adjusted. Similarly, managers will continually review the outcomes of the business relative to the plan, and will adjust polices if the business is not meeting targets.

Economists are also very interested in the time period being considered. Conditions in the short term may be very different from conditions in the long term, for example. In economics we often look at the short term in markets where there are an existing number of providers and compare this to the long term, when we assume it is possible for businesses to enter or leave. This means the structure of the industry can change over time. Short- and long-term issues also arise in considerations about how resources in an economy should, or could, be allocated. For example, there is a danger that individuals will focus on consuming as much as they can now and not plan enough for the future. This may mean that the government will want to intervene to ensure that more resources are allocated to investment for the future rather than being consumed today.

READ MORE

Peter Drucker was one of the great writers on management. To find out more about what managers actually do, you might want to read

Drucker, P.F. (1954), *The Practice of Management*, New York: Harper.

MANAGEMENT TASK

Your shareholders want more of the profits paid out now in dividends. You want to retain more of them, believing this is in the shareholders' best interests. Explain to your investors why you believe this.

BUSINESS CASE QUESTIONS: CAN YOU NOW ANSWER . . .

What do you think the managers of Facebook do?

How might economists and managers approach problems differently?

Managers will be juggling many constraints when making a decision. They will have many different stakeholders involved, such as employees, customers, suppliers, investors, and the local community. To keep all these groups happy, a manager may not be able to focus purely on profit. Managers' decisions may focus on financial factors but are also likely to include a range of other factors less easy to quantify, such as the impact of a decision on employee morale or on the company's brand. Economists are likely to concentrate on the measurable costs and revenues. The economist will want to identify the likely returns on any project; she will want all aspects of a project measured in financial terms.

READ MORE

If you want to know more about how economists can help managers make better decisions, you could read

Casson, J.J. (1996), 'The Role of Business Economists in Business Planning', *Business Economics* Vol. 31, No. 3 (July), pp. 45–9.

   This article highlights the value that economists can add to decision making but also the fact that their skills are often not fully utilized.

1.3 QUICK CHECK

For each of the following statements, say whether it is true or false.

a.   There are unlimited resources in an economy.

b.   Economic models fully reflect reality.

c.   The resources of business are goods and services.

d.   A company is owned by its managers.

KEY CONCEPT

Short-termism occurs when decision makers focus on relatively short-term rewards rather than planning for the longer term.

● ●

SUMMARY

There are several different legal forms of business which have their own characteristics and features. Most businesses in the UK are sole proprietorships—individuals set up and run their own businesses. In some cases they take on partners. In other cases they create a separate legal identity called a company. A company provides limited liability, which makes it more attractive to investors. This enables there to be managers who specialize in running the businesses financed by investors. Managers have several roles including informational, interpersonal, and decision-making activities. Managers, like economists, have to understand how best to use limited resources to achieve their objectives.

KEY LEARNING POINTS

- There are different forms of business you can choose from, such as a sole proprietorship, partnership, or company.
- Limited liability means there is a limit to your financial risk if you invest in a company.
- Managers' roles include informational, interpersonal, and decision-making activities.
- Managers and economists are problem solvers.
- There may be pressure on managers to be short-termist in their thinking.
- Economic models do not necessarily reflect reality—they are a simplification of it.
- Economic models can be used to anticipate outcomes and estimate the effects of changes in policy.

BUSINESS CASE EXTENSION QUESTIONS

1. Research the performance of Facebook since it became a public limited company. Does it seem to have changed its approach in any way?
2. What has happened to Facebook's share price since it became a public limited company? Can you explain how it has changed?
3. Can you find an example in the news of a shareholder revolt? Is there a company at the moment where the shareholders are demanding a change in management and approach? Why?
4. Research a senior manager who has resigned recently. What caused this resignation?

QUICK QUESTIONS

1. What are the key features of a business?
2. In what way are businesses involved in a transformation process?
3. What are the functions of a business?
4. What is the significance of limited liability?
5. What is the difference between the primary, secondary, and tertiary sectors?
6. What do managers do?
7. What are the typical roles of managers, according to Mintzberg?
8. Why do investors buy shares?
9. Why might a manager be short-termist?
10. What is meant by the macro environment of business?

Mission and objectives

I joined the company a few months ago and I still don't know what it is I am sup-posed to be focusing on. One minute I am being told to get costs down. The next minute someone asks me how we can get sales up. Then there will be a request about new overseas options—with Brexit happening we are all suddenly looking for new markets outside of Europe. It's just not clear what the priorities are supposed to be. I can probably get the sales up but it will cost us money and we may have to cut prices. I am not sure I can get sales up, revenue up, and costs down!

It makes life very difficult when I am trying to organize my time and resources and I don't know what the priority is. I wish someone would ask me what I think, put it into a plan and then tell me what it is!

Managers will sometimes be unsure of exactly what they should be doing or how they will be measured. The role of a mission and objectives is to clarify for everyone what the targets are. However, as we shall see, these objectives can vary between organizations and over time.

BY THE END OF THIS CHAPTER YOU WILL BE ABLE TO . . .

- explain what a mission is and how objectives differ from mission
- explain why managers may want to maximize profits
- explain other common objectives of business
- explain what is meant by corporate social responsibility

BUSINESS CASE: AMAZON—IT'S ALL ABOUT THE LONG TERM

The following statement was made to Amazon's shareholders in 1997. It is sent out to them each year to reinforce Amazon's message about its ongoing commitment to growth.

We believe that a fundamental measure of our success will be the shareholder value we create over the long term. This value will be a direct result of our ability to extend and solidify our current market leadership position.

The stronger our market leadership, the more powerful our economic model. Market leadership can translate directly to higher revenue, higher profitability, greater capital velocity, and correspondingly stronger returns on invested capital.

Our decisions have consistently reflected this focus. We first measure ourselves in terms of the metrics most indicative of our market leadership: customer and revenue growth, the degree to which our customers continue to purchase from us on a repeat basis, and the strength of our brand. We have invested and will continue to invest aggressively to expand and leverage our customer base, brand, and infrastructure as we move to establish an enduring franchise.

Because of our emphasis on the long term, we may make decisions and weigh tradeoffs differently than some companies. Accordingly, we want to share with you our fundamental management and decision-making approach so that you, our shareholders, may confirm that it is consistent with your investment philosophy:

- We will continue to focus relentlessly on our customers.

- We will continue to make investment decisions in light of long-term market leadership considerations rather than short-term profitability considerations or short-term Wall Street reactions.

- We will continue to measure our programs and the effectiveness of our investments analytically, to jettison those that do not provide acceptable returns, and to step up our investment in those that work best. We will continue to learn from both our successes and our failures.

- We will make bold rather than timid investment decisions where we see a sufficient probability of gaining market leadership advantages. Some of these investments will pay off, others will not, and we will have learned another valuable lesson in either case.

- When forced to choose between optimizing the appearance of our GAAP accounting and maximizing the present value of future cash flows, we'll take the cash flows.

- We will share our strategic thought processes with you when we make bold choices (to the extent competitive pressures allow), so that you may evaluate for yourselves whether we are making rational long-term leadership investments.

- We will work hard to spend wisely and maintain our lean culture. We understand the importance of continually reinforcing a cost-conscious culture, particularly in a business incurring net losses.

- We will balance our focus on growth with emphasis on long-term profitability and capital management.

- At this stage, we choose to prioritize growth because we believe that scale is central to achieving the potential of our business model.

- We will continue to focus on hiring and retaining versatile and talented employees, and continue to weight their compensation to stock options rather than cash.

We know our success will be largely affected by our ability to attract and retain a motivated employee base, each of whom must think like, and therefore must actually be, an owner.

We aren't so bold as to claim that the above is the 'right' investment philosophy, but it's ours, and we would be remiss if we weren't clear in the approach we have taken and will continue to take.

Source: Amazon Annual Report 1997 and 2016

https://blog.aboutamazon.com/working-at-amazon/amazons-original-1997-letter-to-shareholders

www.amazon.com/p/feature/z6o9g6sysxur57t

BUSINESS CASE QUESTIONS

This chapter will help you answer the following questions.

1. What do you think the mission of Amazon might be?
2. Why do you think Amazon has set an objective of growth?
3. How might this objective affect its decisions within the business?

Mission

The mission of an organization sets out why it exists. What was it set up to achieve and what its owners see as the reason for its existence? Defining the mission of an organization can have very significant impact on decisions within the business; it should influence everything the business does. A mission is a general outline of what a business wants to be. This is then turned into more specific targets in the form of objectives. The mission will be shaped by the owners. Some organizations may have constitutions that set out some aspects of why they exist—for example, if they are a charity, or if they are owned by their employees as in the case of John Lewis. When a company is formed it must set out some description of what it is there to do; this can be changed, but at any moment it defines at least the scope of its activities.

KEY CONCEPT

The **mission** of an organization sets out why it exists.

2.1 BUSINESS INSIGHT: MISSIONS OF GOOGLE AND UBER

The mission of a business can be the subject of much debate. Take Google, for example. Is it a content provider or a search engine? It argues that it is a search engine—this means it helps people to find the information they want. Whatever people might find on the web, it is not Google's problem; it is not there to monitor, police, or control what is shown. For Google, this is a useful interpretation of its mission because it means it does not have to take responsibility for what people find from Google searches. However, if Google defines itself as a content provider then it clearly is responsible for what can be found through searching and should therefore act as a censor.

The question of 'who and what are we?' also became significant with Uber. Uber sees itself as a technology company, but many governments define it as a taxi business. As a taxi business, it needs to be licensed and to meet a number of regulations that would not apply to a technology business.

Question
Do you think Google should take more responsibility for content on the internet?

BUSINESS CASE QUESTIONS: CAN YOU NOW ANSWER . . .

What do you think the mission of Amazon might be?

MANAGEMENT TASK

a. You have a senior position within the police force. Some say the police are there to prevent crime. Some say they are there to solve crime. How might these different missions affect the way you allocate resources?

b. You are the chief executive of a health trust. Should the mission of your trust be to save lives or reduce pain? Why might these two potential missions conflict?

RESEARCH TASK

1. Find the mission statement of the pharmaceutical company Johnson & Johnson (called 'Our Credo'). How do you think this might affect behaviour within the business?

2. Compare and contrast the mission statements of two other public limited companies of your choice.

Objectives

An objective is a target that managers aim to achieve. To be effective, an objective should be SMART. This means it should meet the following criteria.

- Specific: it should specify exactly what is being measured.
- Measurable: it should be possible to quantify it.

- Agreed: a target should not just be imposed on people but should be agreed between those setting it and those who have to achieve it.

- Realistic: a target should be achievable, otherwise people will not be committed to it.

- Time-specific: there should be a clear time limit setting out when the target will be achieved.

Objectives are important for managers because they set out what is to be achieved. They also determine how a manager's performance will be assessed—did she achieve the target in the given time to the agreed standard? Objectives should, therefore, clarify what you are there to do. You can then focus on how to achieve this. The objective will determine how you allocate resources and what your priorities are.

Profit as an objective

For many managers, profit is a very common objective. Profit occurs when the value of the output produced is greater than the value of the inputs that have been used to produce and sell the items involved. It is measured by the difference between total revenue and total costs. If a business generates a profit, this shows that the managers have used the resources effectively in that they have produced something worth more than it cost to provide them. If a profit is made, the business is adding value. If a loss is made, this means that the value of the output is less than the resources used up to provide it.

2.1 DOING THE BUSINESS MATHS

Complete the table.

Output (units)	Total revenue (£)	Total costs (£)	Profit (£)
10	100	20	
20	150	100	
30	300	120	
40	600	220	
50	1,000	700	

Questions

1. At which output is revenue maximized?
2. At which output are costs the lowest?
3. At which output is profit maximized?

2.1 QUICK CHECK

For each of the following statements, say whether it is true or false.
   A business objective should be

a.   specific.

b.   measurable.

c.   ambiguous.

d.   reductionist.

e.   tentative.

Return on investment

Of course, simply making a profit may not, in itself, justify a particular investment in resources. What is important is to consider the scale of the profit relative to the inputs used to achieve it. If, for example, you worked all year to make a £32 profit this may not be regarded as worthwhile. For a particular project, managers will generally be assessed on their return on investment (ROI). This is measured as a percentage.

   ROI = (profit ÷ investment) × 100

For example, if a business makes a profit of £10 million on an investment of £50 million this is a return of (£10 ÷ £50) × 100 = 20%.

Return on capital employed

In terms of the overall performance of the business, the measure of return on investment often used is actually called the return on capital employed (ROCE).
   The capital employed is the total long-term finance that the business has. It is made up of funds from

• loans

• shares

• retained profit

The return on capital employed measures the profit generated by the business in a year.

   ROCE = (profit ÷ capital employed) × 100

Table 2.1 Calculating and analysing the return on capital employed

	Business A	Business B	Business C
Profit	£1m	£2m	£200m
Capital employed	£10m	£20m	£5000m
Return on capital employed	(£1 ÷ £10) × 100 = 10%	(£2 ÷ £20) × 100 = 10%	(£200 ÷ £5,000) × 100 = 4%

If, for example, the capital employed is £20 million and the profit generated in a year is £1 million, this is 5% return on capital employed.

If the capital employed is £200 million and the profit generated in a year is £1 million, this is 0.5% return on capital employed.

If the return on capital employed is too low, managers may be criticized because funds could have been used more profitably elsewhere. Remember there is always an opportunity cost. Whenever funds are being used by managers, the questions will always be—what else could they be used for? Investors will consider the possible returns in alternative investments.

The value of profit is measured in absolute terms, i.e. the number of pounds of profit. Profitability measures the profit in relation to something else such as the capital employed. Profitability is measured as a percentage.

YOU, THE MANAGER

You are considering major expansion and need to raise long-term funds. Should you borrow, or should you recommend issuing more shares?

In Table 2.1, Business B has generated more profit in absolute terms than Business A (£20m vs. £10m). However, given that it had more funds invested in the business to begin with it is a similar rate of return. Business C makes much more profit than the other two businesses. However, it is a much bigger business and relatively its performance is not as good.

Why do profits matter?

Profits matter because they mean that all the endeavours of the managers and staff have generated a financial surplus over a given period. Provided that profit is high enough as a rate of return in the investment, the project was worthwhile in financial terms.

This profit has several functions.

- It can be paid to investors as dividends. Dividends are part of the rewards that investors get; shareholders also benefit if the share price increases (this is called a capital gain).

- It can be used for funds for investment. This will be cheaper than having to borrow funds, as interest will have to be paid on borrowed funds.
- It can be used as an indicator of how successful the managers are in financial terms; this may matter for their career and rewards.

ANALYSING THE BUSINESS DATA: TESCO PLC

The table shows Tesco's return on capital employed over an eight-year period. Comment on Tesco's ROCE.

Year	Return on capital employed
2017	0.55%
2016	0.67%
2015	−26.13%
2014	7.85%
2013	6.29%
2012	12.05%
2011	11.99%

Source: FAME; www.tescoplc.com/investors/

2.2 BUSINESS INSIGHT: DIVIDEND PAYOUTS IN THE UK

Here is an extract from an article published in the *Financial Times* on 17 December 2017.

> Large asset managers have recently warned British companies to reconsider their dividend policies as fears grow that UK business is shunning investment in favour of investor payouts. [. . .] Global dividends grew at the fastest pace in three years in the third quarter of 2017. UK payouts picked up dramatically, rising 17.5 per cent— the fastest underlying rate in the world—as commodity prices increased, according to the Janus Henderson Global Dividend Index report. [. . .] According to the Janus Henderson report, published last month, payouts by UK companies stood at $93bn last year, down 3 per cent on 2015.

The article reports a fear that the dividends being paid out by business were not sustainable and that not enough was being put into research and development. Some businesses were even taking on debt to pay out dividends.

Source: www.ft.com/content/02081042-d391-11e7-a303-9060cb1e5f44

Questions

1. What do you think managers need to consider when deciding how much to pay as dividends?
2. Why would managers borrow money to pay dividends?

Profit maximization

Standard economic theory assumes that businesses will aim to maximize their profits, i.e. generate the maximum possible positive difference between the total revenue and total costs possible. This may well make sense in theory—as a rational decision maker, if you want to make a profit then presumably you will want to make the most possible. However, this assumption may not match what happens in reality, not least because of information problems. Managers may not actually know exactly what the different cost and revenue implications are of any decision they make. They may not therefore be able to maximize profits even if they want to. You cannot be certain what the revenue will be at different prices, for example; you can only estimate. By the time you have gathered all the relevant cost data on production, this may not reflect the current cost of the production that is now happening. Although developments in technology mean that information can be gathered and analysed much faster than in the past, there is still likely to be a difference between what is happening in 'real time' and what the business has measured in terms of costs and revenues.

> **KEY CONCEPT**
>
> **Profit maximization** occurs when there is the highest possible positive difference between revenue and costs.

Other objectives

What managers are aiming to achieve will depend in part on what their rewards are linked to. In some cases, this will be the sales revenue. It may well be that the bigger the sales revenue the business generates, the higher the manager's bonus, for example. In this case, revenue rather profit may be the priority. To generate revenue, managers may be willing to incur additional costs. Profit may fall while revenue increases.

The rewards of other managers may be linked to the overall size of the business; the bigger the output, the more they might receive in some form of rewards. Again, this may not be compatible with profit maximization, at least in the short term. Businesses may invest to grow, and profits may fall as a result. More staff, more capital equipment, more premises, more stock may require heavy spending and thus lower profits in any given period. Another motive for growth may be to dominate markets and benefit from being a larger-scale company. The long-term objective of Amazon may be profit, but to get there it invests heavily to grow.

Whatever drives the rewards of managers is likely to drive their decision making. In many cases this may not be profits, not least because managers may argue that many aspects of their costs are out of their control and may therefore not want this as part of their reward package. The profit figure declared in accounts can also be manipulated by creative accounting (see 2.2 Doing the business maths), and so managers and investors may prefer to link rewards to a slightly less ambiguous target.

2.2 DOING THE BUSINESS MATHS

To an accountant, the 'costs' incurred by a business means the value of resources used up in a given period. Often this requires assumptions to be made about how resources have been used. These assumptions are stated in the company accounts. Changes in assumptions will affect the profits declared for any given period.

For example, imagine a business buys equipment for £100,000. If it is assumed that the equipment will last 4 years, the cost per year (called 'depreciation') is £25,000. If the accountants change the assumption to a lifetime of 5 years, the cost per year is now £20,000. Changing to this assumption would reduce the annual costs for the first four years by £5,000, boosting profits in those years. In year 5, the depreciation would have been £0 under the first assumption but will be £20,000 under the second assumption. Depreciating over 5 years reduces the costs (and boost profits) for years 1 to 4 but increases costs (and reduces profits) in year 5. Overall, £100,000 is allocated as a cost in both cases, but what differs is the timings of this allocation which affects declared profits within the 5-year period.

Example

A computer system is purchased for £50,000 and has a resale value of £10,000. Show the effect on the annual costs in the accounts if the asset is expected to last (i) 2 years or (ii) 5 years.

Year	Annual cost (£000) Expected life span of 2 years	Annual cost (£000) Expected life span of 5 years
1		
2		
3		
4		
5		

Questions

1. What is the overall effect on profits of allocating over 2 or 5 years?
2. What is the impact on profits in (a) Year 1 and (b) Year 5 of the two different methods?

The shareholders, however, may be very keen on profits, as this may affect their dividends and the share price. They may worry that managers are pursuing their own interests rather than shareholders' interests, and they may fear that this will be difficult to discover. This is because of 'asymmetric information': that is, the two groups do not have the same information available. Managers will be very close to all aspects of the business and know what is happening inside and out. Investors may have nothing to do with the business on a day-to-day basis. They will elect a board of directors to represent them, but even then they will only really know what managers tell them. There is an information imbalance.

Shareholders might therefore develop reward packages to incentivize managers to pursue the same objectives as shareholders have. For example, they may link rewards directly to profits through bonuses, or they may give managers share options. This can fix a price at which managers can buy shares at a given point in the future. Imagine you are given the option to buy 100,000 shares at £1.50 in three years' time. If, in three years, the share price has fallen to £0.90, you will not take up this option. If the share price has gone up to £2.00, you can buy 100,000 at £1.50 according to the deal and them immediately resell at £2.00. You have just made 50 pence on 100,000 shares, i.e. £50,000. If you have managed to get the share price even higher you will have made even more money. This type of deal gives you an incentive to get the share price as high as you can; you will focus on whatever drives up the share price, and this will benefit both you and your investors.

RESEARCH TASK

Visit the website of a public limited company and go to the section called 'Investor Relations'. Look for the most recent annual report and read the chief executive's review of the year. Summarize your findings in terms of the actions the business took and the environment in which it operated.

How in theory do managers know when they are maximizing profit?

Profits are measured as total revenue minus total costs. Profits will be maximized when there is the biggest positive difference between total revenue and total costs.

Economists often analyse decisions by looking at what happens at the margin, i.e. when an extra unit (a marginal unit) is sold.

- If the marginal revenue on the unit is greater than the marginal cost of the unit, this means the extra revenue from selling a unit is greater than the extra cost of producing and selling that unit. A profit is made on this extra unit, and total profits will increase if this unit is sold.

- If marginal revenue is equal to marginal cost, this means the extra revenue from selling the unit is equal to the extra cost of producing and selling it. No more profit is made on this extra unit because profits are maximized.

- If the marginal revenue is less than the marginal cost, this means the extra revenue from selling a unit is less than the extra cost of producing and selling it. A loss is made on this extra unit, and total profits will decrease if this unit is sold.

The marginal condition for profit maximization is that this occurs at the level of output where marginal revenue = marginal costs.

2.3 DOING THE BUSINESS MATHS

Example
The table shows how many units are produced, and the marginal revenue and marginal cost for each number of units. Complete the table.

Units	Marginal revenue (£)	Marginal cost (£)	Produce or not?	Impact on profits
1	10	5		
2	10	7		
3	10	10		
4	10	13		
5	10	17		

Question

How many units should be produced? Why?

Figure 2.1 compares marginal costs and revenue with total costs and revenue. In the top diagram, we have assumed every unit is sold at the same price. This means the marginal revenue equals the price (for example, if every unit is sold at £10 the price, and the extra revenue, is £10). Marginal costs are assumed to rise: to produce more it costs more, as resources are scarcer. On the units up to Q1 the extra revenue is greater than the extra cost and so there is an extra profit to be made. At Q1 MR = MC there is no extra profit to be made, in other words profits have been maximized. Above Q1 the extra revenue is less than the extra costs, and so profits start to fall if these are produced.

Figure 2.1 The profit-maximizing output

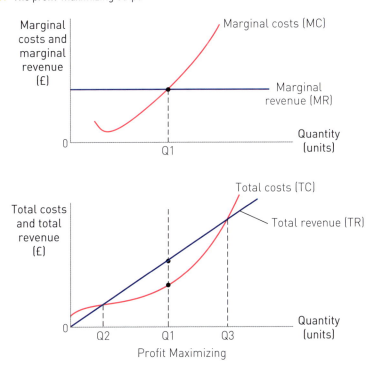

This can also be shown on the bottom diagram. The total revenue line is a straight line because it increases by the price each time a unit is sold. The total costs rise by more each time as the marginal costs are rising. At Q1 there is the biggest positive difference between the total revenue and total costs; profits have been maximized. You can also see from this diagram that below output Q2 and above output Q3 a loss is made because total revenue is less than total costs. Between Q2 and Q3 a profit is made because the total revenue is above total costs but profits are maximized at Q1.

What if managers wanted to maximize sales revenue?

If managers wanted to maximize revenue, this means they should be producing at an output where total revenue cannot increase any more. Again, economists tend to analyse this by looking at what happens with the marginal (extra) unit.

- If marginal revenue is positive, this means that selling the extra unit would increase total revenue. This means that total revenue is not maximized at this output.

- If marginal revenue is zero, this means that selling the extra unit would not increase total revenue. This means that total revenue is maximized at this output.

- If marginal revenue is negative, this means that selling the extra unit would decrease total revenue. This means that total revenue is not maximized at this output.

According to the marginal condition, sales revenue is maximized when marginal revenue is zero.

In Figure 2.1 the revenue would be maximized by selling the most units possible, as each one is sold at the same price. This is not the same as maximizing profits because of the costs involved in producing more units. Profits actually fall after Q1. In reality to sell more managers would, at some point, need to lower prices and revenue would not keep increasing. There would come a point that the effect of lowering the price meant that even though more units were sold the lower price meant there was no more revenue overall. Marginal revenue would be 0 and total revenue would be maximized at this output.

YOU, THE MANAGER

You are the manager of a hotel. You want to increase the revenue from your hotel. Should you increase or decrease the price of your rooms? Explain your reasoning.

What if managers wanted to maximize growth, e.g. output, without making a loss?

If managers wanted to operate at the highest output possible without making a loss, i.e. to achieve the highest non-loss-making growth, they would operate where total revenue equals total costs. On Figure 2.1 this is at Q3. Notice again that this is not the same as maximizing profits. If your focus is growth you will produce units which may actually decrease profits but increase your sales.

This can also be expressed as the output where the average revenue (the price per unit) equals the average cost (the cost per unit).

KEY CONCEPT

The **marginal condition for profit maximization** is that a business should produce at the output where marginal revenue equals marginal cost.

The **marginal condition for revenue maximization** is that a business should produce at an output where marginal revenue equals zero.

Managers may want growth for one or more reasons.

- Growth gives the business more power over suppliers and distributors and weakens the power of rivals.
- Growth may increase brand awareness.
- Growth may lead to cost advantages by spreading certain costs over more units (e.g. the costs of research and development).
- Growth may give a sense of personal development.

BUSINESS CASE QUESTIONS: CAN YOU NOW ANSWER . . .

1. Why do you think Amazon has set an objective of growth?
2. How might this objective affect its decisions within the business?

Will managers really maximize profits?

In reality, profit maximization may not occur. There are several possible reasons.

Priorities in decision making

Decisions will be taken by managers. They cannot necessarily process very complex data to make the right decision—people are not perfect decision makers. People find shortcuts, make assumptions, and make decisions that 'will do'. A manager might think 'Provided I increase profit by at least 5 per cent this year, that will be enough.' Managers will also be dealing with many different groups that have a stake within the business, not least all the different departments within her business—the marketing team, the sales team, the operations staff, the human resources employees, the finance people, and so on. Each of these groups may have a different perspective on problems. A proposal by the finance team to reduce staffing may not be popular with human resources, who have to help manage the redundancies. A proposal by the marketing people to adapt the product may not be welcomed by operations if this means a significant change in the way things are done.

Satisficing

A business is made up of groups of people with their own agendas. The managing director has to juggle these different interests and, according to Herbert Simon, it is possible you will end up 'satisficing' them rather than maximizing profits. Satisficing means doing what is needed to reach a satisfactory solution—you make enough profit to please shareholders while also reaching a compromise internally with the different groups to keep them all working together. Simon argues that even if you had enough information, you would not be able to process it effectively enough to make the maximum profit possible—there are simply too many variables and we, as decision makers, have 'cognitive limits'.

2.2 QUICK CHECK

For each of the following statements, say whether it is true or false.

a. If revenue increases, profits must increase.

b. Maximum profit occurs when revenue is maximized.

c. Higher profits mean higher returns on investment.

d. Profits are maximized when there is the biggest difference between marginal revenue and marginal cost.

e. Maximum revenue occurs when total revenue is zero.

READ MORE

Herbert Simon wrote that 'Whereas economic man maximizes, selects the best alternative from among all those available to him, his cousin, administrative man, satisfices, looks for a course of action that is satisfactory or "good enough".' If you want to find out more about Simon's work on satisficing different stakeholder groups, you could read

Simon, H. (1948), *Administrative Behaviour: A Study of the Decision Making Processes in Administrative Organization*, New York: Macmillan; 4th edn (1997), New York: Free Press.

Taking the long-term view

Managers may be aiming for long-term profit maximization rather than short-term. If managers are planning ahead, they may not make the highest possible profit this period because they are investing for the future. Companies such as Twitter and Ocado have spent years building their brands and customer loyalty and expanding their provision. This has meant years of loss in search of longer-term profits.

Other priorities

There may be other priorities. Like all of us, managers are likely to be affected by the rewards offered to them. They are likely to behave in a way that increases these rewards. If more revenue generates more earnings for managers, they will probably focus on revenue rather than profit. Remember profits and revenue are not the same: you can boost revenue while also increasing investment in marketing, for example, and so profit may actually fall. It may be, therefore, that managers are more focused on revenue maximization than on profit maximization.

MANAGEMENT TASK

- You have become the manager of a company that produces confectionery. Your directors appointed you to improve profits within the next year. What actions do you think you can take to boost short-term profits?

- You are the chief executive of a large but still relatively young social media business. Your investors have asked for dividends to be paid for the first time this year, but you are reluctant to do so. What would you put in an email to investors to explain why you do not recommend paying dividends?

Ownership and objectives

The objectives of a business will be influenced by many factors, including the values of the senior managers and the external environment. A key factor will be the demands of the owners. After all, managers are accountable to owners, so what they want should be an important influence on what the business set out to achieve. Shares in public limited companies, for example, are often owned by financial institutions such as pension funds. These institutions need to generate a return for their own investors, and therefore there will be pressure on the business to deliver financial returns via dividends and share price increases. With such external pressure, the managers are likely to be very focused on the financial performance of the business. By comparison, another organization may have a different ownership structure. John Lewis, for example, is a partnership (see 2.3 Business insight). This means it is owned by its employees, who are all partners. All the partners have one vote, making this a very democratic organization, and will vote on key issues. The constitution of John Lewis sets out that the organization should look after the welfare of its partners. This is not to say that profit does not matter (and partners vote on what happens to the profit) but that the welfare of employees is also a very significant influence on decision making and that employees are involved in this decision making.

2.3 BUSINESS INSIGHT: THE JOHN LEWIS PARTNERSHIP'S CONSTITUTION

The following is an extract from the John Lewis website.

> The John Lewis Partnership exists today because of the extraordinary vision and ideals of our Founder, John Spedan Lewis, who signed away his personal owner-

ship rights in a growing retail company to allow future generations of employees to take forward his 'experiment in industrial democracy'. Not unreasonably, he wanted to leave some clear guidelines for his successors, so that the values which had motivated him would not be eroded with the passage of time.

[. . .] Spedan Lewis was committed to establishing a 'better form of business', and the challenge for Partners of today is to prove that a business which is not driven by the demands of outside shareholders and which sets high standards of behaviour can flourish in the competitive conditions of the third millennium. Indeed, we aim to demonstrate that adhering to these Principles and Rules enables us over the long term to outperform companies with conventional ownership structures.

The Constitution states that 'the happiness of its members' is the Partnership's ultimate purpose, recognising that such happiness depends on having a satisfying job in a successful business. It establishes a system of 'rights and responsibilities', which places on all Partners the obligation to work for the improvement of our business in the knowledge that we share the rewards of success.

The Constitution defines mechanisms to provide for the management of the Partnership, with checks and balances to ensure accountability, transparency and honesty. It established the representation of the co-owners on the Partnership Board through the election of Partners as Directors (Elected Directors) and it also determines the role of the Partners' Counsellor.

Source: www.johnlewispartnership.co.uk/about/our-founder/our-constitution.html

Question

John Lewis is owned by its employees. How might this affect the objectives it sets and the decisions taken by its managers?

2.4 BUSINESS INSIGHT: BUILDING SOCIETIES

You can see the significance of ownership by comparing a bank and a building society. A bank is owned by investors. The managers of a bank will aim to make profits to reward their owners. Customers are important because they provide the finance that allows the business to make a profit. By contrast, a building society is owned by its savers. Profits are used to improve the service and returns for savers, not for outside investors. Decisions are therefore made to benefit those who use the building society's service, not outsiders. This is what Nationwide Building Society says about its objectives:

> The Nationwide is a building society . . . We're a mutual, which means we're owned by and run for the benefit of our members. Because of the way we're run, we're free to reinvest more of our profits into improving products and services for you.
>
> You're a member when you have a current account, mortgage or savings account with us.

We give our members:

- Up to £500 a year for recommending us to your friends (terms and conditions apply)
- A tiered interest rate on our Loyalty Saver based on your length of membership with us
- Cashback offers through Simply Rewards
- Access to personal loans, credit cards, home insurance, protection and investment products
- Flexclusive products when your main current account is with us

You're not just a customer—you're part of our Society. You can vote at our Annual General Meeting [. . .] meet our directors at Member TalkBack sessions across the country, and tell us what you want from our products and services. You can get as involved as you like.

Source: www.nationwide.co.uk/about/why-choose-nationwide/all-about-membership

Question

How might the fact that Nationwide is a mutual lead to different decisions compared to decisions made by a bank (owned by shareholders)?

Corporate social responsibility

Another possible consideration for managers when setting objectives is the impact of their actions on society as a whole. The concept of corporate social responsibility (CSR) highlights that business decisions impact on stakeholders and that managers may want to consider the social effects of their decisions. They may want to take actions over and above their legal requirements to help the different groups they affect (called stakeholders). Some businesses set targets that are much broader than just profit. For example, they may set targets in relations to employee satisfaction, environmental emissions, recycling, or accidents. Most businesses will have several targets, and while profit is often one of them, there are usually others that focus on social issues. And of course some organizations have very clear social objectives and are not profit-making—charities, for example, will aim to benefit a particular disadvantaged group and will not measure their success in terms of the profits made.

As a manager you (and the owners of your business) may accept various responsibilities to society because you feel it is the right thing to do; e.g. the owners may think it is right to use some of the business's funds for charity. At the same time, there may be financial gains from social responsibility: more recycling can save costs; a stronger environmental track record can attract investors and staff. It is possible, therefore, that CSR can be profitable in the long run. One reason why so many companies now have a CSR policy could well be that customers and investors expect this and without it the business would suffer.

2.5 BUSINESS INSIGHT: PUMA'S ENVIRONMENTAL ACCOUNTS

Some businesses, including Puma, are now producing environmental profit and loss accounts (EP&L) that try to value the impact of their activities on the environment. Rather than just using the price paid for an item to represent its costs, environmental accounting attempts to calculate the true cost to society.

The monetary value of the EP&L is the amount that would need to be paid if the environment billed us for providing clean water and air, restoring soils and the atmosphere, and decomposing waste.

The monetary value of Puma's environmental impact expresses the value of impacts such as air pollution, carbon emissions, land use, waste generation, water usage, and water pollution.

Puma produces these results and then aims to lower the monetary value of its impact on the environment each year. This is achieved by working more closely with suppliers and looking at its processes.

Source: https://about.puma.com/en/sustainability/environment

Question

Do you think all businesses should produce an environmental profit and loss statement?

2.3 QUICK CHECK

For each of the following statements, say whether it is true or false.

a. Satisficing occurs when different stakeholder groups are satisfied.

b. CSR acknowledges that business may have social objectives.

c. Achieving growth does not necessarily mean achieving maximum profits.

d. Profits are measured by total revenue plus total costs.

2.6 BUSINESS INSIGHT: SMARTPHONES AND YOUNG PEOPLE

Some of Apple's biggest investors have asked the company to develop software to limit how long children can use its smartphones. The demands have come from two investment groups that hold $2bn (£1.48bn) of Apple shares between them. One of them represents the pensions of Canadian teachers. These investors were worried about the possible effect of the excessive use of smartphones on the mental health of young people.

Many studies suggest excessive phone use can disrupt lessons, harm students' ability to concentrate on school work, and deprive them of sleep. These investors believe that Apple needs to take responsibility for its products and the effect they have on users.

Questions

1. Do you think companies should be responsible for how their customers use their products?

2. If you were running Apple would you try and limit the amount of time young people use your smartphone?

YOU, THE MANAGER

The famous economist Milton Friedman said that 'the business of business is business' (see the article cited in 'Business case extension questions' at the end of this chapter). He did not believe managers should worry about issues such as corporate social responsibility. They should simply focus on maximizing profits for their investors. Anything else was a distraction. Do you agree?

• •

SUMMARY

A mission defines why an organization exists. This mission can then be turned into objectives. These are specific targets that have to be achieved in a given time period. Economists tend to assume that businesses want to maximize profits. However, other objectives include growth and revenue maximization. Managers may also seek to meet a range of stakeholder needs and to act in a socially responsible way.

KEY LEARNING POINTS

- A mission sets out why a business exists.
- Objectives are specific and time-specific targets.
- Objectives help managers allocate resources.
- Profit maximization occurs at the output where marginal revenue equals marginal costs.
- Revenue maximization occurs at the output where marginal revenue equals zero.
- Growth maximization occurs at the highest output where average revenue equals average costs.
- Corporate social responsibility assumes that businesses have responsibilities to society over and above their legal responsibilities.

BUSINESS CASE EXTENSION QUESTIONS

1. Visit the Amazon website, find Amazon's annual report and read the latest review of the company's activities by the chief executive. What does she or he identify as key issues in the business environment that have influenced Amazon's success?

2. Produce a summary of the key business activities of Amazon at present.

3. To what extent do you think Amazon behaves in a socially responsible way? Review the information on Amazon's website and combine this with your own research to answer.

4. In 1970 Milton Friedman wrote a famous article called 'The Social Responsibility of Business is to Increase Profits' for the *New York Times Magazine* (30 September 1970). Read this and discuss whether you agree with Friedman's view.

QUICK QUESTIONS

1. What is the difference between a mission and an objective?
2. What is the value to a business of setting objectives?
3. How is profit measured?
4. Why is profit a common objective of a business?
5. What is meant by corporate social responsibility?
6. Why is maximizing revenue different from maximizing profit?
7. Why might achieving growth be different from maximizing profit?
8. What is meant by satisficing?
9. What is the difference between marginal revenue and total revenue?
10. What is meant by a return on investment?

Managing demand

You are the Chief Executive of a large sports goods retailer. The latest sales revenue figures are just in, and your revenue is down by 2 per cent. With less sales revenue, your profits are going to fall unless you can get costs down. Lower profits will need explaining to the Board of Directors . . . .

Sales matter to businesses. Sales generate revenue, and revenue drives the profits. The level of sales of a business is determined by the demand for the firm's products. Managers will, therefore, want to understand what determines the demand for their products and how they can influence it, because this determines their revenue. Some factors outside the control of the business will affect demand, but managers will try to manage demand where they can.

BY THE END OF THIS CHAPTER YOU WILL BE ABLE TO . . .

- explain what factors may influence the demand for a product
- explain the relationship between price, quantity demanded, and revenue
- analyse the importance of the elasticity of demand
- analyse how managers might influence demand

BUSINESS CASE

Tesla, the US car company set up by entrepreneur Elon Musk, has made a very successful entrance into the automotive market with its electric cars and more recently trucks. The financial research company CSIMarket quotes Tesla as reporting:

We believe the primary competitive factors in our markets include but are not limited to:

technological innovation;

product quality and safety;

service options;

product performance;

design and styling;

brand perception;

product price; and

manufacturing efficiency.

Source: https://csimarket.com/stocks/compet_glance.php?code=TSLA

Here is an extract from Tesla's 2017 annual report.

We believe that our vehicles compete in the market both based on their traditional segment classification as well as based on their propulsion technology. For example, Model S and Model X compete primarily in the extremely competitive premium sedan and premium SUV markets with internal combustion vehicles from more established automobile manufacturers and Model 3 competes with small to medium-sized sedans. Our vehicles also compete with vehicles propelled by alternative fuels, principally electricity. [. . .]

Many established and new automobile manufacturers such as Audi, BMW, Daimler, General Motors, Toyota and Volvo, as well as other companies, have entered or are reported to have plans to enter the alternative fuel vehicle market, including hybrid, plug-in hybrid and fully electric vehicles. [. . .] Overall, we believe these announcements and vehicle introductions promote the development of the alternative fuel vehicle market by highlighting the attractiveness of alternative fuel vehicles, particularly those fueled by electricity, relative to the internal combustion vehicle. [. . .] Electric vehicles have also already been brought to market in China and other foreign countries and we expect a number of those manufacturers to enter the US market as well.

Source: https://www.sec.gov/Archives/edgar/data/1318605/000156459018002956/
tsla-10k_20171231.htm

BUSINESS CASE QUESTIONS

This chapter will help you answer the following questions.

1. Which factors do you think influence the demand for electric cars?

2. Do you think demand for electric cars has been growing or shrinking in recent years? Why?

3. How important do you think the price of an electric car is in terms of influencing the decision to buy an electric car? Why?

4. Do you think demand for electric cars in general is likely to be more or less sensitive to price than the demand for a particular brand of electric car? Why?

5. As more producers move into the electric car market, what do you think this will do to demand for Tesla cars? Why?

6. The UK government is increasing taxes on diesel cars. What effect will this have on demand for electric cars?

What is demand?

The demand for a good or service is the quantity that customers are willing and able to purchase. As a business we are not just interested in what people would like to buy; we need to know whether they can afford it as well. That's why we measure the quantity customers are willing *and* able to buy. Many marketing activities aim to generate interest in the product; however, some may be focused on helping more people to be able to afford the product—for example, through payment by instalment schemes, or trade-in deals. The car market is a good example of this. Most car manufacturers will lend you the money to buy their cars; they will also offer you the ability to rent the car for a number of years and then decide if you want to buy it or trade up.

The demand for a product drives the sales and revenue of a business. Not surprisingly, then, managers will want to know what influences the demand for their products. One of the key factors influencing demand is likely to be price.

When we, as customers, are thinking of buying something, we think about its value to us (economists call this 'utility') and we think about the cost to us—i.e. the price. We often talk about whether something is 'good value for money': this means that we are thinking about whether the price we paid was worth it. Provided we think the benefits of something are at least equal to the price we are paying, we are likely to demand it. We won't demand something if we think it is overpriced: that is, if the benefits we think it offers do not justify the price being asked. A £5 meal at McDonald's can be regarded a good value for money; so can a £100 birthday celebration meal at an exclusive restaurant, provided that the benefits of the whole experience are worth the price paid.

3.1 BUSINESS INSIGHT: BOWMAN'S STRATEGY CLOCK

Different strategies that businesses adopt can be shown on Bowman's strategy clock.

This shows that businesses can be competitive with relatively high prices provided that the benefits they provide are also relatively high. To travel with Qatar Airways is quite expensive, but you may well feel the service you receive justifies the price. Equally, a business can be competitive by offering relatively basic products and services, provided the price is also low. Ryanair and EasyJet offer a more basic service than Qatar Airways, but given that their prices are so much lower they can still be competitive. A business will not be competitive if the benefits it offers are the same as, or less than, those offered by competitors but the price is higher.

Over time, businesses may rethink their strategies. Recently, for example, Sports Direct has launched some new flagship stores with huge investment in the location, the store layout, and the decor. The company's chief executive, Mike Ashley, says it will become the Selfridges of sports retailing. It may end up with higher prices than in the past, but the products and stores may justify this. Burberry, already perceived as quite an upmarket product, has announced it wants to become even more of a premium brand. Where a business positions itself in a market compared to its rivals will affect decisions throughout the organization, such as where it locates, how it produces, what it stocks, and what level of customer service it provides.

Bowman's strategy clock

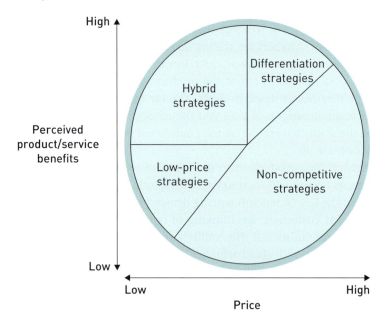

Courtesy of Professor Cliff Bowman

Question

Where would you place the following businesses on the strategy clock?

- Poundland
- Gucci
- Travelodge
- Montblanc pens
- IKEA

In economics, the impact of the price on the quantity demanded of a product is shown by a demand curve.

A demand curve shows the quantity of a product demanded at each and every price for a given time period.

The revenue earned by a business (also called the 'sales', 'sales revenue', 'total revenue', or 'turnover' generated) is measured by the price multiplied by the quantity sold.

Revenue = price × quantity sold

Obviously, businesses tend to sell more than one product. For example, Unilever's brands include Bertolli, Domestos, Knorr, Hellman's, Lipton, Magnum, Sure, Persil, Surf, Toni & Guy, Ben & Jerry's, and Brut. The revenue for the business as a whole is the sum of the revenues from each product.

3.2 BUSINESS INSIGHT: ANALYSING REVENUE

Managers will analyse different elements of the overall business revenue to identify how different parts of the organization are performing. A business may have different divisions representing different types of products, and so managers might analyse the performance of each division. For example, Manchester United will earn revenue from ticket sales, from sponsorship, and from merchandising, and will measure revenue in all these areas over time and in relation to competitors.

How revenue is analysed will depend on a company's operations. In the case of Marks & Spencer plc, for example, revenue might be analysed by product (e.g. food vs. clothing), by region (e.g. UK vs. Europe), source (e.g. physical store vs. online), and type of store (e.g. small stores vs. larger ones). This analysis could help shape strategy in the future. In recent years, for example, Marks & Spencer's revenue for food has performed well, but the revenue from clothes has been disappointing (as shown in the table); this might highlight the need for a change in the business strategy. Managers at M&S may decide to put more resources into clothing or may consider withdrawing from this sector.

	Revenue 2015/16	Annual change
Food (UK)	£5.6bn	+4.2%
Clothing and home (UK)	£3.8bn	−2.8%
M&S.com	£836.3m	+5.6%
International	£1.2bn	+10.7%

Source: http://annualreport.marksandspencer.com/M&S_AR2017.pdf. By permission of Marks & Spencer.

Question

In what ways might Marks & Spencer's analysis affect the decisions it takes?

MANAGEMENT TASK

Look at the data on Marks & Spencer plc shown in the table in Business insight 3.2. If you were the managing director of Marks & Spencer, how might this data affect your plans for the coming years?

A demand curve

A demand curve shows the quantity demanded of a product at each and every price, all other factors unchanged. A given demand curve therefore shows the effect of change in price on the quantity demanded, all other factors unchanged. A change in price will lead to an increase or decrease in the quantity demanded and is shown by a movement along the demand curve (Figure 3.1).

Figure 3.1 Price changes are shown by a movement along a demand curve

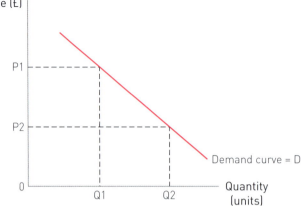

Generally we assume the demand curve is downward-sloping, meaning that more is demanded at lower prices (assuming all other factors remain unchanged).

This is because:

- with a lower price customers can afford to buy more with the same income (this is called the income effect);

- with a lower price this product is cheaper than it was, compared to other rival products, and this will attract customers to switch to this one (this is called the substitution effect).

The income and substitution effects usually combine to increase the quantity demanded.

KEY CONCEPT

A **demand curve** shows the quantity demanded of a product at each and every price, all other factors held constant.

3.3 BUSINESS INSIGHT: TOP LINE AND BOTTOM LINE

Revenue is called 'the top line' in business. This refers to the top line of a profit and loss account (also called an income statement), which forms part of a company's accounts.

The profit and loss account shows the income and costs of a business over the preceding 12 months. The profit is measured by the revenue minus the costs; the profit figure is called the 'bottom line'.

An increase in the 'top line' (revenue) will lead to an increase in the 'bottom line' (profit) provided that costs don't rise by more than revenue.

Notice that there are in fact many different measures of profit, such as profit before interest payments, profit before tax, and profit after tax. Whenever there is a story about the profits of a business, be careful to look at which measure it is using: it may be worth asking why the company chose to report that particular measure.

Table 3.1 shows the accounts for Manchester United in its financial year 2016.

Table 3.1 Manchester United's income statement data, 2016

Revenue			£515, 345
	Analysed as		
	Commercial revenue	£268,318	
	Broadcasting revenue	£140,440	
	Matchday revenue	£106,587	
Operating expenses			−£436,709
	Analysed as		
	Employee benefits	−£232,242	
	Other operating expenses	−£204,467	
Loss from disposal of assets			−£9,786
Operating profit			£68,850
Net finance costs			£20,017
Profit before tax			£48,833
Tax			−£12,462
Profit for the year			**£36,371**

Source: Manchester United plc, 20-F, September 15, 2016

Questions

1. Which profit do you think Manchester United would tend to use in any press statements? Why?
2. Do you think Manchester United should cut employees benefits to boost profits?

RESEARCH TASK

a. Look in the news for two companies announcing their profits. Which profit figure is being used in the press (e.g. before tax or after tax) for each of the two companies? Why do you think they have chosen this one? What are the profits being compared to in the media?
b. Some managers prefer to increase profits by reducing costs. Others seek to invest in order to differentiate what they offer, so that they can then charge a higher price, boost sales, and increase revenue. Can you find examples of these strategies in the news? Which strategy do you think is better?

MANAGEMENT TASK

Explain to your employees how you intend to improve the bottom line of your business without increasing its top line.

ANALYSING THE BUSINESS DATA

1. What does the data in the charts show about the predicted value of sales of beer in the UK from 2017 to 2022 and the predicted volume of sales?

2. Can you explain the difference between the expected trend in volume and value of sales?

Forecast value of UK beer sales, 2017–22

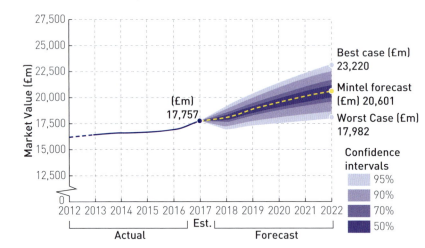

Source: Mintel Beer (December 2017)

Forecast volume of UK beer sales, 2017–22

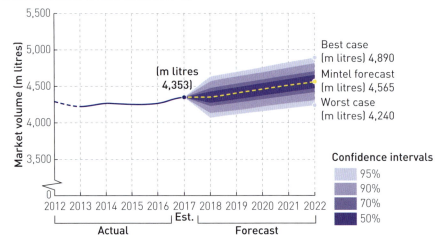

Source: Mintel Beer (December 2017)

The confidence interval shows how confident the researchers are that the actual result will be in this range.

KEY CONCEPT

Profit is measured by total revenue minus total costs.

Of course, what will be of interest to managers is not just whether the quantity demanded increases or decreases but how much the quantity demanded changes in response to price changes. This is because managers will need to plan for issues such as:

- how much to produce to meet the quantity demanded;
- how much to keep in stock ready for an increase in quantity demanded;
- staffing levels if sales are going to increase or decrease;
- the impact on cash flow of a change in sales.

All of these plans will be linked to expected levels of demand. The sales forecast is a key planning tool in business (see Figure 3.2)—most other plans within the organization, such as production planning, human resource planning, and financial planning are linked to the sales forecast. It is not enough for a manager to know that sales will fall if the price is increased. He or she will want to try to estimate exactly how much the decrease will be.

The sensitivity of demand to price changes is measured by the price elasticity of demand. If the quantity demanded is relatively sensitive to price (i.e. the percentage

Figure 3.2 Sales forecasts drive plans

change in quantity demanded is greater than the percentage change in price), demand is said to be price elastic. If the quantity demanded is relatively insensitive to price (i.e. the percentage change in quantity demanded is less than the percentage change in price), demand is said to be price inelastic.

The price elasticity of demand and pricing

The sensitivity of demand to price is likely to affect a firm's pricing policies.

If demand is price inelastic, a price increase will lead to a smaller fall in quantity demanded (in percentages) and sales revenue will increase (see Figure 3.3). Although less is sold, the revenue increases because of the higher price.

If demand is price elastic, increasing the price will reduce revenue (see Table 3.2). This is because the fall in quantity demanded is greater (as a percentage) than the increase in price; although more is charged per item, the fall in sales is so high that

Figure 3.3 Price change and revenue: price inelastic

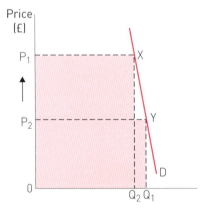

Table 3.2 The relationship between price changes, price elasticity of demand, and revenue

Price change	Effect on revenue if demand is price elastic	Effect on revenue if demand is price inelastic
Lower price	Increases revenue	Decreases revenue
Increase price	Decreases revenue	Increases revenue

overall revenue falls. If demand is price elastic a fall in price would increase revenue: although the price is lower, the increase in sales leads to more revenue.

An understanding of how sensitive demand is to price is therefore an important element of a firm's pricing strategy. Remember, however, that while a manager will be interested in the impact of price changes on the firm's revenue, she will also be concerned about costs. Lowering the price may lead to more revenue if demand is sensitive to price; but if more has to be produced, managers need to be careful that any increase in costs does not outweigh the increase in revenue. If it does, profits may fall.

Note that in reality a business will not know the exact price elasticity of demand for its products. However it can use past data and research to estimate the likely impact of any change in price.

3.1 QUICK CHECK

For each of the following statements, say whether it is true or false.

a. If demand is price inelastic, the quantity demanded won't change at all when the price changes.

b. An increase in price increases revenue if demand is price elastic.

c. A heavily branded item is more likely to be price inelastic than price elastic.

Calculating elasticity

So far we have looked at the price elasticity of demand which shows how quantity demanded changes when price changes. The concept of "elasticity of demand" can be extended to changes in other variables which affect demand such as income and promotional spending.

Calculating an elasticity of demand involves the percentage change in quantity demanded in relation to the percentage change in a variable. To calculate the percentage change in the value of a number, you calculate

(difference between new value and original value ÷ original value) × 100

For example, if quantity demanded increases from 200 units to 250 units, the percentage change in quantity demanded is:

$[(250 - 200) \div 200] \times 100$

$= +50 \times 100$

$= +25\%$

If this was caused by a price cut from £10 to £8, we need to calculate the percentage price change:

$[(new\ value - original\ value) \div (original\ value)] \times 100$

$= (8 - 10) \times 100$

$= -20\%$

The equation for the price elasticity of demand is:

(% change in quantity demanded) ÷ (% change in price)

$= +25 \div -20$

$= -1.25$

Using elasticity

Some people find it useful to use a triangle to help with their elasticity calculations and with using elasticity. The values you know are put into the triangle, and then you can easily calculate the missing value.

If you have a number on the top part of the triangle, you divide it by the number you have below to get the other number you need below.

If you have the two numbers below, you multiply them to get the number missing in the top part.

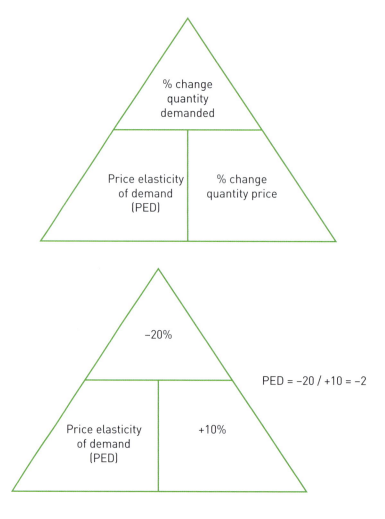

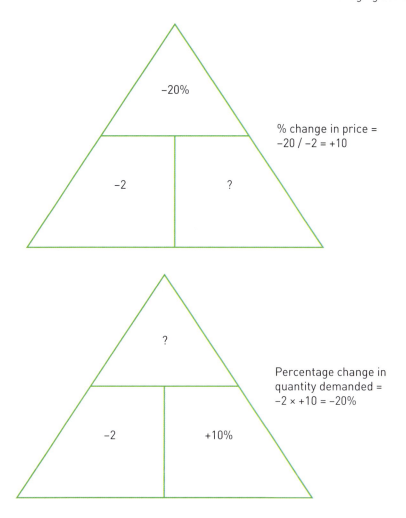

Interpreting elasticity

Having calculated elasticity, how do you interpret it? The key when thinking about the relationship between demand and a variable is to consider two things about the answer to your calculation: the sign of the answer, and the size of the answer (ignoring its sign).

The sign of the answer

If the answer is negative, the change in quantity demanded and the change in the variable are in opposite directions. This would be the case if, for example, a price increase reduces quantity demanded, or if a decrease in income increases demand. If the answer is positive, the quantity demanded and the variable move in the same direction: for example, when an increase in income increases demand. The sign of the answer shows whether the quantity demanded and the variable move in the same direction or opposite directions.

The size of the answer (ignoring the sign)

If the answer is bigger than 1 (ignoring whether it is positive or negative), then demand is elastic. The size of the answer shows how much the quantity demanded changes in percentage relative to the percentage change in the variable. For example:

- a value of 3 means that the percentage change in quantity demanded is 3 times the change in the variable;
- a value of 0.5 means that the percentage change in quantity demanded is 0.5 times the change in the variable.

Remember that if demand is inelastic, this means the change in percentage quantity demanded is smaller than the percentage change in the variable. It does not mean there is no change—just that is it smaller.

For example, the quantity demanded may fall by 40% which is quite a lot; but if this is following a price increase of 70% demand is still price inelastic because the percentage change in quantity demanded is less than the percentage change in price.

Calculating the price elasticity of demand

Example 1

Let's say that quantity demanded increases by 10% when price falls by 5%.

price elasticity of demand =

percentage change in quantity demanded ÷ percentage change in price

$= +10\% \div -5\%$

Because the price and quantity demanded move in different directions (one increases when the other falls), the answer will be negative.

Because the quantity demanded changes by twice as much as price (10% ÷ 5%) the value of the price elasticity of demand is 2.

The price elasticity of demand is therefore

$+10\% \div -5\% = -2$

Demand for this product would be described as price elastic because the percentage change in quantity demanded is more than the percentage change in price.

The value of the price elasticity (i.e. the size of the answer, ignoring the sign) shows how much the quantity demanded changes (in percentages) compared to the percentage change in price: in this case, 2 times as much.

Example 2

Let's say that quantity demanded increases by 10% when price falls by 20%.

price elasticity of demand =

$+10\% \div -20\%$

Because the price and quantity demanded move in different directions (one increases when the other falls) the answer will be negative.

Because the quantity demanded changes by half as much as price (10% ÷ 20%), the value of the price elasticity of demand is 0.5.

The price elasticity of demand is therefore

$+10\% \div -20\% = -0.5$

The percentage change in quantity demanded is 0.5 times as much as the percentage change in price.

Demand for this product would be described as 'price inelastic' because the percentage change in quantity demanded changes is more than the percentage change in price.

Price elasticity of demand

value	0	<1	1	>1	∞
description	perfectly price inelastic	price inelastic	unitary elastic	price elastic	perfectly price elastic

3.1 DOING THE BUSINESS MATHS

Complete the table.

Change in quantity demanded (units)	Change in price (£)	% change in quantity demanded	% change in price	Price elasticity of demand
50 to 40	£2.00 to £2.20			
50 to 75	£2.00 to £1.80			
200 to 195	£20.00 to £21.00			
100 to 100	£50.00 to £60.00			

MANAGEMENT TASK

You want to increase the number of applications to your university for undergraduate business and economics courses. You have been allocated a budget of £200,000. Produce a short proposal on how you think these funds would be best used. Justify your ideas.

3.2 QUICK CHECK

a. If price elasticity of demand is negative, the demand curve is downward sloping: true or false?

b. Is a price elasticity of demand of −3 more or less elastic than a price elasticity of demand of −0.3? Explain.

c. If the price is cut and revenue increases, demand is price elastic: true or false?

d. If a price change has no effect on the quantity demanded, demand is perfectly price elastic: true or false?

3.4 BUSINESS INSIGHT: AMAZON AND WHOLE FOODS

In 2017 Amazon took control of the food and grocery business Whole Foods in the USA. Amazon said it would immediately cut the prices of a number of products at Whole Foods. It also said it would start selling Whole Foods products on its website.

   Amazon said that it would not cut prices on all products because of the impact on its profit margins. The profit margin is a measure of the profit per sale. However, Amazon would target specific items and cut prices on these to increase traffic and sales. Prices at Whole Foods are typically 15 to 20 per cent higher than those charged by rivals.

Question

How could a food and grocery business successfully charge 15 to 20 per cent more than its rivals?

MANAGEMENT TASK

If you were the marketing director of Amazon and you were going to recommend which products to cut the price on, would you choose price elastic or price inelastic products? Why?

What determines the price elasticity of demand?

The sensitivity of demand for a product in relation to changes in price will depend on a number of factors (see Figure 3.4).

Figure 3.4 Influences on the price elasticity of demand

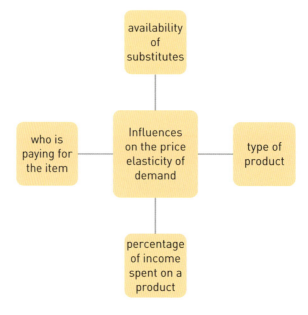

Availability of substitutes

If a customer can easily switch to a product that is similar, or appears similar, to yours, then any price increase is likely to lead to a relatively large fall in the quantity demanded, and demand will be price elastic. Customers will switch to the cheaper alternatives. If, however, managers can convince customers that their product is in some way different from, or better than, their rivals' products, demand will be price inelastic and it may be possible to increase price. The price of a season ticket at Chelsea, or the price of a ticket to see Taylor Swift, will be high because their loyal supporters and committed fans think there is no alternative (Liverpool is not Chelsea, and Selina Gomez is not Taylor Swift); demand for these tickets will be price inelastic. This is why businesses often invest heavily in developing their brands, and in promoting the benefits of their products. The aim is to make customers aware of why their product is better than others (or at least try to persuade them it is). The more closely a product can meet a customer's need, and the greater the value of the benefits provided to customers, the higher the price that a business can set. Are you a Coca-Cola or Pepsi drinker? A Costa or Starbucks fan? An Apple or Microsoft user? All of these companies will try to make you loyal to them so that you won't be put off by high prices.

READ MORE

If you are interested in marketing, you should read

Baines, P., Fill, C., and Rosengren, S. (2016), *Fundamentals of Marketing*, Oxford: Oxford University Press.

Kotler, P., Armstrong, G., Wong, V., and Saunders, J., *Principles of Marketing*, Upper Saddle River, NJ: Prentice Hall.

3.5 BUSINESS INSIGHT: PRICE AND BENEFIT

A key determinant of the price people will be willing to pay and how sensitive they are to price changes is the benefit that they think they get from buying a product. Marketing managers invest heavily in trying to understand customers' wants and needs, developing products to meet them, and communicating to make them aware of the benefits of their products. Sometimes the benefits may be clear from the start. For example, many of us are worried about a virus wiping our documents. Think of the horror of losing a document you have been working on for weeks, or all of the documents you have saved over the years? What if you lost a key assignment hours before the submission? The benefits of anti-virus software to those needing to protect documents is clear, and therefore a relatively high price can be charged.

Other motivations for why we buy things may not be immediately obvious. The watch companies Rolex and Patek Philippe, for example, stress the value of their watches as heirlooms to pass on to your family. They do not promote the fact that their watches enable you to tell the time—there are many other ways we can get the time, not least from our mobile phones. So, why spend hundreds or even thousands of pounds on a Patek watch? Because it is about family, inheritance, and memories. Other watches such as Swatch position themselves more as fashion items—they want you to buy them not because they tell the time, but because they look good and reflect your mood. Swatch want you to have several Swatches—one for work, one for the weekend, one for going out, and so on.

Question

1. Why do people buy flowers, do you think? How might this affect the marketing activities for a business selling flowers?

2. Pandora jewellery is often bought as a gift and to mark a special occasion. How might this affect its marketing activities?

RESEARCH TASK

Look at three adverts in the press and identify the benefits that are being promoted.

MANAGEMENT TASK

- Your business sells burglar alarms for houses. You advertise online and in print. You are the sales manager responsible for training your team when they are handling enquiries generated by these advertisements. Produce a short brief for your sales team to help them justify the price of £1,000 for your alarms.

- Your business produces photocopying paper. The paper has a particularly good finish, which means it does not jam the photocopier. It does, however mean that you are selling it for 10 per cent more than more other providers. Your sales manager has a meeting with the purchasing manager of a large chain of language schools about becoming their sole provider of photocopying paper. Produce a short brief for the sales manager explaining how she should approach the discussion and close the deal.

Type of product

Some products may be regarded by the customer as essential—they will be very reluctant to give them up. The more a product is regarded as a 'necessity', the more price inelastic demand will be. For some people, Sky TV may be a necessity for the sports coverage; some people might be very reluctant to give up their morning coffee at Starbucks on the way to work; others may find it difficult to stop smoking. If, however, an item is regarded as more of a luxury—something that can be given up easily—the demand will be more sensitive to price changes, i.e. more price elastic.

Percentage of income spent on product

If a product is a substantial investment—for example, a new car or a holiday—customers are likely to spend quite a long time finding out information and comparing prices with alternative products. The price of such an item for most people will be a relatively significant proportion of their income (compared to a cup of coffee, for example) and customers are likely to be more sensitive to price changes. In comparison, change in the price of milk may be far less noticeable and so demand is more price inelastic.

Who is paying for the item

If you are not paying for a product, you are probably less sensitive to price then if you are. If your travel is being paid for by your business, you may be more likely to travel business class and get a taxi from the airport to your hotel. If it is your own money, you might look for cheaper alternatives.

Time period

Customers are used to making certain choices at certain moments. You have a favourite cereal, you like a particular restaurant, and you have particular shops you tend to go to. We all tend to stick to a fairly limited range of choices. This means that a change in price may have relatively little impact on the quantity demanded because we are used to the products we have been using already. If the price increases, we may reduce the quantity demanded by only a relatively small amount. Over time, however, we may come across—or actively seek—alternatives and switch away. This makes demand more price elastic over time. In some cases we can be extremely apathetic as consumers, The government regularly asks us to compare our energy prices and the returns offered by banks, for example, because in the UK we are notoriously bad at switching to cheaper alternatives—we either could not be bothered or think somehow we will be worse off.

Breadth of definition

The demand for any individual brand will be more price elastic than demand for the product category as a whole. If the price of one music streaming service increases, we can switch to another one relatively easily, so demand is relatively price elastic. If demand for all music streaming services increases, demand will be less sensitive and the price elasticity will be lower.

1. How important do you think the price of an electric car is in terms of influencing the decision to buy an electric car? Why?
2. Do you think demand for electric cars in general is likely to be more or less sensitive to price than the demand for a particular brand of electric car? Why?

The impact of technology on price sensitivity

Developments in technology are enabling businesses to gather more information on customers' buying habits and their sensitivity to price. This allows firms to estimate price elasticity of demand more accurately and therefore adjust prices more appropriately.

Thanks to technology, businesses are also able to use dynamic pricing with online transactions. This involves changing the price frequently, depending on factors such as:

- how often you have visited the site
- what else you have bought
- what else you have been searching for
- when you are searching (for example, are you trying to book a last-minute flight or are you booking months ahead?)
- what time of day you are searching
- what browser you are using
- your postcode
- your credit rating

Technology will also help the buyer. As customers we can search more easily for alternatives—we can even use price comparison sites to do it for us (if we trust that they are really doing a comparison rather than leading us to producers that pay them to do this). The internet should, therefore, make customers more price sensitive because it is so much easier to compare with other providers.

Dynamic pricing

Although we have tended to talk of 'the price' of a product in our analysis, in reality there is no such thing. For most products there are many different prices, depending on factors such as who the business is selling to or what time of the day or year it is. More and more stores now use electronic tags that allow the business to change the price of a product throughout the day. Some of these electronic tags will change in response to your mobile phone; your phone feeds data about you to a store system which then increases or decreases the price accordingly.

Examples of dynamic pricing include:

- sites such as Expedia, which offer thousands of different prices for a room in a particular hotel every day;
- Uber, the taxi business, which uses surge pricing, making rapid changes to the fares when demand is high (during a recent tube strike in London, Uber fares rose by 400%).

Technology also allows businesses to identify all kinds of factors that might affect the price they charge different customers.

- The travel site Orbitz calculated that Apple Mac users were prepared to pay 20 to 30 per cent more for hotel rooms than users of other brands of computer, and adjusted its pricing accordingly.
- The office supply store Staples and the furniture retailer Home Depot showed customers different prices based on a range of characteristics they could discover about the buyer. This included how far a customer was from a physical store outlet, as this could then be taken into account when setting prices for heavier items; customers in locations with more competitors nearby were shown lower prices.

Do you think businesses should be allowed to charge different prices to different people for the same product?

MANAGEMENT TASK

You run a hotel chain in the UK. You have used a standard pricing policy, charging the same amount per room in all your hotels at all times. Put together a short proposal outlining opportunities to increase or decrease prices to increase the overall revenue. Justify your recommendations.

Shifts in demand

A change in price leads to a movement along the demand curve (see Figure 3.5). A price change leads to a change in the quantity demanded. A change in other factors that influence demand (Figure 3.6) will change the quantity demanded at each and every price. This is shown by a shift in the demand curve. An increase in demand means more is demanded at each and every price. The demand curve moves outward. A decrease in demand means that less is demanded at each and every price. The demand curve shifts inward. In this section we will look at various factors that may influence demand.

Figure 3.5 (a) An increase in demand (b) A decrease in demand

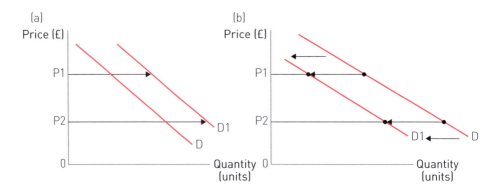

Figure 3.6 Influences on demand

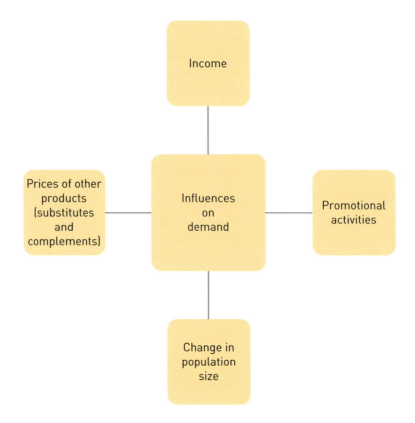

Income

Imagine, for example, your income has increased. At each and every price you can now buy more—this would be shown by an outward shift of the demand curve, as in Figure 3.5 (a). This is an increase in demand.

Equally, with a fall in income you may be willing and able to buy less at each and every price. In this case the demand curve shifts inwards, as shown in Figure 3.5 (b). This is a fall in demand.

If demand increases with an increase in income, and decreases with a decrease in income, a product is called a 'normal good' by economists (see Table 3.3). With more income you might take more holidays, for example.

However, in some cases customers may demand less of a product with more income and more of it with less income. These products are called 'inferior'. For example, in recent years some people have found they have less income to spend and have switched from supermarkets such Tesco and Waitrose towards discounters such as Aldi and Lidl. Because they have lower incomes, they have moved from well-known brands to the less familiar own-label brands that are produced by the discounters.

Table 3.3 The effect of income on demand

Change in income	Normal product	Inferior product
Income increases	Demand rises	Demand falls
Income decreases	Demand falls	Demand rises

KEY CONCEPT

A **shift in demand** occurs when more or less of a product is demanded at each and every price.

Of course, as with price changes, what matters is not just whether demand increases or falls in relation to a change in income; what also matters is how great the change is. Being able to forecast the scale of a change in demand is important for many business decisions such as staffing and deciding on inventory levels.

The sensitivity of demand in relation to income is measured by the income elasticity of demand. This measures the percentage change in the quantity demanded of a product in relation to percentage change in income.

income elasticity of demand = *percentage change in quantity demanded ÷ percentage change in income*

If the demand is sensitive to income (i.e. the percentage increase in quantity demanded is greater than the percentage increase in income, so the value is greater than 1), demand is said to be income elastic. Demand for products such as overseas holidays, sports cars, and membership of a private gym are likely to be income elastic.

If the demand is relatively insensitive to income (i.e. the percentage increase in quantity demanded is less than the percentage increase in income, so the value is less than 1), demand is said to be income inelastic. Demand for salt, socks, and tomato ketchup is likely to be income inelastic; changes in income levels may have relatively little effect on sales.

The **income elasticity of demand** measures the percentage change in the quantity demanded of a product in response to a percentage change in income. All other factors unchanged.

Calculating the income elasticity of demand

Example 1

If the quantity demanded of a product increases 20% when income increases 10%, then this means:

Income elasticity of demand = +20% ÷ +10% = +2

This is a normal good because the quantity demanded increases with more income (and vice versa) and so it has a positive answer. The value of 2 shows that the percentage change in quantity demanded is 2 times the percentage change in income. This is elastic (because it is greater than 1).

Example 2

If the quantity demanded of a product decreases 5% when income increases 10%, then this means:

Income elasticity of demand = −5% ÷ +10% = −0.5

This is an inferior good because the quantity demanded decreases with more income (and vice versa) and so it has a negative answer. The value of 0.5 shows that the percentage change in quantity demanded is 0.5 times the percentage change in income. This is inelastic (because it is less than 1).

An understanding of the income elasticity of demand, as explained in Table 3.4, will be useful to managers as it will show how demand might change in relation to changes in income. If the economy grows fast, for example, it would be useful to

Table 3.4 An explanation of income elasticity of demand

Income elasticity	Description
Positive	Normal good. With more income, demand increases. Demand curve shifts outwards.
Negative	Inferior good. With more income, demand decreases. Demand curve shifts inwards.
Luxury good	Percentage change in quantity demanded is more than the percentage change in income. Value of income elasticity is greater than 1.
Necessity	Percentage change in quantity demanded is less than the percentage change in income. Value of income elasticity is less than 1.

know which products will experience a significant increase in quantity demand, which will be relatively unaffected, and which will experience a fall in sales? This understanding of income elasticity might also affect which regions to target. For example, the growth of incomes in what have been relatively low-income countries, such as China and India, has created a big middle class. This has created a big increase in demand for ovens, microwaves, kitchen equipment, bathrooms, etc. This, in turn, has created massive opportunities for companies such as Unilever, which sells such things as household cleaning products.

3.2 DOING THE BUSINESS MATHS

Complete the table.

Change in quantity demanded (units)	Change in income (£000)	% change in quantity demanded	% change in income	Income elasticity	Normal or inferior? Elastic or inelastic?
20 to 30	10 to 11				
50 to 45	40 to 44				
3 to 2	100 to 98				
80 to 60	50 to 60				

3.3 QUICK CHECK

For each of the following statements, say whether it is true or false.

a. An inferior good has a negative income elasticity of demand.

b. An income elasticity of demand of +2 means demand is income elastic.

c. An increase of 10% in income leading to an increase in demand of 1% means demand is income inelastic.

d. A luxury good will probably have an income elasticity of more than 1.

Promotional activities

Businesses will use a range of promotional activities to communicate about their businesses and products. These promotions will shape and influence demand for their products. Promotional activity can take many forms such as TV advertising, billboards, press, and online advertising; the form of promotion chosen by a business will depend on the target audience and budget.

Promotional activities can be used in different ways:

- to inform people, e.g. that an event is happening, or a new version of the product is to be launched;

- to make people aware, e.g. of the features of a new product;

- to persuade people, e.g. of the benefits of one product compared to another.

Promotion may be used to increase the overall demand for a product or to increase it at certain times; for example, a hotel may be busy in the summer but quieter in the winter, and the business wants to increase demand in the less busy seasons. Similarly, a store may be busy on Saturday but quieter during the week, and so the manager may want to increase demand on weekdays.

Promotional activities will also be used to make demand for a product more price inelastic; by highlighting the particular benefits of a product, it may be possible to make demand less sensitive to price changes.

Managers may measure the sensitivity of demand to different forms of promotional spending. The promotional elasticity of demand could be measured:

percentage change in quantity demanded ÷ percentage change in promotional spending

This could be calculated for different forms of spending and for different campaigns to assess their effectiveness. Does an increase of 20% on Google adwords spending lead to a 1% or 40% increase in quantity demanded, for example? This could affect the size and composition of the promotional budget.

A change in population size

The term 'population' can refer to everyone within a country. In marketing, however, the 'population' refers to the overall target group of customers. The number of customers in the target market will influence the total demand. The relevant population size in a market may change due to demographic change. For example, changes in the birth rate or death rate may affect the number of potential customers in any given age group. Similarly, net migration may increase or decrease the population size in a country and this may lead to a change in the target population for a given product.

The population for any given product will depend not just on the total number of people but also on their tastes and preferences. Greater interest in environmental issues, locally produced goods, and ethically sourced products has increased demand for this type of good, for example. There may also been moves toward particular parts of a market. In the brewing industry, for example, there has been a major shift in recent years toward craft beers produce by small, local breweries rather than mass produced beers.

BUSINESS CASE QUESTIONS: CAN YOU NOW ANSWER . . .

What factors do you think influence the demand for electric cars? You should also be able to show the changing demand on a diagram.

Again, the sensitivity of demand to changes in population could be measured to assess the impact of future changes. The demand for healthcare and education, for example, is likely to be quite sensitive to population changes.

3.6 BUSINESS INSIGHT: POPULATION AND DEMAND

The population pyramid

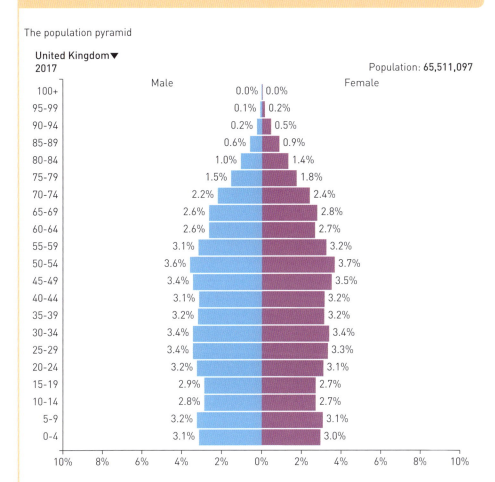

United Kingdom▼
2017   Population: **65,511,097**

Source: Courtesy of https://www.populationpyramid.net/united-kingdom/2017/

The population pyramid illustrated shows the proportion of males and females at different age ranges. These population structures will affect demand for different products—the proportion of very young would affect demand for nappies, while the proportion of elderly people might affect demand for retirement homes.

Question
Can you think of two other products which have a demand that is likely to be closely linked to the age of the population?

MANAGEMENT TASK

The population of the UK is ageing. You are the manager of a business producing a range of ready-made meals. Produce a short report on how the ageing of the population might affect your products and their marketing.

Managers will monitor changes in the size of their target populations and this will influence their marketing activities. For example, managers may decide to target new regions within a country or new countries around the world to reach new target populations; or they may try and broaden the appeal of the product—for example, by trying to make the product appeal to a wider age range, thereby reaching new target groups.

The importance of the prices of other products

A customer's decision to buy a product will be influenced by the prices of other products. For example, when you are buying a new pair of jeans, booking a flight, or getting car insurance, you will probably compare prices. In fact you may use a business such as www.gocompare.com to do it for you. If you are trying to choose between two flights to Paris, both of which are comparable in terms of flight times, you will probably choose the cheaper one. A reduction in the price of a substitute will therefore lead customers to switch to the substitute. This leads to a fall in demand for the original product. At each and every price, the quantity demanded falls and the demand curve will shift in.

Equally, an increase in the price of a substitute means customers will switch from the substitute to this product (see Figure 3.7). Energy companies and credit card companies are regularly trying to get you to switch from more expensive rivals by offering price incentives. Similarly, some companies will push their price competitiveness to stop you switching. John Lewis, for example, claims that it is 'Never knowingly undersold'.

Figure 3.7 (a) A fall in the price of a substitute will lead to an inward shift in demand (b) A rise in the price of a substitute will increase demand

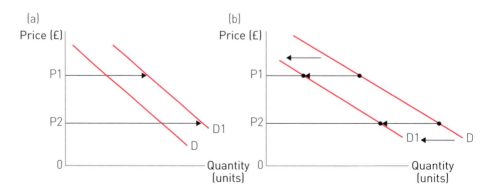

However, businesses will not just be concerned about the prices of substitutes; they will also be interested in the price of products that complement their products (see Figure 3.8). If the amount of milk consumed is linked to how much tea and coffee is drunk, then changes in the price of tea and coffee will affect sales of milk. If the price of a complement falls, the quantity demanded of the complement will increase and the demand for the other product will increase as well. Cheaper coffee may increase the quantity demanded of coffee and of milk. Similarly, a fall in the price of wine may increase sales of wine glasses. By comparison, an increase in the price of a complement may reduce the quantity demanded of the complement and reduce demand for this product.

Figure 3.8 (a) A rise in the price of a complement will lead to an inward shift in demand (b) A fall in the price of a complement will increase demand

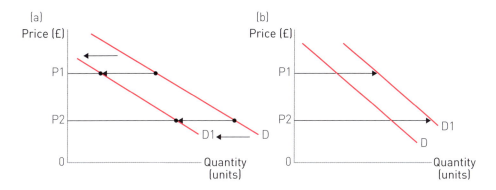

RESEARCH TASK

Research a product in the news that has experienced a major increase in demand. Explain why this has happened.

3.7 BUSINESS INSIGHT: RICHER SOUNDS

Here is an extract from the Richer Sounds website.

We don't just claim to be the cheapest—we guarantee it!
All we ask is that products are brand new, boxed, in stock at time of purchase and carry a comparable guarantee.
We're confident that our prices are amongst the very keenest out there, however in the unlikely event that you do find a genuine lower price our Price Beat ensures we'll beat that price (not just match it) as well as give you the reassurance that comes from buying from us. We also guarantee to beat web prices, and our Price Beat is even valid for 7 days after purchase. If you've seen a cheaper price, let us know, and we'll happily beat that price by up to £100!

> We go to great lengths and huge expense to keep as much stock on site at all our branches for our valued customers to take away immediately. Please be sure when checking out our competition that the stock you are interested in actually exists!
>
> https://www.richersounds.com/information/pricebeat

Question

By focusing on offering lower prices than the competition, what do you think Richer Sounds is assuming about the price elasticity of demand for its products?

MANAGEMENT TASK

You are the Chief Executive of an airline. You want to be the cheapest airline possible. Outline the service you will provide and the marketing mix you will use to achieve this.

Once again, a key issue is not just *whether* a change in the price of another product changes demand, but *how much* it changes demand. The direction and size of the effect of the change in price of one product on demand for another, all other factors held constant, is measured by the cross price elasticity of demand.

Note: once again we are assuming that we are holding all other factors constant. This is essential in order to isolate the effect of just one variable changing. In reality this is difficult to do.

Calculating the cross price elasticity of demand

The equation for cross price elasticity of demand for product A is:

percentage change in quantity demanded of product A ÷ percentage change in price of product B

A positive answer for the cross price elasticity of demand shows that an increase in the price of B increased the quantity demanded of A or a decrease in the price of B decreased the quantity demanded of A. These products are substitutes (see Table 3.5).

A negative answer to this shows that an increase in the price of B leads to a decrease in the quantity demanded of A, or that a decrease in the price of B increased the quantity demanded of A. These products are complements.

The size of the cross price elasticity of demand shows how sensitive the demand for a product is to changes in the price of other products.

If the answer is greater than 1, the cross price elasticity is cross price elastic. A given percentage change in the price of the other product has the effect of a bigger percentage change in the quantity demanded of the product.

If the answer is less than 1, the cross price elasticity is cross price inelastic. A given percentage change in the price of the other product has the effect of a smaller percentage change in the quantity demanded of the product.

Table 3.5 Cross price elasticity of demand

Cross price elasticity of demand	Relationship between product A and product B
Positive	Substitutes. An increase in the price of B increases the demand of A. The demand curve for A shifts outwards.
Negative	Complements. An increase in the price of B decreases the demand of A. The demand curve for A shifts inwards.
Elastic	Value of more than 1. The percentage change in quantity demanded of product B is greater than the percentage change in the price of A.
Inelastic	Value of less than 1. The percentage change in quantity demanded of product B is less than the percentage change in the price of A.

KEY CONCEPT

The **cross price elasticity of demand** measures the percentage change in quantity demanded of one product in response to the percentage change in price of another, all other factors held constant.

Example 1 of calculating cross price elasticity of demand

If the quantity demanded of a product increases 20% when the price of another good increases 10%, then this means:

cross price elasticity of demand $= +20\% \div +10\% = +2$

These products are substitute goods because the quantity demanded of one product increases when the price of another rises (and vice versa). The equation has a positive answer because customers switch to product A when product B becomes more expensive. The value of 2 shows that the percentage change in quantity demanded is 2 times the percentage change in the price of the other good. This is cross price elastic (because it is greater than 1).

Example 2 of calculating cross price elasticity of demand

If the quantity demanded of a product decreases 5% when the price of the other good increases 10%, then this means:

cross price elasticity of demand $= -5\% \div +10\% = -0.5$

These products are complements because the quantity demanded of one product increases when the price of another falls (and vice versa). The equation has a negative answer because customers stop buying as much of product A when product B becomes more expensive. The value of 0.5 shows that the percentage change in quantity demanded is 0.5 times the percentage change in the price of the other good. This is cross price inelastic (because it is less than 1).

BUSINESS CASE QUESTIONS: CAN YOU NOW ANSWER . . .

The government is increasing taxes on diesel cars. What effect will this have on demand for electric cars?

3.8 BUSINESS INSIGHT: SUBSTITUTES

To understand which products are likely to be substitutes and complements managers need to understand their customers fully. If people are thinking about buying a new sofa, they may be weighing it up against a new carpet or new dishwasher—these would be substitutes. Customers may be deciding whether to go to the cinema or out for a meal—again, these are substitutes. Customers may buy flowers or wine as a present—again, these are substitutes.

Managers must not take too narrow a view of their business and only look at other firms producing the same products; they must look at other ways in which the demands of customers may be satisfied.

Question
What do you think are substitutes and complements for a visit to the cinema?

MANAGEMENT TASK

You run a flower shop. Produce a short report setting out what you believe are possible substitutes and complements for your products. Justify your choices.

READ MORE

If you want a fascinating insight into what influences our decisions in a range of areas (including our desire to cheat whenever we can!) then read Dan Ariely's excellent book:

Ariely, D. (2011), *The Upside of Irrationality: The Unexpected Benefits of Defying Logic*, New York: Harper Perennial.

3.4 QUICK CHECK

For each of the following statements, say whether it is true or false.

a.   If the cross price elasticity of demand for two products is positive, they are substitutes.

b. If the cross price elasticity of demand for product A in relation to product B is negative, this means that an increase in the price of B reduces the demand for A.

c. If the cross price elasticity of demand is +0.5, a price change of one product has a smaller effect on the quantity demanded of the other product in percentage terms.

3.9 BUSINESS INSIGHT: INFLUENCES ON DEMAND

The factors influencing demand for a category of products will depend on the nature of the product.

- The demand for breakfast cereals will be influenced by factors such as the size of the population, social trends affecting whether people grab snacks on their way to work, the impact of taxes on sugar, regulations on advertising sugary cereals, and the price of alternatives such as fruit.

- The demand for air travel will depend on income, the value of one currency in terms of another, and concerns over safety of air travel.

- The demand for DIY products will depend on the housing market and the number of houses being sold; this will be affected by the ease and cost of borrowing.

Question

What do you think are key influences on the demand for:

- Music festivals?
- Perfume?
- Energy drinks?
- Pubs?

Other forms of elasticity of demand

The concept of elasticity of demand can be used in relation to any variable that affects demand, such as price, income, the price of other goods, the weather, and the population size. In all cases, the sign shows the direction in which the variable and quantity demanded move in relation to each other. The size shows the strength of the relationship between the variable and the quantity demanded.

Marketing managers will consider the variable that might affect demand for their products. Warm weather will affect sales of barbecues and beers. Big sports tournaments affects sales of TVs. The number of 16-year-olds will affect sales of English GCSE textbooks.

The marketing mix

As we have seen, the price is one tool available to managers to influence demand. Managers can also try to manage demand through promotional activities such as advertisements and promotional offers. Managers will try to include the amount

Figure 3.9 The 4 Ps of the marketing mix

of demand and consider the timing, e.g. to avoid seasonal patterns and to match demand to capacity. However, price and promotion are just two of the various tools a manager can use. The combination of all factors that can be used in marketing is often called the 'marketing mix' (see Figure 3.9).

The basic version of the marketing is called the 4 Ps, namely:

- price, i.e. the cost of the product for the customer and the terms and conditions of payment;
- product, i.e. the product itself: for example, this includes what the product looks like, its features and specifications, and how it is packaged;
- promotion, i.e. the various activities to communicate about the product, such as advertising and promotional offers;
- place: this actually refers to the distribution of the product, for example whether it is sold online, through outlets etc.

Each of these Ps can be changed by the marketing team to influence demand. Price is only one element of the many tools available to marketing managers.

READ MORE

You can find out more about the marketing mix by reading

Anderson, L.M., and Taylor, R.L. (1995), 'McCarthy's 4Ps: Timeworn or Time-Tested?', *Journal of Marketing Theory and Practice*, Vol. 3, No. 3, pp. 1–9.

Borden, N.H. (1964), 'The Concept of the Marketing Mix', *Journal of Advertising Research* Vol. 4 (June), pp. 2–7.

Shapiro, B.P. (1985), 'Rejuvenating the Marketing Mix', *Harvard Business Review* Vol. 63, No. 5 (September), pp. 28–34.

SUMMARY

Managers will be interested in the factors that determine the demand for their products. The demand determines sales and revenue.

Managers will want to anticipate how changes in different factors will affect demand because this affects other plans, such as staffing, production scheduling, and stock levels. Managers will attempt to achieve target levels of demand through their pricing and marketing activities. The elasticity of demand measures how sensitive demand is to changes in variables such as the price, the price of other factors, promotional spending, and income. Managers will want to understand this to help them prepare for changes in sales.

KEY LEARNING POINTS

- A demand curve shows the quantity customers are willing and able to buy at each and every price, all other factors held constant
- A change in price leads to a change in quantity demanded (a movement along the demand curve)
- A change in factors other than price, such as income or population size, leads to more or less being demanded at each and every price and shifts demand
- Elasticity of demand measures how sensitive demand is to changes in variables such as price, the price of other products, and income
- If the change in quantity demanded is less than the change in the variable in percentages, demand is inelastic
- If the change in quantity demanded is more than the change in the variable in percentages, demand is elastic
- A normal good has a positive income elasticity of demand
- An inferior good has a negative income elasticity of demand
- Substitutes have a positive cross price elasticity of demand

BUSINESS CASE EXTENSION QUESTIONS

1. If Tesla has established its brand and a reputation for innovation, how do you think this affects the price elasticity of demand for its products? If, in the future, more competitors start producing electric cars, what effect do you think this has on the price elasticity of demand for Tesla cars? How might this affect its pricing?

2. Do you think electric cars are likely to be a normal or an inferior good? Why?

3. Do you think demand for electric cars is likely to be income elastic or inelastic? Why?

4. With increasing concerns about the environmental impact of diesel cars, diesel fuel and cars are likely to be taxed more in the future. Explain the impact of this on demand for electric cars. How would you show this using a demand curve diagram?

Economics for Business

5. Do you think electricity and electric cars are substitutes or complements? Why?

6. If the price of electricity increased, how might this affect demand for electric cars? Can you illustrate this with a demand curve diagram?

7. Look at the data in the table relating to new car sales in the UK. Summarize and explain the key trends in the data.

UK sales of new cars by fuel type, 2011–16

	Diesel		Petrol		Alternative fuel		Total	
	000	%	000	%	000	%	000	%
2011	982	50.6	934	48.1	26	1.3	1,941	100.0
2012	1,039	50.8	978	47.8	28	1.4	2,045	100.0
2013	1,127	49.8	1,105	48.8	33	1.5	2,265	100.0
2014	1,240	50.1	1,184	47.8	52	2.1	2,476	100.0
2015	1,277	48.5	1,284	48.7	73	2.8	2,634	100.0
2016	1,285	47.7	1,319	49.0	89	3.3	2,693	100.0

Source: https://store.mintel.com/cars-in-uk-2016-market-sizes.

8. Look at the data on the evolution of the global electric car stock. Summarize the key elements of the data. Why do you think the levels of sales of electric cars varies between countries?

Evolution of the global electric car stock, 2010–16

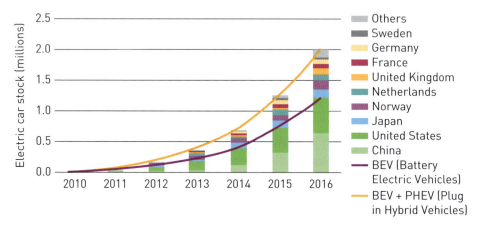

Source: © OECD/IEA 2017 *Global EV Outlook 2017*, IEA Publishing. Licence: www.iea.org/t&c. IEA analysis based on EVI country submissions, complemented by EAFO (2017a), HIS Polk (2016), Marklines (2017), ACEA (2017a, 2017b) and EEA (2017).

Notes: The electric car stock shown here is primarily estimated on the basis of cumulative sales since 2005. When available, stock numbers from official national statistics have been used, provided good consistency with sales evolutions.

QUICK QUESTIONS

1. What is the difference between a change in quantity demanded and a change in demand?
2. If demand is price sensitive, should you increase or decrease price to increase revenue? Why?
3. Explain why an increase in revenue may not increase profits.
4. Explain the effect on demand of an increase in income if the product is inferior.
5. Explain the effect on the demand for product A if the cross price elasticity of demand for A in relation to B is positive and the price if B increases. Explain your answer.
6. If price decreases from £10 to £8, and the quantity demanded increases from 20 units to 30 units, what is the price elasticity of demand?
7. If income increases from £15,000 a year to £18,000, and the quantity demanded of a product increases from 20,000 units to 22,000 units, what is the income elasticity of demand?
8. If price of product B decreases from £10 to £8, and the quantity demanded of A increases from 20 units to 22 units, what is the cross price elasticity of demand?

Managing costs

WHY DO I NEED TO KNOW ABOUT MANAGING COSTS?

Your employees are asking for a significant pay increase after a couple of years during which their pay has been held relatively constant. The rents on a number of your stores are increasing by 10 per cent this year, and you are also being hit by higher energy bills. You operate in a very competitive market where increased market share is hard to come by, and putting up prices would not be a good move at the moment. Unless you can find some ways of getting costs down or revenue up, your annual profits are going to be lower than last year. This won't be good for your bonus or your company's share price. It may not be good for your long-term future, as you were brought in to get the profits up.

You know there may be some areas where costs could relatively easily be cut back, but you think you have quite a lean organization as it is. Staff are already suspicious, and there are rumours of redundancies already circulating. You would like to get the unit costs down without job losses if you can, but it may not be easy.

Managers will be interested in what happens to the costs of the business because this has an impact on their profits. In this chapter we consider the different types of costs and how managers might control them.

BY THE END OF THIS CHAPTER YOU WILL BE ABLE TO . . .

- distinguish between the different types of costs that a business may have
- explain why costs and cash outflow are different
- explain the importance of the concept of contribution to business
- explain the importance of productivity
- analyse how a business might try to control and manage its costs

BUSINESS CASE

The supermarket Sainsbury's announced in 2017 that it would be cutting up to 2,000 jobs from its human resources staff as part of cost reduction plans. A BBC report from October 2017 said:

> The UK's second biggest supermarket chain says the 'difficult decision' will affect roles in stores, as well as in the company's central offices. It plans to make 1,400 payroll and HR clerks redundant and other changes could see another 600 other posts removed.

Sainsbury's is looking to save £500m amid fierce competition from discounters and rising food costs. The majority of the headcount losses will be from within its supermarket stores.

Sainsbury's [. . .] employs nearly 200,000 people in total. It said it would offer affected staff alternative roles wherever possible, or redundancy packages. [. . .]

Its biggest rival Tesco is also shrinking its headcount. Tesco said in June that that it would cut 1,200 jobs from its head office, just days after revealing that more than a thousand jobs were going at its Cardiff call centre.

All the big established food retailers are juggling rising costs and increased competition from the discounters.

Source: © BBC: www.bbc.co.uk/news/business-41652424

BUSINESS CASE QUESTIONS

This chapter will help you answer the following questions.

1. Why is cutting costs a priority for Sainsbury's at the moment?
2. How do you think cutting costs will help the competitiveness of the business?
3. Why do you think Sainsbury's cut these particular costs?
4. Why doesn't Sainsbury's try and cut costs further?

Introduction

Most people think they have a fairly clear understanding of costs. We happily talk about the 'cost' of something. However the word 'costs' is in fact a very technical term in economics; it is defined differently by business people and economists and that technical sense is widely misunderstood by the general public. One assumption most people make, for example, is that if you pay £100 for some resources, this is shown in the accounts that year as the cost of them; believe it or not, this is not the case in the eyes of business people. So, in this section we will explain why the cost of resources is not necessarily the amount spent on them, and why accountants and economists view costs slightly differently.

Costs and cash flow

Costs measure the value of the resources used up over a given period. Managers measure the value of the resources used based on the price paid. These costs are not necessarily the same as cash outflow. If, for example, a business bought 12 units of inventory at £10 each and then used up 3 of them in production, the cost of these resources for that accounting period would be £10 × 3 = £30 (because only 3 were actually used up and sold); the remaining 9 units are classified as inventory (or stock) because they are there to be used and sold in the future. They would appear as assets of the business on its balance sheet when it produces its annual accounts.

KEY CONCEPT

Inventory (or **stock**) is an asset of the business; it is product or materials that the business owns and that can be used in coming periods.

4.1 DOING THE BUSINESS MATHS

A business buys 20 units of supplies at £5 each in cash and produces 20 items using the supplies. The costs of labour and other inputs per item produced are £4 in cash. The business sells 12 items at £20 on credit.

a. Cash flow for this period
   Cash in: £0 because items are sold on credit
   Cash out: £100 on the supplies plus £80 on labour and other costs = £180
   Net cash flow = −£180

b. Profit/loss for this period

   Revenue = value of the sales = 12 × £20 = £240.

Although the cash has not been received yet, the items sold are worth £240.

   Costs of the goods sold = 12 × £5 = £60

Only 12 units of supplies have been used up, so these are the only costs relevant to the 12 sales. The other 8 units are in store to be sold in the future. At the moment they are an asset of the business.

   Labour and other costs = £4 × 12 = £48
   Profit = revenue − costs = £240 − (60 + 48) = 240 − 108 = £132

The 8 unsold units are inventory for the business. This would show as an asset in the financial statements of the business.

   Inventory = 8 × £5 = £40

   This highlights how a business can have a negative cash flow even though it is making a profit. It shows how important it is for managers to understand the difference between costs and cash flow.

Questions

1. A business buys 200 units of materials at £5 each on credit. It sells 40 of them for £9 each in cash. The labour cost per unit is £2 paid in cash.
   As a result of these transactions what is:

   a. the level of profits?

   b. the cash position of the business?

   c. the stock level of the business?

2. A business buys 200 units of materials at £5 each in cash. It sells 40 of them for £9 each on credit. The labour cost per unit is £2 paid in cash.

As a result of these transactions what is:

a. the level of profits?

b. the cash position of the business?

c. the stock level of the business?

4.1 QUICK CHECK

For each of the following statements, say whether it is true or false.

a. A business buys 20 units of a product for £6 each on credit. The cash outflow is 0.

b. A business buys 20 units of a product for £6 each on credit and uses them all up. The cost in accounting terms is 0.

c. A business buys 20 units of a product for £6 each on credit and uses 5 of them up. The cost in accounting terms is £120.

d. A business buys 20 units of a product for £6 each on credit and uses 5 of them up. The cost in accounting terms is £30.

Economists and costs

As we saw above, costs measure the value of the resources used up. How much was paid for the labour used? The transport used? The materials used in the sold items? However, an economist also includes an estimate of opportunity cost of the resources used in a business. Opportunity cost is the loss of the next best alternative when one alternative is chosen, i.e the benefit missed out on when one option is chosen over another. To an economist, if the revenue of a business covers the costs, this means that it covers the value of the resources used up plus the opportunity cost. This means that a business may declare a profit in its accounts because its revenues are greater than its business costs, but to an economist this might be regarded a loss. This would be the case if, when the opportunity cost is included the revenue, the income is not sufficient to make this economically viable in the long run.

Costs and profits

Costs matter because profit is measured by revenue minus costs. If costs are too high, profits will be low and investors will be unhappy with the return on their investment. As a manager you will be held to account for the low profits of the business. A failure to deliver the expected profits may lead to lower rewards for managers and may even cost them their jobs.

DOING THE BUSINESS MATHS

Table 4.1 Calculating profits

	Business A (£m)	Business B (£m)	Business C (£m)
Revenue	100	100	100
Costs	60	60	60
Profit (to an accountant)	40	40	40
Estimated opportunity cost	30	70	40
Profit (to an economist)	?	?	?

In Table 4.1 the opportunity costs of the resources being used have been estimated. Business B declares a profit in its accounts. However, an economist would say that these profits are not sufficient given the resources it is using; in fact, given what these resources could be earning elsewhere, this business is making a loss.

Question
What would an economist's view of Business C be?

KEY CONCEPT

The **opportunity cost** measures the benefit of the next-best alternative that is foregone by choosing another alternative.

BUSINESS CASE QUESTIONS: CAN YOU NOW ANSWER . . .

- Why is cutting costs a priority for Sainsbury's at the moment?
- How do you think cutting costs will help the competitiveness of the business?

Types of costs

The costs of a business are measured by the value of all the resources used. Managers will be interested in the overall costs of a business for a given period but will also want to analyse their costs further—for example, they may be interested in the costs associated with a given region or product. Costs will also be categorized in different ways, such as those which are to do with production, those to do with administration, those to do with marketing, and so on.

ANALYSING THE BUSINESS DATA: MARKS & SPENCER'S UK OPERATING COSTS 2016–17

Table 4.2 Marks & Spencer's UK operating costs

	52 weeks ended		Change on previous year (%)
	1 Apr 17 (£m)	26 Mar 16 (£m)[1]	
Store staffing	1,010.3	974.4	3.7
Other store costs	1,000.7	974.4	2.7
Distribution and warehousing	519.6	475.4	9.3
Marketing	162.7	186.1	–12.6
Central costs	697.1	655.8	6.3
UK operating costs	**3,390.4**	**3,266.1**	**3.8**

1. Certain prior year costs have been reclassified to reflect changes in UK organization structure.

Source: corporate.marksandspencer.com

Questions

1. Why do you think Marks and Spencer plc measures its costs in this way?
2. How might such data be useful to managers?

Fixed and variable costs

One way of analysing costs is to distinguish between those that change with output and those that don't. These are known as fixed costs and variable costs.

- **Fixed costs** are costs that are unrelated to output levels: for example, the rent on a building. These costs can change—for example, rent can increase over time—but the rent on a store is not related to how many customers the store attracts.
- **Variable costs** are costs that do change with output. For example, in McDonald's the more burgers that are sold, the more the company will use up meat and pickles.

KEY CONCEPTS

Fixed costs are costs that do not change with output. **Variable costs** are costs that do change with output.

Figure 4.1 Example of fixed, variable, and total costs

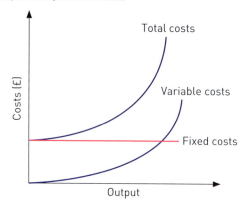

In this example the variable cost per unit is assumed to increase as more is produced, perhaps because because more has to be paid to acquire materials or labour.

MANAGEMENT TASK

You run a multinational consumer electronics business similar to PC World and Currys.

Explain how you might analyse the cost data of the business to help you make useful management decisions.

Fixed costs are shown as a straight line against output. In a given time period they do not change for given levels of output, although it may be that fixed costs increase, e.g. if more office space has to be rented.

Variable costs increase with output; variable costs may increase by varying amounts as output increases, which we will explore later. In Figure 4.1 the variable costs are assumed to be increasing at an increasing rate (for example, because resources become scarcer and more expensive).

Total costs measure the fixed costs plus variable costs at any level of output.

4.3 DOING THE BUSINESS MATHS

Look at the chart and answer the questions.

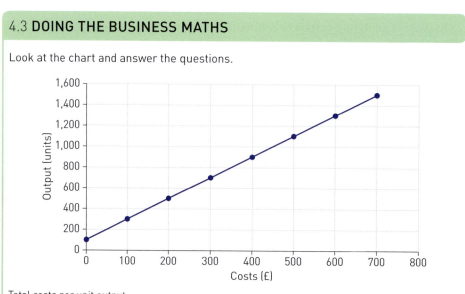

Total costs per unit output

Questions

1. What is the level of fixed costs when output is 300 units?
2. What is the level of variable costs when output is 500 units?

KEY CONCEPT

Total costs equals fixed costs plus variable costs.

4.2 QUICK CHECK

For each of the following statements, say whether it is true or false.

a. Fixed costs never change.

b. When output is zero, total costs equal fixed costs.

c. Total costs equals fixed costs plus variable costs.

d. Profit equals total revenue minus total costs.

4.1 BUSINESS INSIGHT: HOUSE OF FRASER PREMISES

Faced with poor profits, managers will focus on different ways of reducing costs. One aspect of this might be looking for cheaper, or lower-cost, premises to reduce fixed costs.

This is exactly what the House of Fraser department store chain did recently when it sought to reduce the rent on some of its stores. It wrote to some of its landlords asking for their support. This followed a disappointing Christmas period for sales at the end of 2017. According to a BBC report of January 2018, House of Fraser said that

> like for like sales in the UK fell 2.6% for the 17 weeks to 30 December amid a 'volatile and competitive' market. [. . .] The *Guardian* reported that the chain wanted to reduce the size of its 59 stores by close to a third over the next decade by getting rid of top floors or basements. House of Fraser was bought by Chinese firm Sanpower for £480m in 2014. Last month the Moody's credit agency downgraded its credit rating for the retailer.

The retailer group Arcadia also wrote to its suppliers asking them to reduce prices.

Source: BBC, www.bbc.co.uk/news/business-42581940

Questions

1. What do you think will determine how suppliers respond to being asked to reduce their prices?
2. Should managers care about the effect that reducing the amount they pay to suppliers might have on those businesses?

KEY CONCEPT

Like for like sales measure the sales of certain stores in a business over a period of time and compare sales from the same stores over the same period in a previous year. This means, for example, that it would not include sales that occur from new stores that opened during that period.

The importance of fixed and variable costs

The level of fixed costs is important because in the short run these must be paid even if the business is not producing any output. The business is committed to paying these costs for a given period. Even if output is zero, the business will still pay fixed costs: i.e. it will make a loss of this amount. When considering whether to go ahead with a venture, managers should consider the risks involved and what would happen if sales were low. Fixed costs would be a significant consideration in this case. The higher the fixed costs, the higher the losses if sales are low.

However, what this also means is that a business may still produce in the short run even if it is making a loss, provided the loss is smaller than the fixed costs.

KEY CONCEPT

The **short run** is the period of time when at least one factor of production is fixed. In the **long run**, all factors are variable.

Imagine the fixed costs of a restaurant are £3,000 a week. If the business has no customers it will make a loss of £3,000 in the short run. Now imagine that the variable cost of making and serving a meal is £5. If the business can sell a meal and cover this £5, then anything on top of this is going to help pay off the £3,000 that are incurred no matter what. For example, if there was one customer who paid £8 for a meal, this would mean the £5 of making the meal are covered and there is £3 that can be used to put towards the fixed costs. This £3 is called the 'contribution per unit' because it contributes towards the fixed costs (as shown in Figure 4.2).

Imagine the business now has two customers, each paying £8 for a meal. This would mean it had $2 \times £3 = £6$ total contribution to put towards the fixed costs. The losses would still be £3,000 − £6 = £2,994 but this is less than £3,000.

If you look at Table 4.3 you can see that with every customer another £3 is earned, which helps reduces the losses. At 1,000 customers the restaurant would have enough contribution to pay off the fixed costs. This is called the break-even output. At levels of output above 1,000 customers, the contribution exceeds the fixed costs and a profit is made. The concept of contribution is very important to

Figure 4.2 A contribution to fixed costs

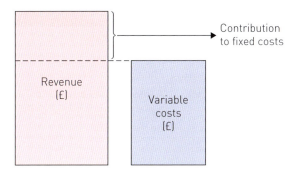

Table 4.3 Contribution and profits

Output (units)	Total contribution (£)	Fixed costs (£)	Profit or loss = total contribution minus fixed cost (£)
0	0	3,000	−3,000
50	150	3,000	−2,850
100	300	3,000	−2,700
250	750	3,000	−2,250
500	1,500	3,000	−1,500
100	300	3,000	−2,700
1,000	3,000	3,000	0
2,000	6,000	3,000	3,000
3,000	9,000	3,000	6,000

managers—provided a contribution is made on a unit, it is worth producing financially in the short term.

What this analysis helps explain is why businesses may continue even when they are making a loss—in the short term they are locked into certain costs, and the loss incurred by shutting down the business may be even greater. In the long term, however, the business would not want to produce when making a loss—it would, for example, not renew the rent on buildings and would stop production. The analysis also explains why some businesses seem to offer unbelievably low prices. Imagine that an airline has a flight that it is committed to run. Most of its costs have to paid regardless of how many passengers there are—for example, the salary of the crew and the landing fees. Even if a passenger only pays £30, then provided this covers any variable costs a contribution is paid towards the fixed costs, which is better than having no contribution at all (see Table 4.4).

Table 4.4 Relationship between total contribution and fixed costs

Relationship	Consequence
Total contribution is greater than fixed costs	A profit is made
Total contribution equals fixed costs	The business breaks even (no profit)
Total contribution is less than fixed costs	A loss is made but it is less than if there had been no output (because the loss would then be fixed costs)

4.4 DOING THE BUSINESS MATHS

A business sells a product for £20. Its variable cost per unit is £15. Its fixed costs are £150,000.

Complete the table.

Output (units)	Revenue (£)	Variable costs (£)	Contribution (£)	Fixed costs (£)	Profit/ loss (£)
10,000					
20,000					
30,000					
40,000					
50,000					

KEY CONCEPTS

The **contribution per unit** is measured by the price minus the variable cost per unit. **Total contribution** equals the contribution per unit multiplied by the number of units sold. **Break-even output** is the level of output at which revenue and costs are equal; no profit is made.

Shut-down point and break-even point

In the short run, a business will continue to operate provided that it can make a contribution from the sales it makes to put towards the fixed costs. Any contribution made will reduce the losses that would be made if no sales were made. The shut-down point in the short run will occur when the revenue just covers the variable costs. At this point, there is no contribution being made to fixed costs and so the loss made (equal to the fixed cost) would be the same as if the business shut down (Figure 4.3). A business would not produce if the revenue could not cover the variable costs because the loss would be bigger than if it shut down.

Figure 4.3 Shut-down point

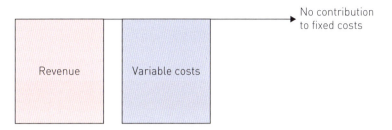

4.5 DOING THE BUSINESS MATHS

Complete the table.

Units (000)	Price (£)	Variable cost per unit (£)	Contribution (£)	Fixed costs (£)	Profit or loss (£)
10	10	6		120,000	
20	10	6		120,000	
30	10	6		120,000	
40	10	6		120,000	
50	10	6		120,000	

MANAGEMENT TASK

You have empty rooms in your hotel for this coming weekend. A customer has rung up to make a booking for a group of friends for 30 rooms. She is asking for a room rate of £100 a room; the published rate is £175. Should you accept this price?

The long run in economics is defined as the period of time when all factors of production are variable. There are no fixed costs; for example, the business can move offices if it needs to. In the long run a business will only continue if the revenue at least equals its total costs: i.e. it must at least break even. The break-even point occurs when the revenue equals the total costs.

KEY CONCEPTS

The **shut-down point** occurs when revenue equals variable costs. The **break-even point** occurs when revenue equals total costs.

MANAGEMENT TASK

You are the chief executive of a social media app launched three years ago to rival Twitter. You have yet to make a profit. Why would you keep the business open?

4.3 QUICK CHECK

For each of the following statements, say whether it is true or false.

a. The break-even point occurs when total revenue equals total costs.

b. The break-even point occurs when price equals average costs.

c. The shut-down point occurs when total revenue equals fixed costs.

d. Profit equals total contribution minus variable costs.

e. Break-even can be calculated using the equation fixed costs ÷ contribution per unit.

4.6 DOING THE BUSINESS MATHS

If the price per unit and the variable cost per unit are constant, the break-even output can be calculated using this formula:

  break-even output = fixed costs ÷ contribution per unit

Imagine the selling price per unit is £12 and the variable cost per unit is £8. This means the contribution per unit is

  price − variable cost per unit = £12 − £8 = £4

If fixed costs are £20,000, then £20,000 ÷ £4 = 5,000 units need to be sold for the contribution to cover the fixed costs.

Questions

1. Imagine the selling price is now £15, the variable cost per unit is still £8, and fixed costs are still £20,000. What is the break-even output now that the price is higher?

2. Imagine the selling price remains at £15, the variable cost per unit is reduced to £5, and fixed costs are still £20,000. What is the break-even output now that the variable cost per unit is lower?

Increasing your contribution per unit

If managers can increase the contribution per unit (CPU), this means that more contribution is made from every sale to put towards the fixed costs. Fewer units have to be sold in order for the business to break even. If fixed costs are £5,000 and the CPU is £5, you need to sell 1,000 units to cover the fixed costs and break even. If the CPU was £10 you would only need to sell 500 units.

To increase the contribution per unit, you may decide to do either or both of the following things.

- You might increase price. However, you will wish to consider the impact of this on sales; this will depend on the price elasticity of demand. If demand is price elastic, a price increase will reduce total revenue because the percentage fall in quantity demanded is greater than the percentage increase in price.

- You might reduce the unit costs. To do this, you must consider how to reduce costs without impacting on the quality, and therefore sales. If, for example, you can improve the efficiency of the process by reducing waste, this may boost the contribution per unit without affecting quality. You need to look for efficiency gains—can you find ways of doing what we do faster, or with fewer mistakes? Can you find ways of saving money where we are wasting money at the moment? Managers often talk of making the organization 'leaner'; this means finding 'excess fat' which can be removed from the business without having a negative impact on the business operations as a whole. If, however, reducing costs reduces quality, sales may fall. You must therefore look for areas of the business where costs can be cut without having a negative impact on the quality of your product or service.

BUSINESS CASE QUESTIONS: CAN YOU NOW ANSWER . . .

Why do you think Sainsbury's cut these particular costs?

4.2 BUSINESS INSIGHT: MANAGING COSTS

Managing costs is a key aspect of management. However, managers cannot simply reduce costs without considering the possible impact on the quality of product or service provided. Reducing the number of staff in a restaurant may cut employment costs, but customers may be unhappy with the longer wait involved. Cutting costs can be seen as a short-term fix in terms of profits, but the longer-term consequences must also be considered.

An example of manufacturers cutting costs, and being closely watched as they do so, can be seen in the chocolate industry.

Over recent years, manufacturers of chocolates have been reducing the amount of chocolate in their products, and thereby increasing the contribution per unit. For example, as reported in the *Telegraph* (January 2017):

- The segments of Terry's chocolate orange have been 'hollowed-out' [. . .] 'The treat, first manufactured in York in 1932, has been reduced from 175g to 157g in weight—a cut of 10 per cent.'

- 'Mondelez International has increased the gap between the peaks' in Toblerone in the UK.

- Nestlé cut the standard tin of Quality Street from 1kg to 820g in 2012. In 2014 consumers got only 780g.

Source: www.telegraph.co.uk/news/2016/11/21/9-chocolates-have-become-smaller-expensive-due-shrinkflation/

Questions

1. Why do you think managers have chosen to reduce costs in this way?
2. What do you think are the dangers of chocolate manufacturers reducing the cost per unit in this way?

MANAGEMENT TASK

You own a chain of restaurants. You are worried about profit margins. The manager of one of your restaurants has suggested cutting the amount of food per portion. Do you think this is a good idea?

Labour productivity

Managers will monitor costs and want to control them as a percentage of revenue because of the impact on profits. In the case of labour, managers will be interested in what staff are paid (their wages and salaries) and how much is produced on average by employees. The output per employee is called the labour productivity.

labour productivity = total output ÷ number of employees

For example, if 100 units are produced by 5 employees,

labour productivity = 100 ÷ 5 = 20 units each on average

If 100 units are produced by 2 employees,

labour productivity = 100 ÷ 2 = 50 units each

Why this matters is because the amount produced by employees will determine the labour cost per unit.

Imagine, for example, that you paid an employee £1,000 a week and she produced 20 units; the labour cost per unit is

£1000 ÷ 20 = £50 per unit

Imagine she now produced 40 units; the labour cost per unit is

£1000 ÷ 40 = £25 per unit

From a business perspective, if wages remain constant and labour productivity increases, this reduces the labour cost per unit.

Table 4.5 The relationship between labour productivity and labour costs per unit

Number of employees	Wage bill if each employee paid £500 a week	Output per week	Labour productivity per week	Labour cost per unit (£)
10	£5,000	10,000	10,000 ÷ 10 = 1,000	£5,000 ÷ 10,000 = 0.50
10	£5,000	20,000	20,000 ÷ 10 = 2,000	£5,000 ÷ 20,000 = 0.25
10	£5,000	50,000	50,000 ÷ 10 = 5,000	£5,000 ÷ 50,000 = 0.10
10	£5,000	100,000	100,000 ÷ 10 = 10,000	£5,000 ÷ 100,000 = 0.02

As we can see in Table 4.5, greater labour productivity, assuming total labour costs are constant, means that the labour cost per unit falls. With lower unit costs a business may be able to reduce the price and still maintain the profit per unit; or the business might keep the price the same but enjoy higher profit per unit. This is why increasing labour productivity is often a key focus of management.

4.7 DOING THE BUSINESS MATHS

Complete the table.

Number of employees	Wage bill if each employee paid £500 a week	Output per week	Labour productivity per week	Labour cost per unit (£)
20	£6,000	20,000		
20	£6,000	40,000		
20	£6,000	80,000		
20	£6,000	120,000		

How to increase labour productivity

Increasing labour productivity is a constant management challenge. Managers will want to improve productivity because this can help to reduce unit costs.

Increasing productivity may be achieved in a variety of ways.

- Changes to reward systems that encourage more productivity: for example, if it is easy to measure the output of an employee, then paying per unit produced may provide an incentive to produce more.

- Changes to the work processes: by more effectively managing job design, the flow of work, or the layout of resources it may be possible to speed up production and increase productivity,

- Training of staff so they can do their jobs more effectively.

- Investment: employees will usually be more productive if they have the right equipment and the latest technology. You can try and build a house by hand, but you are probably a lot faster doing it with machinery.

KEY CONCEPT

Labour productivity measures the output per worker.

4.3 BUSINESS INSIGHT: LABOUR PRODUCTIVITY IN THE UK

Labour productivity in the UK has been very low in recent years, and this has been a real concern because of its potential impact on unit costs and the international competitiveness of UK businesses. To address this issue, the UK government is aiming to invest more in new roads, research and development, and skills training. UK productivity has fallen behind that of Germany, the US, France, and Italy. According to the UK chancellor, as reported by the *Guardian* in November 2016, it takes a German worker four days to produce what a UK worker make in five days; this means that too many British people work longer hours for lower pay. In the time a British worker makes £1 worth of output, a German worker makes £1.35 worth. The Office for Budget Responsibility (OBR) suggested that the rate of productivity growth was low and was unlikely to climb back up to the long-term trend of 2% until 2020.

Possible causes of the low productivity in the UK may be

- lack of investment when banks restricted lending after the global economic crisis in 2008;

- the growth of low-level service jobs such as delivering online orders and working in coffee shops—these jobs have limited opportunity for productivity growth;

- cheap labour, prompting businesses to hire employees rather than invest in technology.

These points are further discussed in Chapter 6, Business insight 6.2.

Source: www.theguardian.com/business/2016/nov/24/why-is-uks-productivity-still-behind-that-of-other-major-economies

Question
Why would managers in a business be concerned about labour productivity levels?

MANAGEMENT TASK

The sales per employee at your Oxford store are lower than in branches elsewhere in the country, but the number of people visiting the store is not lower.

How are you going to improve the productivity of your staff in Oxford?

Different types of productivity

Marginal productivity

Economists call the extra output added by adding an employee the 'marginal productivity of labour'. This is calculated by:

change in total output ÷ change in number of employees

For example, if output increases from 200 units to 240 units when another employee is hired, the marginal productivity is 40 units.

In the short run, it may not be possible to change the amount of equipment or machinery in a business. To increase output, managers may need to hire more staff. The problem then is that there are increasing numbers of staff trying to use a given amount of equipment or other resources. This can lead to a decrease in the output of extra employees, i.e. the marginal product (see Figure 4.4). This effect is known

Figure 4.4 The relationship between marginal product and marginal cost

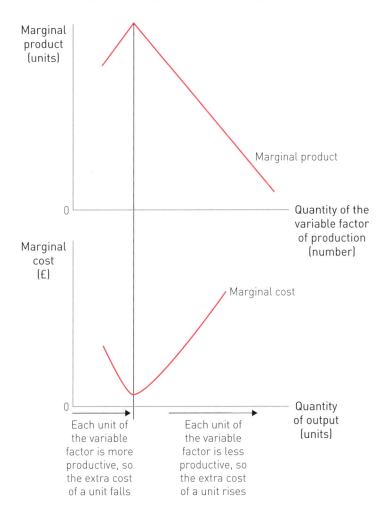

as the law of diminishing returns, which means that marginal product starts to fall after some point as extra resources are less productive. The effect of this is that, other factors being constant, the extra costs of production increase. The marginal costs are the inverse of the marginal product. In the short run, all other things being equal, adding extra units of a variable factor to fixed factors will eventually lead to less marginal product. In the long run, the amount of machinery and equipment can be changed in order to avoid diminishing returns.

KEY CONCEPTS

The **law of diminishing returns** states that, in the short run, additional units of a variable factor added to a fixed factor will lead to a fall in marginal product. **Marginal product** measures the extra output from an additional employee. **Average output** is total output divided by the number of employees.

Average productivity

This measures the output per employee. It is measured as

   total output ÷ number of employees

For example, if 400 units are produced by 40 employees this means the average productivity is

   400 units ÷ 40 employees = 10 units per person

Marginals and averages

If the marginal product of an employee is higher than the average productivity (see Figure 4.5 and Table 4.6), this will increase the average product. Imagine, for example, that a team scored an average of 2 goals a game; if the club then scored 4 goals in an extra (marginal) game this would pull up its average. Similarly, if a team scored 2 goals per game and then scores no goals in an extra (marginal) game, this pulls down the average.

4.4 QUICK CHECK

For each of the following statements, say whether it is true or false.

a. Labour productivity is measured by output ÷ number of employees.

b. Marginal product measures the output per employee.

c. If labour productivity increases, all other factors unchanged, the labour cost per unit should fall.

d. If marginal product is above average product, average product should fall.

4.8 DOING THE BUSINESS MATHS

Complete the table.

Number of employees	Output = total product (units)	Marginal product	Average product
2	20	n/a	
3	40		
4	90		
5	120		
6	140		
7	150		

Question

At which number of employees does the marginal product start to decline?

Figure 4.5 The relationship between marginal product and average product

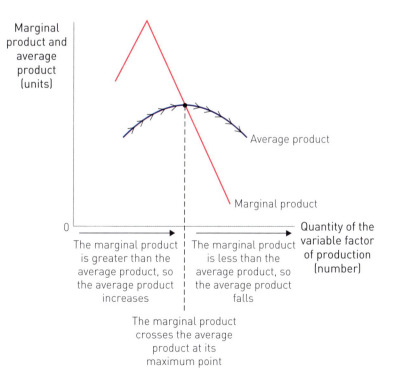

Table 4.6 The relationship between marginal product and average product

Number of employees	Output (units)	Marginal product	Average product	Marginal and average
10	100	n/a	100 ÷ 10 = 10	n/a
11	121	21	121 ÷ 11 = 11	Marginal above average so average increases
12	140	19	140 ÷ 12 = 11.66	Marginal above average so average increases
13	150	10	150 ÷ 13 = 11.53	Marginal below average so average decreases
14	155	5	155 ÷ 14 = 11.07	Marginal below average so average decreases
15	158	3	158 ÷ 15 = 10.53	Marginal below average so average decreases

Productivity and costs

The more productive the extra employees are, i.e. the higher the marginal product, the lower the extra cost of units in terms of labour, i.e. the lower the marginal cost (see Figure 4.6). Imagine we pay an employee £300 for a week's work and they produce 3,000 units; the labour cost is 10 pence a unit. If an extra employee produces 6,000 units, the labour cost of these extra units is now 5 pence. Similarly, if the extra employee is less productive, then the extra cost of a unit will rise. The marginal cost is therefore the inverse of the marginal product curve, assuming other factors are constant. If, on average, employees are more productive, this means that the labour cost per unit falls (i.e the average variable costs).

You can see in Figure 4.6 the marginal and average relationship. If marginal product is above average product, the average increases; if it is below, the average falls. This means the marginal product curve cuts the average product curve at its maximum. Similarly, if the marginal cost is below the average variable it pulls the average down. If it is above the average variable it pulls it up. This means the marginal costs curve crosses the average variable cost curve at its minimum.

In Figure 4.7 we can see the shape of the average cost curve. In the short run the average costs is made up of average fixed costs plus average variable costs. The average cost is U-shaped.

Difficulties measuring productivity

Although the concept of productivity is very important, how to measure it will vary from industry to industry. In some cases, it may be relatively straightforward: for example, the number of burgers served per shift or the number of sales calls made by your sales team. However, in other cases it may be less clear what to measure—how would you measure the productivity of a teacher? a receptionist? a nurse?

Figure 4.6 The relationship between (a) the marginal product and the average product; and (b) the marginal cost and the average variable cost

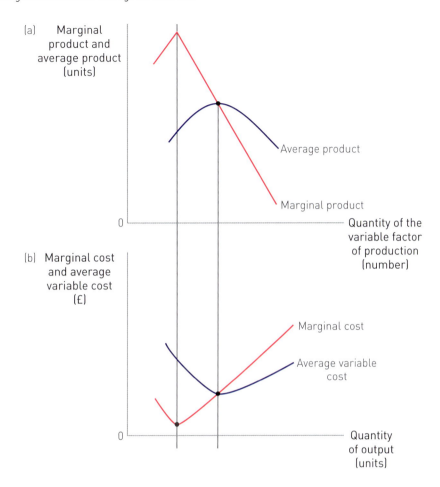

MANAGEMENT TASK

What do you think would be the best way of measuring the productivity of:

- check-out staff?
- reception staff?
- maintenance staff?
- IT staff?
- sales staff?
- university lecturers?

Productivity and quality

While increasing productivity seems desirable in terms of its impact on the costs of units, in reality it can cause problems. One reason is that there can be a

Figure 4.7 The relationship between the average cost, the average variable cost, and the average fixed cost

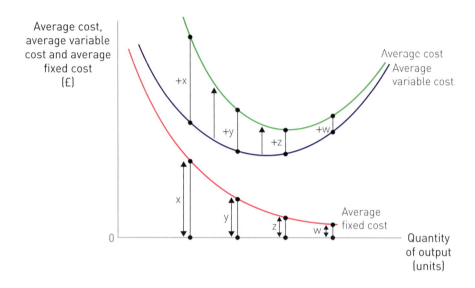

trade-off between productivity and quality—in an effort to achieve output targets the quality of production or the quality of service may suffer. For example, in an attempt to see more patients per hour doctors may spend less time with a patient and so the quality of care may differ in an attempt to be more productive. Managers can find there are unintended consequences when they focus on increasing productivity—employees rush to produce more, but the defects increase or the quality of service suffers. Productivity targets usually need to have some quality criteria as well.

Total, marginal, and average costs

Total costs measure all of the costs incurred in a business in a given time period. Marginal costs show the extra costs of an added unit.

The equation for marginal cost is

change in total costs ÷ change in output

The marginal cost shows what happens to total costs when an extra unit is produced.

- If marginal costs are positive, this means that total costs increase.

- If marginal costs are positive and increasing, this means that total costs are increasing at a faster rate.

- If marginal costs are positive and decreasing, this means that total costs are increasing at a slower rate.

- If marginal costs are negative, this means that total costs decrease.

Average costs measure the cost per unit.

average cost = unit cost = total cost ÷ output

To calculate the profit of a business we measure the total revenue minus the total costs. Average (or unit) costs are very important because they are a major factor in determining the profit margin, i.e. the profit per unit.

Marginal costs and average costs

If marginal costs are above the average costs, this will pull up the average costs. If the marginal costs are below the average costs, this will pull down the average costs (see Figure 4.8 and Table 4.7).

   Imagine the cost per unit was £10 each and you then produced an extra (marginal) unit for £2; this would pull down the average.

   Imagine the cost per unit was £10 each and you then produced an extra (marginal) unit for £10; this would maintain the average at £10.

   Imagine the cost per unit was £10 each and you then produced an extra (marginal) unit for £15; this would pull the average up.

Figure 4.8 Relationship between marginal cost and average cost

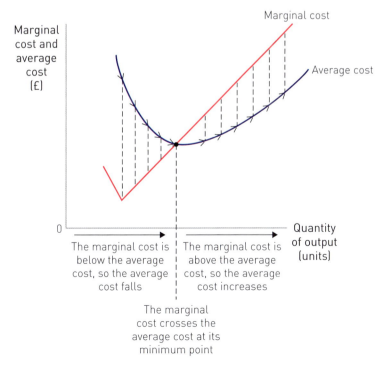

Table 4.7 Relationship between marginal cost and average cost

Output (units)	Total cost £	Marginal cost = change in total cost £	Average cost = total cost/ output £	
1	100	n/a	100	
2	130	30	65	Marginal cost (£30) below previous average cost (£100) brings down average cost
3	150	20	50	Marginal cost (£20) below previous average cost (£65) brings down average cost
4	180	30	45	Marginal cost (£30) below previous average cost (£50) brings down average cost
5	250	70	50	Marginal cost (£70) above previous average cost (£45) pulls up average cost
6	360	110	60	Marginal cost (£110) above previous average cost (£50) pulls up average cost

4.9 DOING THE BUSINESS MATHS

Complete the table. Explain the relationship between the marginal cost and average cost in the table.

Output (units)	Total cost (£)	Average cost (£) = total cost ÷ output	Marginal cost	Relationship between marginal cost and average cost (e.g. higher or lower and impact on average)
1	10		n/a	
2	18			
3	27			
4	36			
5	50			
6	66			
7	84			

4.5 QUICK CHECK

For each of the following statements, say whether it is true or false.

a. Average costs is calculated using total costs ÷ number of units.

b. Marginal costs are the extra fixed costs from producing another unit.

c. If marginal cost is above average cost, average costs should rise.

d. Marginal cost crosses the average cost at its minimum point.

Price and average costs

When setting the price of a product, the business must consider the average cost. To make profits, the price must at least cover average costs (see Figure 4.9).

Price and average costs	Profit or loss
Price is less than average costs	A loss is made
Price equals average costs	Normal profit is made
Price is greater than average costs	Abnormal profit is made

However, the price set will influence sales and this will in turn affect the average costs.

Imagine you run a mobile phone network business. A huge part of your costs will be setting up the network in the first place. These are fixed costs—whether or not

Figure 4.9 Price and average cost

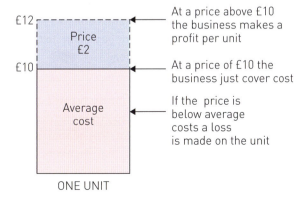

you have any customers, you will still have the costs of establishing the network. This investment represents a huge risk because if there are no customers you will lose all these funds invested. However, once you start getting customers the cost per customer will begin to fall. This is because the huge initial costs can be spread over more units.

Imagine you spent £500 million setting up the network. Table 4.8 shows what happens as more customers join the network.

Table 4.8 Cost per call

Fixed costs (£)	Number of customers	Average cost per customer (£)
500,000,000	1	500,000,000
500,000,000	1000	500,000
500,000,000	10,000	50,000
500,000,000	100,000	5,000
500,000,000	1,000,000	500
500,000,000	10,000,000	50
500,000,000	100,000,000	5

4.6 QUICK CHECK

For each of the following statements, say whether it is true or false.

a. If total revenue equals total cost, abnormal profit is earned.

b. If total revenue is greater than total cost, normal profit is earned.

c. If total revenue is less than total cost, a loss is made.

MANAGEMENT TASK

You are the managing director of a newspaper company. You find that any newspapers not sold by lunchtime tend to not to sell at all and are therefore returned to be pulped. Your usual selling price is £1, but your sales director has suggested that you cut the price to 50p after 1.00pm. Do you think this is a good idea?

Volume is therefore key in this type of industry because it allows the fixed costs to be spread over more units. The same is true in industries such as rail transport, car manufacturing, and chemical production. The marginal cost of providing the service to a customer is very low. A low price may therefore be set to generate more customers. With more customers, a lower price can be charged and still a profit can be made because average costs can fall. By comparison, a high price may lead to lower sales and therefore higher average costs; this may mean a loss is made even though the price is higher.

At output Q1 a price of P1 is required to cover the unit costs. At output Q2 the unit costs are lower and a price of only P2 would cover the unit costs. The business could charge a lower price at the higher output because the unit costs are lower.

Understanding unit costs and price, and the effect of price changes on demand and therefore output, is crucial for managers. Imagine the business is at P1Q1 making normal profits. If the managers feel that a price cut to P3 will increase demand to allow output to increase to Q2 it would then make a profit on each unit. If, however, sales remained at Q1 the business would be making a loss.

MANAGEMENT TASK

You are the manager of mobile phone network. You are arguing for a significant price cut to increase the number of customers. You believe this could increase profits. Outline the logic of your recommended price cut.

4.4 BUSINESS INSIGHT: AIRBUS COSTS AND PROFIT

The cost per passenger of a flight on an airbus A320 (which has a capacity of 154 passengers) for a 260-mile flight from New York to Washington, DC have been estimated by Wendover Productions as follows.

Fuel cost: $2.50 (£1.72)

Crew cost: $1.50 (£1.03)

Landing fees at two airports: $13.50 (£9.27)

Taxes: $15.60 (£10.72)

Price of the aircraft: $11.50 (£7.90)

Maintenance: $14 (£9.62)

Non flying cost: $10 (£6.87)

Insurance: $0.25 (17p)

Total $68.50 (£47.06)

These figures assume the flight is full.

The typical price of a flight on this route is $80, suggesting that the profit per passenger is only $12.50.

Source: www.youtube.com/watch?v=6Oe8T3AvydU

Questions

1. If these figures are accurate, what would the profit on this flight be for the airline?

2. What would happen to these cost per flight figures if the flight was only half full?

Controlling costs in a business

Using resources efficiently

Controlling costs involves using resources efficiently. To achieve this, managers may use one or more of the following measures.

- Use budgeting to set targets that staff can work to. This can help ensure there is sufficient thought about what is being done, what resources are needed and whether the return justifies the investment. Budgets are used to help managers with planning and to review performance. If the targets for expenditure are not achieved, there is a 'variance'; this variance needs to be analysed to understand why it occurred and what the consequences are for the business.

- Use techniques to reduce waste. Lean production is a Japanese approach to production that seeks to remove all wastage, such as wasted time and wasted materials, by constantly reviewing the operations process.

- Use techniques to make the organization more flexible so that money is not invested in idle resources. Just-in-time production aims to hold as little inventory as possible. Inventory is minimized because the business prices to order. As the orders come in, the business produces and at that point orders supplies.

- Reusing materials to reduce wastage.

- Improving quality to reduce the re-working of materials and having to throw items away.

- Manage suppliers effectively. The costs of a business will be influenced by the suppliers they work with. The price of the inputs provided by suppliers will affect the firm's costs. The ability of suppliers to increase prices and therefore the firm's costs will depend on their power relative to the business. The more powerful suppliers are, the more they can increase prices.

Reactions to cost cutting

Although cutting costs may help the business as a whole, this does not mean that everyone will respond positively to such decisions. For some people it may mean a cut in their budget and may even mean a loss of jobs. Employees may also feel that this strategy is short-termist and that cutting costs will damage the quality of service or the ability to innovate and deliver the right products in the future. Managers need to be careful which costs they cut and consider the long-term effects.

BUSINESS CASE QUESTIONS: CAN YOU NOW ANSWER . . .

Why doesn't Sainsbury's try and cut costs further?

4.5 BUSINESS INSIGHT: FAST FASHION

Zara is renowned as a fast fashion retailer that is able to design and distribute new designs to its stores quickly. However, some online brands are now even quicker at getting new designs into stores than Zara. ASOS and BooHoo use social media to keep on top of trends and are able to design a product and have it ready for sale in a couple of weeks. An article in *Business Insider UK* from May 2017 gives an account of a report by Fung Global Retail and Technology. The report says of these companies:

> They've streamlined their supply chain and moved production closer to key markets, enabling them to speed up the design and manufacturing process. According to the report, it takes ASOS between two and eight weeks to get a product from concept to sale. It takes Boohoo two weeks and Missguided as little as one, beating Zara's formerly speedy five-week turnaround and far outpacing H&M, which can take up to six months.
>
> 'Fast fashion is becoming ultrafast fashion', said the report. This is an issue for chains such as Zara and H&M, whose success was built around this unique business model. These new online stores are also constantly refreshing their products to drive customer frequency. [. . .]
>
> They also have an 'agile supply chain', said the report. Initial designs are made in small batches, and if they're popular, more are rolled out. This strategy allows them to match supply with changing demand. [. . .]
>
> Lastly, these online retailers also use Zara's tactic of keeping production close to the headquarters and in key customer markets. According to the report, Inditex, the parent company of Zara, sources 60% of its products in Europe. Boohoo similarly sources over 50% of its products from the UK.

Source: Hanbury, M. (2017), 'Zara is Facing a Massive Threat', *Business Insider UK* (23 May), uk.businessinsider.com/fast-fashion-is-getting-faster-2017-5

Question
How can effective management of the supply chain reduce the costs of a business?

4.6 BUSINESS INSIGHT: AIRLINES REDUCE COSTS

Every day airlines transport people over 40 milllion air miles around the world. They do this safely and quickly. However, they are also very inefficient in many ways. Aircraft are often sitting idle on the runway in between flights, and this costs millions if not billions of pounds a year.

Up to 45 percent of an airline's costs are linked to maintenance, ground handling, in-flight services, and call centres. Airlines therefore have a major opportunity to cut costs in these areas. An example of how lean techniques may help reduce costs by reducing waste and altering the different aspects of the process can be seen in Figure 4.10.

Figure 4.10 Eliminating delays

	Turnaround time between flights[1]		Lean techniques
	Average number of minutes per step	Best practice: minimum number of minutes per step[3]	
Unload passengers[3]	6:14	4:38	1. Stricter controls on carry-on bags, lower passengers moving back in aisle to find bag
Wait for cleaning crew to board aircraft	0:24	0:18	2. Cleaning crew in position ahead of time
Clean airplane	11:48	9:40	3. Standardized work flow, timing, and methods, such as cleaning supplies in prearranged kits
Wait for transmission to gate of cabin crew's approval to board	4:11	0	
Wait for first passenger to board	4:06	0	4. Visual signal from cabin crew to agent when plane is ready to board— for example, light flashing at top of ramp
Load passengers	19:32	16:00	
Wait for passenger information list	1:58	0:13	5. Active management of overhead storage bins by flight attendants
Close aircraft door	0:57	0:09	
Detach boarding ramp	1:39	0:43	6. Passenger information list delivered by agent following last passenger to board
Total time (including initial steps[3])	52:18	33:11	7. Agent ready at aircraft to close door

[1]For Airbus A320 single-aisle medium-range airfinger (disguised example)
[2] Assumes rudimentary application of lean techniques; further reductions may be possible.
[3]Initial steps (attaching boarding ramp, opening aircraft door, and waiting for first passenger to decline) can't be significantly reduced

Source: Exhibit from 'The Hidden Value in Airline Operations', November 2003, McKinsey Quarterly, www.mckinsey.com. Copyright (c) 2018 McKinsey & Company. All rights reserved. Reprinted by permission.

Questions

1. How is this airline described trying to reduce costs?

2. Are there are dangers with reducing costs in this way, do you think?

4.7 BUSINESS INSIGHT: AIRLINES GENERATE REVENUE

In Business Insight 4.6 we saw how airlines are working at improving their efficiency. This is one way of increasing their profits. Airlines are also looking for more ways to generate revenue from passengers. They charge for additional legroom, for food, for selecting your seat, and so on, to increase the average income per person. They are also looking for ways of getting more passengers on per plane. This is difficult, because if the seats are too close together passengers will complain. In 2017 American Airlines announced that it would add 12 more seats (two rows) into its economy class on its Boeing 737-800 fleet and nine seats into its Airbus A321s. JetBlue said it would add 12 seats into its A320s.

The aircraft interiors industry, which includes seat manufacturers, is worth $17bn today, according to the *Los Angeles Times,* and is forecast to grow to $29bn by 2021. That is partly explained by high demand for new planes: Boeing expects airlines to require more than 37,000 jets over the next two decades. But it is also because of the need for more compact seats.

Source: www.economist.com/gulliver/2017/10/11/airlines-are-trying-to-cram-ever-more-seats-onto-planes; www.latimes.com/business/la-fi-airline-seats-20171001-story.html

Question

How will the changes to the seats help the airlines?

Economies of scale

Internal economies of scale

One significant factor that influences the average costs of a business is the scale at which it operates. In many cases, unit costs will fall when the scale of the business increases. When this occurs it is called 'internal economies of scale'.

There are various different types of internal economies of scale (see Figure 4.11).

- Purchasing: when a business gets bigger it has more purchasing power. This means it can negotiate better deals with suppliers and the media, bringing down unit costs.

- Financial: as the scale of a business increases it is likely to have more assets. These can act as collateral and be used to help raise finance at lower interest rates because the banks know they can take the assets to pay back the loan if necessary.

Figure 4.11 Examples of internal economies of scale

- Technical: as a business expands it can benefit from a number of technical economies of scale, such as:

  a. specialization—this occurs when work is divided into small units so that individuals become specialized in their work and more productive. McDonald's divides up its process into small, well-defined jobs so that employees can be relatively easily trained and become more efficient through standardization and repetition.

  b. indivisibilities—some equipment incurs high average costs if used on a small scale but has relatively low unit costs when used on a large scale. If a manufacturer invests in a production line, for example, the average cost per unit is high at low levels of output. At high levels of the output the costs of the production line can be spread over a large number of units, reducing the average cost.

  c. increased dimensions (see Figure 4.12). Imagine a storage unit in the form of a cube with sides of 1m. The volume of this cube is $1 \times 1 \times 1 = 1\text{m}^3$. The area of one face is $1 \times 1 = 1\text{m}^2$. There are six faces, so the total surface area is $6 \times 1 = 6\text{m}^2$. Now imagine the length of the sides of this cube is doubled to 2m. The volume is $2 \times 2 \times 2 = 8\text{m}^3$. The area of one face is $2 \times 2 = 4\text{m}^2$. The total surface area is $6 \times 4 = 24\text{m}^2$. This means that the materials to build the bigger cube would cost four times as much as those for building the smaller cube, because the surface area is four times as big. However, the amount that the cube could hold inside is eight times as big. Therefore, the storage costs per unit would fall. This is important when designing storage space, container vessels, and transportation vehicles, as there are economies of scale by building them on a bigger scale.

Figure 4.12 Economies of scale through increased dimensions

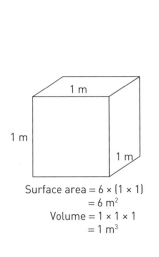

Surface area = 6 × (1 × 1)
= 6 m²
Volume = 1 × 1 × 1
= 1 m³

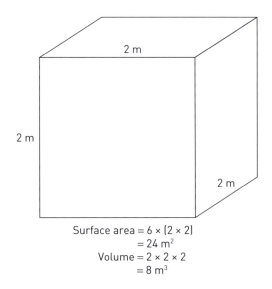

Surface area = 6 × (2 × 2)
= 24 m²
Volume = 2 × 2 × 2
= 8 m³

KEY CONCEPT

Internal economies of scale occur when the unit costs fall as the scale of production increases.

4.8 BUSINESS INSIGHT: REDUCING COSTS ON THE *EMMA MAERSK*

Costs can be reduced in many ways, including the way items are transported.

The *Emma Maersk* is a container ship that is often featured in the news around December when there is a story on the toys it is bringing to the UK for Christmas. The *Emma Maersk* was the largest container ship in the world when she was launched in 2006. She is able to carry at least 11,000 large containers (called 20-foot-equivalent units) which means she can ship millions of items across the world. The ship typically has a crew of 13 people.

Questions

1. What is the productivity of a crew member in terms of number of containers?

2. How does the principle of increased dimensions apply to container ships?

Internal economies of scale and market structure

The extent to which internal economies of scale exist is likely to have a significant impact on the structure of the market. If there are major economies of scale this means that it is in the interests of business to expand to benefit from lower unit costs.

The first level of output at which economies of scale stop occurring is called the minimum efficient scale (MES; see Figure 4.13). If the MES is relatively small relative to demand, this means there can be many efficient businesses operating in a market. If, however, the MES was, say, 50 per cent of demand, this means there would only be two efficient businesses in the industry. Of course, it may be possible for inefficient businesses to exist. This depends on the cost disadvantage of not being at the MES. For example, how much higher are unit costs if a business is operating at, say one-third of MES? The bigger the cost disadvantage of not being at MES, the less likely it is that smaller inefficient businesses will survive; their unit costs will be much higher than the unit costs in bigger businesses, which will be able to undercut them and force them out. If, however, there is little difference in the unit costs of producing less than MES, this means there may be many inefficient businesses.

The number of businesses operating in an industry is likely to be high if:

*   the MES is low compared to demand, and

*   the cost disadvantage of operating below MES is small.

Figure 4.13 The relationship between the minimum efficient scale (MES) and market structure

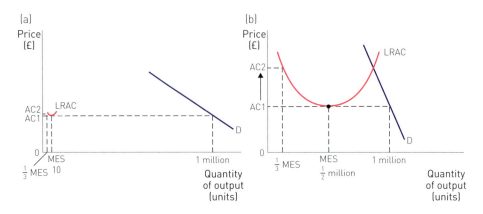

The number of businesses competing in an industry is, therefore, likely to be relatively small if:

- the MES is a high relative to demand—so there is incentive to get bigger—and

- the cost disadvantage of operating below MES is high—so inefficient businesses cannot survive.

In Figure 4.13(a), the MES is low relative to the market demand and the cost disadvantage of operating below the MES is also low. This means that this market is likely to be very competitive, with many firms competing. In Figure 4.13(b), the MES is high relative to the market demand, and the cost disadvantage of not operating at the MES is also high. This industry is likely to be dominated by a few firms—probably two, given that the MES is half of the market demand.

If the MES is actually more than the demand in the market and the cost disadvantage of operating below MES is high, this means that the industry is a natural monopoly. Only one business is likely to exist because of the benefits of expansion and the cost disadvantages of being below MES.

Natural monopolies often occur in utility industries such as gas, electricity, and water, which require heavy investment to set up the infrastructure. These investment costs are high fixed costs which can then be spread over increasing numbers of customers to bring down the unit cost. In a natural monopoly, as shown in Figure 4.14, the internal economies of scale are so great that one firm will keep expanding and supply the whole market. A smaller business, e.g. at Q1 in Figure 4.14, will face much higher unit costs and will not be able to be price competitive. The major unit cost advantage of operating on a large scale make it difficult for any other business to compete. Having a natural monopoly does give the dominant business major power over consumers, which could lead to higher prices and a poor-quality service. In a situation of natural monopoly, the government must decide whether to run the organization itself, to ensure customers are protected, or to regulate private providers.

Figure 4.14 A natural monopoly

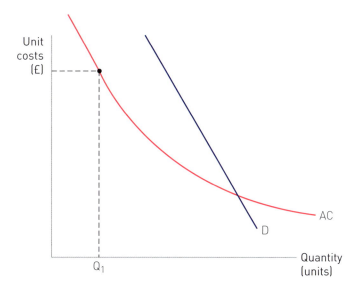

Getting too big

While there are potentially cost advantages of getting bigger, there are also some potential disadvantages if a business gets too big. If the cost per unit increases as you increase the scale of your production, this is known as internal diseconomies of scale (as shown in Figures 4.15 and 4.16). Essentially these higher unit costs relate to the difficulties of running a bigger business with more products, more bases in more locations, and more employees.

Internal diseconomies of scale may arise from various factors.

- Communication problems—when a business is too large, there can be problems in communication between employees. Communication can become slow while people wait for responses and as decisions are passed from one committee to another.

- Coordination problems—as a business grows, there tend to be more products and divisions involved. The business tends to operate in more areas, and simply coordinating the business becomes more complex. Tim Martin, the chairman of Wetherspoons, liked to visit each of his pubs at least once year. This was easily done when the business was small, but not so easy when he has 1,000 pubs under his control (he still manages to visit several hundred a year).

Figure 4.15 Examples of internal diseconomies of scale

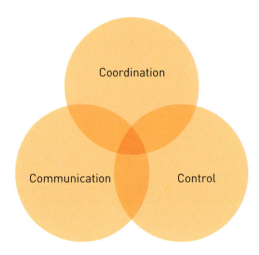

Figure 4.16 Internal economies and diseconomies of scale

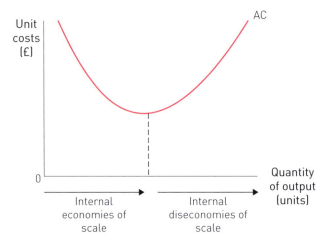

- Control problems—as a business grows, there are increases in the amount of information that needs to be managed, the number of decisions that have to be made, and the number of people who need to understand the culture of the business. This can lead to a loss of control and to inefficiency.

KEY CONCEPT

Internal diseconomies of scale occur when the unit cost increases as the scale of production increases.

4.7 QUICK CHECK

For each of the following statements, say whether it is true or false.

a. Internal economies of scale occur when total costs fall with greater scale.

b. Internal economies of scale occur when average costs fall with greater scale.

c. Internal diseconomies of scale occur when average costs rise with greater scale.

d. The minimum efficient scale is the first level of output at which the average cost is at its lowest.

4.10 DOING THE BUSINESS MATHS

Complete the table.

Units	Total cost (£)	Average cost per unit (£)
100	200,000	
200	220,000	
300	250,000	
400	280,000	
500	300,000	
600	350,000	
700	470,000	
800	600,000	

Question
At what level of output do internal diseconomies of scale start?

MANAGEMENT TASK

Your business is growing and you want to make sure you avoid diseconomies of scale.

Outline the actions you might take to avoid communication, coordination, and control problems.

READ MORE

A big influence on productivity and unit costs is the way in which operations are managed. A classic text on operations management is

Slack, N., Chambers, S., and Johnston, R. (2004), *Operations Management*, 4th edn, Harlow, Essex: FT Prentice Hall.

You might also want to read about lean production in the best-selling

Womack, J.P., Jones, D.T., and Roos, D. (1990), *The Machine That Changed the World*, London: Simon & Schuster.

Figure 4.17 External economies of scale

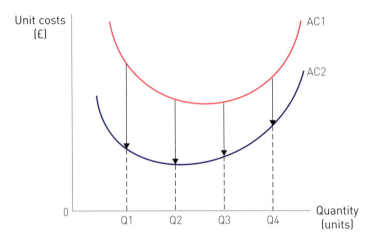

Costs and external economies of scale

Factors which affect the costs of a business are partly internal and partly external. External economies of scale (Figure 4.17) refer to a situation where the cost per unit is lower as a result of an external factor. For example, one of your suppliers may have increased in size; it has therefore benefited from internal economies of scale, allowing it to pass on a lower price to you. You therefore find that at every level of output your unit costs have fallen. External economies are often linked to location decisions. Locating near key suppliers, or near a university that specializes in your industry, can facilitate lower unit costs for all levels of output.

• •

SUMMARY

Managing costs is a key aspect of management. Whatever management role you have, you will have objectives and you will have a budget which will determine what you can spend. You will want to achieve your targets and be within budget. If you can reduce your cists within a given quality target, you will increase your profits and/or allow the business to be more price-competitive. Reducing costs may be achieved in a number of ways, such as improving labour productivity, managing supplies effectively, being leaner generally, and looking at the scale of production.

KEY LEARNING POINTS

- Profits are calculated by measuring total revenue minus total costs.
- Costs measure the value of resources used up in producing and selling an item in a given period.
- Costs may be variable costs or fixed costs; this distinction examines how costs change with output.
- Economists include opportunity costs when assessing costs; accountants don't include opportunity costs.
- When normal profits are earned, businesses in the industry are earning returns that justify them being there but which are not so high that they attract other firms in from other industries.
- If revenue is greater than total costs, abnormal profits are earned.
- If revenue is equal to total costs, normal profits are earned.
- If revenue is less than total costs, a loss is made.
- Contribution per unit equals price minus average variable costs; this contributes to the fixed costs.
- Break-even occurs when the total contribution pays for the fixed costs.
- Shut-down point occurs when price equals the average variable costs.
- Break-even point occurs when price equals the average costs.
- Internal economies of scale occur when unit costs fall as the scale of production increases.
- Internal diseconomies of scale occur when unit costs rise as the scale of production increases.
- External economies of scale occur when unit costs fall at every level of output due to factors external to the business.
- The minimum efficient scale and the cost disadvantage of not operating at the MES are important determinants of market structure.

BUSINESS CASE EXTENSION QUESTIONS

1. Visit the investor relations of the Sainsbury's website and identify its current strategy.
2. Look at its most recent annual report. Read the chairman and chief executive's statement and identify economic factors that Sainsbury's believe are important to its success.
3. Look at the annual reports and identify key costs in Sainsbury's operations.
4. What do you think determines the inventory Sainsbury's will hold at any moment?
5. How could Sainsbury's increase the contribution per unit? What difficulties might it face doing this?
6. How might Sainsbury's measure labour productivity in its stores?
7. Why would labour productivity matter to Sainsbury's?
8. As a large retailer what economies of scale do you think Sainsbury's might benefit from?

QUICK QUESTIONS

1. In what way is an economist's view of costs different from an accountant's?
2. What is the difference between fixed and variable costs?
3. What is meant by labour productivity and why does it matter?
4. How might managers increase labour productivity?
5. What are internal economies of scale and why do they matter?
6. What are internal diseconomies of scale and why do they matter?
7. What is the difference between shut-down point and break-even point?
8. What is meant by the contribution per unit, and why is it important?
9. Why might a focus in productivity lead to a reduction in quality?
10. What are external economies of scale and why do they matter?

How markets work

WHY DO I NEED TO KNOW HOW MARKETS WORK?

You run a coffee chain throughout the UK. It is a competitive market with lot of small independent stores as well other big chains. You differentiate your chain where you can with the environment of the outlets, the customer service, and the overall brand, but profit margins are not very big and your overall returns rely on volume. The economy has not been doing especially well recently, and customers are being a little bit more careful before buying a coffee.

Of course, you could try and get costs, such as wages, down. However, despite the state of the economy overall, unemployment remains quite low and you don't have people queuing up to work with you. If anything, you may need to increase wages in the labour market; so employee costs are not going to fall easily.

A major part of your costs is the price of the coffee itself. In the last few months, the worldwide price of coffee has been increasing. The problem has been that a disease has hit the main crops in Colombia. This has reduced supply, and that in turn has pushed up global prices of the bean. Your profits are being squeezed, and you don't think it is your fault! Your ability to make profits is heavily influenced by the markets you sell in and the markets for your inputs.

Managers will often find that their business is affected by factors beyond their control. Managers deal with, and operate in, a range of markets, and changes in market conditions can affect their costs and revenues. In this chapter we examine the effect of market forces on prices and output.

BY THE END OF THIS CHAPTER YOU WILL BE ABLE TO . . .

- explain what is meant by a market
- explain how markets work
- analyse the role of the price mechanism
- analyse the effect on prices of changes in market conditions

BUSINESS CASE

In 2017 the world price of copper reached its highest level since 2010. This followed years of oversupply. The price increased by around 40 per cent, thanks to high levels of demand. This demand was generated by strong global economic growth, especially in China. An article in the *Financial Times* in December 2017 reported:

> Copper has become a favourite metal for global mining companies such as Glencore and Rio Tinto, which now forecast a lack of supply by the end of the decade as old mines come to the end of their lives and are not replaced. Demand for the metal is also expected to increase from a buildout of charging networks required for electric cars. [. . .]
>
> Copper staged a spectacular rally to more than $10,000 a tonne in early 2011 after China launched a huge stimulus package following the financial crisis. It then fell to just over $4,000 a tonne in early 2016, as new copper projects came to fruition and demand weakened. [. . .] This year, however, copper prices have clawed their way back up to more than $7,000 a tonne. [. . .] Higher copper prices are also likely to lead to calls for a greater share of the wealth from miners in Chile and Peru, which could also halt supply to the market. Analysts at Citibank estimate that nearly 30 labour contract negotiations are set to take place in copper mining countries next year, potentially affecting 25 per cent of global mine supply.

Source: https://www.ft.com/content/cebd9cfc-eaf6-11e7-bd17-521324c81e23

QUESTIONS

This chapter will help you answer the following questions.

1. What might influence the supply of copper?
2. Why might the price of copper increase?
3. Why might it decrease?
4. How might changes in copper prices affect businesses?

Introduction

A market is made up of buyers and sellers who want to trade with each other. The buyers demand the good or services. The sellers want to sell their goods and services. Economies are made up millions of markets. For example, there are markets for:

- the final goods and services produced
- the supplies that are used to produce the final goods and services
- the labour that works in businesses
- the money that is borrowed to finance business
- the shares sold by businesses to raise finance
- the currency of a country, affecting the exchange rate

Many of these markets are interrelated. More demand for one product can lead to less demand for another. More demand for one product can increase demand for a specific type of labour. It is important, therefore, for you as a manager to understand how these markets work, how they relate to each other, and the possible impact of future changes on your business.

Changes in market conditions can affect the selling price or the price of inputs such as land, labour, or capital. That's why managers need to understand the changes that are happening and very importantly the changes that might occur. Markets are critical to business—for example, they drive share prices, exchange rates, oil prices, and labour prices—so managers need the tools to analyse possible changes and take a view on where prices will go. This will affect a whole host of decisions such as investment decisions, employment decisions, and decisions on how and why to compete.

Markets can create opportunities for business, but they can also generate threats. Watch or listen to the news and you will almost certainly hear managers blaming market conditions for high costs, low profit margins, or poor sales due to factors that they cannot control. You may also hear about 'headwinds' in the economy; this is when managers anticipate unfavourable market conditions coming up in the future. These might include a fall in demand due to lower incomes, or higher costs as a result of higher wage demands by employees. However, while market conditions can and do play a significant role in the performance of a business, it is often easier to blame the market rather than your own decisions. Sometimes the fault lies with the managers for not anticipating what was going to happen or not responding quickly and effectively enough.

Market forces

There are some markets which have many sellers and many buyers. In such cases, no one seller is large enough to control supply in the industry—they are too small to have any significant influence on the total output. Similarly, any one buyer is insignificant in relation to the total demand. In these circumstances, what happens in the market is determined by market forces. This is called a 'competitive market' situation.

In competitive markets, the decisions of buyers and sellers are brought together by the price mechanism. Sellers want to achieve their own objectives, which we assume are to maximize profits. Buyers want to achieve their objectives, which we assume are to maximize their satisfaction (utility). The buyers and sellers have their own interests and make their own decisions, but these independent decisions are aligned via the price.

Imagine that demand for a product is much higher than the quantity supplied by providers. In this case there is excess demand in the market. This is called a 'shortage'. As the price increases, this will start to reduce the quantity that consumers want to buy and are able to afford. At the same time, the higher price is an incentive for producers to produce more—financially this product becomes more attractive.

The price therefore increases, increasing the quantity produced and reducing the quantity demanded. This is the price mechanism in action. The price increases until the quantity demanded equals the quantity supplied in the market; when these are equal and the position in the market is stable, this is called equilibrium. As a manager of a business in this situation, you will have noticed high levels of demand initially leading to higher prices, enabling you to produce more.

Another situation that might occur in a market is that there is more supply of a product than is demanded at the given price. This means there is an excess supply; this is called a 'surplus'. Again, the decisions of producers and customers have been made independently but, at the given price, the quantity demanded is less than the quantity supplied. The price would begin to fall, and this means that customers will want, and can afford, a higher quantity: more of the product is demanded. At the same time, the falling prices means there will be less ability and less incentive for producers to supply the product. The price will keep falling until the decisions of producers and customers are aligned and equilibrium is reached. As the manager of a producer in this market you would initially have noticed a surplus leading to the market price falling. This would reduce your incentive to sell as much while stimulating demand.

Table 5.1 lists some of the likely causes of shifts in demand and supply.

KEY CONCEPTS

The price mechanism describes how the price adjusts in competitive markets to equate supply and demand and bring about equilibrium.

A **shortage** occurs when the amount demanded at the given price is greater than the amount supplied.

A **surplus** occurs when the amount supplied at the given price is greater than the amount demanded.

BUSINESS CASE QUESTION: CAN YOU NOW ANSWER . . .

What might influence the supply of copper?

Table 5.1 Factors which might cause shifts in demand and supply

Shifts in demand might be caused by changes in	Shifts in supply might be caused by changes in
Income	Number of producers
Market population	Technology
Marketing	Input costs
Price of substitute	Taxes on producers
Price of complements	Weather

A demand curve

A **demand curve** shows how much consumers are willing and able to purchase at any price, all other factors held constant. We usually expect the quantity demanded to increase as the price falls and vice versa, assuming all other factors are held constant (see Figure 5.1).

A price increase leads to less quantity demanded (all other factors constant); an economist calls this a 'contraction of demand'. This is shown in Figure 5.2(a).

A price decrease leads to more quantity demanded (all other factors constant); an economist calls this an 'extension of demand'. This is shown in Figure 5.2(b).

An increase in demand occurs when more is demanded at each and every price. This can occur because of factors such as increase in income or better marketing activities.

A decrease in demand occurs when less is demanded at each and every price. This can occur because of factors such as lower prices of substitutes or more expensive complements.

Figure 5.1 A movement along a demand curve (caused by a price change)

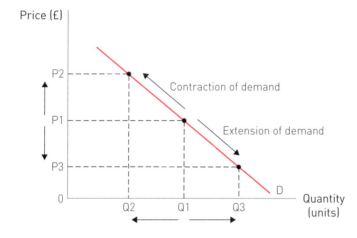

Figure 5.2 Shifts in demand (a) An increase in demand (b) A decrease in demand

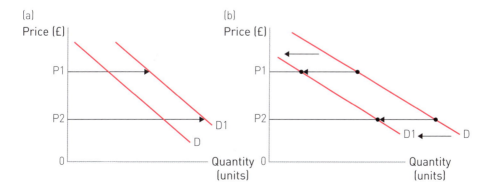

Figure 5.3 A completely price inelastic demand curve (price elasticity of demand = 0)

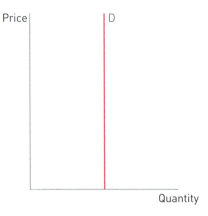

How sensitive the quantity demanded is to changes in price is measured by the 'price elasticity' of demand.

If the percentage change in quantity demanded is less than the percentage change in price, demand is said to be price inelastic (not very sensitive to price).

If the percentage change in quantity demanded is greater than the percentage change in price, demand is said to be price elastic (sensitive to price).

If the percentage change in quantity demanded is equal to the percentage change in price, demand is said to be unit price elastic.

If the quantity demanded remains the same regardless of price, demand is said to be completely price inelastic, as illustrated in Figure 5.3.

A supply curve

A **supply curve** shows how much producers are willing and able to produce at each and every price, all other factors held constant. We usually expect the quantity supplied to decrease as the price falls and vice versa, assuming all other factors are held constant.

An increase in price, all other factors held constant, increase the quantity supplied because producers can now afford to cover higher costs and produce more, as shown in Figure 5.4. An economist calls this increase in quantity supplied an 'extension of supply'.

A decrease in price, all other factors held constant, decrease the quantity supplied because producers must cut costs and produce less, as shown in Figure 5.5. An economist calls this decrease in quantity supplied a 'contraction of supply'.

An increase in supply (S1 in Figure 5.6) occurs when more is supplied at each price; this may be due to better technology or more producers.

A decrease in supply (S2 in Figure 5.6) occurs when less is supplied at each price; this may be due to an increase in costs or a fall in the number of producers.

How sensitive the quantity supplied is to changes in price is measured by the price elasticity of supply. If the percentage change in quantity supplied is greater than the percentage change in price (all other factors unchanged), supply is said to be price

Figure 5.4 A movement along the supply curve: an extension of supply

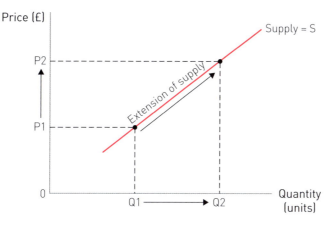

Figure 5.5 A movement along the supply curve: a contraction of supply

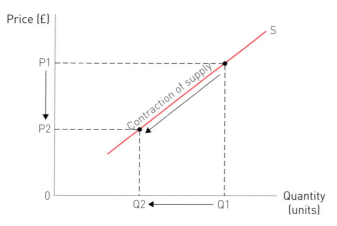

Figure 5.6 Shifts in the supply curve

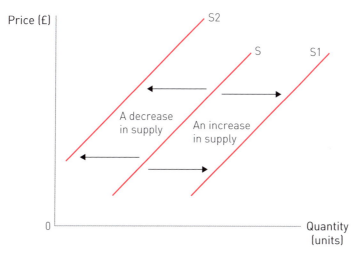

elastic. If the percentage change in quantity supplied is less than the percentage change in price (all other factors unchanged), supply is said to be price inelastic.

Markets occur when demand and supply come together and the price moves to bring the two into equilibrium. Table 5.2 is an example of the price mechanism at work, showing the price at which equilibrium occurs.

At any price, we can see the quantity demanded and the quantity supplied. In theory, the price will adjust until the quantity demanded equals the quantity supplied and equilibrium is reached. Equilibrium occurs when at the given price the quantity demanded equals the quantity supplied and there is no incentive or pressure for change in the market.

In Figure 5.7, at P1 there is excess supply in the market. The price will fall, increasing the quantity demanded and decreasing the quantity demanded, until equilibrium is reached at P2Q2.

Table 5.2 How the price mechanism brings about equilibrium in a market

Price (£)	Quantity supplied (units)	Quantity demanded (units)	Market outcome (units)	Impact on price
10	200	5	Surplus of 195	decrease
9	180	40	Surplus of 140	decrease
8	150	80	Surplus of 70	decrease
7	110	110	Equilibrium	no change
6	70	140	Shortage of 70	increase
5	20	170	Shortage of 150	increase
4	5	200	Shortage of 195	increase

Figure 5.7 At prices above equilibrium, there is excess supply. The price will fall

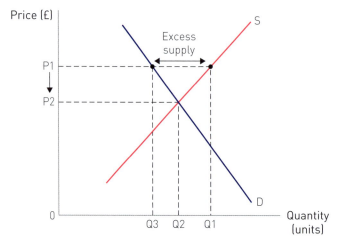

Figure 5.8 At prices below equilibrium, there is excess demand. The price will rise

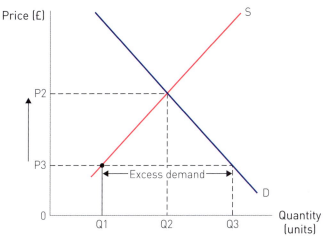

In Figure 5.8, at P1 there is excess demand in the market. The price will rise, decreasing the quantity demanded and increasing the quantity demanded until equilibrium is reached at P2Q2.

5.1 DOING THE BUSINESS MATHS

Complete the table.

Price (£)	Quantity supplied (units)	Quantity demanded (units)	Market outcome (units)	Impact on price
10	320	50		
9	250	80		
8	180	120		
7	150	150		
6	90	200		
5	20	250		
4	15	300		

Questions

1. What would be the equilibrium price and quantity given the supply and demand conditions in the table?

2. What would be the equilibrium price and quantity if demand increased by 50 per cent at each price?

5.1 BUSINESS INSIGHT: SNAP SHARES

The specific factors affecting demand and supply in a market depend on the particular market being considered. The demand for the shares of a business can be influenced by speculation and rumours about how the business might do in the future.

In February 2018, demand for shares in Snap (the business that owns Snapchat) fell suddenly, leading to a drop in share price and a reduction in the value of the company of £1.3bn. The cause? Reality TV star Kylie Jenner tweeted to her 24.5 million followers that she no longer used the Snapchat messaging app, and this led to a major sale of the company's shares. Snapchat has been facing intense competition from Facebook's Instagram, and Jenner's attack worried investors.

Source: www.bbc.co.uk/news/business-43163544

Question
What are the main factors that influence the demand for a company's shares, do you think?

5.2 BUSINESS INSIGHT: LIMITED SUPPLY

The supply of some products is limited. For example, at any moment there are a fixed number of seats in a sports stadium. This means that whatever happens to demand will affect the price rather than the quantity available. If demand was expected to be very high for tickets, the price could increase. If the demand was expected to be low, the price would need to be low to fill the venue.

The supply of works of art is also limited, which means the price can fluctuate depending on demand. Leonardo da Vinci died in 1519, and fewer than 20 of his paintings are known to exist. In 2017 a 500-year-old painting of Christ that is believed to have been painted by Leonardo da Vinci was sold for a record $450m (£341m). The painting, known as *Salvator Mundi* ('Saviour of the World'), shows Christ with one hand raised, the other holding a glass sphere. In 1958 it had been sold at auction in London for a mere £45. At that time the painting was generally reckoned to be the work of a follower of Leonardo and not the work of Leonardo himself. The 2017 price was the highest auction price for any work of art to date. *Salvator Mundi*, believed to have been painted sometime after 1505, is the only painting by Leonardo thought to be in private hands.

Question
Can you draw a supply curve to show a market where there is a fixed supply regardless of the price?

MANAGEMENT TASK

Thanks to a change in market conditions, the price of chocolate used in your confectionery business has increased significantly. What actions do you think your business could, or should, take to cope with this? Explain your reasoning.

Changes in market conditions

Many factors can change supply and demand in a market. When this happens, there will be excess supply or demand which puts pressure on the price to change, as shown in Table 5.3 and in the four scenarios described below.

- If demand increases, this creates a shortage and the price will increase, leading to less being demanded and more supplied. The new equilibrium will have a higher price and quantity. In Figure 5.9, at the original price P2 there is excess demand. This pulls up price, increasing the quantity supplied and decreasing the quantity demanded until equilibrium is reached. This increase in demand might be caused by factors such as a fall in the price of a complement (discussed in Chapter 3), an increase in the price of a substitute, effective marketing by the business, or an increase in consumers' income leading to people being willing and able to buy more of a normal good.

- If demand decreases, this creates a surplus and the price will decrease, leading to more being demanded and less supplied. In Figure 5.10, at the original price P0

Table 5.3 Changes in market conditions affect the equilibrium price and quantity

Change in market conditions	Impact on equilibrium price	Impact on equilibrium quantity
Increase in demand	Higher	Higher
Decrease in demand	Lower	Lower
Increase in supply	Lower	Higher
Decrease in supply	Higher	Lower

Figure 5.9 An outward shift in demand leads to a higher equilibrium price and output

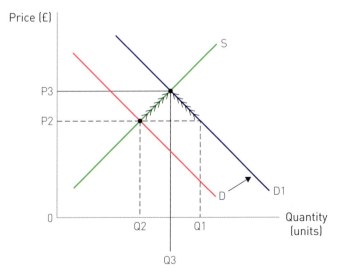

Figure 5.10 An inward shift in demand leads to a lower equilibrium price and output

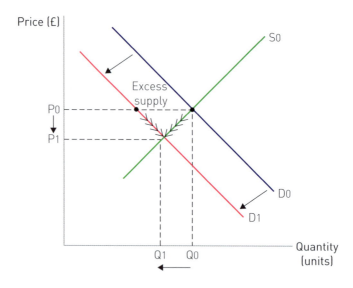

there is excess supply. This pulls down price, increasing the quantity demanded and decreasing the quantity supplied until equilibrium is reached at P1Q1. The new equilibrium will have a lower price and lower quantity. This decrease in demand may occur because of a fall in the population size, effective marketing by competitors, or a fall in the price of a substitute.

• If supply increases, this creates a surplus and the price will decrease, leading to more being demanded and less supplied. In Figure 5.11, at the original price P2 there is excess supply. The price will fall, reducing the quantity supplied and

Figure 5.11 An outward shift of supply leads to a lower equilibrium price, but a higher equilibrium quantity

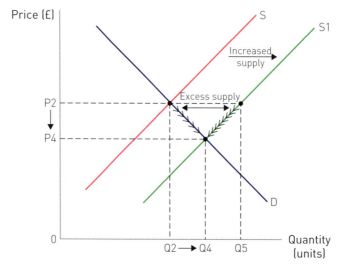

Figure 5.12 An outward shift of supply leads to a lower equilibrium price and a higher output

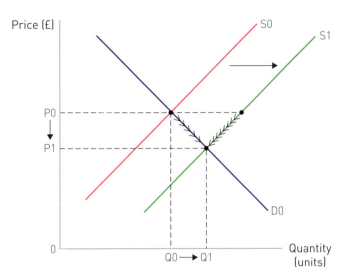

increasing the quantity demanded until a new equilibrium is reached. The new equilibrium will have a lower price and higher quantity. This increase in supply may occur with an increase in the number of producers, an improvement in technology, or lower input prices.

- If supply decreases, this creates a shortage and the price will increase, leading to less being demanded and more supplied. In Figure 5.12, at the original price P0 there is excess demand (a shortage). The price will rise, reducing the quantity demanded and increasing the quantity supplied until a new equilibrium is reached at P1Q1. The new equilibrium will have a higher price and lower quantity. This decrease in supply may occur due to a fall in the number of producers, higher wage costs, or higher taxes on producers.

BUSINESS CASE QUESTIONS: CAN YOU NOW ANSWER . . .

Why might the price of copper increase?
Why might it decrease?
How might changes in copper prices affect businesses?

5.3 BUSINESS INSIGHT: SUGAR PRODUCTION IN THE UK

In agricultural markets, there can be major shifts in supply leading to significant price fluctuations. These shifts can be due to changes in the weather, crop disease, or changes in government regulations. Governments often regulate to try to protect their own countries' food production, and changes to government regulations can affect what can be produced.

Until 2017, under an agreement with the European Union, UK producers could sell only 1.056 million tonnes of sugar beet, even though they had the capacity to produce over 1.4 million. In 2017, after nearly 50 years, the limits on the amount of sugar beet that British producers could sell were lifted. For the first time since 1968, UK farmers could produce and sell as much sugar around the world they wanted. The changes in restrictions also meant that French, German, and other European Union producers could sell more sugar into the UK. The likely effect of this is lower prices. According to the BBC (September 2017):

> The 3,500 British farmers that grow beet [. . .] and British Sugar, which is the main processor of British-grown beet, see the change as a huge opportunity.
>
> British Sugar—which also makes Silver Spoon sugar—plans to step up production immediately and is looking to sell 1.4 million tonnes next year, up from 900,000 this year. It's also planning to export sugar to the world market for the first time in at least a decade. [. . .] Britain's other big sugar producer, Tate & Lyle Sugars, processes sugar cane, and so is not directly affected by the changes.
>
> How big is the UK sugar beet industry?

- There are nearly 10,000 workers in the industry's UK supply chain
- The UK consumes 2 million tonnes of sugar a year
- 60% of that comes from UK beets
- Another 15% comes from EU beets and 25% from imported sugar cane

Source: British Sugar; www.bbc.co.uk/news/business-41412717

Questions

1. What factors have affected supply in the sugar beet industry?
2. Can you think of any factors that might affect demand?

5.1 QUICK CHECK

For each of the following statements, say whether it is true or false.

a. A demand curve shifts outwards or inwards when the price changes.

b. A change in quantity supplied occurs when there is a change in price.

c. If the price is above equilibrium there is excess demand, assuming a downward-sloping demand curve and an upward-sloping supply curve.

d. If the price is below equilibrium there is excess demand, assuming a downward-sloping demand curve and an upward-sloping supply curve.

e. With excess supply in a market, the price will tend to fall to restore equilibrium.

f. With excess demand in a market, the price will tend to fall to restore equilibrium.

5.4 BUSINESS INSIGHT: THE CO_2 SHORTAGE

In the summer of 2018, the supermarket chain Asda announced it was to ration the amount of some carbonated drinks that its online customers could buy. This was because of the national shortage in CO_2. According to the BBC:

[Asda] has restricted shoppers to six bottles or multipacks of soft drinks online. Those affected are its own-label soft drinks, plus Pepsi, Pepsi Max, Coca-Cola, Diet Coke, Coke Zero, 7Up, Irn Bru and Fanta. [. . .] The carbon dioxide scarcity has already forced beer, fizzy drink, crumpet, and meat firms to curb production. [. . .]

CO_2 is widely used in the food processing and drinks industries. It puts the fizz into beer, cider and soft drinks, and is used in food packaging to extend the shelf life of salads, fresh meat and poultry.

The gas is also used to stun pigs and chickens before slaughter, and create dry ice to help keep things chilled while in transit.

However, several UK and mainland European producers of carbon dioxide [. . .] have been closed for maintenance or scaled down operations. [. . .] Meanwhile the World Cup football, hot weather, and barbecue season has created an added demand for beer, just when the CO_2 plants have gone offline.

Source: www.bbc.co.uk/news/business-44673648

Question
In the free market, what would you expect to happen to the prices of products such as carbonated drinks and beer when there is a shortage of CO_2? Why has Asda had to ration the amount bought?

5.2 QUICK CHECK

What changes in supply or demand could cause

a. higher equilibrium price and lower quantity?

b. higher equilibrium price and higher quantity?

c. lower equilibrium price and lower quantity?

d. lower equilibrium price and higher quantity?

READ MORE

The Austrian Economist Friedrich Hayek believed that the prosperity of society was generated by creativity, entrepreneurship, and innovation and that these occurred with free markets. Hayek also argued that in a planned economy, with prices, quantities, and jobs set by central planners, there is a loss of freedom which can lead to totalitarianism. You can read more about this in

Hayek, F.A.V. (1994), *The Road to Serfdom*, Chicago: University of Chicago Press.

How much will the equilibrium price and quantity change with a change in market conditions?

The change in the equilibrium price and quantity following a change in demand will depend on two factors:

- the extent to which demand changes—this will depend on how sensitive demand is to the factor that caused the change in conditions. For example, if demand is very income elastic then any given percentage change in income will lead to a relatively high shift in demand. The percentage change in demand is greater than the change in income.

- how price inelastic supply is—the more price inelastic it is, the more any change on demand will affect the equilibrium price rather than quantity. Some factors that affect the price elasticity of supply are listed in Table 5.4.

The change in the equilibrium price and quantity following a change in supply will depend on the extent to which supply changes, which will in turn depend on two factors:

- the extent to which there is a change in factors such as technology, capital equipment, production costs, production taxes and number of suppliers;

- how price elastic demand is. The more price inelastic it is, the more any shift in supply will affect the equilibrium price rather than quantity, as shown in Figure 5.13. Some factors that affect the price elasticity of demand are listed in Table 5.4.

Understanding these issues will help managers to anticipate the effect of any change in market conditions. Agricultural products such wheat and coffee have very volatile prices because

- supply will often shift with a change in the weather or crop diseases;

- demand and supply are both relatively price inelastic, so demand and supply shifts have a relatively large effect on price.

Table 5.4 Factors affecting price elasticity of demand and supply

Price elasticity of demand is affected by	Price elasticity of supply is affected by
Percentage of income spent on the product	Ease of substituting alternative factors of production
Availability of alternatives	Time period, e.g. short- or long-term periods
Nature of the product, e.g. necessity or luxury	Availability of spare production capacity

Figure 5.13 The more price inelastic demand is, the greater the effect of a shift in supply on price

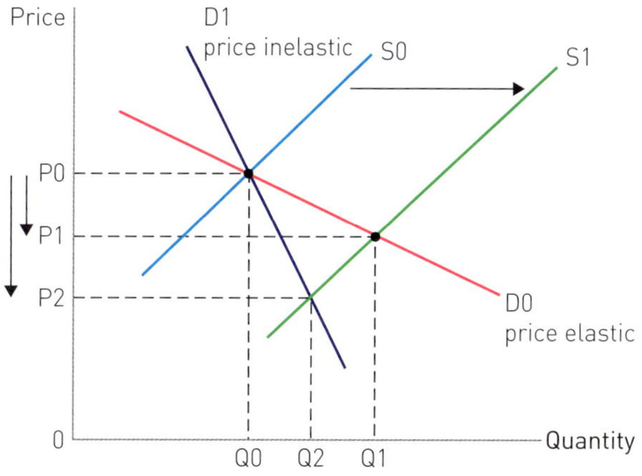

5.3 QUICK CHECK

For each of the following statements, say whether it is true or false.

a. An increase in demand is likely to increase equilibrium price and decrease the quantity in a market.

b. An decrease in demand is likely to increase equilibrium price and increase the quantity in a market.

c. An increase in supply is likely to increase equilibrium price and decrease the quantity in a market.

d. An increase in demand is likely to decrease equilibrium price and decrease the quantity in a market.

Does the price mechanism work?

In reality, the price mechanism may not work quite as well as has been described. One problem is that prices can be 'sticky'. They may be fixed for a period of time and it may not be able to adjust them easily. Businesses have to anticipate in advance the likely demand and set the price accordingly. They may then find that demand is higher or lower than expected, but if there is a published price or a price that has been agreed in a contract it may not be easy to change this. Imagine you are a restaurant with a printed menu with prices in it. If your restaurant is very popular and you are full every evening you might decide to increase prices, but in the short term you will be committed to the prices on the printed menu. (Perhaps that's why many restaurants and cafés put their prices on a blackboard—that way they are easier to change!) It may be that reducing prices in the short term is easier than increasing them, because you can introduce special offers and discounts; asking for a higher price than has already been publicized is not so easy.

The problem facing many managers when setting price, therefore, is one of information—they don't know exactly what supply and demand conditions will be, and so when they set the price there is a risk of there being a surplus until they have the opportunity to review prices. Having said this, online businesses are able to track demand conditions much more easily and can adapt their prices more easily and more rapidly than traditional businesses.

Secondary markets

Sometimes a secondary market springs up if a shortage exists. Imagine a band is going on tour. Its managers estimate the likely demand and set the price. If the demand is much higher than supply at this price, there is a shortage. Some people who manage to get hold of tickets may then sell them on to other people at a much higher price; this is a secondary market. This is a common occurrence for big concerts and sports events. Interestingly, some performers and teams deliberately set the ticket price lower than they could, to try and make attending affordable for more people; they recognize that this means the price mechanism is not allowed to work, and they try to prevent ticket touts from buying up ticket and reselling them.

5.5 BUSINESS INSIGHT: SHARE PRICES

Companies can try to raise money from selling shares. Investors then own a part of the company. They will receive a return via dividends, which are payments made as income to investors and through changes in the share price. The shares can then be bought and sold. In the case of public limited companies, there are usually share available and they are traded daily on the stock exchange. A stock exchange is a secondary market for shares. Whether the price rises or falls does not directly affect the company that issued the shares—it affects whoever is holding them.

The demand for shares will depend on

- the price;
- the expected price in the future;
- the expected dividends.

On the final day of trading in 2017, share prices in the UK reached the highest level there had been. According to the BBC:

> Both the FTSE [a measure by the Financial Times of the share prices of the largest 100 companies listed on the Stock Exchange] [. . .] and the FTSE 250 [a measure by the Financial Times of the share prices of the largest 250 companies] reached new records at the close of trading. US stock markets have also hit new peaks over the year, helped in part Donald Trump's sweeping tax reforms. [Under the changes, the US corporate tax rate was to fall from 35% to 21% in 2018.]
>
> The FTSE 100 finished up 7.6% at 7,687.77 compared with the last day of trading in 2016. Meanwhile, the FTSE 250 ended 14.7% ahead at 20,726.26 compared with the end of last year.

Figure 5.14 Best and worst performing FTSE 100 companies, percentage change in 2017

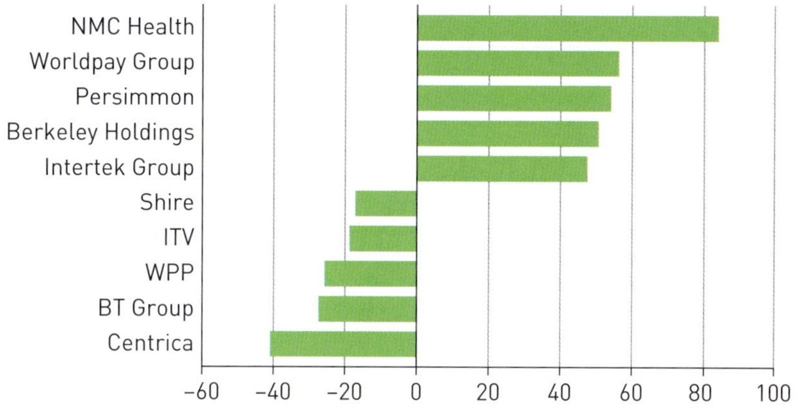

Source: www.bbc.co.uk/news/business-42512023

George Salmon, an equity analyst at Hargreaves Lansdown, said the FTSE 100 had been lifted by natural resource giants such as Shell and BP which have benefited from a rise in oil prices.

[. . .] Housebuilders were among the best performing companies on the FTSE 100 in 2017 [see Figure 5.14]. Berkeley Group, which mainly builds luxury homes in London, rejoined the blue chip index in September and has seen its share price rise by more than 50% this year. Businesses such as advertising giant WPP and broadcaster ITV were among the worst performers as companies reduced investment in marketing.

Source: www.bbc.co.uk/news/business-42512023

Question
What factors do you think might affect the price of a company's shares?

MANAGEMENT TASK

You are the managing director of a printing company. The share price of your company has been falling. Explain why you are concerned about this.

ANALYSING THE BUSINESS DATA: THE PRICE OF OIL 2008–17

The chart in Figure 5.15 shows the price of oil over a number years. Explain, using supply and demand analysis, the key price changes over the last few years.

Figure 5.15 The price of oil, 2008–17

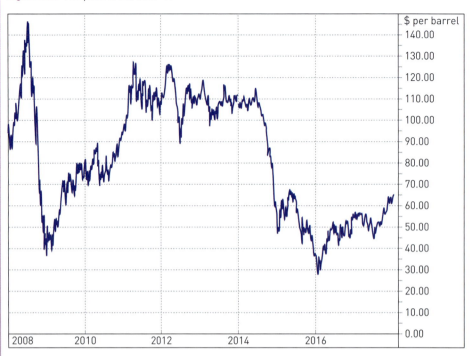

Source: 2018 MoneyAM.com

5.6 BUSINESS INSIGHT: BITCOIN

Bitcoin is an online (crypto) currency. As reported by the BBC:

> Bitcoins are created through a complex process known as 'mining', and then moni-
> tored by a network of computers across the world. There's a steady stream of about
> 3,600 new bitcoins a day—with about 16.5 million now in circulation. [. . .] The rules
> underpinning bitcoin say that only 21 million bitcoins can be created—and that fig-
> ure is getting ever nearer.

Every single bitcoin transaction is recorded in a public list called the blockchain. This
makes it possible to trace the history of bitcoins to stop people from spending coins they
do not own, making copies, or undoing transactions.

In 2017 the value of bitcoin fluctuated significantly. Towards the end of the year its value
fell sharply to around one-third of its value from a record of nearly $20,000 (£15,000).
Bitcoin is traded globally. The currency started 2017 at a price of around $1,000. The
market for bitcoin is driven heavily by speculation about what the value will do next. Some
speculators will have taken the view that £15,000 was its peak and they started to sell;
this provoked concern in other holders, who then decided it was a good time to get out of
the currency, increasing supply further.

The Danish government said that buying bitcoin was a 'deadly' gamble. The head of
one of the UK's leading financial regulators warned people to be ready to 'lose all their

money' if they invested in bitcoin. The head of the UK's Financial Conduct Authority said that neither central banks nor the government stood behind the 'currency' and that it was therefore not a secure investment.

Explain how speculation will affect the price of bitcoin.

Source: BBC; www.bbc.co.uk/news/business-42150512

SUMMARY

Markets are made up of buyers and sellers who want to trade with each other. The price adjusts in a free market to equate supply and demand. If there is excess demand, the price will rise, which usually reduces quantity demanded and increases quantity supplied until a new equilibrium is reached. If there is excess supply, the price is likely to fall to bring about equilibrium.

Changes in supply or demand will lead to a change in the equilibrium price and quantity. Markets are often interrelated—a change in demand in one market may lead to more demand for resources while reducing demand for a substitute product.

KEY LEARNING POINTS

- Markets are made up of buyers and sellers.
- It is assumed that buyers act rationally and want to maximize their satisfaction (utility) and sellers want to maximize their profits.
- If demand is greater than the quantity supplied at the given price, there is excess demand (a shortage).
- If demand is less than the quantity supplied at the given price, there is excess supply (a surplus).
- At equilibrium, the quantity supplied equals the quantity demanded at the given price and there is no incentive for change.
- The effect of a change in market conditions will depend on the extent to which supply and demand shifts and the price elasticity of demand and supply.

BUSINESS CASE EXTENSION QUESTIONS

1. Research the price of copper in the last year. Analyse the reasons for any changes during this period.

2. Copper is a commodity. It is traded globally and there is a world price. Research the market for another commodity. Analyse the factors affecting supply and demand of this commodity. Use this analysis to explain changes in the price of the commodity in recent years.

QUICK QUESTIONS

1. What is a market?
2. What is shown by a demand curve?
3. What is shown by a supply curve?
4. What is the likely effect in a market of an increase in demand?
5. Explain why demand for a product might increase.
6. What is the likely effect in a market of an increase in supply?
7. Explain why supply of a product might increase.
8. What is the likely effect on price and quantity in a market of a decrease in demand?
9. What is the likely effect on price and quantity in a market of a decrease in supply?
10. What is the difference between a surplus and a shortage?

Labour market

Your football team is struggling to win a match, even at home. You have lost the last three matches and the local press is calling for you to resign as manager. You have lasted longer than many, having managed the team for three seasons already.

At the moment you have the support of the fans, but you are not sure how much longer this will last. You have invested in more training for the team. You have changed the players' diets. You have had motivational speakers come in. You have shouted and screamed. You have played attacking football and defensive football, and still no joy. You are clear now that you need some new players—two more upfront and, ideally, a strong defender. The problem is the cost. Players' salaries just seem to go up and up, and the players you want will cost you millions. Football is your life, but even you wonder how people can earn so much for kicking a circular object around on a piece of grass. Shouldn't there be a limit to what they earn, so that more clubs can afford some of the top players? But that won't happen this season, so you had better call the bank to borrow some money. A lot of money.

Labour is an important resource and, like any resource, it needs careful management. In this chapter, we consider the factors that determine the price of labour, and what factors can influence its productivity and value.

BY THE END OF THIS CHAPTER YOU WILL BE ABLE TO . . .

- explain the importance of labour as a factor of production
- analyse factors influencing the demand for labour
- analyse factors affecting the supply of labour

BUSINESS CASE

In 2017 there was considerable media coverage of the rewards being received by the senior staff (called vice-chancellors) at UK universities. Many university vice-chancellors were earning £300,000 a year, and some more than £400,000. The government responded by creating a new regulator called the Office for Students. This office would have the power to fine universities if they could not justify high pay. Any pay over £100,000 could be referred to the office. The BBC reported:

Universities have argued that their leaders are managing large institutions, have enormous responsibilities and huge budgets, and therefore command large salaries. [. . .]

Jo Johnson [the government's minister for universities and science] said 'It's important there's confidence fees are put to the uses we intend them to be—we want fees to deliver great teaching and world-class research.' [. . .]

The overall cost of salary and benefits for vice-chancellors rose 2.5% to an average remuneration of £257,904 in 2015–16 on the previous year. When pension contributions are included, the rise was 2.2% to an average of £280,877. And several high profile cases revealed pay levels substantially higher than this. Imperial College London pays its vice-chancellor [. . .] a £430,000 yearly wage and pension package. She was recruited from an American university some years ago where she was paid £679,754. The University of Birmingham pays [its vice-chancellor] £426,000 in salary and pensions.

Defenders of these earnings say that universities operate in a competitive market and argue that 'salaries help to maintain the UK's position as a "world leader in science and innovation"' (BBC).

Source: www.bbc.co.uk/news/uk-england-bristol-42260090

BUSINESS CASE QUESTIONS

This chapter will help you to answer the following questions.

1. What do you think determines the pay of a vice-chancellor?

2. Is £300,000 too much to pay a vice-chancellor? Is it too much to pay anyone?

3. Do you think the government should intervene to determine how much vice-chancellors are paid? What about other jobs?

Labour

Labour is one of the resources you will be responsible for as a manager. As with any other resource, such as land and capital, you will want to manage it well to get the most from it. As with any resource you will be making an investment—in this case, investing in people. You will pay to recruit and hire them, and you will often fund their training and development. Imagine you employ someone at £25,000 for 20 years; that's half a million pounds just on salary costs. Now add in the likely costs for other taxes you pay, training costs, and pensions, as well as any other benefits you might provide, such as healthcare, and you are getting closer to a million pounds.

Used well, labour has enormous potential as a resource—people can find solutions to problems, can develop new processes and products, and can be creative. Managed badly, labour can walk away, can have motivational issues, or can even disrupt your production.

How much should you pay your employees?

One of the key decisions when it comes to employees is how to reward them, and what level of rewards to set. In terms of how to pay staff, there are numerous systems such as paying by the hour, paying on output, or paying a salary. The total rewards an employee receives is called their remuneration.

As well as basic pay, remuneration may include factors such as:

- pension arrangements
- additional benefits such as healthcare
- holiday period
- sickness benefits

Many managers will have share options. This is the right to buy shares of the business at a given price at a point in the future. For example, you might be given the option to buy 200,000 shares at £1.50 in two years' time. This gives you an incentive to do all you can to get the share price to be higher than this. If the share price rises to £2.00 you can buy your shares at £1.50 (this is known as 'exercising your options') and sell them for £2.00. You make 50 pence profit on 200,000 shares, which is £100,000. Share options are a way of aligning managers' behaviour with what shareholders want.

The right system of remuneration will depend in part on the nature of the work—for example, if you want the focus to be on sales, then paying commission on the revenue generated may make sense. If it is easy to measure an individual's output and the focus is on productivity, then a piece rate may be suitable.

KEY CONCEPT

An employee's **remuneration** is the total rewards he or she gets.

MANAGEMENT TASK

You are reviewing the way your staff are remunerated in your retail outlets. Should you pay your sales staff on commission for the sales they make? What might the outcome of this be? Should it be individual or team commission? Why?

Decisions about the overall level of rewards you give to staff are likely to depend on labour market conditions, i.e. demand and supply of labour. Of course, managers may decide to ignore market conditions and pay more than they have to because they think it is right.

Managers may also pay more than the market rate because they think this will encourage more productivity from employees and end up justifying the higher wage. The higher wage may also means people may stay longer, which reduces the labour turnover (the proportion of the workforce that leave over a given period).

By reducing labour turnover, you also reduce the costs of recruitment and training. The suggestion that paying more than the market rate can actually lead to sufficient productivity gains and costs savings is known as the 'efficiency wage' theory.

KEY CONCEPT

Efficiency wage theory suggests that it may be efficient for managers to pay more than the market wage because of the consequent productivity gains and cost savings.

There may also be occasions where market conditions do not apply—for example, within the public sector. However, you will usually want to consider what market conditions are, and what others in your industry are paying; your employees will certainly be considering this.

6.1 BUSINESS INSIGHT: REAL EARNINGS

When it comes to pay negotiations, your staff will be interested in how much they will be earning now and how much this will increase in the future. However, they will also want to know what is happening to prices; after all, what really matters is the purchasing power

Figure 6.1 How inflation compared to wage growth, 2016–17

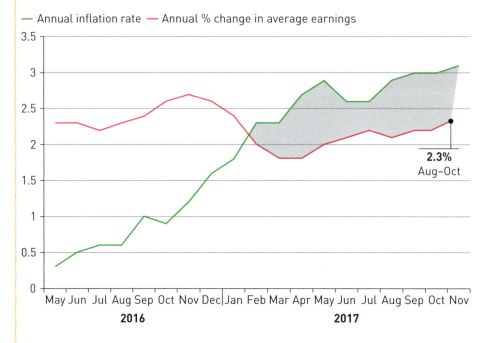

— Annual inflation rate — Annual % change in average earnings

Note: Earning figures are three-month averages, excluding bonuses.

Source: Office for National Statistics / BBC

of the money you get—what can you afford with the money you are earning? Real earnings show the purchasing power of your money.

In recent years the average earnings growth for employees in the UK has been falling behind inflation (see Figure 6.1). This means that real earnings have been falling.

In 2017 unemployment declined by 26,000 to 1.43 million, while the jobless rate remained at 4.3 per cent, the lowest since 1975. Average weekly pay in 2017, excluding bonuses, reached £478, which is the lowest since February 2006.

Source: www.bbc.co.uk/news/business-42337659

Question
What might be the consequences in an economy if real wages are falling?

KEY CONCEPT

Real wages are nominal wages adjusted for inflation (price increases). They show the purchasing power of earnings.

MANAGEMENT TASK

Some of your employees want to meet to negotiate higher pay. Employees' real wages have been falling. But so have your profits. Should you meet with your employees? If so, what would you say?

ANALYSING THE BUSINESS DATA

Figure 6.2 Great Britain's average weekly earnings nominal and real, January 2005 to November 2017, seasonally adjusted

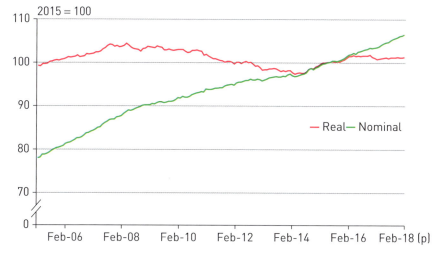

Source: Contains public sector information licensed under the Open Government Licence v3.0.

Questions

1. Did pay levels ever actually fall in the period covered above? When, and how do you know?

2. Why do you think pay grew faster from August 2015 onwards compared to the period from 2012 to August 2015?

The demand for labour

Your demand for labour will be linked to the demand for your output. You want and need employees to produce the goods and services that are demanded. The demand for them is derived from the demand for the product you are producing: labour is a 'derived demand'. The higher the demand for your products and the more customers are willing to pay for the product, the higher the demand for employees in general is likely to be, and this is likely to pull up wages and salaries.

> ## KEY CONCEPT
>
> Labour is a **derived demand**. Demand for labour is derived from demand for the final product.

Another factor that influences your demand for labour is how productive employees are. If employees are productive then they produce more, and this extra output can be sold. This means that you are likely to be willing and able to pay them high earnings. If, however, employees are not very productive, this means there is not much you can earn from their output.

Employment decisions

In a rational world you will employ additional people up to the point where the value of the extra output produced by one additional person (known as the value of the marginal product) is equal to the extra costs of employing that person. This is the marginal condition of employment for a profit-maximizing employer.

*   If the value of the extra output from employing someone is more than the extra cost of employing them, the profits will rise if they are employed (see Table 6.1). This person should be employed.
*   If the value of the extra output from employing someone equals the extra cost of employing them, the profits will not change if they are employed. This is because profits are maximized. Managers should recruit up to this person.
*   If the value of the extra output from employing someone is less than the extra cost of employing them, the profits will fall if they are employed. This person should not be employed.

Table 6.1 Making employment decisions

Condition	Impact on profits by employing extra person	Employment decision
Value of extra employee's output is greater than extra cost of employing them	increases	employ
Value of extra employee's output is equal to extra cost of employing them	same	employ
Value of extra employee's output is less than extra cost of employing them	decreases	do not employ

KEY CONCEPT

The **marginal value product** is the value of the extra output of the extra employee.

6.1 DOING THE BUSINESS MATHS

Complete the table.

Number of employees	Extra cost of employing employee (£)	Value of marginal product (£)	Employ or not? (yes or no)
1	10	90	
2	20	60	
3	30	30	
4	50	10	
5	70	5	

6.1 QUICK CHECK

For each of the following statements, say whether it is true or false.

a. Demand for labour is a derived demand.

b. Efficient wage theory means managers may pay more than the market wage.

c. Profit-maximizing managers will employ staff up to the point when the value of marginal product equals the marginal cost of labour.

Productivity and pay

Productivity is obviously a key element in the likely earnings of employees. If some-one is not producing, they are not earning for the business. As a manager, you will be very interested in productivity and how to increase it. You will want to examine every stage of the operational process to look for ways of saving time, of reducing waste, of improving quality, and of helping employees to become more productive. Higher productivity is potentially a win–win situation: the business can earn more, and so can employees.

Improving productivity benefits the whole of the UK economy. It enables workers to produce more for the same number of hours worked. This in turn raises profits for companies and benefits households, as firms can pay higher wages and offer goods and services at lower prices.

However, this depends on what actually happens to any additional profits gener-ated. Some employees may be very wary of efforts to improve productivity, as this may simply be a way that the business earns more; the employees may not benefit from this and may therefore regard initiatives to increase productivity as unwelcome change, and potentially extra effort.

The low levels of productivity in the UK in recent years is of some concern (as discussed in Business insight 6.2); without more productivity, employees will not be generating more output and so this will limit growth and incomes.

How to increase labour productivity

Increasing labour productivity is a constant management challenge. Managers will want to improve productivity because this can help to reduce unit costs.

Increasing productivity may be achieved in several ways.

- Changes to reward systems: for example, if it is easy to measure the output of an employee, then paying per unit produced may provide an incentive to produce more.

- Changes to the work processes: managing job design and the flow of work more effectively or changing the layout of resources may make it possible to speed up production and increase productivity.

- Training of staff: training may help them do their job more effectively.

- Investment: employees will usually be more productive if they have the right equipment and the latest technology. You can try and build a house by hand, but you are probably a lot faster doing it with machinery.

However, increasing productivity may face opposition from employees. They may worry about extra work, and they may resent the business earning more if they do not earn more themselves.

MANAGEMENT TASK

You need an increase in productivity from your workforce to match your competitors' productivity. Employees have heard that this is on the agenda and are talking of a strike. They say they already work hard and cannot do any more. Even if they could, why should they? It would only benefit management. What actions would you take to achieve an increase in productivity in these circumstances?

KEY CONCEPT

Labour productivity measures the output per worker.

READ MORE

You can find more data about how the labour market in the UK works from the Office of National Statistics:

www.ons.gov.uk/employmentandlabourmarket

6.2 BUSINESS INSIGHT: SLOW PRODUCTIVITY GROWTH

'Productivity isn't everything, but in the long run it is almost everything,' said Paul Krugman, the Nobel-Prize-winning economist, in 1994. Productivity—or output per hour by workers—is the key driver of economic growth. In the UK this is a critical issue at the moment. Productivity is no higher now than it was just before the 2008 financial crisis; this compares with the average annual growth of 2.1 per cent in the decade before the crash. If the pre-crisis trend had continued, productivity would now be 20 per cent higher.

The lack of productivity growth since the crisis has been concentrated in a small number of industries: finance, telecoms, energy, and management consulting. Over the past 18 months this issue has been accentuated by a pick-up in employment in less productive service sectors.

As discussed in Chapter 4 (Business insight 4.3), there are various possible reasons for this lack of productivity.

1. Lack of investment in new equipment and better technology: since 2008 business investment has been growing relatively slowly. Companies' capital spending is only 5 per cent above its pre-crisis peak, compared with a 60 per cent increase over the decade after the 1980s recession and 30 per cent following the 1990s slowdown. Part of the issue here may have been the difficulty accessing funds from banks after the financial crisis—banks were wary of lending and so companies struggled to borrow.

This situation has now improved, with banks in a healthier financial position, but the difficulty now is the uncertainty in the economic environment. This means that businesses are reluctant to invest even if the funds are available.

2. Low interest rates have meant that because it is cheap to borrow and because the returns generally available are low, some businesses have survived that would not otherwise have done. They have been able to survive even while generating low returns because investors have little choice and because this covered the costs of borrowing. These so-called zombie companies are unproductive and under normal circumstances would not have kept going. The cost of borrowing in recent years has been around 5 per cent; it was around 10 per cent in the early 1990s recession.

3. Businesses have retained employees even when they are not very productive, much more than in the past. Unemployment peaked at just 8.5 per cent of the workforce after the 2008–9 recession compared with 10.7 per cent reported in the 1990s. Keeping hold of workers was costly in the short term and hit productivity as demand fell but employment held up. Possibly businesses have held on to employees rather than investing in more expensive technology.

4. There are an increasing number of low-level service jobs in the UK, such as delivering online orders and serving at coffee shops. These jobs have limited opportunity for productivity growth.

5. Labour is relatively cheap, so businesses hire employees rather than invest in technology.

Sources: www.ft.com/content/41be9e38-e521-11e4-bb4b-00144feab7de;

Questions

1. Why does low labour productivity matter (a) to businesses; (b) to the economy; (c) to the government?

2. What can a business do about low productivity? What can the government do?

The supply of labour

The earnings of employees in a market will depend on the supply conditions as well as the demand. It's not just whether you want to hire people as a manager, it is also how easy it is to recruit them!

The supply of labour (i.e. the number of people who are willing and able to work in a particular profession at a given wage) will depend on a range of factors:

• the amount of training required—the supply of doctors, for example, is relatively limited at any moment because it takes years to train them;

• the skills involved—for example, there are many would-be footballers but relatively few who have the skills required for the premiership;

- the ease of movement—how easy it is for employees to move locations to accept a job; the cost of accommodation in some areas, such as the south-east of England, can lead to geographical immobility.

When deciding whether they want to work in a given industry or job, employees will also consider factors such as:

- the working environment
- the opportunities for promotion
- perceived job security

Generally more people are likely to want to accept a job that has good conditions and good promotion prospects than one that is dangerous, involves unsociable hours, or is in a location that is difficult to travel to.

The more limited the supply of labour, the higher the earnings of employees is likely to be.

The reservation wage

The reservation wage is the minimum amount that an employee would need to accept a job.

This will depend on many factors, such as

- the nature of the job
- the working conditions
- the hours of work
- an individual's personal and family circumstances

KEY CONCEPT

The **reservation wage** is the minimum amount that an employee would require to accept a job.

In many markets, the wage will need to increase to attract the right number of employees; some of these may have a lower reservation wage than the market wage. They are being paid over what they need to do the job.

However, if the market wage is below the reservation wage then employees will not accept work and would rather be unemployed. In the UK, some argue that migrant labour has driven down wages in some sectors such as fruit picking and that the local labour force is reluctant to work for the given wage. Local labour might have a higher reservation wage than the migrant labour.

6.2 QUICK CHECK

For each of the following statements, say whether it is true or false.

a.   The reservation wage is the minimum someone is prepared to work for.

b.   A change in the wage rate will shift the supply of labour.

c.   Net migration is likely to shift the supply of labour outwards.

d.   An increase in the retirement age will increase the supply of labour.

6.3 BUSINESS INSIGHT: SEASONAL WORKERS

A BBC report of June 2017 highlighted problems faced by producers of fruits and vege-tables in the UK.

> UK summer fruit and salad growers are having difficulty recruiting pickers. [. . .]
> About 80,000 seasonal workers a year pick and process British fruit and veg. Most
> of them are from the European Union, mainly Romania and Bulgaria. [. . .] British
> Summer Fruits, the body which represents soft fruit growers, says labour short-
> ages are now the worst seen since 2004. [. . .]
>
>   Recruitment was getting harder even before the vote to leave the EU. But the in-
> dustry believes Brexit is exacerbating the problem and if access to non-UK workers
> dries up, it could cripple home-grown berry production.

In theory, the farmers might be able to recruit local UK employees. However, these fruit and vegetable farmers are located in areas of low unemployment. This means there simply are not the employees they need locally.

This reliance on migrant labour is not unique to the UK. In Australia and New Zealand, businesses often source labour from the Pacific Islands. In the US, businesses recruit labour from Mexico and the Caribbean countries.

Question

What is the likely impact on fruit and salad growers if there is a shortage in the supply of labour in their industry?

Source: www.bbc.co.uk/news/business-40354331

KEY CONCEPT

Geographical immobility occurs when employees cannot easily move between regions to accept a job.

ANALYSING THE BUSINESS DATA

The unemployment rate measures the number of unemployed as a percentage of the number of people in the labour force (see Figure 6.3).

Figure 6.3 UK unemployment rates

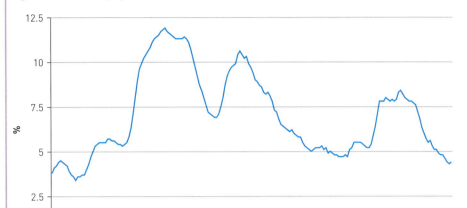

Source: Contains public sector information licensed under the Open Government Licence v3.0.

Questions

1. What is happening to the unemployment rate in the UK over the given period?

2. What might the impact of this be for businesses, do you think?

3. How might unemployment rates affect wages and the ease of recruiting?

Market forces

The labour market is, in fact, made up of millions of markets. The demand and supply of labour in a given region is different from those in another region; the demand and supply for one type of job is different from those for another type.

In any particular market the wage level may be determined by the market forces of supply and demand.

• If demand for labour increases, this leads to a higher wage; the extra demand pulls up the wage level. Computer programmers and data analysts are in high demand at the moment and tend to be relatively well paid.

• If demand for labour decreases, this leads to a lower wage; the lack of demand pulls down the wage level. There is relatively little demand for newspaper deliveries these days, and so these staff would tend to be relatively poorly paid.

• If the supply of labour to a market decreases, this limits the number of people available and wages are pushed up. There is a shortage of skilled medical professionals in the UK at the moment, which should lead to higher earnings.

Figure 6.4 Equilibrium in the labour market

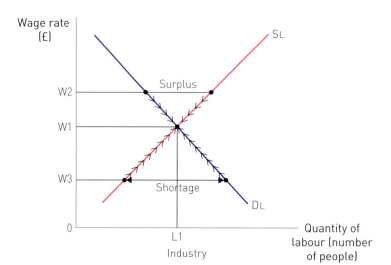

- If the supply of labour to a market increases, this increases the number of people available and wages fall. The inflow of employees from Eastern Europe in recent years has led to relatively low wages in some sectors, such as agriculture.

Figure 6.4 illustrates the interaction between wage rate and the quantity of labour. At W2 there is excess supply of labour. The wage falls, increasing the quantity demanded and reducing the quantity supplied until equilibrium is reached at W1L1.

At W3 there is excess demand of labour. The wage rises, decreasing the quantity demanded and increasing the quantity supplied until equilibrium is reached at W1L1.

Changes in market conditions

Looking at Figure 6.5, imagine the labour market is in equilibrium at W1L1. If demand for labour increases, this leads to excess demand at the existing wage. The wage is pulled up, decreasing the quantity demanded and increasing the quantity supplied. This continues until the new equilibrium at W2L2, with a higher wage and higher number of people employed.

Looking at Figure 6.6, imagine the labour market is in equilibrium at W1L1. If supply of labour increases, this leads to a surplus at the existing wage. The wage is pulled down, increasing the quantity demanded and decreasing the quantity supplied. This continues until the new equilibrium at W2L2, with a lower wage and higher number of people employed.

The effects of changes in demand for labour and supply of labour are summarized in Table 6.2.

Figure 6.5 A shift in the demand for labour

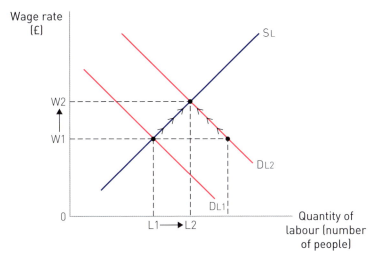

Figure 6.6 A shift in the supply of labour

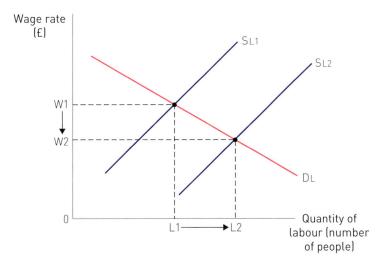

6.3 QUICK CHECK

For each of the following statements, say whether it is true or false.

a.   If the wage rate is above the equilibrium rate there will be excess supply.

b.   If the wage rate is below the equilibrium rate there will be excess supply.

c.   An increase in demand for labour is likely to increase wages.

d.   An decrease in supply for labour is likely to increase wages.

Table 6.2 The effects of changes in labour market conditions

Change	Possible causes	Effect on the equilibrium wage and quantity of labour
Increase in demand for labour	More demand for final product	Higher wage and quantity
Decrease in demand for labour	Less demand for final product	Lower wage and quantity
Increase in supply of labour	Net migration	Lower wage and higher quantity
Decrease in supply of labour	Net emigration	Higher wage and lower quantity

BUSINESS CASE QUESTIONS: CAN YOU NOW ANSWER . . .

What do you think determines the pay of a vice-chancellor?

6.2 DOING THE BUSINESS MATHS

In terms of shifts in supply of and demand for labour, what might cause
a) an increase in the equilibrium wage and quantity of labour?
b) an increase in the equilibrium wage and a decrease in the quantity of labour?
c) a decrease in the equilibrium wage and quantity of labour?
d) a decrease in the equilibrium wage and an increase in the quantity of labour?

Monopoly and monopsony

Not all labour markets will be competitive, and so not all wages will be determined by market forces. In some markets, the labour force may be well organized and form a trade union to control the supply of labour. The trade union may, for example, restrict the supply to those who are union members. This can shift supply inwards, pushing up wages. Trade unions may also bargain to force managers to retain the same number of employees that would occur in the free market but insist on a higher wage than the market suggests. Managers may fear industrial action (such as strikes) and so feel obliged to pay to ensure that production continues.

If a trade union controls the supply of labour it is a monopoly supplier, and it can force up wage levels (and the costs of the business).

In other markets there may be one main 'buyer' of a particular type of employee: e.g. the health service will be the main buyer of doctors. If there is one buyer of labour, this is known as a 'monopsony'. A monopsony is likely to drive down wages.

6.4 BUSINESS INSIGHT: NET MIGRATION

Figure 6.7 Long-term international migration, UK, 2007 to 2017 (year ending June 2017)

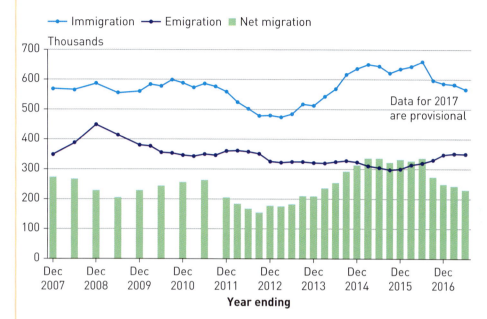

Source: Office for National Statistics

Net migration is the difference between the number of people coming to live in the UK, and the number of people leaving to live elsewhere. This fell to 230,000 in the year ending June 2017. This was down from the recent peak seen in the year ending June 2016 and is now at a similar level to 2014 (see Figure 6.7).

Table 6.3 Age distribution of the UK population, 1976 to 2046 (projected)

	0 to 15 years (%)	16 to 64 years (%)	Aged 65 and over (%)	UK population
1976	24.5	61.2	14.2	56,216,121
1986	20.5	64.1	15.4	56,683,835
1996	20.7	63.5	15.9	58,164,374
2006	19.2	64.9	15.9	60,827,067
2016	18.9	63.1	18.0	65,648,054
2026	18.8	60.7	20.5	69,843,515
2036	18.0	58.2	23.9	73,360,907
2046	17.7	57.7	24.7	76,342,235

Source: Office for National Statistics

- In 2016 the population of the UK was 65.6 million, its largest ever.

- The UK population is projected to continue growing, reaching over 74 million by 2039.

- The population in the UK is getting older, with 18% aged 65 and over and 2.4% aged 85 and over (see Table 6.3).

- In 2016 there were 285 people aged 65 and over for every 1,000 people aged 16 to 64 years ('traditional working age').

- Births continue to outnumber deaths, and immigration continues to outnumber emigration, resulting in a growing population.

Source: www.ons.gov.uk/peoplepopulationandcommunity/populationandmigration/internation-almigration/bulletins/migrationstatisticsquarterlyreport/november2017

Questions

1. Why does the size of the UK population matter to businesses?

2. Why does net migration into the UK matter to businesses?

3. Why does the age distribution of the UK population matter to businesses?

KEY CONCEPTS

Migration refers to the flow of people in and out of a country. **Immigration** means people are coming into a country. **Emigration** means they are leaving a country. **Net migration** means that more people are entering a country than are leaving.

Why do labour costs matter?

The earnings of employees are costs of the business and, as with any costs, managers will want to make sure they are getting value for money. For any given level of revenue, the higher the cost of labour the lower the profits. Managers will want to measure costs relative to revenue and compare this with other businesses in the industry to assess the profit being earned per employee.

The proportion of labour costs compared to revenue will vary from industry to industry. For a football club, for example, labour costs are a very significant part of the total costs, and managing employees is particularly vital because it is such a labour-intensive industry. The same is true of consultancies businesses, universities, and the health service.

However, in a business producing soft drinks or a telecommunications business labour costs will be a lower proportion of overall costs because these are more capital-intensive industries. Managers will want to be sure that the amount spent on labour is generating a sufficient return.

This means managers must consider

- whether the remuneration they are offering is at an appropriate level to attract and retain the right numbers and calibre of staff;
- whether the productivity and quality of work of employees is appropriate.

Managers may then take various actions:

- investing in further training and development;
- adjusting the remuneration levels of systems;
- changing the numbers of staff, perhaps through recruitment, relocation, re-deployment, or potentially redundancies.

KEY CONCEPTS

A **labour-intensive** business uses a relatively high proportion of labour relative to capital.
A **capital-intensive** business uses a relatively high proportion of capital relative to labour.

Employment and costs

If employees are paid a salary, then these labour costs are fixed. Regardless of what the sales of the business are, the same amount must be paid as a salary in a given time period. (Over time, redundancies may have to be made if the business cannot cover its costs.) These fixed costs are a risk to the business. Some managers will, therefore, try to make employee rewards (or at least some of them) variable costs, i.e. linked to output and sales. This means that if revenue falls, costs will fall as well, which reduces the risk to the business of making a loss. This is a feature of what is known as the 'gig' economy.

Flexible organizations will often try to have workforce levels that can be increased or decreased easily depending on demand; this would include using part-time workers, seasonal workers, agency staff, or temporary staff rather than having everyone on full-time contracts. This gives the organization the ability to match supply to demand more easily and to have more of its costs variable rather than fixed.

6.5 BUSINESS INSIGHT: THE GIG ECONOMY

The gig economy refers to labour markets that have a high level of short-term contracts or freelance work, as opposed to permanent jobs. Rather than receive a salary, workers are paid for the work they do—for each 'gig', such as delivering a product. For some this is attractive because it offers flexible working—this can suit employees and employers. However, for others it represents exploitation of employees.

The relationship between a business and people who work for it is subject to much legal action at the moment. The debate is whether workers are 'employed' by the business, in which case the employer has a host of additional legal responsibilities. In the UK it's estimated that five million people are employed in this type of capacity. Workers in the gig economy are classed as independent contractors. That means they have no protection against unfair dismissal, no right to redundancy payments, and no right to receive the national minimum wage, paid holiday, or sickness pay. Last year Uber drivers in the UK won the right to be classed as workers rather than independent contractors.

Workers in the gig economy differ slightly from those on zero-hours contracts. These are the—also controversial—arrangements used by companies such as Sports Direct, JD Wetherspoons, and Cineworld. Like workers in the gig economy, zero-hours contractors—or casual contractors—don't get guaranteed hours or much job security from their employer.

People on zero-hours contracts are seen as employees in some sense, as they are entitled to holiday pay. But, like those in the gig economy, they are not entitled to sick pay.

Question

Do you think the gig economy is a good thing?

ANALYSING THE BUSINESS DATA

Table 6.4 Marks & Spencer's UK operating costs, 2017 and 2016

	52 weeks ended		Change on previous year (%)
	1 April 1017 (£m)	26 March 2016 (£m)	
Store staffing	1,010.3	974.4	3.7
Other store costs	1,000.7	974.4	2.7
Distribution and warehousing	519.6	475.4	9.3
Marketing	162.7	186.1	−12.6
Central costs	697.1	655.8	6.3
Total UK operating costs	**3,390.4**	**3,266.1**	**3.8**

Note: Certain prior year costs have been reclassified to reflect changes in UK organization structure.

Source: https://corporate.marksandspencer.com/annualreport

Questions

1. What proportion of Marks & Spencer's operating costs are store staff costs?

2. What would managers of Marks and Spencer's want to analyse in order to decide if this is too high a figure or not?

MANAGEMENT TASK

You are the chief executive of a home delivery service. Many of the people who deliver for you are self-employed. Your drivers have been asking for a guaranteed number of hours' work each week. Should you agree to this?

Why does productivity matter?

Productivity matters because it affects how much is produced and can be sold; this can affect the demand for labour. Productivity also affects the costs of the business and therefore how much can be supplied at any price.

Imagine, for example, that you paid an employee £1,000 a week and she produced 20 units; the labour cost per unit is £1,000 ÷ 20 = £50 per unit.

Imagine she now produced 40 units; the labour cost per unit is £1,000 ÷ 40 = £25 per unit.

From a business perspective, if wages remain constant and labour productivity increases this reduces the labour cost per unit.

As we can see in Table 6.5, greater labour productivity, assuming total labour costs are constant, means that the labour cost per unit falls. With lower unit costs, a business may be able to reduce the price and still maintain the profit per unit, or the business might keep the price the same but enjoy higher profit per unit. This is why increasing labour productivity is often a key focus of management.

6.3 DOING THE BUSINESS MATHS

Complete the table.

Number of employees	Wage bill if each employee paid £600 a week	Output per week (units)	Labour productivity per week	Labour cost per unit (£)
50		50,000		
50		60,000		
50		100,000		
50		200,000		

Trade unions

Employees within your business may belong to a trade union. Unions exist to represent employees and protect their interests. By being part of a union, employees have more power in negotiations because they are acting as a group, rather than

Table 6.5 Effects of labour productivity

Number of employees	Wage bill if each employee paid £500 a week	Output per week (units)	Labour productivity per week	Labour cost per unit (£)
10	£5,000	10,000	10,000 ÷ 10 = 1,000	£5,000 ÷ 10,000 = 0.5
10	£5,000	20,000	20,000 ÷ 10 = 2,000	£5,000 ÷ 20,000 = 0.25
10	£5,000	50,000	50,000 ÷ 10 = 5,000	£5,000 ÷ 50,000 = 0.10
10	£5,000	100,000	100,000 ÷ 10 = 10,000	£5,000 ÷ 100,000 = 0.02

individually. This means they might be able to push up wages. If union members feel they are being exploited by management, they may organize a strike. This means they withdraw their labour. The threat of a strike may support employees' demands for higher wages.

A trade union might use its power to insist that employers allow only union members to work. This was known as a 'closed shop' but is now not legal in the UK. It had the effect of increasing wages (see Figure 6.8) and ensuring that employees belonged to a union.

A trade union might use its power to insist on higher wages without job losses: for example, as in Figure 6.9, it might push wages up to W2 but insist that L1 employees are employed. This would force managers off their demand curve for labour.

Figure 6.8 The effect of a restriction of the supply of labour

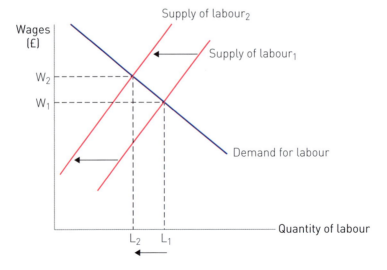

Figure 6.9 The effect of higher wages without job losses

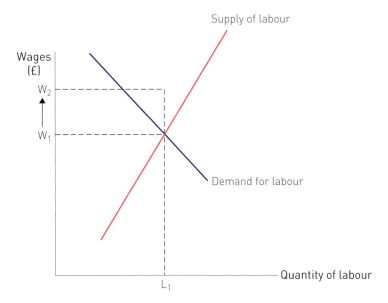

Unions may work with managers to find ways of increasing productivity. This co-operation can lead to higher wages and more employment (as shown in Figure 6.10). It therefore can be in the interests of both managers and employees to boost productivity.

Figure 6.10 The effect of increased productivity

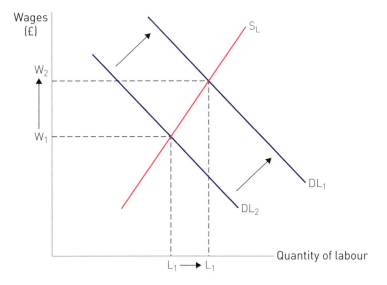

6.6 BUSINESS INSIGHT: TRADE UNIONS

The Trade Union Congress (TUC), which represents many trade unions in the UK, sets out reasons to join a union.

- On average, union members get **higher pay** than non-members. They are also likely to get better sickness and pension benefits, more paid holiday and more control over things like shifts and working hours. This is because workers join together to negotiate pay and conditions rather than leaving them up to managers.

- Unions make sure working people are **treated with respect**—for example, opposing managers closing pensions schemes and stopping new workers being employed on worse terms and conditions.

- Unions push managers to make workplaces **more inclusive** for women, LGBT workers, Black and minority ethnic workers, older workers and disabled workers. When there's a strong trade union, women are far less likely to face problems at work while pregnant, on maternity leave or when they return to work.

- Workplaces where there are unions are **safer workplaces**. Every year, unions train 10,000 reps to spot unsafe working practices and cut accident rates. That's why workplaces with union representation have significantly lower injury rates.

- If you run into problems at work, **your union has got your back**. The union's legal team can make sure you are treated fairly—without you having to worry about paying. Every year, unions win millions in compensation for members who suffer injuries or are treated unfairly at work.

- Unions help our members **get on in life**. Every year, unions help more than 200,000 working people get the skills they need to get better-paid jobs. And we push employers to make sure ordinary working people get chances for training and promotion.

- Unions make sure working people get **a voice at work**. Companies where workers are involved in decisions have better training opportunities, are fairly rewarded and can help companies survive bad times.

Source: www.tuc.org.uk/why-join-unionwww.tuc.org.uk/

Questions

1. Outline the benefits to managers of working with trade unions in their organization.
2. Outline the potential disadvantages.
3. How might trade unions affect the conditions in a labour market?

In 2017, Ryanair chief executive Michael O'Leary wrote to the airline's pilots to offer them better pay and conditions. The BBC reported on the situation in October 2017.

The improved conditions came after the airline was forced to cancel thousands of flights in recent weeks. In a letter to pilots, Mr O'Leary also apologised for changes that caused disruptions to their rotas and urges them not to leave the airline.

The Irish Air Line Pilots' Association was sceptical, saying the letter gave no details of the cost of the promises. [. . .]

Mr O'Leary's apology came after he accused the pilots of being 'full of their own self-importance'. But in the letter he urges pilots to stay with Ryanair 'for a brighter future'.

Ryanair has been in crisis after the rota changes—brought about to comply with new aviation rules—led to a shortage of pilots because the airline failed to plan for enough leave. [. . .] Many of the airline's 4,200 pilots had joined unions over the past two weeks over discontent with the disruptions caused by the rota changes. Mr O'Leary's letter implored the pilot team not to leave the airline and offered them improved terms and working conditions. Ryanair's sweetener included pay increases, loyalty bonus payments, improved rotas and better compensation for pilots forced to work away from their home base. Mr O'Leary stressed that Ryanair was a 'very secure employer in a very insecure industry' and he emphasized that the airline's pilots 'are the best in the business'. And he asked them not to allow competitor pilots or their unions 'to demean or disparage our collective success'. The Ryanair boss also urged the airline's pilots not to join 'one of these less financially secure or Brexit-challenged airlines'. Mr O'Leary's letter asked the pilots to take note of 'the recent bankruptcies of Air Berlin, Alitalia and Monarch', as well as the difficulties faced by another budget airline, Norwegian Air, which has been under pressure to boost its finances.

Ryanair announced its first wave of 2,100 cancellations in the middle of September, after it rearranged pilots' rosters to comply with new aviation rules requiring a change in how their flying hours are logged.

Towards the end of September, Ryanair announced 18,000 further flights would be cancelled over the winter season. These moves affect more than 700,000 passengers.

The airline blamed the flight fiasco on its own mistaken decision to force its pilots to take their remaining annual leave before the end of this year, rather than by the end of the financial year next March. That left Ryanair without enough pilots to fly all its scheduled flights in September and October.

Source: www.bbc.co.uk/news/business-41520970

Questions

1. What do you think determines the pay of pilots?
2. Why did Ryanair offer pilots better pay and conditions?
3. What might be the impact on Ryanair of a continue shortage of pilots?

6.8 BUSINESS INSIGHT: WAGES AND RANKINGS IN THE PREMIER LEAGUE

Figure 6.11 Premier League clubs' revenues and wage costs, 2015/16 (£m)

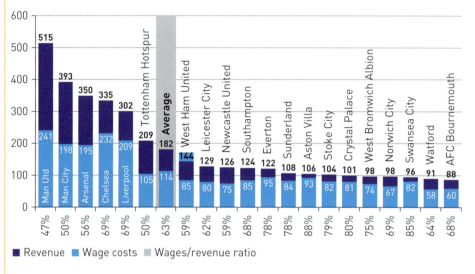

■ Revenue ■ Wage costs ■ Wages/revenue ratio

Source: Deloitte

Correlation measures the apparent relationship between two variables. A positive correlation shows that the two variables move in the same direction—for example, an increase in one apparently leads to an increase in the other. A negative correlation suggests that an increase in one variable is linked to a decrease in the other (e.g. an increase in price is linked to a fall in sales). The size of the correlation coefficient ranges from 0 to 1. The higher the figure, the stronger the apparent relationship between the two variables.

In the world of football, the salaries of key players can be extremely high. However, there is not always a strong correlation between what is paid and how well the team does, as shown by the report from Deloitte below and illustrated in Figure 6.11.

> The Spearman's rank correlation coefficient, which measures the relationship between league position and total wage cost rank, was 0.54 in 2015/16, with only four clubs finishing within one place either side of where one would expect given their wage bill. This was down from 0.74 (and ten clubs) in the previous season, and is the lowest level of correlation ever seen in our analysis of Premier League finances.
>
> The remarkable success of Leicester City, who ranked 15th in wage costs, outperforming their wage spending to an extent never before achieved in Premier League history, and the relative on-pitch struggles of the defending champions Chelsea heavily contributed to this figure, with the latter finishing tenth, eight places lower

than their wage costs rank of second. Relegated Aston Villa also finished twelve places lower than their wage costs rank of eighth, further contributing to the low level of correlation in 2015/16.

Indeed, had Leicester City not won the league and incurred bonuses as a result, their wage costs would have been even lower, which makes their achievement even more remarkable.

Two of the three promoted clubs, AFC Bournemouth and Watford, successfully avoided relegation despite recording the lowest wage costs in the division. This illustrates that there are other factors beyond wage spend which contribute to clubs' on-pitch performance.

Source: Courtesy of Deloitte. www2.deloitte.com/content/dam/Deloitte/uk/Documents/sports-business-group/deloitte-uk-annual-review-of-football-finance-2017.pdf

Questions

1. Why might you expect wage costs and the performance of a football club to be positively correlated?
2. What factors do you think might have contributed to the performance of clubs apart from wage costs?

Gender equality

An important issue in pay that has been in the media a great deal is that of gender equality. Differences in pay may occur because women in general are in lower roles within an organization (and therefore may be paid less based on the responsibilities of the job). Questions should then be asked about why this is, and whether this is due to discrimination. There may be discrimination where women are just not offered the same amount as men for a comparable job; although this is illegal under the Equal Pay Act, those involved may not be aware of this discrepancy if contracts are negotiated separately and secretly, or the organization may argue that the jobs were not comparable. A number of high-profile cases have been made public of significant differences in earnings between men and women in the media and film industry. Several male presenters on the BBC agreed in 2018 to take pay cuts to make their pay more comparable with that of their female colleagues.

MANAGEMENT TASK

You have been asked to make all the earnings of you staff transparent to everyone.
Should you do this?

6.9 BUSINESS INSIGHT: THE GENDER PAY GAP IN THE UK

Under UK government legislation, companies with 250 or more employees have to publish the pay of their male employees relative to female. The BBC reported on this in January 2018.

> Ladbrokes, Easyjet and Virgin Money are among the major companies that recently revealed gender pay gaps of more than 15% in favour of men for mean hourly pay. [. . .]
>
> Women's hourly pay rates are 52% lower than men's at Easyjet. On average, women earn 15% less per hour at Ladbrokes and 33% less at Virgin Money.
>
> All three firms say men and women are paid equally when in the same role.
>
> At Easyjet, for example, 6% of its UK pilots are women—a role which pays £92,400 a year on average—whereas 69% of lower-paid cabin crew are women, with an average annual salary of £24,800. The carrier said it had set a target that one in five of new entrant pilots should be female by 2020. [. . .]
>
> The gender pay gap is the pay discrepancy between men and women irrespective of their job or position. That is distinct from equal pay—when companies are required to ensure that men and women carrying out the same or similar roles are paid the same for the amount of work they do. [. . .]
>
> The firm to publish the biggest gender pay gap so far is women's fashion chain Phase Eight—with a 64.8% lower mean hourly rate for female staff. Phase Eight's chief executive Benjamin Barnett said the figure did not reflect the 'true story' of the business, since most male employees worked in head office roles rather than in shops.

Question

What are the consequences for businesses of paying women less than men?

Source: www.bbc.co.uk/news/uk-42580194

MANAGEMENT TASK

You are the managing director of a large insurance business. You have reviewed the pay of your staff and have discovered significant differences between the pay of men and women. Should you take action?

The earnings of senior staff

While there will be economic factors influencing individuals' pay, there may also be a question of fairness. Some managers may be concerned about the ratio of the pay of senior staff relative to more junior staff and may wish to ensure that the gap is not too wide. This may be partly because of public scrutiny and criticism if senior staff are regarded as earning 'excessive amounts of money'.

6.10 BUSINESS INSIGHT: EXECUTIVE AND EMPLOYEE PAY

According to a report from the TUC (the Trade Union Congress, which represents many of the trade unions in the UK) in October 2014:

- Executive pay levels in the UK remain excessive.

- The gap between executive pay and employee pay within the same companies is far too high and is damaging firm performance, employee morale and social cohesion.

- Current reporting requirements are inadequate and do not allow fully accurate and comparable figures on employee pay and therefore pay gaps within companies to be produced. [. . .]

- Worker representation on remuneration committees should be implemented. This should be mandatory and remuneration committees should include a minimum of two worker representatives.

Executive Excess provides a snapshot of top company directors' pay and how it compares with that of their own employees in the FTSE 350. It finds that median total earnings for FTSE 100 top directors were £3,195,353, while within the FTSE 250 median earnings for top directors were £1,284,361. It finds that the ratio between top directors' pay and average employees at their own companies varies hugely, from 1,601:1 at the top to 3:1 at the bottom.

[. . .] the report also finds that publicly available information on employees' pay is woefully inadequate and that it is currently not possible to calculate robust figures for average employee pay from company annual reports. The report therefore calls for standardised mandatory disclosure on employee earnings to be included in annual reports. It also calls for worker representation on remuneration committees to tackle excessive executive pay and help companies take into account employee pay and conditions within their company when setting directors' pay, as they are required to do by the Corporate Governance Code.

Source: www.tuc.org.uk/research-analysis/reports/executive-excess-gap-between-executive-and-employee-pay-within-companies

Question
Do you think businesses should be made to provide more information on remuneration?

BUSINESS CASE QUESTIONS: CAN YOU NOW ANSWER . . .

Is £300,000 too much to pay a vice-chancellor? Is it too much to pay anyone?

MANAGEMENT TASK

Should you worry if your senior managers earn over 50 times more than you junior employees? Can you justify it?

Minimum wage

Market conditions may lead to a wage that brings about equilibrium in a particular labour market, but which society feels is too low. This desire to see employees earn a 'reasonable amount' led to the government introducing the National Minimum Wage in 1999. There is now a National Living Wage for those aged 25 and over.

These rates are for the National Living Wage and the National Minimum Wage. The rates change every April.

Year	25 and over	21 to 24	18 to 20	Under 18	Apprentice
April 2018	£7.83	£7.38	£5.90	£4.20	£3.70

The effect of a minimum wage

A minimum wage is the lowest amount an employee can be legally paid. If this is set below the equilibrium wage (see Figure 6.12) it has no effect. However, if it is set above the market wage it will lead to excess supply. At the higher wage, the quantity demanded falls and the quantity supplied increases (compared to the equilibrium wage and output).

The impact of the minimum wage is that the number of people employed falls compared to equilibrium but the wage rate they receive is higher. The impact on total earnings depends on the wage elasticity of demand. If demand for labour is wage inelastic, the number losing their jobs because of higher wages is relatively

Figure 6.12 The effect of a minimum wage in the labour market

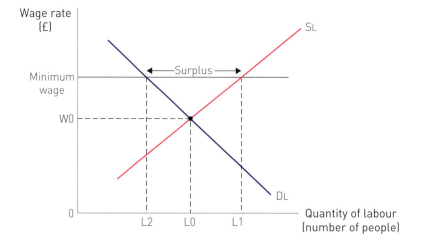

small and the total earnings increase. If demand for labour is wage elastic, the number losing their jobs because of higher wages is relatively large and the total earnings decrease.

The wage elasticity of demand will depend on various factors.

- How easy it is for employers to switch other resources for employees: with the rise of artificial intelligence it may become easier in many jobs to use computers rather than people, making demand for labour more sensitive to any wage increases.

- Wage costs as a proportion of total costs: if labour costs are a significant proportion of total costs, then any wage increase is likely to lead to a bigger price increase for the final product. This then reduces the demand for the product by a greater amount and so reduces demand for employees by more than if wage costs were relatively insignificant.

- How price elastic demand for the final product is: if demand for the final product is very price sensitive, then any wage increase leading to a price increase will lead to a relatively large fall in the quantity demanded of the product and of labour.

Government influences on pay

The government can influence pay through the minimum wage. In the past, the UK government has also tried to limit pay increases through what was called an 'incomes policy'; however, organizations usually found other ways of increasing rewards without an actual pay rise (e.g. additional benefits). Any attempt to limit pay increases or ensure a minimum pay intervenes in the market mechanism and will lead to surpluses or shortages. However, it may lead to a more equal income distribution in the economy and what is perceived a fairer outcome. Earnings can also be influenced by pay awards to employees in public sector organizations such as the healthcare and education systems.

BUSINESS CASE QUESTIONS: CAN YOU NOW ANSWER . . .

Do you think the government should intervene to determine how much vice-chancellors are paid? What about other jobs?

6.11 BUSINESS INSIGHT: BEN & JERRY'S AND ECONOMIC JUSTICE

The 'About Us' section of ice cream producers Ben & Jerry's website includes a statement about the company's board of directors.

> Ben & Jerry's is a wholly-owned subsidiary of Unilever, but we're betting you've never met our independent Board of Directors . . .

It's not a governing body in the conventional sense, but a (very!) independent B.O.D. that's empowered to protect and defend Ben & Jerry's brand equity and integrity. AND our product quality! They also make sure our entry level folks come into the company making a livable wage!

Their mission:

Preserving and expanding Ben & Jerry's social mission, brand integrity and product quality, by providing social mission-mindful insight and guidance to ensure we're making the best ice cream possible in the best way possible.

All in all, they're an enterprising group of mover-shakers and difference-makers who really know their stuff.

Best of all, they're not stuffy about it.

Among its values Ben & Jerry's supports economic justice. Its 'How We Do Business' statements says:

Ben & Jerrry's commitment to economic justice starts with our employees. That's why we're committed to paying all of our Ben & Jerry's Vermont full time workers a livable wage—enough to allow for a quality of life that includes decent housing, health care, transportation, food, recreation, savings, and miscellaneous expenses.

Every year, we recalculate the livable wage to make sure it's keeping up with the actual cost of living in Vermont. In recent years, Ben & Jerry's livable wage has been nearly twice the national minimum wage, landing at $16.92 in 2015.

Source: https://www.benjerry.co.uk/about-us/how-were-structured; http://www.benjerry.com/values/how-we-do-business/livable-wages.

Question
Do you think Ben and Jerry's approach to 'economic justice' is a good one?

6.4 QUICK CHECK

For each of the following statements, say whether it is true or false.

a. If men get paid more than women this means there must be discrimination.
b. Labour productivity will affect the demand for labour.
c. A minimum wage above equilibrium will not affect the equilibrium.
d. A minimum wage below equilibrium leads to excess demand for labour.

SUMMARY

The remuneration of employees is important to attract the right number and calibre of staff. Employees' costs are also a significant cost of the business and must be monitored and assessed to ensure the investment is worthwhile. The pay that individuals receive will usually be affected by the demand and supply conditions in the relevant labour market. Low pay may be associated with low levels of demand and/or high levels of supply. High pay is likely to be associated with limited supply and/or high levels of demand.

KEY LEARNING POINTS

- The demand for labour is a derived demand; it depends on the value of workers' output.
- The supply of labour represents the number of people who are willing and able to work at the given wage.
- Wages will often be determined by market forces.
- A trade union represents employees and protects employee interests.
- The minimum wage is the lowest amount of money per hour that someone can legally be paid.

BUSINESS CASE EXTENSION QUESTIONS

1. What factors do you think affect the demand for vice-chancellors?
2. What factors do you think affect the supply of vice-chancellors?
3. How would you measure the productivity of a vice-chancellor?
4. What would you link the pay of a vice-chancellor to?
5. Do you think vice-chancellors tend to belong to a trade union? Explain your answer.
6. In what way do you think market forces determine the pay of vice-chancellors?
7. Do you think the government should set a maximum for the earnings of those in senior positions in universities? What do you think the effects of this would be?

QUICK QUESTIONS

1. Why is demand for labour a derived demand?
2. What factors affect demand for labour?
3. What factors affect the supply of labour?
4. How can trade unions influence the labour market?
5. What makes the demand for labour sensitive to wage changes?
6. What is the impact of a minimum wage if it is set above the equilibrium wage?
7. Why do some people get paid more than others?
8. Why does labour productivity matter?
9. What is meant by the gig economy?
10. What is meant by net migration?

Do markets work?

WHY DO I NEED TO KNOW ABOUT HOW WELL MARKETS WORK?

You have a small business producing a range of soft drinks aimed at children. They are tasty but not especially healthy. You have seen moderate sales growth in your local region and are trying to expand nationally. You have had amazing reviews for your products in the media. Customers seem to love them and say they taste very different from anyone else's drinks. You have approached the national retailers and, although they say they like your drinks, they are reluctant to take them. The huge drinks companies are apparently putting pressure on them not to stock your products. If they do, they will lose the ability to sell these much bigger global brands. One of the bigger companies has approached you recently and offered to buy your business at an insultingly low price. Their representative said that 'you will never be able to grow without our help—we are too big, and if we want to we will get you.' In the past you probably would have pushed on regardless, but the recent government sugar tax and the increasing pressure on companies such as yours to change their recipes has made life increasingly difficult for you.

Unfortunately, having a good product is not enough to guarantee success in business. You need a whole series of other factors to fall into place, including the distribution. And you need to be able to fend off rivals who may be keen to see you fail. While markets can lead to efficiency and innovation, unregulated they can also lead to exploitative behaviour. This is one of many potential failings in the free market that may require government intervention. In this chapter we consider some of the potential failings of markets and how and why governments intervene in them.

BY THE END OF THIS CHAPTER YOU WILL BE ABLE TO . . .

- explain why markets might not work
- analyse how and why the government may intervene in markets
- analyse how intervention may affect your business

BUSINESS CASE

Philip Morris International (PMI) is a major tobacco producer selling cigarettes all over the world. However, its chief executive has said that the company wants to have a 'smoke free future' where the business is made up entirely of alternatives to cigarettes.

The chief executive of British American Tobacco (BAT), one of PMI's biggest rivals, says that investing in lower-risk products is important for shareholders, consumers and society. Tobacco companies are now investing heavily in finding alternatives to cigarettes. They have already developed and promoted e-cigarettes. They are now working on cigarettes that heat but do not burn the tobacco (HNB) in nearly 40 countries. It is claimed that HNB products have between 50 and 90 per cent fewer 'harmful and potentially harmful' compounds compared with traditional cigarettes.

The chief executive of PMI wants at least 40 per cent of its revenue to come from e-cigarettes and HNB-type products by 2025. In part this will depend on how easy regulators make it to launch these newer products and to be able to claim they are safer than traditional cigarettes. Tobacco companies are therefore in the process of producing products than can 'save lives' but which are still addictive and cause fatal diseases.

The business case for continuing to sell conventional cigarettes is very appealing in that they are extremely profitable. The average profit margin on a cigarette is about 80 per cent. And the ban on advertising has not necessarily harmed the major tobacco companies—it has reduced their marketing costs and made it more difficult for new entrants to come into the market. As smoking rates decline in much of the West, firms have been able to raise prices for cigarettes in relatively high-income countries while promoting smoking elsewhere.

The new alternatives to cigarettes also offer attractive returns. The big established producers were initially slow to get involved in e-cigarettes, but they caught up quickly by buying up brands and now have around four-fifths of the market. E-cigarette sales doubled between 2014 and 2016 (although they still make up under 5 per cent of total tobacco revenues). New products are also harder for rivals to replicate than conventional cigarettes. BAT points to $2.5bn of investments in new, lower-risk products since 2011; PMI has invested more than $3bn since 2008. Big companies have the resources to seek regulatory approval for new products, whereas smaller firms may struggle to do so.

How regulators deal with these products seems to vary. In the US, the main focus of the Food and Drug Adminstration (which regulates this market) is on looking to reduce the amount of nicotine in traditional cigarettes. This will take years to take effect, giving the big companies plenty of time to make more money. Outside the US rules vary considerably. In Britain, the Royal College of Physicians has said that e-cigarettes are a sensible, promising way to help smokers quit. Regulators in other countries fear that e-cigarettes and tobacco-heating products will make the habit of smoking more acceptable again, and lead to people going on to cigarettes. In 2016, a group within the World Health Organisation invited those who had signed its anti-tobacco treaty to 'prohibit or restrict' e-cigarettes.

PMI hopes to influence the debate. In September the firm announced it would give $80m a year for the next 12 years to a new foundation to research ways to speed the shift away from tobacco, including through the use of lower-risk products.

Meanwhile the tobacco industry is changing rapidly. In July BAT paid more than $49bn to acquire Reynolds American, America's second-biggest tobacco company after Altria. Even bigger scale gives tobacco firms the ability to increase their profit margins on conventional products, as well as more funds to invest in new ones. In buying Reynolds, BAT won access both to the American market and to Reynolds' portfolio of e-cigarettes. Many investment analysts expect PMI to buy Altria, which sells PMI's portfolio of brands in America.

Source: www.economist.com/news/business/21732828-new-safer-products-such-heated-tobacco-devices-and-e-cigarettes-mean-tobacco-industry

BUSINESS CASE QUESTIONS

This chapter will help you answer the following questions.

1. Why might governments want to intervene in the tobacco market?

2. How do governments intervene in the tobacco market?

3. What are the potential advantages and disadvantages of this intervention by government?

Competitive markets

Competitive markets occur when there are many businesses competing against each other.

This competition can be beneficial for customers because businesses may

- try to increase efficiency to reduce price;

- improve their product or service to gain competitive advantage;

- innovate and develop new products to meet customer needs more effectively than the competition.

Competition can act as an incentive to businesses to keep improving. This is why most governments encourage market forces because they think such forces lead to progress, greater output, and greater incomes, moving the economy forward. From a business perspective, efficient markets mean more choice for inputs. In theory, then, markets can lead to efficiency and innovation.

MANAGEMENT TASK

You are the manager of a clothes retailer in a newly built shopping centre. Other clothes retailers have recently opened up near your store. Why might you welcome this competition?

To encourage market forces, governments might

1. make it easier for businesses to enter markets;

2. prevent unfair means of competition to ensure that businesses that do compete fairly are protected.

However, there are some reasons why as managers (and indeed as consumers) we might worry about the market system and the problems it can bring.

Can markets be trusted?

While market forces may well help buyers (and businesses are themselves buyers of many different inputs), they also bring dangers. Markets are likely to experience imperfections and failures, and so there are many areas where society might want the government to intervene.

Some examples follow.

Accuracy

To win customers, a business may deliberately mislead them. They may exaggerate the benefits or performance of the product and not identify its limitations. Governments may want to regulate to ensure that customers and employees are not misled.

Vulnerable groups

Managers may deliberately target those who may not be in a good position to make well-informed decisions, such as young children, and therefore behave unethically. They may use persuasive promotional methods and encourage people to overspend or to consume products that are not good for them. This is why the government regulates the advertising of tobacco products and restricts the sale of alcohol to certain age groups.

Collusion

Businesses may abuse their market position to collude and fix prices. Businesses may join together to form a cartel, where they act as a monopoly and push up prices.

KEY CONCEPT

A **cartel** occurs when businesses join together to act like a monopoly.

Employee protection

Businesses may exploit staff to keep labour costs down; for example, they may insist on long hours, poor working conditions, and low wages. Governments may need to intervene to allow trade unions to protect the interest of employees or to introduce laws such as the minimum wage and equal pay legislation to ensure that people are fairly treated.

MANAGEMENT TASK

Your policy is to pay staff as little as you can. You employ many staff on the minimum wage. You have been criticized in the media for this. You are due to appear on *Newsnight* on television to defend your approach. What are you going to say?

Equal service provision

Businesses will only provide products to those who can pay, and this may be regarded as socially unfair, e.g. in the case of health care and transport. A private postal business, for example, would deliver post to those areas where a profit could be made but would not be interested in delivering to the more isolated areas if earnings would be small. A government may want to subsidize the provision of such a service, or directly provide it itself.

Long-term planning

Managers may be short-termist in their decision making. They may focus on projects that bring rewards while they are still at the business: i.e. they may have a relatively short time horizon in their planning and be reluctant to invest in projects that are long term. There are major infrastructure projects in the UK at the moment, such as a new runway for Heathrow or the high speed rail link, which need government involvement to get them completed.

Income distribution

There will be unequal income distribution. Some people will earn a lot more than others in a free market. In jobs which do not generate high revenues and/or which have a high supply of labour—perhaps because the jobs are unskilled—wages will be low. In jobs where supply is scarce—such as senior managers—and where their output generates high revenue—such as players in top football teams—earnings will be high. Governments may want to intervene to make incomes fairer. Managers will also have to consider within their own businesses what the differential between senior managers and the lowest-paid employees should be.

Market stability

There will be instability in markets. Prices will change when supply and demand conditions change. In some markets these changes will be frequent—for example in agricultural markets, where changes in the weather can lead to significant and sudden shifts in prices. This can make it difficult for business to plan, as their costs can change significantly. A government may intervene through what is known as a buffer stock system, discussed in the next section, where it buys and sells the products to remove shortages and surpluses.

7.1 BUSINESS INSIGHT: IS CAPITALISM DELIVERING?

According to Lord Adair Turner, a former head of the Confederation of British Industry (an organization that represents many businesses in the UK), capitalism is not delivering on its promise to raise living standards. As reported by the BBC in October 2017, Lord Turner said:

'Everybody knows that capitalism is not egalitarian, but the broad promise has been that, over a ten year period, you can be pretty confident that a rising tide raises all boats and everybody feels somewhat better off, and that's gone wrong.' [. . .] He pointed to a toxic mix of stagnant productivity, falling real wages and rising inequality.

'The combination of that is a lot of people do not feel the system is delivering for them. This is a big challenge for economists. Why, in a world of apparently extraordinary capabilities of technology, do we have these very low productivity growth rates? [. . .] The UK economy has grown a bit in the last five years and we have created lots of jobs, but they have been low productivity jobs', he said.

Lord Turner noted certain sectors such as manufacturing, retail and logistics have managed to improve productivity through automation, replacing human workers with robots. But those workers displaced by technological change have ended up in low paid jobs—Deliveroo cyclists working in the gig economy, for example. 'I think paradoxically that we should expect to see in a world of huge automation the continued proliferation of low paid, low tech jobs', Lord Turner said.

'We are going to have to face as a society the question of how do we make sure that people have a good enough standard of living to be equal citizens of society even if the wages they get will be relatively lower?'

Source: www.bbc.co.uk/news/business-41744127

Questions

1. Do you think the government needs to intervene to make sure living standards are high enough for everyone?

2. If so, how should it do this?

Buffer stocks

Buffer stocks occur when the government intervenes in a market to stabilize the price. In agricultural markets, for example, supply can increase or decrease due to

Figure 7.1 A buffer stock scheme

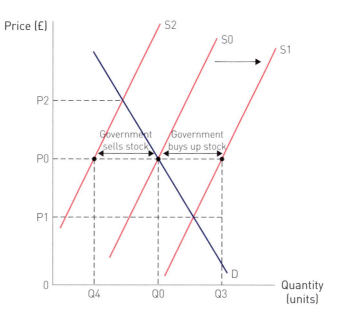

environmental issues. A crop disease can reduce supply and prices may increase significantly. Next year, bumper harvests cause the price to drop radically. This means that farmers' incomes are volatile and may cause many to leave the sector for a more stable life! To avoid this (after all, governments may be keen to keep a domestic food supply just in case of poor relations with overseas countries), the government may intervene to keep prices stable.

When supplies are high, the government may buy up the excess and this can prevent the price falling. This surplus can be stored and sold on the market when supplies would otherwise be short. This prevents a shortage and avoids an increase in the price.

Figure 7.1 illustrates the effects of this. In a free market, the price would fluctuate between P0, P1, and P2 with changes in supply. In a buffer stock scheme, the government maintains the price at P0. In a good year (that is, with an increase in supply), the government buys up the quantity Q3 minus Q0; this is the buffer stock. In a bad year (i.e. when supply falls) the government sells the quantity Q4 minus Q0 to increase supply and to keep the price at P0.

Of course, the effectiveness of this policy depends on the price the government intends to keep in the market, and the actual supply and demand conditions in the market over time. If it sets too high a price and/or there are a series of good crops, the government will end up buying every year, accumulating more and more supplies. This incurs the costs of warehousing and the opportunity cost of how those funds might otherwise have been used.

7.1 DOING THE BUSINESS MATHS

Imagine the government is operating a buffer stock system to keep the price of a product at £10. Complete the table.

Market price (£)	Quantity demanded (units)	Quantity supplied (units)	Excess demand or supply (units)	Government action: buy or sell?
8	200	40		
9	150	70		
10	100	100		
11	80	120		
12	50	150		

MANAGEMENT TASK

You manage a farm in Wales. The government is threatening to withdraw subsidies for farmers. How would you justify the need for farmers to be subsidized?

Externalities

A major failing of the free market system is that you, as a manager, will focus on the private costs and benefits of your actions: what it will cost you, and what you will earn as a result. You are unlikely to worry about any wider impact on society as a whole. And why should you? After all, if your responsibility is to your investors and they want higher financial returns, then that is what you may understand-ably think you should concentrate on. This means you will not automatically be interested in any external costs of your actions. So what if you create noise and pollution that upsets and even harms others? So what if your waste pours into the local river and pollutes it? So what if your fishing levels are so high that you are destroying the fishing stock in the sea? There are no private costs to you in these effects, and so there are no reasons for you to measure or care about them. The result of this is that you underestimate the costs of your actions in the eyes of society and are likely to over-produce. It is up to the government to make you appreciate the costs of your actions through taxes, or fines, or even by limiting what you can produce, or how you produce it. If your production generates a cost to society, this is called an external cost. The total cost to society is the private cost plus the external cost.

Equally, it may be that your actions have positive external benefits to society. Your new wonder drug reduces flu in the country and earns you money; however, it also means more people are at work, boosting the economy as a whole. This means the total social benefit is greater than the private benefit. In this case private businesses will under-produce because they do not place the same value on what they produce as it has in the eyes of society as whole. In this situation the government may want to intervene to encourage more production through subsidies, or by directly providing the product itself. The total benefit to society is the private benefit plus the external benefit.

KEY CONCEPTS

Social cost = private cost + external cost
Social benefit = private benefit + external benefit

A **positive externality** occurs when the social benefits are greater than the private benefits.
A **negative externality** occurs when the social costs are greater than the private costs.

There will be projects where the costs to society are greater than the private costs; this is because of negative external effects. For example, when transport companies decide which routes are viable in the private sector, they would consider only the private costs of operating the routes. However, there are external costs of operating transport, such as pollution and congestion. Where the social cost of producing a product is greater than the private cost, a negative externality exists. These products will be over-provided in a free market.

BUSINESS CASE QUESTION: CAN YOU NOW ANSWER . . .

Why do governments need to intervene in the tobacco market?

The effect of externalities

Negative production externalities occur when there are external costs to society that occur with production, such as pollution. The total costs to society are called the social costs. Social costs = private costs + external costs (see Figure 7.2).

If there is no intervention in a market, the equilibrium is at P0Q0. However, this does not take account of social costs. Society as a whole would want equilibrium to be at P1Q1. The government might intervene by taxing your business to raise your costs or by legislating to restrict output.

The social marginal cost is above the private marginal cost due to external costs. In the free market the equilibrium would be P1Q1, but the socially optimal equilibrium

Figure 7.2 A negative externality

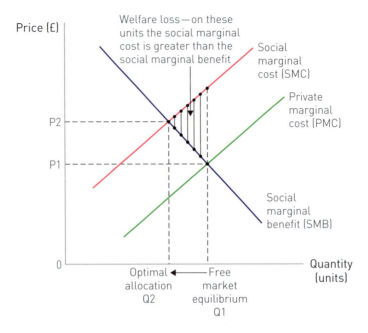

taking account of the full social costs would be P2Q2. In the free market there is over-production of Q2Q1, and in these units the extra costs to society exceeds the extra benefit. Economists talk of a welfare loss, as shown by the shaded area.

Positive production externalities occur when the benefit to society is greater than the private benefits (see Figure 7.3). The demand curve for society is at D1, not D0.

Figure 7.3 A positive consumption externality

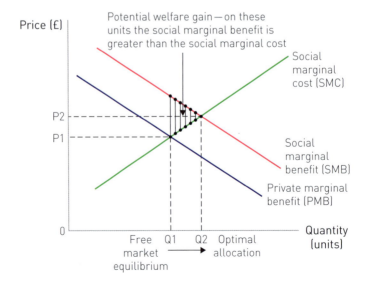

This means that the socially desirable output is higher than would be achieved by market forces. To encourage consumption, the government might subsidize or legislate to make everyone consume a given amount of it.

The social marginal benefit is greater than the private marginal benefit due to external benefits. The free market equilibrium is P1Q1, but the socially optimal level is P2Q2. The product is under-provided in the free market. On units Q1Q2 the extra benefit to society is greater than the extra cost, and so there is a potential welfare gain by producing these units.

7.2 BUSINESS INSIGHT: DISPOSABLE CUPS

Governments may intervene to make businesses more aware of the external costs of their activities. This may affect the objectives a business sets. For example, some members of the UK parliament have recently asked for a 25p 'latte levy' on disposable coffee cups, and a complete ban unless there are improvements in recycling. As the BBC reported in January 2018:

> A report by the Environmental Audit Committee says the tax should be used to improve the UK's recycling and reprocessing facilities. The MPs say throwaway cups should be prohibited altogether by 2023 if they are not all being recycled. In response, Starbucks said it would try out a 5p cup charge in 20 to 25 central London outlets. [. . .] The government agrees plastic waste is a problem and will seek evidence on a tax on single-use plastics. [. . .]
>
> The UK throws away 2.5 billion disposable coffee cups every year.
>
> The British Coffee Association [. . .] welcomed the report's broad principles, but said a levy was not the answer. A representative said 'It places an unfair and additional cost on coffee drinking consumers only—despite paper cups only contributing 0.7% of total paper packaging waste', [. . .] [and that] the industry should continue to focus on other environmental issues such as cutting water use, carbon reduction, and turning waste coffee grounds into biofuel.

Source: BBC: www.bbc.co.uk/news/business-42564948

Question
Do you think taxing paper cups is a good idea?

MANAGEMENT TASK

The government has introduced a fee for plastic bags. Is this a good idea? Justify your answer.

7.2 DOING THE BUSINESS MATHS

Based on the table, answer the questions below.

Output	Marginal benefit (£)	Private marginal costs (£)	Social marginal costs (£)
10	50	5	15
20	40	25	40
30	30	30	50
40	20	40	70
50	10	50	85

Questions

1. What would be the equilibrium output in a free market?
2. What about if businesses took full account of the external costs of their actions?

7.3 BUSINESS INSIGHT: A CIRCULAR ECONOMY?

Some economists and managers are now considering the value of thinking about business in the context of a 'circular' rather than linear economy. In a traditional economy, managers think how best they can transform resources into outputs and sell their products, but they do not think about what happens to their goods and services once sold. With a growing world population and some natural resources becoming more scarce, there is greater interest in the whole life cycle of products and in how resources can be conserved.

One model being put forward is to plan for a more 'circular economy' which aims to restore materials, energy, and other inputs used up in any process. It aims to move away from the 'take, make, and dispose' system by designing and optimizing products or parts of products to be re-used. Designers and producers need to think of what happens once their product is about to be disposed of.

Examples are described in an article in *McKinsey Quarterly* of February 2014.

- Ricoh, a global maker of office machines, designed its GreenLine brand of office copiers and printers to maximize the reusability of products and components, while minimizing the use of virgin materials. Products returning from their leasing contracts are inspected, dismantled, and taken through an extensive refurbishing process that includes replacing components and updating software before the machines reenter the market. By designing the components to be reused or recycled in Ricoh facilities, the company reduces the need for new materials in production and creates a tight 'inner circle' of use that allows it to employ less material, labor, energy, and capital. GreenLine products are now offered in six major European markets, where they account for 10 to 20 percent of Ricoh's sales by volume and earn margins that are as much as two times higher than those of the company's comparable new products—without a reduction in quality.

- Michelin [. . .] offers tire upgrades, maintenance, and replacement to optimize the performance of trucking fleets and to lower their total cost of ownership. By maintaining control over the tires, Michelin can collect them when they wear out and can extend their technical utility by retreading or regrooving them for resale. The company estimates that retreads, for example, require half of the raw materials new tires do but deliver up to 90 percent of the performance. [. . .]

- B&Q is piloting a take-back program for its power tools. Customers can exchange used ones either for cash or a charity donation. The company plans to refurbish the tools it collects in Europe for resale locally or to recycle them and thus recover raw materials that could be used to make new power tools in the company's facilities in China. Our research suggests that the margin-improvement potential, primarily resulting from savings in the cost of materials, could be as high as ten percentage points. [. . .]

- Global apparel retailer H&M launched an in-store collection program encouraging customers to bring in old clothes in exchange for discount vouchers on new H&M clothing. [. . .] The majority of items collected are dispatched to the global secondhand-apparel market. Clothes that are no longer suitable to wear are used as substitutes for virgin materials in other applications—for example, as cleaning cloths and textile yarns or as inputs for damping and insulation materials in the auto industry or for pipe insulation in the construction industry.

Source: H. Nguyen, M. Stuchtey, and M. Zils (2014), 'Remaking the Industrial Economy', *McKinsey Quarterly* (February), www.mckinsey.com/business-functions/sustainability-and-resource-productivity/our-insights/remaking-the-industrial-economy

Question

How might the concept of the circular economy affect car producers?

MANAGEMENT TASK

You are the chief executive of a consumer electronics company. You have been urging your managers to think about the circular economy, but have had little buy-in so far. You want to remind your managers why this should feature prominently in their thinking and planning, and you are about to send a memo around.

What should your memo say?

KEY CONCEPT

A **stakeholder** is any individual or group affected by the actions of a business.

Public goods

Another problem of leaving markets to themselves is that by allowing businesses and households to pursue their own interests, a situation may arise when certain products are not produced even though people want them! Imagine if the road outside your house was not provided by the government but was left to individuals to look after. You selfishly hope your neighbour will be so keen to have the road in excellent condition that she will pay for it to be maintained. You can then drive up and down it quite happily, benefiting from the road she has built and maintained! The neighbour, of course, knows this and decides not to do anything because you will benefit without contributing (unless she can find a way of not letting you use it). The result is no road, as you are both hoping the other one will pay. That's the danger of self-interest—you can both lose. You want to be a 'free rider', i.e. benefit from something without paying, and so do not reveal your true intentions. These types of products are called 'public goods' by economists.

Public goods have the features of non-diminishability and non-excludability. A public good is non-diminishable because if one person consumes it, it does not affect the amount available for others. Non-excludability means that it is not possible to prevent people from consuming this product. Take, for example, a nuclear deterrent system. If this is provided it does not matter if the population is 60 million or 70 million—having more people living in the country does not reduce the protection available to others. Similarly, once it is made available, all benefit from whatever protection there is—you cannot only protect some people. The result of these features is that there is the free rider problem; even if people want the service, they will want to be free riders and try to benefit from it without paying. If it is not possible to charge people for a service, private sector businesses will not provide it.

KEY CONCEPT

A **public good** is non-diminishable and non-excludable.

Markets can, therefore, bring benefits to consumers (and businesses as consumers) but there are also many failures and imperfections that exist which may require government intervention. There is, therefore, a constant debate between economists, politicians, and other groups in society about the extent to which markets should be left to themselves or whether the government should intervene.

MANAGEMENT TASK

You are the chief executive of a bank. In order to recruit some of the best banking talent in the world, you are thinking of paying high salaries and big bonuses. What do you think you should consider before deciding?

Asymmetric information

How well markets work will depend in part on how much information buyers and sellers have. If one party has more information than others, this can prevent the market working efficiently. This was highlighted in a study of the second-hand car market by George Akerlof (details in the 'Read more' feature in this chapter). When you are buying a second-hand car from someone, you do not know as much about it as they do. They know exactly the problems that they have had with it, and it is not in their interest to tell you. Of course, you can limit the risk by getting inspections done by a garage, or the AA, and asking for the service history, but even then you might not get to know all the issues the owner has had with the car. Given that it is in the interests of the seller not to tell you the truth, and given that you may not be able to tell whether they are being truthful or not, you have to assume the car has a fault. This means you won't be prepared to pay as much as you would if you would if you were 100 per cent sure it was fine. In the words of Akerlof, you assume all second-hand cars are 'lemons'; you base your decisions on the assumption they have more faults than have been declared. This means the price you can get selling a second-hand car is too low in many cases, so not enough people sell them and the market is distorted.

Differences in the information between buyers and sellers happen all the time. Buying off e-bay, renting on Airbnb, buying a new house—all bring with them dangers, and this distorts the price. From a business perspective, what you are offering may be regarded as a lemon when it is not. This means you might want to find ways of 'signalling' that your product is not a lemon—you may do this through testimonials, through building the brand reputation so people know exactly what you offer because you do it consistently, or through guarantees.

Information asymmetry is not just in the market for goods and services—it is also in the labour market. How do you know how good an employee really is? This means that employees will try and 'signal' that they are not lemons through qualifications and references.

Meanwhile, when you are deciding what to pay a new employee, can you believe they are as good as their CV says?

READ MORE

If you would like to find out more about Akerlof's theory, you can read

Akerlof, G. (1970), 'The Market for "Lemons": Quality, Uncertainty and the Market Mechanism', *Quarterly Journal of Economics* Vol. 84, No. 3 (August), pp. 488–500.

Too big to fail

One of the interesting aspects of the banking crisis of 2008 was the reckless behaviour of many financial institutions. There were various factors at play here, including a lack of regulation. Regulations had been eased to allow the banks to lend more, in the belief that this would stimulate the economy. The problem was that banks went all out for lending and seemed to care little whether households or businesses could pay them back. This focus on lending more and more was exacerbated by the fact that the rewards systems for many senior bank officials were linked to the volume, not the quality, of lending. This high-risk lending was also encouraged by a belief among the banks that they were too big to fail. Too many jobs and too much lending relied on them continuing to exist; without them, economies would come to a halt. So, if you think that whatever happens, someone (in this case, the government) will save you, you might as well take whatever risks you want in pursuit of profit. You don't care if it goes wrong. Post-2008, governments have been keen to intervene in financial markets to ensure that no one bank is too big and, therefore, so that the owners and managers of these banks know that if they do get it wrong, they will not be bailed out.

7.4 BUSINESS INSIGHT: BENEFITS AND PROBLEMS OF THE FREE MARKET

At the Conservative Party conference in 2017, the UK prime minister, Theresa May, defended free market capitalism, saying that the British should never forget the value of a free market economy. She argued that a free market economy led to a fall in absolute poverty and helped raise living standards in a country.

At the same conference, the chancellor, Philip Hammond, said 'The market economy frees people and businesses, encourages them to create, take risks, give ideas a go because they can see the results and benefit from their success.'

Just days before, Jeremy Corbyn, the Labour Party leader, promised that if he got into government he would introduce rent controls. As reported by the BBC:

> He said 'the capitalist system still faces a crisis of legitimacy' after 2008's financial crash and the time had now come for a new economic model, with a bigger role for the public sector, renationalised energy companies and more government investment in infrastructure and skills.

Sources: www.bbc.co.uk/news/business-41419858; www.bbc.co.uk/news/uk-politics-41408150

Questions

1. What do you think are the benefits of the free market?
2. What issues that are in the news currently do you think highlight some of the problems of free markets?

MANAGEMENT TASK

In what areas of your economy do you think there should be more intervention by government to help business? Why?

READ MORE

Milton Friedman was a very well known writer about the benefits of the free market. He famously wrote that 'the business of business is business'. You can read more about the benefits of the free market here:

Friedman, M. (1962), *Capitalism and Freedom*, Chicago: University of Chicago Press.

7.1 QUICK CHECK

For each of the following statements, say whether it is true or false.

a. A negative production externality occurs when the social cost are greater than the private costs.

b. A public good is both diminishable and excludable.

c. A positive production externality means that a product is over-provided in the free market.

d. Asymmetric information occurs when one party in a market knows more than the other.

What actions can governments take to intervene in markets?

As we have seen in the various examples of potential market failures, there are many ways in which governments can intervene. The primary ones are shown in Figure 7.4.

- Governments may legislate to control behaviour. For example, a government might control the promotion of products to ensure that consumers are not misled by advertising. A government might protect employees and ensure they are treated fairly.

- Governments may regulate behaviour. For example, the government might set up regulatory bodies to oversee the behaviour of certain businesses. The government has a number of agencies, such as the communications regulator Ofcom, to ensure that business behaviour is acceptable.

- Governments may tax or subsidize. If a government wants to discourage the provision of consumption of certain products, it might tax them (such as diesel fuel). If the government wants to encourage the provision or consumption of certain products, it can subsidize production.

- Governments may directly provide. If a government feels that the free market could lead to exploitation of consumers, or an unacceptable level of service, it might provide the goods and services itself. In the case of education and health,

Figure 7.4 Government interventions in the market

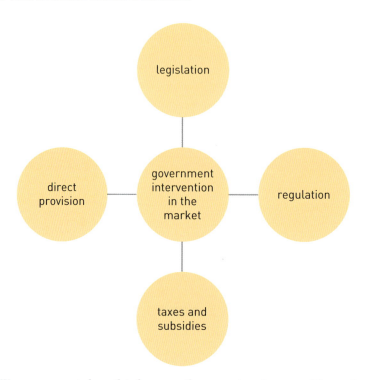

the UK government does this because these services have positive externalities. In the case of the police and the armed forces, it does because these are forms of public goods. In the case of energy and transport services, the UK government has provided these in the past to ensure these were available at a suitable price and on a suitable scale. When the government takes over a business or industry this is called 'nationalization', whereas when a government sells an industry to the private sector this is called 'privatization'.

There are various scenarios that might lead a government to intervene in a market. Some examples are given in Table 7.1.

KEY CONCEPTS

Nationalization occurs when a government transfers the assets of a business from the private sector to the public sector.

Privatization occurs when a government transfers the assets of a business from the public sector to the private sector.

MANAGEMENT TASK

Your company produces alcoholic drinks. It has been criticized heavily recently for producing a product that can cause major health problems. How should your company respond to this criticism?

Table 7.1 Reasons for, and types of, government interventions in markets

Market failing	Consequence in a market system	Possible intervention
Monopoly power	Pushing up prices as customers have few alternatives	Prevent businesses becoming too big, fine businesses if exploiting consumers
Price instability	Difficult for businesses to plan	Buffer stock scheme
Income inequality	Social unrest—perceived as unfair	Use tax and benefits system to redistribute income
Public goods not provided	Social needs not met	Directly provide
Positive externalities under-provided	Perception of unfairness	Subsidize and/or provide
Negative externalities over-provided	Perception of unfairness	Tax, or legislate to limit provision, or take over provision
Asymmetric information	Buyers or sellers make the wrong decisions due to lack of information	Legislate for fair information to be provided

BUSINESS CASE QUESTIONS: CAN YOU NOW ANSWER . . .

How do governments intervene in the tobacco market?

What are the potential advantages and disadvantages of this intervention?

7.5 BUSINESS INSIGHT: NATIONALIZATION

Different views on privatization and nationalization come in and out of fashion. In the late 1940s and 1950s, for example, there was a desire in the UK for the government to run the key industries in the economy. The government wanted to own the iron, steel, and communications industries, as well as airlines, and even Pickfords, the removal business. In the 1980s there was much more interest in privatization. It was believed that this would lead to more competition, better services, and improved investment as businesses could pursue profits and were run by businesspeople rather than government officials. Industries such as water, energy, and the railways were privatized.

In 2017, nationalization was back on the agenda of the UK Labour Party under its leader Jeremy Corbyn. He argued that services such as rail had not served the customer well, and should be renationalized.

A study by David Parker (2003) on the performance of industries post-nationalization suggested there was a huge variation in the results. Sometimes investors did well; sometimes there was an improvement in productivity; sometimes prices fell. However, the results were not guaranteed. In part it has depended on how the nationalized industry has been run. There is a difference, for example, between the government providing a service where consumers can still switch to something else and the government having a complete monopoly.

Source: D. Parker (2003), 'Performance, Risk and Strategy in Privatised, Regulated Industries: The UK's Experience', *International Journal of Public Sector Management* Vol. 16, No. 1, pp. 75–100.

Questions

1. Would you prefer to be a manager in a private-sector business or a public-sector one? Why?
2. What services does the government provide in the UK?
3. Do you think there are more services it should provide? Why?

READ MORE

If you are interested in how privatized businesses perform relative to state owned you could read

Parker, D. (2003), 'Performance, Risk and Strategy in Privatised, Regulated Industries: The UK's Experience', *International Journal of Public Sector Management* Vol. 16, No. 1, pp. 75–100.

How might government intervention affect your business?

The impact of government intervention on your business will depend on the form of intervention. It may have negative impacts, including

- limiting the options available when making a decision, e.g. limiting the options for a takeover or for promoting your product;
- increasing costs, perhaps through imposing minimum wages or raising taxes on foreign goods;
- reducing demand—for example, government legislation restricting the promotion of cigarettes has reduced demand for these in the UK.

However, government intervention may protect you. For example:

- it may prevent unfair competition from your rivals, such as larger businesses, undercutting you to force you out of business;
- it may encourage competition amongst your suppliers, leading to better services and lower prices.

7.6 BUSINESS INSIGHT: HOTEL BOOKING SITES

The UK's competition regulator—the Competition and Markets Authority (CMA)—exists to make sure that markets work efficiently. It has the right to investigate businesses that it suspects might be abusing their power. In 2018 the CMA announced it would investigate any hotel booking sites it is concerned about to see if consumers are being misled. It said that it was concerned about the clarity, accuracy, and presentation of information on some sites. The investigation was to consider aspects of the site such as hidden charges, search results and the presentation of information on sites. The CMA is also concerned that businesses use 'pressure selling' techniques, creating a 'false impression of availability or rush customers into making a booking decision'.

According to the CMA, about 70% of people who shop around for accommodation use hotel booking sites.

Source: https://www.gov.uk/government/news/cma-launches-enforcement-action-against-hotel-booking-sites

Question
Why might hotel booking sites need to be regulated?

MANAGEMENT TASK

You are an independently owned bookseller. You are concerned by the growth of some of the major chains in your industry, including online retailers, and you believe that customers are suffering.

What arguments might you make to the government to persuade it that it should take action to protect you?

Should the government intervene in markets?

As a manager, you will almost certainly be in favour of some aspects of government intervention. You may value the legal protection you have when dealing with other businesses. You may be delighted that bigger competitors cannot use anti-competitive practices to remove you from the market. You will enjoy the benefits of interventions that help the economy grow and so boost demand. However, you may object to some aspects of intervention that you see as bureaucratic (perhaps some elements of health and safety), or expensive (perhaps some parts of employee protection), or that restrict you (perhaps restricting what you can say in adverts). It is unlikely that you will welcome all forms of government intervention. It is also unlikely you would want none. What you will do is try to shape policy through your own vote, through lobbying your local MP, and by joining others in your industry to address issues specific to your industry or region.

7.7 BUSINESS INSIGHT: LIMITS ON ENERGY PRICES?

In 2017 the UK government announced it was considering limiting the prices charged by gas and electricity companies. The government's energy regulator, Ofgem, would use its powers to restrict prices increases by energy companies. Around 12 million people are on energy companies' Standard Variable Tariffs (SVTs), which tend to be the most costly tariffs.

According to a BBC report, 'The Competition and Markets Authority has said consumers have been collectively overcharged £1.4bn by energy providers.' The companies themselves disputed this, one representative saying that 'the figure was equivalent to the industry's entire profit so it was not possible for companies to have overcharged by such a sum'. He also said that a price cap would restrict competition and limit choice for consumers.

Source: https://www.bbc.co.uk/news/business-41509232

Question

Do you think the government should limit price increases by energy companies? What might be the consequences of this?

7.2 QUICK CHECK

For each of the following statements, say whether it is true or false.

a. A government will want to tax products that have positive externalities.

b. A government is likely to directly provide some public goods.

c. A government may use a buffer stock scheme to stabilize the output produced in a market.

d. Nationalization occurs when a government transfers a business from government control to private control.

MANAGEMENT TASK

To attract new customers to your credit card business, you often offer low interest rates. These are lower than the rates charged to existing customers. This practice has recently been highlighted on a popular consumer radio programme. Should you change your approach?

● ●

SUMMARY

Markets can be glorious things. They can provide an incentive for business to compete more effectively and be innovative with each other, which is good for consumers, and for you as a manager when your business is consuming other products such as supplies.

However, markets have limitations and failings and so require some degree of government intervention. As a manager you will be affected by legislation, taxes, and direct intervention by the government. You will operate in a regulated arena. Quite how regulated it is, and how much governments want to be involved, depends in part on government policy and the perception of how many failings there are in the market. In recent years, several trends—reckless unregulated lending bringing the financial system close to collapse, scandals involving pay discrimination, and low wages in the gig economy—have led more people to question whether markets are indeed regulated enough.

KEY LEARNING POINTS

- Competitive markets can lead to efficiency and innovation.
- Markets can lead to many failures and imperfections.
- Some products may be over- or under-produced in a free market.
- Governments may intervene in several ways, such as legislation, direct provision, taxes, and subsidies.

BUSINESS CASE EXTENSION QUESTIONS

1. Analyse the factors that influence the demand and supply of tobacco.

2. The consumption of tobacco creates a negative externality. Show the impact of this on the market and explain how it creates a market failure.

3. Discuss the ways in which the UK government intervenes in the market for alcoholic drinks. Do you think further intervention is likely? Explain why.

4. Research a current market failure. Show why and how the government is intervening to remedy this failure.

QUICK QUESTIONS

1. What is meant by a public good?
2. How does a negative production externality affect a market?
3. How does information asymmetry distort a market?
4. How might monopoly power distort a market?
5. How does a government use buffer stocks to stabilize price?
6. What is the difference between nationalization and privatization?
7. How do markets lead to income inequality?
8. Why might prices in a market may be unstable?
9. How might governments might intervene in markets?
10. What might happen if managers think their business is too big to fail?

Different market forms

You have been running a taxi business in your city for the last 15 years. You have had to bid for the contract from the council every three years, but you have always been able to submit the best bid in terms of what it would cost the city, the level of service provided, and the safety of passengers. The contract means that you are the only taxi business within the area that is allowed to be flagged down by people. Other car hire businesses have to be pre-booked.

You have done very well financially in the last few years and have been planning on even higher earnings in the future; this optimism led to your investment in more cabs last year.

But six months ago, Uber arrived in your city and overnight the competitive landscape changed. Because passengers order an Uber car via their phones, this does not break your contract with the council and so you are suddenly facing a lot of competition. The number of passenger journeys booked with your business is falling dramatically. Some people may welcome competition. You don't.

You need to call an emergency meeting with your managers to see how you can fight back. You had been thinking for some time of an app to allow your customers to book more easily and to show them where there driver was. This is suddenly looking essential. You wonder what else you are going to need to do now that Uber are here. You wonder: will you be able to find a way to get the council to force Uber out?

There are many different market forms. In some markets, there are many businesses competing with a similar offering; in others, there may only be one provider in a given region. Differences in the market forms will affect the prices charged, the quality of service, and the degree of innovation. Market forms are not static—they will change with new competition, new laws, and new technology, enabling competition from different types of providers. The changing shape of markets will affect both customers and businesses. Once-great businesses may collapse and new business champions emerge. Some markets may disappear and other grow from nowhere to be huge. In this chapter we look at models of different forms of markets that help us anticipate what might happen in the short run and long run to prices, quality, innovation, and output. These models help shape government attitudes and policy in relation to different market forms.

BY THE END OF THIS CHAPTER YOU WILL BE ABLE TO . . .

- explain what is meant by a competitive market
- explain why competition may be desirable
- explain why competition may bring dangers and unwelcome consequences
- analyse the appeal of monopoly position for businesses
- analyse the possible effects of a monopoly position on consumers
- explain what an oligopoly is and how this affects the decisions of businesses
- explain what is meant by a monopolistically competitive industry and the implications of this

BUSINESS CASE

The beer industry is dominated by a few large businesses globally, as illustrated in Figure 8.1.

In 2017 the output of the main producers was as follows, in billions of litres of beer:

- AB InBev 41.1
- SAB Miller 19.2

Figure 8.1 Global market share of the leading beer companies, 2016

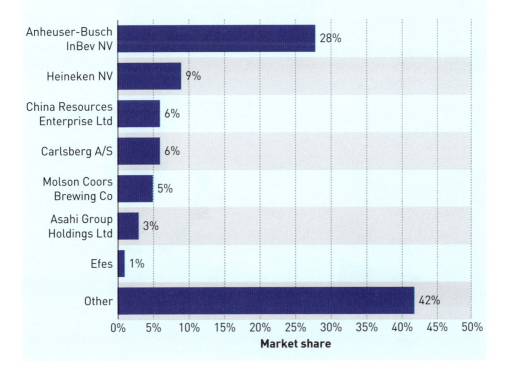

- Heineken 18

- Carlsberg 12.1

- China Resources Enterprise 11.8

These huge market shares of the top producers have been gained though their own expansion and the acquisition of other brands. In 2017, AB InBev actually joined together with SAB Miller, creating an even bigger organization that provided nearly a third of all the beer sold in the world.

However, there are also an increasing number of tiny craft breweries (microbreweries) starting up in many markets, as shown on the map in Figure 8.2.

The Economist reported in December 2017:

> These new small, craft producers have been rapidly taking market share away from the big established brewers. Since 2010, the number of micro-brewing businesses in Europe has nearly tripled and is now over 7,000.
>
> The success of small-scale brewing is due to a change in tastes so that consumers are increasingly looking for more distinctive, local products rather than mass-market brands. Microbreweries are relatively cheap and easy to establish: they can be housed in industrial estates, old plant works, farm sheds and even campsites. Britain has well over 2,000 microbreweries. Forecasts for the craft beer industry look good and are expected to grow revenues by around 10% annually until 2021.

> Sources: www.statista.com/statistics/257677/global-market-share-of-the-leading-beer-companies-based-on-sales/; https://www.economist.com/graphic-detail/2017/12/28/europes-microbreweries-are-barrelling-along

Figure 8.2 Number of microbreweries in Europe, 2016

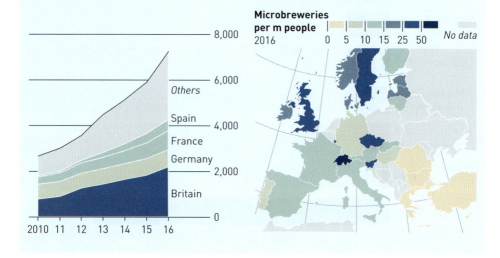

Understanding markets

Managers will want to assess different markets to decide whether they want to compete in them. To evaluate how attractive a market is, a manager might be interested in various factors.

Size of market

The overall size of the market may be measured by the volume of sales, i.e. the number being sold and the value of sales i.e. the value of the revenue earned. It is possible for the volume and values of sales to be moving in different directions. For example, if there is a move towards the premium end of the market the volume of sales might fall but with higher prices the value of sales could rise.

Market growth

Market growth is measured by the percentage change in sales over the year. The growth of a market is significant because it can influence the degree of competition. If a market is growing, all of the firms in the industry could potentially sell more. If, by comparison, sales were falling in a market then one firm can only sell more if another one sells less. This can lead to very aggressive competition between businesses.

Market share

The market share of businesses in the market: market share measures the sales of one business as a percentage of the market as a whole. Economists often measure the concentration ratio. This measures the market share of the largest n number of businesses. For example, the five-firm concentration ratio measures the combined sales of the largest five businesses as a percentage of the total market.

KEY CONCEPTS

The **size of a market** can be measured in terms of the value or volume of sales.
The **market share** of a business is its sales as a percentage of the total market sales.
The **n-firm concentration ratio** shows the market share of the largest *n* firms.

MANAGEMENT TASK

You are considering entering the banking sector. This is already dominated by a few businesses. Outline the challenges you might face entering this market.

Measuring market growth and market share

Market growth

Market growth is measured by the percentage change in the market size.
   To calculate the percentage change use the equation

(change in value ÷ original value) × 100

For example, if the market was worth £250 million and then grew to £300 million this is a growth of

$(300 - 250) \div 250 \times 100 = (50 \div 250) \times 100 = 20\%$

You may need to calculate how big the market is if it grows by a given percentage. For example, imagine a market has a size of £400 million and then grows by 5%.
   You need to calculate 5% of £400 million.

$$\frac{5}{100} \times £400 \text{ million} = £20 \text{ million}$$

The market size now is

£400 million + £20 million = £420 million

If the market growth is negative this means it is actually shrinking in size.

Market share

Market share is measured by

$$\frac{\text{The sales of one product (or brand or company)} \times 100}{\text{The total sales in the market}}$$

For example, if sales of a product were £200,000 and the total sales in the market were £500,000, this means

market share = (£200,000 ÷ £500,000) × 100 = 40%

8.1 DOING THE BUSINESS MATHS

a. Calculating market growth

$$\frac{\text{change in size of market}}{\text{original size of market}} \times 100$$

For example, imagine that market size was £40,000 and is now £50,000.

$$\text{Market growth} = \frac{+£10,000}{£50,000} \times 100 = 20\%$$

Complete the table.

Original market size (£)	New market size (£)	Market growth (%)
10,000	12,000	
60,000	62,000	
500,000	500,000	
500,000	490,000	

b. Calculating market share

$$\frac{\text{Sales of a business}}{\text{Total sales in a market}} \times 100$$

For example, imagine that sales made by a business were £5,000 and total market size was £20,000.

$$\text{Market share} = \frac{£5,000}{£20,000} \times 100 = 25\%$$

Question
Complete the table.

Sales of one business (£)	Total market size (£)	Market share (%)
10,000	120,000	
60,000	620,000	

ANALYSING THE BUSINESS DATA

In 2017 the market shares of the leading supermarkets in the UK were as follows:

Tesco (27.8%)

Sainsbury's (15.8%)

Asda (15.3%)

Morrisons (10.4%)

Aldi (7%)

Co-op (6.3%)

Lidl (5.2%)

Waitrose (5.1%)

Iceland (2.1%)

Ocado (1.4%)

Questions

1. What is the three-firm concentration ratio for this industry?
2. What is the four-firm concentration ratio for this industry?
3. What do you think is the significance of your results?

8.1 QUICK CHECK

For each of the following statements, say whether it is true or false.

a. If the market share of a business increases it must be selling more.
b. A five-firm concentration ratio of 20% means each business has a 20% market share.
c. The size of a market can be measured in terms of volume or value.
d. If the market is growing, the market share of your business will fall.

RESEARCH TASK

Using Mintel, research a market of your choice. Produce a market summary showing the size, the growth (past and projected), and the market share of the major competitors. Summarize the key segments and trends in the market.

Competitive markets

Competitive markets occur when there are many firms with a relatively small market share. Businesses will compete with each other to win the available demand. This can lead to businesses

• improving the quality of their offering to attract customers;

- investing in innovation to add additional features to what they do, in order to distinguish themselves from other firms;

- developing new approaches to increase efficiency and keep costs down, enabling lower prices.

Competition can therefore drive innovation, creativity, better quality and service, and lower prices; this can be good for customers. This is why governments often try to promote more competition in markets by encouraging startups and trying to ensure that a high level of competition exists. In the UK, the Competition and Markets Authority (CMA) is a government body that aims to ensure that markets work well and that they have competition within them.

8.1 BUSINESS INSIGHT: FOOD DELIVERY

The food delivery business was experiencing high levels of competition in 2018. UberEats had a presence in 20 countries and was operating in around 100 cities, providing nearly a tenth of Uber's overall revenue figures. However, it was still not profitable and had low profit margins and high competition. Facebook had launched its food delivery business in the US in 2017, and Amazon's restaurant delivery service was launched in 2016. Smaller rivals such as Postmates, Deliveroo, and DoorDash were fighting for market share. UberEat did have an advantage in that it was able to use its fleet of more than 2 million Uber drivers around the world who could carry either passengers or food. This should have meant it could offer greater convenience for customers and faster delivery, but even so, profits were hard to earn.

Question
What impact do you think more competition will have on the food delivery business?

Who is your competition?

One of the classic mistakes in business is to define your competitors as simply those who produce similar products. 'A bus operator competes against other bus operators.' Except it isn't like that. Imagine you have to go somewhere in town—you might catch a bus, walk, cycle, drive, or get a taxi. All of these methods of transport are competitors to the bus operator. What matters in business is what needs and wants you are fulfilling and what are the different ways of meeting these. If a business focuses only on those who produce the same product, they will miss out on many of their competitors and may lose their market. A marketing guru, Theodore Levitt, called this too-narrow focus 'marketing myopia' (see 'Read more' in this chapter). To truly understand your competition, you must understand the benefit your product provides and what else might perform a similar function. Are customers going to the cinema because they like watching films, or because they like going out with their friends? If they don't go to the cinema, do they go to a café or restaurant instead? If so, these services are competitors with the cinema.

READ MORE

You can find Levitt's classic article here:

Levitt, T. (1960), 'Marketing Myopia', *Harvard Business Review* Vol. 38, No. 4 (July/August), pp. 45–56.

BUSINESS CASE

Alphabet is the organization that owns Google and many other businesses such as Chrome, Android, and YouTube. In its 2007 Annual Report, Alphabet said:

Our business is characterized by rapid change as well as new and disruptive technologies. We face formidable competition in every aspect of our business, particularly from companies that seek to connect people with online information and provide them with relevant advertising. We face competition from:

- General purpose search engines and information services, such as Microsoft's Bing, Yahoo, Yandex, Baidu, Naver, and Seznam.
- Vertical search engines and e-commerce websites, such as Amazon and eBay (e-commerce), Kayak (travel queries), LinkedIn (job queries), and WebMD (health queries). Some users will navigate directly to such content, websites, and apps rather than go through Google.
- Social networks, such as Facebook and Twitter. Some users are increasingly relying on social networks for product or service referrals, rather than seeking information through traditional search engines.
- Other forms of advertising, such as television, radio, newspapers, magazines, and billboards. Our advertisers typically advertise in multiple media, both online and offline.
- Other online advertising platforms and networks, including Facebook, Criteo, and AppNexus, that compete for advertisers with AdWords, our primary auction-based advertising program.
- Providers of digital video services, such as Facebook, Netflix, Amazon, and Hulu.
- Companies that design, manufacture, and market consumer electronics products, including businesses that have developed proprietary platforms.
- Providers of enterprise cloud services, including Amazon and Microsoft.
- Digital assistant providers, such as Apple, Amazon, Facebook, and Microsoft.

Competing successfully in our advertising-related businesses depends heavily on our ability to deliver and distribute innovative products and technologies to the marketplace so that we can attract and retain:

- Users, for whom other products and services are literally one click away, primarily on the basis of the relevance and usefulness of our search results and the features, availability, and ease of use of our products and services.

- Advertisers, primarily based on our ability to generate sales leads, and ultimately customers, and to deliver their advertisements in an efficient and effective manner across a variety of distribution channels.

- Content providers (Google Network Members, the parties who use our advertising programs to deliver relevant ads alongside their search results and content, as well as other content providers for whom we distribute or license content), primarily based on the quality of our advertiser base, our ability to help these partners generate revenues from advertising, and the terms of our agreements with them.

Source: abc.xyz/investor/pdf/2015_alphabet_annual_report.pdf

BUSINESS CASE QUESTIONS

1. Why is it important for Alphabet to define its competitors?

2. Why does Alphabet have so many competitors?

3. What is the impact of competition on Alphabet?

Perfect competition

Economists often imagine a world in which there is 'perfect competition' between firms and use this to examine the outcomes. This model shows the consequences of high levels of competition in a market. Perfect competition makes the following assumptions.

- There are many businesses competing against each other.

- The products of the businesses are similar, so customers are not loyal to one brand or product.

- Customers can switch easily between products, so that if the price of one company's product was higher than prices elsewhere in the market, that company would lose sales.

- Customers have perfect information about what is on offer and so will be aware of any price differences.

These assumptions create a perfectly competitive market. Businesses will be competing for customers, but given they have the same products and given that customers know this, they will end up charging the same prices as each other. In this market, businesses cannot afford to be inefficient because that would lead to higher prices and then they would lose their sales.

Any one business is known as a price taker, as it has to accept the price that is prevalent in the market as a whole. That price is determined by the overall demand for the product and the overall supply from all the businesses in the industry. Any change in output by one business is so small, relative to the total output being produced, that it basically has no effect on total supply and so does not change the

Figure 8.3 Perfect competition makes a firm a price taker

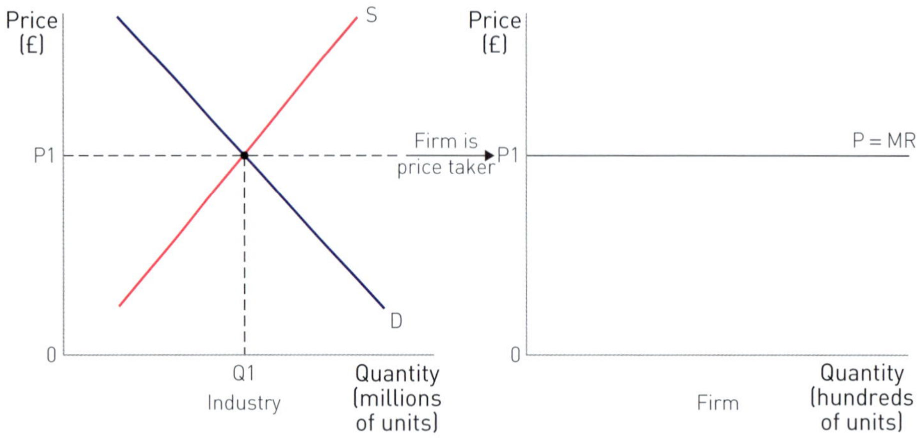

price. Imagine the total world output was 1 billion units and your business decided to produce 2 more units; this would have no noticeable effect on the world supply and therefore, assuming demand conditions are the same, the world price would stay the same.

Given that, in perfect competition, the individual business is a price taker (see Figure 8.3), it can sell as much as it is possible to sell at the given market price. This means that price = marginal revenue. For example, if every unit is sold at £10, the extra revenue from selling a unit is £10.

KEY CONCEPT

A **price taker** has to accept the market price; it cannot charge less or it would make a loss; if it charged more it would lose its customers.

The model of perfect competition can show the effect in competitive markets of changes in demand conditions. If demand increases, this will increase prices. This will in turn increase the profits made by firms that are already established in the industry.

This profit will be above the levels that established firms need to keep their resources in their present use. This abnormal profit will attract new competitors into the industry. The abnormal profit acts a signal to firms in other industries to enter this industry.

With more firms producing, the price will be driven down in the industry. This will continue until the profits are just sufficient to cover the costs, including the opportunity costs. Once normal profit is being earned, there is no incentive for more firms to enter the industry. With normal profit, the rewards to the businesses are just sufficient to keep resources in their present use.

Figure 8.4 Adjustment from short-run abnormal profits to long-run equilibrium in perfect competition

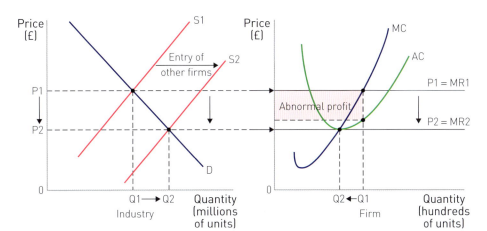

Short-run and long-run equilibrium in perfectly competitive markets

It is assumed that businesses in perfect competition want to maximize profits. This means they produce where marginal revenue = marginal costs (i.e. there is no extra profit to be made).

In the short run it may be possible for these businesses to make abnormal profits (i.e. the price is greater than the average costs), but this leads to entry of other businesses into the market, increasing the total supply and bringing the price down.

Figure 8.4 shows the adjustment process from short-run abnormal profits to long-run equilibrium in a perfectly competitive market. The firm is initially making abnormal profits when the price is P1. This acts as a signal that attracts other firms into the industry, thereby shifting the industry supply curve to the right. With more firms in the industry, the price falls until normal profits are made at P2.

We can see the effect of high levels of profit attracting businesses to shift resources into new areas to try and earn higher rewards all the time. When a particular business idea becomes attractive, new businesses set up to try and benefit from it. Just think how many coffee shops have opened in your area in the last five years. When fidget spinners took off as a craze, how long did it take before the shops were flooded with them?

Similarly, when demand falls, businesses will make a loss (where the price is less than the average costs) and leave industry. We see pubs closing down every week these days, as fewer people go out to them to drink.

Figure 8.5 Adjustment from short-run losses to long-run equilibrium in perfect competition

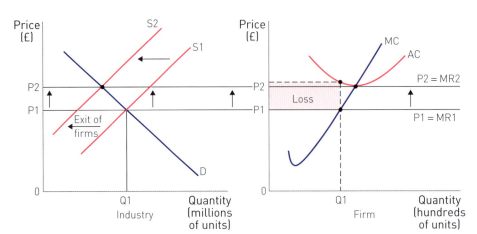

Figure 8.5 shows the adjustment process from short-run losses to long-run equilibrium in a perfectly competitive market. The firm originally makes a loss at the price P1 because this price is less than the average cost per unit. This leads to an exit of firms from the industry. The industry supply curve shifts to the left. This increases the price until only normal profits are made (P = AC). At this point there is no further incentive to leave the industry.

8.2 QUICK CHECK

For each of the following statements, say whether it is true or false.
In perfect competition,

a.   there are many buyers and sellers.

b.   each business sells differentiated products.

c.   it is difficult for businesses to enter and exit the market.

d.   each business is a price maker.

How to prevent entry into a market

While competition may be attractive for consumers, from a business perspective it means you are constantly competing with other businesses. What you might want to do is prevent other firms from entering the industry so that you can make high profits and hold on to them. To stop other businesses entering you will want to develop barriers to entry (see Figure 8.6). This means you can earn abnormal profits without them being reduced through greater competition.

Figure 8.6 Barriers to entry

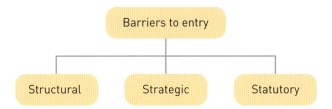

Barriers to entry can be put in three general categories.

- **Structural barriers** ('innocent' entry barriers) occur due to differences in the structure of businesses. For example, the existing businesses may operate on a large scale and therefore their unit costs are so low that entrants (who are likely to be operating at a smaller scale initially) cannot compete.

- **Strategic barriers** may be adopted by existing businesses to prevent others entering a market. For example:
  a. the existing businesses may set lower prices than they should charge in order to deter entry. 'Limit entry' pricing occurs when an established business sets a price specifically to prevent market entry; entrants realize that if they enter and drive down the price further, they will make a loss.
  b. developing a strong brand loyalty means that customers stick with you even if the price is higher. Potential new entrants may see that they would struggle to gain enough demand for entry to be profitable and worth doing. The costs of attacking existing players and gaining your own customers may be too much to make entry likely. The economist George Stigler defined a barrier to entry as 'A cost of producing which must be borne by a firm which seeks to enter an industry but is not borne by businesses already in the industry' (details in 'Read more' in this chapter).
  c. gaining control of resources may stop other firms entering a market. For example, a supermarket business may try and hold the best locations in any given area to make it difficult for others to enter, or a business may try to control the supply of natural resources.

- **Statutory barriers** are legal entry barriers: examples are patent protection given to new inventions, or licenses given to limit the number of black taxis in some cities. Alternatively domestic businesses within an industry may also seek to have the government take protectionist measures to prevent or make it more difficult for foreign firms competing in the country

BUSINESS CASE QUESTIONS: CAN YOU NOW ANSWER . . .

Why do you think the global beer industry is dominated by large brewers such as AB InBev?

KEY CONCEPT

Barriers to entry are features of a market that make it difficult for other businesses to enter, e.g. legal barriers that allow only existing providers to deliver the product or service.

8.2 BUSINESS INSIGHT: UBER

In 2017 Transport for London (TfL) announced that the ride-hailing app business Uber would not be issued with a new private hire licence. TfL decided that Uber was not fit and proper to hold a London private hire operator licence. It stated that it could not renew the licence on the grounds of public safety and security. Uber said that this showed that London was closed to innovative companies. TfL had been concerned that Uber was not carrying out suitable background checks on its drivers or reporting serious criminal offences.

Uber was given 21 days to appeal against TfL's decision. Around 3.5 million passengers and 40,000 drivers use the Uber app in London. Uber operates in over 600 cities, more than 40 of them in the UK.

Uber's view is that this resistance to its service is promoted by the traditional black cab drivers in London. To drive a black cab, drivers must pass a test (called 'The Knowledge'). Supporters of Uber argue that the company has brought much more competition into the transport market in London. They also claim it has forced the black cab companies to improve their service by introducing mobile phone booking and cashless payment.

Source: www.bbc.co.uk/news/uk-england-41358640

Questions

What do you think we learn about the benefits of competition from the Uber example?
What do you think we learn about the dangers of competition from the Uber example?

8.3 QUICK CHECK

For each of the following statements, say whether it is true or false.
Barriers to entry may include

a.   patents.

b.   the introduction of trade restrictions on foreign competition.

c.   limited brand loyalty.

MANAGEMENT TASK

You are a steel producer. You have managed to get your government to protect your industry. Explain the effects of this protection on your industry and the economy as a whole.

8.3 BUSINESS INSIGHT: AIRBNB

Figure 8.7 Is Airbnb really cheaper than a hotel room?

Is Airbnb Really Cheaper Than A Hotel Room?
Average room price per night in selected major cities in January 2018*

Legend: ■ Hotel ■ Airbnb ($) saved through Airbnb

City	Hotel	Airbnb	Saved
New York	$306	$187	$119
Sydney	$240	$191	$49
Tokyo	$220	$93	$127
London	$217	$179	$38
Toronto	$193	$114	$79
Paris	$167	$110	$57
Moscow	$118	$65	$53
Berlin	$114	$92	$22

* Converted from EUR to USD on 1/22/18

Even when you may think you have barriers to entry, competitors may find ways around them! Airbnb is an excellent example of disruptive innovation. The established operators are content with a business model that has worked well for them, when along comes a new form of competition—in this case, a business providing accommodation that has no rooms of its own! By using technology to match suppliers and buyers in an easy-to-use, reliable, and user-friendly way, Airbnb has disrupted the accommodation market globally. It has also brought down prices, putting pressure on traditional operators to cut their prices.

Source: www.statista.com/chart/12655/is-airbnb-really-cheaper-than-a-hotel-room/

Question
Is Airbnb a good thing?

Monopoly

If a business dominates an industry in terms of its market share, it is known as a monopoly. In theory a 'monopoly' has a 100 per cent market share—it is the sole provider of a good or service. At one point in the UK, for example, you could only get a telephone from British Telecom—it was the monopoly provider. In reality, we often regard a monopoly as a business that has a large market share even if it is not 100 per cent. Under UK law a monopoly has a market share of 25% or more.

Of course, what is critical in this definition is what we regard as 'the market'. Imagine you are thinking of going on your weekly shop (if you have a weekly shop!)—how far would you travel? The market that is relevant to you might be the shops within, say, a 20-mile radius. If this is an area where there are several Tesco stores and few other shops, you might say that Tesco is a monopoly in this region. This does not mean that Tesco is a monopoly in the UK as a whole, or in Europe, or the rest of the world.

KEY CONCEPT

A **monopoly** occurs when one business dominates a market.

8.4 BUSINESS INSIGHT: ZILDJAN

Anyone who plays drums will know the name of Zildjan. This company dominates the cymbal industry across the world, with well over 50 per cent of sales. The business was founded nearly 400 years ago, in 1623, in Istanbul. It is still a family business but is based in Norwell, Massachusetts. The appeal of the cymbals is due in part to a secret production process that creates the alloy of copper, tin, and silver that gives the Zildjian cymbals their famous sound. As the BBC reported in June 2012: 'At the Norwell factory, there's a special room that only a few people have access to, where the alloy is mixed by a trusted handful—even the company's head of research and development doesn't know what goes into the mix.'

The family also has an interesting approach to management.

Every Zildjian who wants to work in the family business must get a college degree, preferably in business. They also must intern while in high school or college, to get a taste of the company's standards. [. . .] Another rule requires family members to work elsewhere to get experience outside the company.

Source: BBC, www.bbc.co.uk/news/business-18261045

Questions

What do you think are the barriers to entry into the cymbal market?

Do you think Zildjan is likely to continue to dominate the cymbal industry?

Why would you want to be a monopoly?

If managers can help their businesses to gain market share and become a monopoly, this means they will have more power. As a major player in the market they can demand lower prices or better payment terms from suppliers. They can bargain for better deals from any media business they are using for promotion. They may be able to set the prices in the market.

Monopolies and demand

A monopolist faces a downward-sloping demand curve. To sell more, given existing demand conditions, the price has to be lowered. Assuming one price is charged, this reduces the price on the last unit and all the ones before. Revenue has been sacrificed on the earlier units, meaning the marginal revenue is less than the price, as shown in Table 8.1.

Imagine a business sells one unit for £10; to sell two, it lowers the price to £9. The total revenue is

$2 \times £9 = £18$

This means the extra (marginal) revenue is only £8 (because total revenue has increased from £10 to £18). Why is this? The business earns an extra £9 on the second unit but has lost £1 on the first one:

$£9 - £1 = £8$

The more units that are being sold, the more the price reduction on earlier units will take effect and the more marginal revenue will fall below the price charged. The marginal revenue therefore diverges from the demand curve.

Table 8.1 The relationship between demand and marginal revenue

Quantity demanded (units)	Price (£)	Total revenue = price × quantity demanded (£)	Marginal revenue (£)
1	10	10	—
2	9	18	8
3	8	24	6
4	7	28	4
5	6	30	2
6	5	30	0
7	4	28	−2

Figure 8.8 The price and output outcome in a monopoly

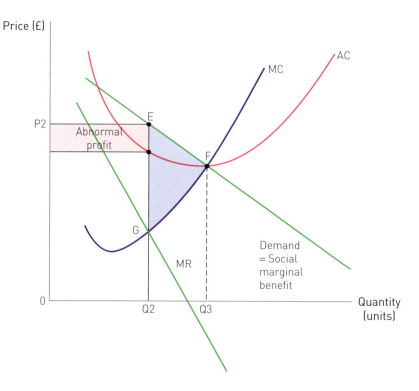

Notice how the marginal revenue at a price of £5 is zero. The reductions in price on the previous units exactly matches the extra revenue from the last unit. At a price of £4 the marginal revenue is actually negative. The effect of the price reduction is so great that total revenue falls.

Figure 8.8 shows how marginal revenue is below the demand curve and diverges from it. To profit-maximize the business produces where marginal revenue = marginal costs. The profit/loss position is then determined by considering the price in relation to the average cost. If the price is above the average costs, this means that there is abnormal profit on each unit. The pink shaded area shows the total abnormal profit being earned. There will be an incentive for other businesses to enter, but they cannot due to barriers to entry.

At the profit-maximizing price and output there is a 'welfare loss'; this is because the extra benefit to society of units Q2Q3 (shown by the price) is greater than the extra cost. Society would benefit, therefore, from these units; however, the business would end up with lower profits, because to sell them the price would have to be lowered on these units and all the ones before. This potential loss of welfare can be a concern to governments.

8.2 **DOING THE BUSINESS MATHS**

Complete the table.

Price (£)	Quantity (units)	Total revenue (£)	Marginal revenue (£)	Marginal cost (£)	Would a profit maximizer produce this unit or not?
20	4		n/a	n/a	
19	5			3	
17	6			7	
15	7			10	
13	8			12	
11	9			17	
9	10			20	

Should the government or society worry about monopolies?

Governments usually have concerns over monopolies. Many governments have set up organizations to monitor the behaviour of monopolies. What worries them is that the monopolist will abuse its strong position in the market and that consumers and the economy will suffer.

The predicted dangers are as follows.

• A monopoly may increase prices, knowing that customers have no choice if they want the product because they cannot switch to another provider.

• A monopoly may provide poor quality-products or service because there is little competition. The business can, essentially, say 'this is what you get whether you like it or not' because customers have limited alternatives.

However, there may be benefits to society involved in having a monopoly.

• It may avoid the duplication of resources that could occur with many providers of the same product.

• It can lead to high profits that may be used for investment, e.g. in research and development that lead to new products.

• It may act as a good way of encouraging other businesses to be innovative in order to try and reduce the monopoly power.

• It may lead to lower unit costs due to a higher scale of output and economies of scale.

MANAGEMENT TASK

You are one of three large cinema chains in the UK. You are the third largest business in the industry, with 22 per cent of the market. You want to be the biggest. Discuss three actions you might take to achieve this.

What might happen to you if your business is a monopoly?

The effect of being a monopoly on a business will depend on the government and its approach to competition policy. In the UK, the Competition and Markets Authority (CMA) is the body that regulates monopolies. It investigates potential abuses of power and can take various actions. It can prevent a merger or takeover from going ahead or impose certain conditions on such a deal. For example, it may insist that certain stores in particular regions are sold off if the takeover deal goes ahead, in order to reduce monopoly power in those areas. The CMA may also impose a fine for anti-competitive behaviour. This could be up to 10 per cent of turnover.

8.5 BUSINESS INSIGHT: GOOGLE'S DOMINANCE

The Guardian reported in 2017 on a fine imposed on Google by the EU.
'The European Union has handed Google a record-breaking €2.42bn (£2.14bn) fine for abusing its dominance of the search engine market in building its online shopping service.' It was claimed that Google was 'artificially and illegally promoting its own price comparison service in searches. The *Guardian* went on to report:

> The EU regulator is further investigating how else the company may have abused its position, specifically in its provision of maps, images and information on local services.
>
> The commission's decision, following a seven-year probe into Google's dominance in searches and smartphones, suggests the company may need to fundamentally rethink the way it operates. It is also now liable to face civil actions for damages by any person or business affected by its anti-competitive behaviour.
>
> As the EU official in charge of competition policy, commissioner Margrethe Vestager, spelled out the case against Google, [. . .] [she commented that] 'What Google has done is illegal under EU antitrust rules. It denied other companies the chance to compete on the merits and to innovate. And most importantly, it denied European consumers a genuine choice of services and the full benefits of innovation.'

Source: www.theguardian.com/business/2017/jun/27/google-braces-for-record-breaking-1bn-fine-from-eu

Questions

Why do you think Google's power might need to be controlled?
What problems might there be in controlling it, do you think?

8.4 QUICK CHECK

For each of the following statements, say whether it is true or false.

In a monopoly

a. there is a single buyer.

b. businesses face an upward-sloping demand curve.

c. marginal revenue is lower than average revenue.

d. profit maximization occurs where marginal revenue equals marginal costs.

RESEARCH TASK

Visit the website of the Competition and Markets Authority (CMA). Research a recent investigation undertaken by the CMA.

Oligopoly

A market where there are several large firms dominating is a common market structure. It might be, for example, that the four-firm concentration ratio is 60 per cent. This type of market structure is called an oligopoly.

An oligopoly is a particularly interesting market structure because businesses within this market have to be aware of how the other firms might respond to any decision they make. In an oligopoly there is a high degree of interdependence—any business will consider the reaction of other businesses. This need to consider the potential responses of other businesses means that what happens in oligopoly depends on what assumptions are made about possible reactions.

The businesses in an oligopoly may decide to compete with each other, or to co-operate with each other.

Collusive behaviour in oligopoly

An example of cooperative or collusive behaviour would be to form a cartel. This occurs when businesses join together and act as one. For example, the major road construction companies may decide on which company bids for which deal and what price they will set.

By colluding, the businesses remove competition and all of them can earn higher profits at the expense of customers.

However, cartels are often very unstable. This is because individual members have an incentive to cheat and secretly undercut their rivals in order to increase their own profits at the expense of the others. If discovered, this leads to aggressive competition. Cartels are only likely to work if the actions of competitors are visible and easily investigated by others.

BUSINESS CASE QUESTIONS: CAN YOU NOW ANSWER . . .

Why might ABinBev have wanted to join with SABMiller?

What might be the possible consequences for the consumers of having a few large businesses dominate the industry?

KEY CONCEPTS

An **oligopoly** is a market which is dominated by several large businesses. A **cartel** occurs when businesses collude and work together as if they are a monopolist.

MANAGEMENT TASK

You are the manager of a leading national construction business. There are only two other major companies that can take on big projects such as motorway repair or construction. A representative of one of the other companies has approached you and suggested the three of you meet up to discuss a common approach to pricing when asked to tender for a contract. Should you agree to meet? What might be the advantages and disadvantages of colluding?

Competitive behaviour in oligopoly

The outcomes in oligopoly depend on what you think your rivals are going to do and how you act based on these assumptions. Imagine the following situation.

You make two assumptions.

- You assume that if you increase your price, then the other businesses in the industry will not follow. This means that the fall in the quantity demanded is likely to be relatively high because customers will switch to your competitors; demand is therefore price elastic.

- You assume that if you decrease your price, then your rivals will follow this price cut (because they do not want to lose sales). This means that the increase in the quantity demanded will be smaller than the price change (in percentages); demand will therefore be price inelastic.

These assumptions take a pessimistic view of how others might react (that is, they assume that you will not get away with a price cut, and that if you increase price, then you will be on your own). The kinked demand curve is a non-cooperative model of oligopoly because firms are assumed to compete with each other. Given these assumptions, the firm being examined is likely to leave price where it is. An increase in price will lead to such a fall in demand that the overall revenue will fall. A decrease in price will lead to such a small increase in sales that, again, revenue will

Figure 8.9 The derivation of the kinked demand curve

fall. If revenue is going to fall whatever you do with the price, then why not leave it where it is?

Figure 8.9 shows how a kinked demand curve arises. The demand curve D2 is price inelastic; it assumes that a price change will have relatively little effect on the quantity demanded because any price change by one firm will be followed by the others, and so there will be little difference between them. By comparison, the demand curve D1 is price elastic; it assumes that a price change will have a relatively larger effect on the quantity demanded because any price change by one firm will not be followed by the others. This means that increasing price will reduce revenue.

Starting from P1Q1 in the kinked demand curve model, it is assumed that a price increase will not be followed, so D1 is relevant—but a price decrease will be followed, so D2 is relevant. This means a price decrease will reduce revenue. This gives the kinked demand curve indicated by the thicker line.

The kinked demand curve model provides an explanation of why prices in oligopolistic markets are often 'sticky'—that is, they do not change very much. Price competition is not common in many markets because it is relatively easy for a firm to copy another firm's price cut. Many firms prefer to try to differentiate their products—for example, by building a brand or developing some unique selling point—and using this as a means of competing rather than using price. It is much more difficult for competitors to imitate a brand image than it is for them to follow a price cut.

MANAGEMENT TASK

You run a cinema chain. You have two other big rivals. One has just cut ticket prices. Should you follow and cut your prices? Explain the factors you would consider before deciding.

READ MORE

You can read more about the kinked demand curve, including the limitations of the model, in the following articles.

Hall, R., and Hitch, C. (1939), 'Price Theory and Business Behavior', Oxford Economic Papers 2, pp. 12–45.

Stigler, G. (1947), 'Kinky Oligopoly Demand and Rigid Prices', *Journal of Political Economy* Vol. 55, pp. 432–49.

Sweezy, P. (1939), 'Demand under Conditions of Oligopoly', *Journal of Political Economy* Vol. 47, pp. 568–73.

Game theory in oligopoly

Game theory has been used to explain how businesses might plan to act given that they know that, in an oligopoly, whatever they do will lead to a reaction from the other firms. Managers may try to anticipate the actions of other businesses in order to decide what is the best action for them to take.

An example of game theory can be seen in the 'prisoner's dilemma', in which two individuals have both been arrested for committing a crime together. The question is whether they should confess to the crime or not, and that, in turn, depends on what they think the other person will do. Unfortunately, they are locked up in separate rooms and cannot communicate, so they have to make assumptions about the other person's behaviour. It is assumed that if they both confess, they will be imprisoned for a long time; if they both refuse to confess, the police cannot prove anything and they will be released. The problem comes if one person refuses to confess and the other one does so: the latter person gets a light sentence and the one who refused to talk gets a very long sentence for non-cooperation. The ideal solution, from the prisoners' point of view, is not to confess and then they would both get off. But if you do not trust your fellow prisoner and think that he or she will confess, you are better confessing as well. On this basis, they will both confess because they do not trust each other.

The prisoner's dilemma highlights how your decisions about what to do depend on your relationship with other prisoners (or businesses in an oligopoly) and your view of whether you think you can trust them or not. You can imagine the manager of one business thinking carefully about what a major competitor might be about to do and trying to work out the best action in different situations. The prisoner's dilemma shows the dangers of oligopoly from a manager's point of view: a lack of

Figure 8.10 The prisoner's dilemma in a business context (the top area of each quadrant shows the payoff for A; the bottom area shows the payoff for B)

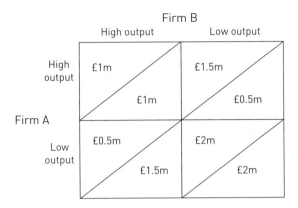

trust may lead to an outcome in which firms are worse off than if they trusted each other.

Figure 8.10 shows the prisoner's dilemma in a business context. Two businesses are considering what level of output to produce: high or low. If they both produce low outputs, this will push the price up and both will win. But if one produces relatively little and its competitor produces a lot, this will increase supply and drive the price down; the first producer will do badly because it will sell a little at a low market price whilst its rival wins the market and is selling more. Both businesses will be suspicious and fear the other one will produce a high output. As a result both producers might flood the market, meaning that both are worse off compared to what they could both have earned if they had restricted output.

The matrix in Figure 8.10 shows that if both firms produce high levels of output, they will gain £1 million each; if both restrict output, they will earn £2 million each.

This model shows the importance of managers' assumptions about what other businesses will do. The past behaviour of businesses becomes very important here: how they have behaved in the past may influence assumptions about what they will do in the future.

Game theory can become much more complex depending on the assumptions that are made. In figure 8.11, imagine that you are the manager of Firm A thinking about your pricing options. Assume that you are pessimistic and look at the worst possible outcome of any decision. If you choose a price of £2, the worst that can happen is that B will charge £1 and you will make profits of £5,000. If you were to charge £1, the worst that could happen is that B would do the same and you would end up with £6,000. If you decide to choose the 'best of the worst', then you choose a £1 price. This is called a 'maximin' strategy because you are maximizing the minimum outcomes. If Firm B were to do the same, it would choose £1 as well and you would both end up with £6,000, whereas you could have had £10,000 had you agreed to charge £2 and believed each other would stick to that price.

Figure 8.11 The prisoner's dilemma: financial outcomes

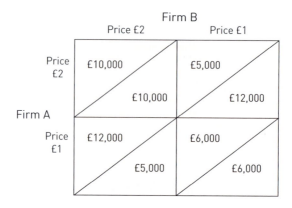

A 'maximax' strategy occurs when a manager is optimistic and bases decisions on the 'best of the best' outcomes. The best outcome if you choose a price of £1 is that your rival chooses £2 and you earn £12,000. The best outcome if you choose a price of £2 is that your rival chooses £2 and you end up with £10,000. To maximize the maximum outcomes, you would choose £1.

In this case the best strategy, whether you adopt a minimax or a maximax approach, is the same—the business should set the price at £1. Because both assumptions give the same solution, this is known as the 'dominant strategy'.

Now let's look at Figure 8.12, which illustrates how a business might decide whether it should increase its promotional spending or not.

If A assumes B will increase its spending, then its best strategy is to increase its spending and earn £4m. If A assumes B will not increase its spending, then its best strategy is not to increase its own spending (which would result in earnings of £6m). This means there is no dominant strategy for firm A.

Figure 8.12 Deciding whether to increase promotional spending

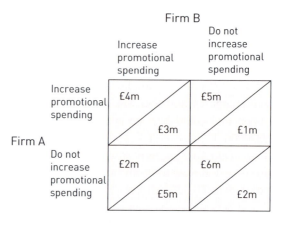

If B assumes A will increase its spending, then its best strategy is to increase its spending to earn £3m. If B assumes A will not increase its spending, then its best strategy is to increase its spending and earn £5m. This means B does have a dominant strategy, which is to increase its spending.

This means that the best strategy for B is to increase its promotional spending regardless of what A does. If A realizes this, it will also increase its promotional spending, so both will end up increasing their spending. This is known as the Nash equilibrium. A Nash equilibrium occurs in a game involving two or more players, in which each player is assumed to know the equilibrium strategies of the other players. If each player has chosen a strategy and no player would benefit by changing his or her strategy while the other players keep theirs unchanged, then the current set of strategy choices and the corresponding payoffs represent a Nash equilibrium.

8.5 QUICK CHECK

For each of the following statements, say whether it is true or false.
   In an oligopoly

a.   there are many businesses.

b.   the five-firm concentration ratio is likely to be low.

c.   businesses may collude or compete.

d.   the kinked demand curve assumes that the price increases of a business are not followed by other businesses.

RESEARCH TASK

Research a recent case of collusion and summarize the issues involved.

Monopolistic competition

In some markets, businesses are able to differentiate what they offer but at the same time it may be relatively easy for other firms to enter the market. Imagine you set up a beach bar and it proves successful. Fairly soon you will have beach bars around you—they may have different names and slightly different decor and menus, so it may be possible to charge different prices, but they are competing closely with each other.

In this type of market a business may be able to benefit from abnormal profits in the short run—perhaps when it gains an advantage with a new promotion. However, over time any abnormal profits will simply bring more firms in. This reduces demand for any one business until only normal profits are made, as shown in Figure 8.13.

Figure 8.13 (a) Short-run abnormal profits in monopolistic competition (b) Long-run normal profits in monopolistic competition when demand has fallen with the entry of new businesses

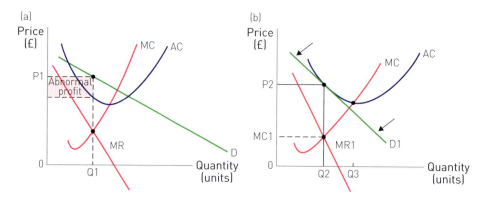

MANAGEMENT TASK

You want to open a restaurant in the city centre. There are already many restaurants based there. You do not want to compete with them on price. How can you compete? What can you do to protect your business from the marketing activities of the existing restaurants?

A business in monopolistic competition faces a downward-sloping demand curve; to sell more, the price must be reduced. The marginal revenue is below the demand and diverges because the price must be lowered on the last unit and all the ones before.

A profit-maximizing business produces where marginal revenue equals marginal costs. In the short run, this is P1Q1 and abnormal profit is earned.

The abnormal profit attracts more businesses into the industry; the demand for any individual business falls, and the demand curve shifts inwards until only normal profits are earned at P2Q2.

8.6 QUICK CHECK

For each of the following statements, say whether it is true or false.
  In monopolistic competition

a. there are many businesses.

b. each business is a price taker.

c. there is freedom of entry and exit.

d. normal profits are earned by businesses in the long run.

8.6 BUSINESS INSIGHT: GOVERNMENT AND MONOPOLIES

In the US, the Council of Economic Advisers (CEA) measured the increase in market concentration in various markets and its implications. In the *Guardian* in May 2016, Joseph Stiglitz wrote:

> In most industries, according to the CEA, standard metrics show large—and in some cases, dramatic—increases in market concentration. The top 10 banks' share of the deposit market, for example, increased from about 20% to 50% in just 30 years, from 1980 to 2010.
>
> Some of the increase in market power is the result of changes in technology and economic structure: consider network economies and the growth of locally provided service-sector industries. Some is because firms—Microsoft and drug companies are good examples—have learned better how to erect and maintain entry barriers, often assisted by conservative political forces that justify lax anti-trust enforcement and the failure to limit market power on the grounds that markets are 'naturally' competitive. And some of it reflects the naked abuse and leveraging of market power through the political process: Large banks, for example, lobbied the US Congress to amend or repeal legislation separating commercial banking from other areas of finance. [. . .]
>
> Joseph Schumpeter, one of the great economists of the 20th century, argued that one shouldn't be worried by monopoly power: monopolies would only be temporary. There would be fierce competition *for* the market and this would replace competition in the market and ensure that prices remained competitive. [. . .] [However,] [t]oday's markets are characteried by the persistence of high monopoly profits. [. . .] If markets are fundamentally efficient and fair, there is little that even the best of governments could do to improve matters. But if markets are based on exploitation, the rationale for laissez-faire disappears. Indeed, in that case, the battle against entrenched power is not only a battle for democracy; it is also a battle for efficiency and shared prosperity.

Source: www.theguardian.com/business/2016/may/13/-new-era-monopoly-joseph-stiglitz

Question
Do you think the government should prevent monopolies existing?

Contestable markets

When thinking about market structure and its impact on the profits of your business, the number of businesses there are now is not the only key issue. What also matters is how many there might be—how contestable is the market? If others could come in easily, then the market is very contestable and those within the industry may keep profits relatively low so as not to attract too much interest. The threat of competition keeps profits and profits down. E-commerce has been a powerful factor in making it easier to start up and compete, increasing the contestability of many markets.

Niche markets

A niche market is a small part of the overall market where businesses meet specific needs and wants. For example, within the overall car market there may be a niche for sports cars. Within the music market there may be mainstream pop and more niche types of music such as catstep. By focusing on a niche, businesses may be able to develop their own market and avoid direct competition with the bigger firms.

Niche producers will tend to have higher unit costs than the mass producers because of the small scale of production. However, it may be possible to charge a higher price for a more specialized product, enabling niche producers to make a profit.

Pricing strategies

In highly competitive markets such as perfect competition the price is determined by the market. Any one business is so small relative to the market as a whole that it cannot influence the market price. If it tries to charge more, customers will easily switch to competitors who offer similar products. Firms in these markets are price takers.

However, if a business is able to differentiate what it offers and have some control over the market (perhaps due to branding or barriers to entry), managers are then price makers.

Methods of pricing include price skimming, cost-plus pricing, and price discrimination.

Price skimming

Price skimming occurs when businesses charge a high initial price when a product is first launched. For example, when a new Apple iPhone is launched there are a group of customers who will be willing to pay a high price to get the product early (in marketing terms, the very first buyers are called 'innovators' and they are followed by the 'early adopters'). Over time the price will be reduced to target other customers (who marketing managers call the 'mainstream', the 'late adopters' and—the final group—the laggards).

Cost-plus pricing

This is a very common approach to pricing in which managers add an amount (or percentage) to unit costs to set the price for their products. This should ensure a certain profit margin of each sale. However, managers do need to take account of demand and the price elasticity of demand when deciding on the amount to add, in order to ensure an appropriate level of sales and overall profits.

Price discrimination

Managers are often selling their products in different markets or in different market segments. This means that they may face different demand conditions. For example, the demand for a good or service in London may be different from the demand for the same good or service in other parts of the UK; or the demand at some times of day may be different from the demand at others. These differences in demand may create opportunities for managers to increase profits. If, for example, you realize that after midnight the demand for taxi journeys is not as sensitive to price as it is during the day, you might increase prices.

Price discrimination occurs when managers can separate markets and charge different prices for the same product. It can be used when there is a difference in the price elasticity of demand for the product in the separate markets. The price will be higher where demand is less sensitive to price. By price discriminating and charging different prices in different markets a business can earn higher profits, as shown in Figure 8.14.

For price discrimination to work, the markets must be kept separate; otherwise customers may buy in the low-price market and resell the product themselves.

KEY CONCEPT

Price discrimination occurs when different prices are charged for the same product.

Figure 8.14 Profit-maximizing by setting different prices in markets with different demand conditions

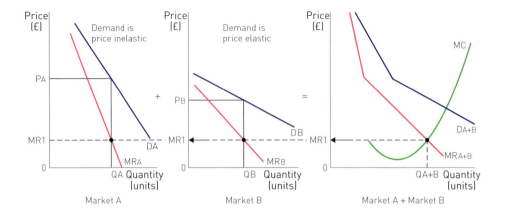

Market A   Market B   Market A + Market B

Markets may be separated by various factors:

- time—for example, train companies may charge more during peak time than off-peak;

- age—it may be possible to charge different prices for those who are retired;

- status—for example, you may decide to have different prices for those who belong to your loyalty club system.

Online retailing allows managers to change the price of products according to many factors, such as the time of day you are buying, the date (e.g. when you are booking your flight relative to the departure date), and where you are booking from.

To determine the profit-maximizing output the manager produces where marginal revenue equals marginal cost. The manager must then decide how much to sell in each market segment and at what price. To do this, managers will consider the marginal revenue from selling another unit in each of the different market segments. If an extra £10 could be achieved selling a unit in market A, for example, and only £5 could be made selling it in market B, then managers will naturally focus more on market A and try to sell more there. Output will be switched to sell more in market A and less in market B; this will drive down the price and marginal revenue in A and increase the price and marginal revenue in B; relocation of output will occur until the marginal revenues are equal. The profit-maximizing allocation of sales occurs when the marginal revenues are equal in all market segments. This will lead to a higher price when demand is price inelastic and a lower price when demand is more price elastic.

Figure 8.15 shows the effect or price discrimination on profits. If a single price (P1) was charged for the output level Q1 the total revenue would be the area 0P1XQ1. If, however, some of the output (Q2) could be sold for a higher price (P2), the total revenue is now the area 0P2YQ2 plus Q2WXQ1. Total revenue has increased, and given that costs would be the same, this means profits are higher.

Figure 8.15 The effect on profits of price discrimination

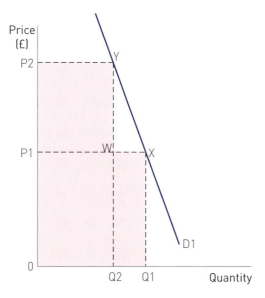

8.7 QUICK CHECK

For each of the following statements, say whether it is true or false.
   Price discrimination

a. occurs when different prices are charged for different products.

b. can lead to higher profits than charging a single price.

c. profit-maximizes when total revenues are equal in each market.

d. requires markets to be kept separate to prevent resale.

BUSINESS CASE QUESTIONS: CAN YOU NOW ANSWER . . .

Why might craft brewing becoming more popular?

How can craft breweries survive against the large breweries?

• •

SUMMARY

There are many different forms of market. At one extreme we have a highly, or in theory perfectly, competitive market where in essence all businesses are the same and the customer can move easily from one to the other. Businesses end up making what economists call normal profit—just enough to cover their costs and opportunity costs. At the other end we have a monopoly, which dominates the market and can make high profits (called abnormal profits) even in the long term if it can keep competitors out. In between, we have various market forms such as oligopoly and monopolistic competition. The nature of a market affects how businesses compete and the profits they can make. The shape of a market can change as regulations change to let more businesses compete, as managers buy up rivals or rivals shut down, or as new markets and competitors emerge with new technologies. Managers cannot be complacent—their market almost certainly will not look the same in five years' time as it does now!

KEY LEARNING POINTS

- There are different degrees of competition in different markets.
- A monopoly exists when one business dominates a market.
- Perfect competition exists when there are many firms competing in a market with similar products and freedom of entry and exit.
- A key influence on competition in a market is the extent to which barriers to entry exist.
- In oligopoly there are a few businesses that dominate a market. This means there is a high degree of interdependence.
- Oligopolies may compete or collude.
- Game theory highlights the importance of your objectives and your assumptions about competitors' possible behaviour in terms of the actions you take.
- The degree of competition can influence how businesses can compete, the quality of service for customers, and the profits that businesses can make in the long term.
- The contestability of an industry depends on how easy it is for businesses to enter it.

BUSINESS CASE EXTENSION QUESTIONS

1. Using Mintel, compare and contrast two markets that have different market structures. Analyse the differences in terms of the number and size of competitors. Discuss the possible reasons why these differences exist.

2. The brewing industry is undergoing major change with new competition from craft brewers. Research another industry that is undergoing major change. Analyse the changes that are occurring and the implications for the established businesses.

QUICK QUESTIONS

1. What is the difference between market size and market share?
2. What is the difference between market size and market growth?
3. Why might managers want their business to become a monopoly?
4. What are the potential dangers of monopolies for consumers?
5. Why might managers want to form a cartel?
6. What are examples of barriers to entry?
7. What is the likely effect of barriers to entry on the market price?
8. What is the difference between collusive and competitive oligopoly?
9. How might interdependence in oligopoly affect the decisions that managers might take?
10. How does the contestability of a market affect the likely returns of a business?

Strategic planning and the economy

WHY DO I NEED TO KNOW ABOUT STRATEGIC PLANNING?

You started your property development business in the early 1990s. At first it was small scale. You bought an existing house, renovated it, and sold it on. However, the business quickly took off and you started building houses from scratch. You would find land, develop it, and sell the houses. The business grew fast, and the scale of the developments got bigger and bigger, involving plots for hundreds of new houses in some areas. To keep the growth going and to manage cash flow, your debt increased, but so did your company and its profits. You specialized in upmarket property and for many years had no problems selling the houses you built. Then came the global crash in 2008, and you found that demand collapsed. Potential households were too worried about the financial situation to take risks, and so if they were going to do anything they would renovate their own houses rather than move. You had interest payments to make and houses that sat empty. In 2011 your business went into administration and was sold to new owners. Since then you have started back at the beginning, but your business remains a small local building company.

Looking back, you clearly made the wrong strategic decision. If only you hadn't undertaken major expansion just as the economy went into decline.

Managers have to make important long-term decisions. These make or break the business. Get it wrong and the business is in trouble. That's why you need to get it right. In this chapter we look at how managers might make these crucial decisions and why understanding the economy matters when they do so.

BY THE END OF THIS CHAPTER YOU WILL BE ABLE TO . . .

- explain what is meant by strategy and why it matters
- explain SWOT analysis and how it influences strategy
- analyse how the economy can affect the choice and success of a strategy
- explain why economic forecasting can be useful
- identify some of the difficulties of economic forecasting

BUSINESS CASE

Monarch—the UK's fifth biggest airline—went into administration in 2017, leaving 110,000 holidaymakers needing to be brought home. Monarch reported a £291m loss in 2016 and employed about 2,100 people. Its managers blamed the problems on terror attacks in Tunisia and Egypt and increased competition pushing prices down. It had also been hit by the weak pound, which increased the fuel costs as fuel is priced in dollars. The weak pound also put people off from travelling abroad from the UK.

The airline carried 14 per cent more passengers in 2016 than in the previous year but earned £100m less revenue. Monarch's owner, Greybull Capital, had been trying to sell part or all of its short-haul operation so it could focus on more profitable long-haul routes. The *Financial Times* reported in October 2017:

> Like its peers, Air Berlin and Alitalia, which both entered administration this summer, Monarch has been unable to compete in Europe, coming up against much larger airlines who have much lower cost bases. Low fuel prices have encouraged stronger rivals to flood the market with capacity, putting pressure on weaker operators.
>
> 'Monarch had somewhat lost its way in recent years, trying to reinvent itself as a low-cost carrier but in a market already well supplied by dominant players like Ryanair and EasyJet', says John Strickland, an aviation consultant. [. . .]
>
> Under Greybull's ownership, Monarch ditched its longstanding business model as a charter airline and repositioned itself as a budget carrier that would compete with EasyJet and Ryanair for holidaymakers. It cut about 700 jobs, reduced its fleet and scrapped long-haul flights, helping to cut £200m in annual costs. [. . .] While the restructuring brought some initial success—alongside cheap fuel prices and a weak euro, it helped Monarch deliver its first profit in three years in 2015—this was ultimately shortlived. [. . .]
>
> Data from OAG, an aviation consultancy, show how the airline had to move about 213,000 seats from Egypt into other, more competitive, markets, such as Spain and Portugal, taking it head-to-head with the big low-cost carriers (see Figure 9.1). [. . .] In its annual report, published in July, Monarch said it was once again reviewing its strategy, with a plan to move away from the short-haul market and return to its old long-haul business model. [. . .] Some commentators say Monarch's failure highlights that there is no place for a 'mid-market' carrier that is not protected by either some geographic or operational quirk. [. . .] 'The thing about the airline industry is that airlines that are widely considered to be financially doomed have been kept alive for years and years if someone is able or willing to inject capital', says Gerald Khoo, an analyst at Liberum. [. . .] 'Monarch was basically in the wrong place at the wrong time. It was sub-scale and failed to adapt to changes in a tough market', says Mr Khoo.

Source: www.ft.com/content/5648b990-a777-11e7-ab55-27219df83c97

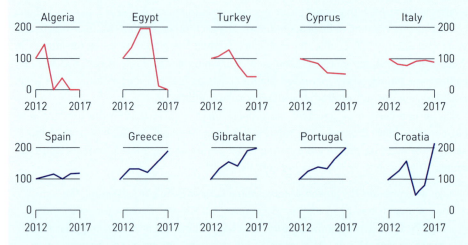

Figure 9.1 How Monarch's grand strategy failed to take off (number of seats, by destination, rebased; 100 = 2012)

BUSINESS CASE QUESTIONS

This chapter will help you answer the following questions.

Some of Monarch's problems seem to be due to its managers choosing the wrong strategy.

1. What do you think this means? And why do you think it might have happened?

2. What other factors seem to explain the problems that Monarch has had?

3. To what extent do you think Monarch's problems were of its own making?

What is meant by strategy?

The strategy of a business is the route it chooses to achieve its objective. For example, you know you want to grow your business, but should you try and do this by selling more of your products to your existing customers? Targeting new customers? Or developing new products? Managers will have choices about what to do with their resources—how best should the resources be deployed to achieve the targets? What if there was more focus on this area and less on that area? Given that resources are limited, managers must decide how best to use them. Strategic choices therefore involve an opportunity cost. If resources are deployed in one area, they cannot be used in another venture. Strategies also involve risk—there is some probability that they will go wrong. When undertaking strategic planning, managers will consider factors such as

- the initial costs
- the amount and timing of the expected returns
- the risk

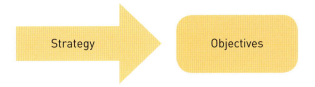

The risks involved could relate to various factors:

- the waste of money and resources if the project fails, and the financial risk if it causes problems due to cash flow issues or debt levels;
- the damage that might be done to the brand image and reputation of the business;
- any legal action that might be taken if the project creates legal problems, such as safety issues with a product.

Every strategy will have some form of risk. Managers must consider the risk they may face relative to the rewards. They will also consider their own appetite for risk, i.e. their willingness to take risks.

KEY CONCEPT

A **strategy** is a long-term plan that sets out how a business will achieve its objectives.

Features of strategic decisions

Strategic decisions could include taking over another business, entering a new market, or investing in new product development.

Typically, a strategic decision will have three main characteristics.

- It will require a large investment of resources.
- It will involve making decisions that cannot easily be reversed. Given the scale of strategic decisions, significant resources need to be committed to them; once resources are committed, it may be difficult to switch them to something else. Once you have invested in your new product, you cannot easily stop and use the funds elsewhere. This means strategic decisions have high levels of opportunity cost.
- It will include a high level of risk. The risk is not only because a strategic decision does usually involve a high level of resources, but also because strategic decisions tend to be ones that do not happen regularly. A decision to target a new region may not happen often; a decision to take over a competitor is not a regular occurrence. This means that the decision makers may not have huge experience in this specific area or much familiarity with the key issues in this decision. This in turn means that the decisions involve a high level of uncertainty.

BUSINESS CASE QUESTION: CAN YOU NOW ANSWER . . .

What was Monarch's strategy in recent years?

9.1 QUICK CHECK

For each of the following statements, say whether it is true or false.
    A strategy is usually

a. short-term.

b. low-risk.

c. a plan involving a high level of investment.

d. a plan made by junior managers.

Forms of strategy

One way of categorizing strategy was developed by Igor Ansoff and is known as the Ansoff Matrix, shown in Table 9.1 (details of Ansoff's book are given under 'Read more' in this chapter).

Ansoff's approach categorized strategy according to the product being offered and the market being targeted. For example, the following are ways that Coca-Cola might apply the different strategy categories.

- Develop its marketing around its existing products in existing markets: it could, for example, develop new promotional strategies to sell more to its current customers. This is called 'market penetration' because the aim is for its existing products to gain a bigger market share.

Table 9.1 The Ansoff matrix

	Existing products	New products
Existing markets	MARKET PENETRATION	NEW PRODUCT DEVELOPMENT
	Sell more in existing markets to existing customers, e.g. through greater advertising	Develop new products for existing customer, e.g. extend the product range or widen your offering to customers
New markets	MARKET DEVELOPMENT	DIVERSIFICATION
	Offer existing products to new market segments, e.g. different age groups or different countries	Offering new products to new customers

- Develop new products for its existing customers: this could, for example, be new flavours, new sizes, or new brands to get current customers to buy more overall. This strategy is called 'new product development'.

- Take its existing products and target new markets: these could be new in the sense of new regions. For example, if there were countries where Coca-Cola was finding it difficult to access, it could focus more on these. Alternatively, it could target a new market segment. For example, if Coca-Cola found consumption did not exist amongst older consumers it might put more resources into targeting this new group. This strategy is called 'market development'.

- Develop new products and target new markets. For example, Coca-Cola might develop new products and target new regions with these. This strategy is called 'diversification'.

READ MORE

If you want to know more about Ansoff's work, you can read

Ansoff, I.H. (1965), *Corporate Strategy*, London: Penguin Books, especially pp. 100–16.

9.2 QUICK CHECK

For each of the following statements, say whether it is true or false.

a. A new product development strategy involves new products in existing markets.

b. A diversification strategy involves new products in new markets.

c. A market development strategy involves existing products in existing markets.

d. A market penetration strategy involves existing products in new markets.

9.1 BUSINESS INSIGHT: COCA-COLA'S BRANDS

Coca-Cola classic	Sprite Zero	Schweppes Lemonade
Coca-Cola Zero Sugar	Lilt	Schweppes Cordials
Diet Coke	Lilt Zero	Schweppes Slimline
Glaceau Smartwater	Oasis	Schweppes Sparkling Juice Drinks
Glaceau Vitaminwater	Oasis Zero	5 Alive
Glaceau Vitaminwater Zero	Minute Maid	Kia-Ora
Fanta	Rose's	Kia-Ora No Added Sugar

Fanta Zero	Powerade	Appletiser
Dr Pepper	Powerade Zero	Honest
Dr Pepper Zero	Schweppes Water	Fuze Tea
Sprite	Schweppes Mixers	Honest Kids

Source: www.coca-cola.co.uk/drinks

Question

Coca-Cola has many brands in the UK (as listed above). Why do you think this is?

Strategies and risk

When assessing these strategies, Ansoff considered the risk involved. For example, market penetration may be seen as low risk in the sense that the business already knows the customers and the product. However, the danger is that if anything happened to hit demand in this market the business could be vulnerable. By diversifying, the business could be spreading risk in that it now has another customer base and product. However, there is an inherent risk in developing products where you may have had no experience and in targeting markets you do not know.

MANAGEMENT TASK

You have a well-known sportswear clothing brand. You are considering moving into the gym and fitness club market. What might be the arguments for and against this?

9.2 BUSINESS INSIGHT: ELECTRIC CARS

Senior managers will constantly be scanning the environment to see where the business should be headed next. As the internal and external environments change, so too will the organization. For example, Sir James Dyson, founder of Dyson, recently announced he wanted the company to develop an electric car to add to its portfolio of vacuum cleaners, fans, and hairdryers that the company already manufacturers. He plans to invest £2bn ($2.7bn), divided evenly between battery technology and vehicle development. A traditional carmaker typically spends £1bn on a new chassis or platform alone. This shows that the barriers to entry in the battery-powered vehicle business are much lower than those in the market for cars with complex internal-combustion engines, which would cost far more to develop. However, success may be more difficult.

Dyson says that he has assembled a team of over 400 people and aims to launch a vehicle in 2020. Dyson is likely to aim first at the luxury market, which is where the electric vehicle producer Tesla has already been operating. The company will face challenges in the car market. Established global car companies sometimes produce in excess of

10 million vehicles a year; this scale brings them financial protection and the chance to spread huge development costs across a large portfolio of models.

And there are other challenges.

- While the market for electric cars is growing, so are the competitors. Jaguar is due to launch the iPace, a competitor to Tesla's Model S, and Porsche, Audi, and BMW all have electric models that will arrive by 2020. They may be joined by others from a host of startups.

- Getting to the buyers will be costly. Tesla has had to spend heavily setting up its own retail network to sidestep the established dealerships of big carmakers.

- The badge on the front of a luxury car is all-important. A brand shared with washroom hand-dryers may fail to entice consumers.

Source: BBC, https://www.bbc.co.uk/news/business-41399497

Questions

1. Why do you think Dyson has chosen to develop a car?
2. Do you think this was a good move by Dyson?

How you might choose a strategy

The strategy of a business depends largely on:

- the internal strengths and weaknesses of a business;
- the external opportunities and threats that exist.

A strategy may attempt to address each of these factors.

- A business may build on its existing strengths and leverage these, for example by extending the brand into a new market or, as Dyson hopes to do, using its technical expertise to develop a new product.

- A business may work to overcome its weaknesses. For example, if the business has a weak online presence it might take over another business that has a strength in this area.

- A business may exploit its opportunities. For example, if there is a growing demand for the product in a particular overseas market, this might be the time to expand there.

- A businesss may aim to protect itself against its threats. For example, if the business was vulnerable to government intervention in its market to regulate pricing, it might look to adjust to prices downwards slightly to avoid further government scrutiny.

MANAGEMENT TASK

You run a coach company around the major cities of the UK. The market is stagnant, and you are looking for growth. Produce an example of four different strategies, according to Ansoff's model, that you might adopt.

Strategic planning

Strategic planning needs to take account of the external environment in which it operates. This is because these changes open up new opportunities and create new threats.

The external environment can be categorized in terms of micro and macro environments.

- The micro environment is the immediate environment of the business, such as its suppliers, distributors, and rivals. This can be analysed using Porter's five forces model, discussed in the next subsection.

- The macro environment is the wider external environment of the business, such as the economy and the population of the country. A business cannot directly control these macro factors but has to anticipate how they might change.

The micro environment

The micro environment can be analysed using Michael Porter's five forces model, illustrated in Figure 9.2.

The relative power of these forces can help explain why some industries appear to be more profitable over significant periods of time than others. The effects of these forces are listed in Table 9.2.

The five forces may be explained as follows.

- The power of buyers (customers): if you are dependent on relatively few customers, then these buyers will have the power to push down prices, and this will reduce the profits of your business.

Figure 9.2 Porter's five forces

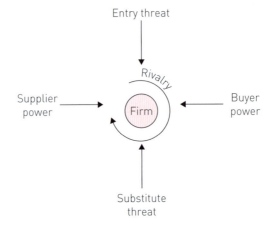

Table 9.2 The effect on profitability of a change in the five forces

Force	Effect
Buyer power	High buyer power reduces profitability as buyers push prices down
Supplier power	High supplier power reduces profitability as suppliers push up their prices
Rivalry	High rivalry reduces profitability profits have to be shared out
Substitute threat	High substitute threat power reduces profitability as customers will switch to alternatives
Entry threat	High entry threat reduces profitability: high profits encourage more entry so that profits have to be shared out among more businesses

- The power of suppliers: if, for example, your business has relatively few suppliers they will have power over you. This means they may be able to push up their prices so they gain more profits at the extent of your business that is buying from them. This reduces the profitability of your business and increases the suppliers' profitability.

- The degree of rivalry in an industry: this describes competition between providers of the same type of good or service, such as two smartphone producers. The greater the rivalry between businesses, the more profits have to be shared out and the lower the profitability of any one business.

- The ease of substitution: a substitute is an alternative way of meeting a customer's requirement. For example, you might put your drink in an aluminium container or a plastic container. If it is easy for buyers to find alternative ways of meeting their needs (e.g. catching a train instead of a bus), then the businesses in the industry will have less ability to push up prices and this will restrict their profitability.

- The entry threat: if it is relatively easy for other businesses to enter the industry, this means that the existing businesses will not be able to make particularly high rates of profit. If they do, other businesses will enter the market to benefit as well, and this brings down any one firm's profitability.

READ MORE

You can read Porter's classic article on the five forces in

Porter, M.E. (2008), 'The Five Competitive Forces That Shape Strategy', *Harvard Business Review* Vol. 86, No. 1 (January), pp. 78–93.

9.3 **QUICK CHECK**

For each of the following statements, say whether it is true or false.
The five forces in Porter's model include

a. supplier power.

b. retention threat.

c. rivalry.

d. complement threat.

e. buyer power.

MANAGEMENT TASK

What can you do to make the five forces in your industry more favourable to your business?

The macro environment

The macro environment includes changes to the law, changes in the social environment, and developments in technology, which can all affect the business in many ways. There are various frameworks used in business to categorize these macro factors, such as PESTEL (political, economic, social, technological, environmental, and legal).

If you do not regularly review the external environment your business might experience strategic drift. This occurs when the strategy adopted falls behind the market trend. For example, Tesco carried on opening hypermarkets at a time when the market was buying more online; the company had to take stock and review its strategy. Nokia was slow to see the appeal of smartphones and lost its mobile phone dominance to the iPhone.

KEY CONCEPTS

The **micro environment** refers to the immediate environment of a business, such as its suppliers and distributors. The **macro environment** of a business refers to factors outside of a business's control, such as the political, economic, social, and technological environments. **Strategic drift** occurs when the strategy of a business is no longer suitable given its strengths and weaknesses and the environment in which it operates.

RESEARCH TASK

Select an industry and undertake a five forces analysis of it. Decide whether each of the forces is high or low and justify your decisions.

MANAGEMENT TASK

What would you say is the biggest issue in the external environment facing UK businesses today? Justify your choice.

9.3 BUSINESS INSIGHT: TOYS R US

If your strategy goes badly wrong your business may end up having to close down. If the business cannot pay its bills, it is illiquid and may declare itself bankrupt. For example, Toys R Us recently filed for bankruptcy protection in the US and Canada in an attempt to restructure its debts. Toys R Us had been a major retailer in the US toy market but it has struggled in recent years against online companies such as Amazon. Toys R Us has nearly 1,600 stores and 64,000 employees.

The BBC reported on the Toys R Us bankruptcy in September 2017.

> The bankruptcy filing is more evidence that traditional retailers are struggling in the US, as online retailers continue to capture market share. [. . .] But the company is also looking to achieve high online sales to secure its future, with recently launched web stores for its products. GlobalData Retail estimates that in 2016 about 13.7% of all toy sales were made online, up from 6.5% five years ago.
>
> 'The past decade has seen a dramatic change in the domestic toy market with new channels, increased competition, and new technology all having a deleterious impact on the sector and traditional toy stores. Unfortunately, Toys R Us has not responded effectively in terms of its strategy to these challenges', said Neil Saunders, managing director of GlobalData Retail. [. . .]
>
> Toys 'R' Us wants to use the bankruptcy process to restructure and make the company viable over the long term. Enormous debt levels are its most immediate problem.
>
> Various lenders, including a JPMorgan-led bank syndicate and some of the company's existing lenders, have committed more than $3bn in new financing to turn the company around.

Source: www.bbc.co.uk/news/business-41316205

Question
Why do you think Toys R Us allowed itself to get in this position?

BUSINESS CASE QUESTION: CAN YOU NOW ANSWER . . .

Some of Monarch's problems seem to be due to its managers choosing the wrong strategy.

What do you think this means? And why do you think it might have happened?

The economy and the macro-economic environment

Changes in the macro environment will affect the strategy of a business. For example, advances in technology mean some businesses are switching from 'bricks' (physical stores) to 'clicks' (online operations). One important factor in the external environment is the economy. Economic factors include economic growth, prices, unemployment levels, and international trade; changes in these can be significant in terms of the right strategy a business needs to adopt. Just think of the impact of the decision by the UK to leave the European Union ('Brexit'). This has led to huge amounts of uncertainty about what will happen politically and economically in the UK. Businesses are unsure about the way in which the UK would end up trading with the Europe and the rest of the world, and what would happen in relation to issues such as the flow of labour into, and out of, the country.

Economic change is largely beyond the control of any one business, and yet it can have a major effect on its costs and revenue. Managers will want to identify possible changes in these economic factors and consider how they might affect their particular business. It is important to plan, therefore, for economic change.

9.4 BUSINESS INSIGHT: RISKS AND UNCERTAINTIES

When public companies produce their accounts they state the potential risks and uncertainties they face. Look at this statement by Starbucks made in 2018.

> These risks and uncertainties include, but are not limited to, fluctuations in U.S. and international economies and currencies, our ability to preserve, grow and leverage our brands, potential negative effects of incidents involving food or beverage-borne illnesses, tampering, adulteration, contamination or mislabeling, potential negative effects of material breaches of our information technology systems to the extent we experience a material breach, material failures of our information technology systems, costs associated with, and the successful execution of, the company's initiatives and plans, including the recently completed purchase of the remaining 50% ownership of our East China joint venture and our continuing growth in China, the acceptance of the company's products by our customers, our ability to obtain financing on acceptable terms, the impact of competition, coffee, dairy and other raw materials prices and availability, the effect of legal proceedings, the effects of the U.S. Tax Cuts and Jobs Act and related guidance and regulations that may be promulgated, and other risks detailed in the company filings with the Securities and Exchange Commission.

Source: news.starbucks.com/press-releases/starbucks-unveils-innovative-growth-strategy-at-2018-annual-meeting

Question

Identify economic factors in Starbuck's macro envirnment that create risks and uncertainty for the business.

SWOT analysis

To develop a strategy, managers may consider the strengths and weaknesses of the internal position of their organization, as well as the opportunities and threats presented by external factors. This approach is known as SWOT analysis (strengths, weaknesses, opportunities, threats).

For example, the strengths of a business might include

- a portfolio of strong brands;
- a good distribution network;
- a healthy cash position.

Weaknesses might include

- a high proportion of faulty items produced;
- low levels of profitability;
- a weak senior management team.

Opportunities in the environment might include

- the opportunity to develop new products and services;
- the opportunity to expand overseas.

Threats in the environment might include

- new competitors entering the market;
- increased energy prices.

KEY CONCEPT

SWOT analysis is a very common technique used to identify a suitable strategy. It involves managers examining the internal position of the business (strengths and weaknesses) and the external position of the business (opportunities and threats).

9.5 BUSINESS INSIGHT: SWOT ANALYSIS OF NEXT

Next plc is a retailer with over 530 stores and a retail area of nearly 8 million square feet. It retails clothes, footwear, electrical and electronic appliances, furniture, furnishings, home decor, shoes, and lifestyle accessories for men, women, and children. The Next Directory segment of the company sells its merchandise through a direct mail catalogue and a transactional website that has 4.7 million active customers in the UK. The catalogue offered by the company features home improvement products and extensive collections for men, women, and children. The catalogue is provided to internet customers to aid their shopping activities.

Strengths

- The company has a multi-channel strategy selling through stores, online, and its directory.
- There is a strong inventory/turnover ratio, meaning its stock levels are relatively low compared to its sales.

Weaknesses

- Revenues fell in 2016 and 2017.

Opportunities

- Next is in a good position to benefit from growing interest in own-label products as shoppers look for more budget products.
- There is an expanding retail market in the UK and the company could continue to build on its sales of apparel for men, women, and children, digital art, lifestyle accessories, footwear, home decor, garden and outdoor products, and electrical equipment through its stores.

Threats

- Foreign exchange risks: Next Plc. operates in many parts of the world and is exposed to fluctuations in foreign exchange rates. The company reports financials in the British pound and therefore its revenue is exposed to the volatility of the British pound against other functional currencies such as US dollar, Euro, Chinese yuan renminbi, Hong Kong dollar, and Korean won, among others.
- Labour costs in the UK are rising. Increasing manpower costs could impact the cost structure of the company. In the financial year 2017, the company employed 31,238 associates. It has taken several initiatives to expand its stores, which requires increasing its employee base. Therefore, rising manpower cost could impact the stability and operational efficiency of the company.
- Fashion trends are evolving. Operating in the fashion retail industry, Next plc's business is subject to a significant risk of constantly changing fashion trends in the market. Fashion has a limited shelf-life, and there is always a risk that a few collections will not be well received by the customers. It is very important for the group to supply the merchandise in the right volumes and achieve the right balance in the mix between fashion basics and the latest trends.

Source: https://store.marketline.com/report/ccc3f8a7-c028-44d4-bc09-0b6d769d0215--next-plc-strategy-swot-and-corporate-finance-report/

Questions

1. How might conducting a SWOT analysis be useful for strategic planning for Next?
2. Why should a SWOT analysis be undertaken regularly?
3. If you were the managers of Next plc, what actions might you take following the SWOT analysis above?

9.1 DOING THE BUSINESS MATHS

State whether you think each of the following is a strength or a weakness. Explain your reasoning.

Item	Index (where industry average is 100)	Strength or weakness? Why?
Labour productivity	80	
Absenteeism	120	
Gearing	300	
Unit costs	130	
Research and development spending	65	
% of repeat sales	110	

9.4 QUICK CHECK

SWOT analysis includes which of the following? Analysis of . . .

a. strengths

b. superiority

c. weaknesses

d. opportunities

e. threats

f. turnaround

RESEARCH TASK

Choose a business you know. Produce a SWOT analysis for it. What do you think are the strategic implications of this SWOT analysis for the business?

9.6 BUSINESS INSIGHT: TRAVEL AND TOURISM

According to the World Travel and Tourism Council, travel and tourism's direct contribution to world income was 3.2% in 2017. The travel and tourism sector continues to grow faster than this and is expected to grow by around 4% per year over the next ten years. Customers are becoming more confident in the world economy, and this means they are more willing to travel. Within the growing leisure travel sector, package travel is particularly popular now compared to ten years ago and continues to grow. As well as being sensitive to changes in the economy, the travel sector is also vulnerable to changes in the political environment and events such as terrorist attacks. Other factors include the regulatory environment—the UK's decision to leave the European Union, for example, may make travel more difficult and expensive. Government decisions can also be important. For example, in the UK the decision by the government to allow the building of a third runway at Heathrow will allow more passenger traffic.

Source: https://www.wttc.org/-/media/files/reports/economic-impact-research/regions-2018/world2018.pdf

Questions

1. What factors influence the demand for travel and tourism?

2. Based on your assessment of the future, do you think travel and tourism is likely to be a growth sector?

3. What future changes in this sector might create opportunities and threats?

Strategic positioning

Once a business has chosen which market(s) to compete in, it will want to decide where it wants to position itself. Does it want to be a budget provider or a premium provider, for example? Consider the hotel market—both Travelodge and Hilton provide hotel rooms, but they compete in different sectors of the market.

The decision on where to position your business will depend on the strengths of your organization and the external environment, including economic factors. In 2008, many economies faced difficult times following a global economic crisis. In the UK there was a great deal of uncertainty about the state of the economy and whether the economy would grow in the future. This led to a shift towards discounters such as Aldi and Lidl, away from the major supermarkets such as Tesco and Sainsbury's.

KEY CONCEPT

Strategic positioning refers to the position of a business relative to others within a market.

MANAGEMENT TASK

You are the manager of Tesco plc. You have seen the market share of discounters such as Aldi and Lidl increase in recent years. Should you change your strategy to compete head-on with the discounters?

READ MORE

The classic text on strategic planning is

Johnson, G., and Scholes, K. (1999), *Exploring Corporate Strategy*, London: Prentice Hall Europe.

Strategic decision makers

Strategic decisions are often one-off decisions. For example, if you decide to bid for a company it is unlikely that you will have done that before for the same business. The same is true when investing in new product development: you may or may not have developed other products before, but you won't have developed this one. This means that strategic decisions involve a high level of uncertainty. This in turn means they involve risk. These decisions are likely to be taken at the highest level by the directors, and therefore it is important that the composition of the board has suitable experience and skills. The quality and experience of the leadership team is a major influence on whether the right strategy is adopted. Selecting and building the right team at the top (as illustrated in Figure 9.3) is, therefore, key to business success.

The shareholders are the owners of a company. Usually a shareholder has one vote per share. Shareholders elect directors to represent them and oversee what the managers are doing. In a company there can be a difference between those that own the business (shareholders) and those that run the business (managers).

Figure 9.3 The leadership team

9.7 BUSINESS INSIGHT: THE CO-OP

Whether or not a company's chosen strategy is the right one is ultimately the responsibility of its senior management team. If a strategy goes wrong, questions will be asked about the quality of the senior management team.

In 2014 the Co-op Bank came close to collapse following a disastrous merging with the Britannia Building Society. A report on the problems suggested that they were mainly caused by poor management and governance. Not enough checks were made by the Co-op's senior managers before the 2009 integration with Britannia. As a result of the deal, the group lost around £3.5bn—half of its net worth—in the four years after the deal.

A government investigation found that the Co-op was led by a board totally unable—because of a lack of experience—to do its job. The BBC reported on this in May 2014:

> The report by former City minister Lord Myners says the group's current board is 'manifestly dysfunctional'. [. . .] [The Co-op's] former chairman Paul Flowers was arrested last year following allegations that he was involved in a drug deal. [. . .]
>
> [Lord Myners] recommended a smaller board for the group, that is made up of members with similar skills and experience to those at competing companies—such as Tesco and Sainsbury's in food and Nationwide in lending.
>
> The Co-op has 48 area committees—the grassroots of the organization—which each have 10–12 members. They elect members of seven regional boards who in turn elect 15 members of a board that can be as large as 23 members. There are also boards for the food business; the bank, which the group no longer fully owns; and specialist businesses, which include the pharmacies and funeral care. The Co-op calls these subsidiary boards.
>
> 'The group's bottom-up, competitive election process provides no rigour for assessing the commercial capability levels of candidates as there is no meaningful competency bar in place. Similarly, it provides no scope to balance the capabilities and fill skills gaps', says the report.
>
> Source: https://www.bbc.co.uk/news/business-27302820

Question
Why do you think the composition of the board of directors is important for strategic success?

9.5 QUICK CHECK

For each of the following statements, say whether it is true or false.

a. Shareholders are owners of a company.

b. All shareholders have one vote.

c. Directors are elected by customers.

d. Company managers are always the owners of the company.

MANAGEMENT TASK

You are trying to create the perfect board of directors for your multinational food retail business. What would the composition of this board look like? Explain your choices.

Why does the strategy of a business matter?

Strategy determines the direction in which a business is headed. Strategic decisions are taken by the senior management of the business and determine the long-term success of the organization. Think of the car industry and the radical changes that are occurring there, with the increasing demand for electric cars and with developments in technology leading to cars that can drive themselves, diagnose their own faults, and plan their own routes. The managers of businesses such as Ford and VW have to ensure they are aware of such trends and are making the right strategic decisions. Which are the key developments that they should be adopting? Which are the ones that will not actually turn into a major shift? These questions will influence where resources are allocated and will determine the long-term survival and success of the business.

READ MORE

If you would like to find out more about strategy, you can read

Porter, M.E. (1996), 'What is Strategy?', *Harvard Business Review* Vol. 74, No. 6 (November–December), pp. 61–78.

Strategic planning and economic forecasting

Effective strategy requires an understanding of where your markets are and making sure you are in the right place in the right form. Newspaper businesses are rapidly reshaping themselves to be online media businesses. Car companies are developing electric cars and more 'intelligent cars'. Music companies are realizing that with the increasing use of streaming, their income will come from tours and merchandising. Universities are looking for ways of leveraging their assets in a digital world. Senior managers need to be visionaries and prepare. Others can manage the here and now, but those at the top have to look ahead. This involves thinking about all the major trends that could be relevant, including changes in the world political systems, population trends, and technological change. Managers must also think about where the economy is headed. The problem is that this is very difficult to do—not even the experts do it very well! However, managers should look at economic forecasts to consider the possible impact on their strategies.

Economic forecasts are predictions of what will happen to key economic variables such as income, inflation, and interest rates. These are all important influences on the environment in which a business operates, and so managers need to reduce their risk by anticipating and planning for them. To do this, economists build models of the economy, trying to establish links between different variables so that they can forecast what might happen next. Of course, these models are not always correct, and so economists are constantly evaluating and refining them. Models are not necessarily intended to directly reflect reality, but provided they are successful at predicting outcomes they can still be valid. However, the accuracy of a model will depend a great deal on its underlying assumptions; if these prove to be inaccurate, then the model's forecast will be inaccurate. Different economists will make different assumptions, which is why we get different economic predictions. The difficulty facing economists is that they are trying to anticipate the outcomes of millions of decisions by businesses, households, employees, and governments and how these all combine. Unfortunately, these individuals do not always act in a way that is predictable.

In a BBC interview with the economist Prakash Loungani, he discussed a study he had done for the International Monetary Fund in which he analysed the accuracy of economic forecasters. He noted that almost everyone failed to predict the decline in economies in 2008 and that economists had failed to predict 148 of the past 150 recessions. Part of the problem, he argued, was that there wasn't much of a reputational gain to be had by predicting a recession that others had missed. If you disagreed with the consensus, you would be met with scepticism. The downside of getting it wrong was more personally damaging than the upside of getting it right (https://www.bbc.co.uk/programmes/p058qrkt).

Forecasts are also made less trustworthy because of a feedback loop. So, if a meteorologist says it will rain, the fact that you take an umbrella out with you does not affect the weather. But if an economist forecasts that inflation will rise by 3 per cent and people react by asking for at least a 3 per cent rise in wages, the model has already changed. Inflation is now likely to rise by more than 3 per cent because of the wage increase. The simple fact that the forecast exists changes the reality it is trying to predict. Economic forecasts therefore need to be treated with some caution.

Emergent strategy vs. planned

What you intend to do to achieve your objective is your planned strategy. However, what you actually end up doing may be different from what you intended. Changes in circumstances, external events, or internal events may lead to a slightly different course of action. What actually happens is known as the emergent strategy. Think of what you imagine you will be doing in the next ten years of your life—that is the plan. What you end up doing could be very different for all sorts of reasons—a strategy may emerge.

What is important is to keep checking where you are and where you want to be. Even if you end up taking a different turn from what you initially imagined, this is fine provided you know where you are and where you are going to. SWOT analysis and strategic planning is an ongoing process and may take you on a very interesting journey. In its history, Nokia has produced paper, toilet paper, and tyres as well as consumer electronics. WPP, the global media business, began as Wire Plastic Products making shopping baskets. Businesses need to keep moving. For example, Sky recently announced it would be making all its channels and content available online. This is a response to greater competition from the likes of streaming services such as Netflix and Amazon and allows it to enter new markets more easily than through satellite TV broadcasting.

SUMMARY

Managers must look ahead and decide what their business should aim to achieve, and how best to get there. The strategy is the plan the business should follow. If the strategy is clear, all the different parts of the business should be able to plan for their part of the business and how it fits in with the overall direction of the business. Strategic decisions are critical to the performance of the business. Managers will look at the possible future changes in the micro and macro environment and try to work out how best to move the business forward in these circumstances.

KEY LEARNING POINTS

- A strategy is a long-term plan for a business to achieve its objectives.
- A strategy usually involves high levels of investment and risk.
- The strategy of a business is usually based on the internal strengths and weaknesses of a business and the opportunities and threats created by the external environment (SWOT).
- The micro environment of a business can be analysed using Porter's five forces. The macro environment can be analysed using PESTEL analysis.
- Strategies will need to change over time to be effective.
- Strategies that emerge may be different from those that were planned.
- The Ansoff matrix shows strategies in terms of new and existing products and markets.
- Strategic positioning decisions show where the business wants to be within the market relative to competitors.

BUSINESS CASE EXTENSION QUESTIONS

1. Select two airlines and analyse the strategies they have adopted.
2. Identify a business that has shut down recently. Analyse the factors that led to its closure.
3. Identify a business that is growing fast. Analyse the reasons why its strategy has been successful.

QUICK QUESTIONS

1. What is meant by strategy?
2. What is the difference between an emergent and a planned strategy?
3. What is meant by SWOT analysis?
4. What is the role of the board of directors?
5. What is meant by the macro-economic environment?
6. What is the difference between market development and market penetration strategies?
7. What is the difference between new product development and diversification strategies?
8. Why is economic forecasting difficult?
9. What is the difference between buyer power and supplier power in Porter's five forces model?
10. What is the difference between rivalry and substitute threat in Porter's five forces model?

Strategies for growth

Your business was recently bought out by a private equity business, and you are being asked to grow your business to get to the scale their investors think is required for high returns. You want to know how best to grow your business and the possible problems you might encounter.

Growing a business is a common business strategy. It leads to 'top line' growth. In this chapter we consider how managers might grow their business, the reasons why they might want to do this, and the problems they might encounter.

BY THE END OF THIS CHAPTER YOU WILL BE ABLE TO . . .

- explain why growth matters
- explain how a business could grow
- analyse the advantages and disadvantages of different forms of growth
- analyse the problems of growth
- analyse how managers might try to overcome the problems of growth

BUSINESS CASE

In 2016 the supermarket chain Sainsbury's made a successful takeover bid of £1.4bn for the Home Retail Group to form a larger food and general merchandise retailer. This was a major strategic decision for the business, as reported in the *Guardian* in February 2016:

> [Sainsbury's] has promised to pay Home Retail shareholders 55p in cash and 0.321 Sainsbury's shares for their shares, valuing Home Retail at £1.1bn [or 143.7p a share based on Sainsbury's share price]. Sainsbury's said the takeover would cre-ate the UK's largest non-food retailer—ahead of John Lewis or Marks & Spencer—with about 2,000 stores and 100,000 products. It plans to put Argos outlets in Sains-bury's large stores [see Figure 10.1].

Excess supermarket space was built up in the 1990s and 2000s when supermarkets com-peted to open giant out-of-town branches. Those stores are now less popular after many

Figure 10.1 Sainsbury's and Argos : information produced to explain the reasons for the proposed merger

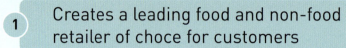

1 Creates a leading food and non-food retailer of choce for customers

Complementary customer base

Sainsbury's   *Over 2/3 of UK households have shopped at Sainsbury's over the last year* [1]

Argos   *c. 2/3 of UK households have shopped at Argos over the last year* [2]

Sainsbury's Argos   *Over 40% of UK households have shopped in both Sainsbury's and Argos* [2-3]

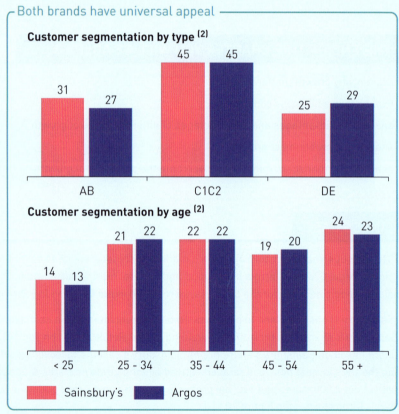

Both brands have universal appeal

Customer segmentation by type [2]

	AB	C1C2	DE
Sainsbury's	31	45	25
Argos	27	45	29

Customer segmentation by age [2]

	< 25	25 - 34	35 - 44	45 - 54	55 +
Sainsbury's	14	21	22	19	24
Argos	13	22	22	20	23

Sainsbury's   Argos

Notes:
1. Source: Nielsen
2. Source: HPI customer survey November 2015 - 2,000 households surveyed of which 1,292 had shopped in Argos in the last 12 months, 1,235 had shopped in Sainsbury's in the last 3 months and 300 had shopped in neither
3. As per HPI customer survey November 2015 there is a c. 40% overlap between customers that had shopped in Argos in the last 12 months and the customers that had shopped in Sainsbury's in the last 3 months

households have stopped doing the big weekly shop in favour of more frequent visits to smaller convenience stores.

Sainsbury's motive was to help it take on Amazon and diversify away from the very competitive food retail market. Closing Argos stores (at no cost, as it just involves not renewing the lease) to open up Argos concessions in Sainsbury's stores may make sense financially at least in the short term. The *Guardian* went on to report:

> Sainsbury's is also interested in Argos's delivery network and IT systems, which it believes will help it take on Amazon, the US online retailer that is increasing its presence in the UK grocery market. [. . .] The rapid growth of the discounters Aldi and Lidl has also created a price war, slashing supermarket profits. Sainsbury's argues that buying Argos will allow it to offer a broader range of goods at its stores and offer a wider delivery service—both to homes and click and collect points in stores. Argos outlets will also provide a useful filler for spare space in Sainsbury's largest outlets.

The combined business offered a multi-product, multi-channel proposition, with fast delivery networks. The company hopes that adding Argos will let it sell more products to customers and give them an extra reason to visit its stores. There is a great deal of overlap between the chains' customers, and a handful of Argos concessions in Sainsbury's shops have traded well.

Sources: https://www.theguardian.com/business/2016/feb/02/sainsburys-agrees-terms-13bn-deal-buy-home-retail-group; Sainsbury's website

BUSINESS CASE QUESTIONS

This chapter will help you answer the following questions.

1. What factors do you think influenced Sainsbury's strategic decision to buy HRG?
2. Why do you think it decided to do this rather than invest in its own internal growth?
3. What risks do you think this strategy of growth brings?
4. What actions can Sainsbury's managers take to reduce these risks?

How do we measure the growth of a business?

There are many different measures of the size of a business. Typically, managers might measure the value of sales or the value of assets. In some cases they might measure the number of employees, the number of stores or the number of vehicles.

In the UK, the size of a business is often measured by the number of employees.

- A small business is a business with 0 to 49 employees.
- A medium-size business has 50 to 249 employees.
- A large business has 250 or more employees.

ANALYSING THE DATA

The vast majority of businesses in the UK are classified as small in terms of the number of people employed. However, large businesses account for most of the turnover. These comparisons are shown in Figures 10.2 and 10.3 and in Table 10.1.

Source: www.gov.uk/government/uploads/system/uploads/attachment_data/file/663235/bpe_2017_statistical_release.pdf

Questions

1. Consider the scale of small businesses in the UK in terms of employment, turnover, and number of businesses. Can you explain this data?

2. Look at the trends in Figure 10.3. What do you think has caused these trends?

Table 10.1: Estimated number of businesses in the UK private sector and their associated employment and turnover, by size of business, start of 2017

	Businesses	Employment (thousands)	Turnover[1] (£ million)
All businesses	5,694,515	26,723	3,739,171
SMEs (0–249 employees)	5,687,230	16,146	1,904,912
Small businesses (0–49 employees)	5,653,375	12,849	1,363,996
With no employees[2]	4,327,680	4,697	271,574
All employers	1,366,835	22,026	3,467,597
of which:			
1–9 employees	1,117,810	4,093	552,637
10–49 employees	207,885	4,059	539,786
50–249 employees	33,855	3,297	540,915
250 or more employees	7,285	10,577	1,834,259

1. Total turnover figures exclude Section K (financial and insurance activities), where turnover is not available on a comparable basis.

2. 'With no employees' includes sole proprietorships and partnerships with only the self-employed owner-manager(s), and companies with a single employee, assumed to be a director.

Figure 10.2 Contribution of different sized business to total population, employment, and turnover, start of 2017 (UK)

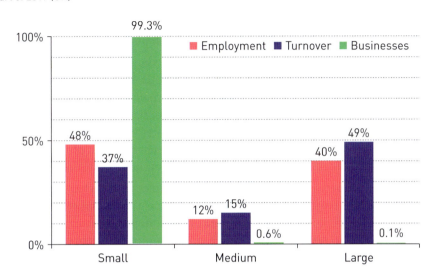

Figure 10.3 Growth in the number of UK private sector businesses by size band, 2000 to 2017 (base year = 2000)

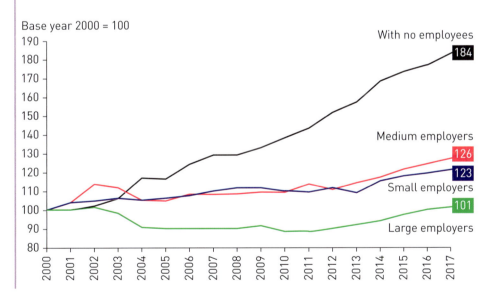

Why do businesses want to grow?

Growth is a common objective of a business. Partly this is because it shows the business is moving forward and it is one way managers can judge their success. 'When I took this business over we had 20 stores; now we have 50' would be a typical way that a manager might measure her own success in the role and use as evidence to others that she has been successful. 'When I started in this business we had 20 stores; now we have 10' might not sound quite so impressive. Growth shows that the business has momentum and is progressing. Standing still might suggest complacency or a lack of initiative.

However, there are many other reasons why growth might appeal.

- A larger scale of operations can generate internal economies of scale which reduce the unit cost. The benefit of lower unit costs is that a business can increase its profit margins if it maintains the same price. Alternatively, it allows the business to reduce its price and still be profitable. Greater scale is therefore an important source of efficiency and provides the ability to lower prices but retain profitability. This is a driving force in industries such as brewing, cars, pharmaceuticals, tobacco, and banking, where there are relatively few huge businesses.

- Greater scale allows a business to dominate a market with higher market share. This dominance may allow the business to become a price maker rather than a price taker. This could allow it to push prices up. It might also reduce the pressure on the business to need to be innovative and to improve efficiency.

- Two businesses may benefit from each other's strengths when they join together. For example, one may have a strong research team while another may have a good distribution network. One may have a good understanding of one part of the world; another may have a good insight into a different region. Combining these strengths may help the combined business become much stronger than the two individual parts. Synergy occurs when the combined business is worth more than the individual parts. Synergy can be summarized as $2 + 2 = 5$.

KEY CONCEPTS

Internal economies of scale occur when unit costs fall as the scale of production increases.
Synergy refers to the benefits from two or more businesses working together and sharing resources, so that the combined business is worth more than the individual ones.

Forms of business growth

Growth may be internal or external. Internal growth occurs when a business sells more of its products. For example, effective marketing increases demand and sales. External growth occurs when one business joins with another; this is known as 'integration'.

Forms of external growth are mergers and acquisitions.

- **A merger** occurs when one business joins together with another to form a new business entity. If you have shares in business A and this merges with business B, you now have shares in the new organization C (which is made up of A and B).

- Acquisition (also called takeover) occurs when one business gains control of another business. If you have shares in business A and this takes over business B, you continue to have shares in business A but these now include ownership of B as well. To take over another company you might offer cash for their shares, or you might offer some shares in your own business (this is called a paper offer), or a combination of the two.

10.1 DOING THE BUSINESS MATHS

Complete the following table to show economies of scale.

Output (units)	Total cost (£)	Unit cost (£) = total cost ÷ output
2,000	30,000	15
3,000	42,000	
4,000	48,000	
5,000	50,000	
6,000	60,000	
7,000	77,000	

Question
At which level of output does the business stop benefiting from internal economies of scale?

KEY CONCEPTS

A **merger** occurs when two or more businesses join together to create a new joint business entity. An **acquisition** (or **takeover**) occurs when one business gains control of another.

MANAGEMENT TASK

You are considering a strategy of growing through takeover. Outline the three key factors you think you should take into account when choosing a target business.

There are different forms of external integration. These are typically categorized in terms of which industries are involved and which stage of production the businesses involved are at.

Types of integration are horizontal, vertical, and conglomerate.

- **Horizontal integration** occurs when businesses in the same industry and at the same stage of the production process join together. Two food retailers joining together or two pharmaceutical companies joining together would be examples of horizontal integration. The motive behind this form of integration is usually to reduce the degree of competition in the market and to gain internal economies of scale and market power. You may decide to undertake horizontal integration to remove a rival and gain more market share, for example.

- **Vertical integration** occurs when a business joins with another business at a different stage of the same production process. This may be 'forward vertical integration', when a producer joins with another business at a stage closer to the customers. For example, a car producer might buy car dealerships. This helps ensure access to a market. 'Backward vertical integration' occurs when a business joins with a business further down the supply chain away from the end customer. This is usually undertaken to gain control of supply and to control costs and quality more effectively.

- **Conglomerate integration** occurs when one business joins with a business in a different industry. This can help reduce the overall risk of the business by operating in different markets and therefore being less vulnerable to changes in any one of them. If you are worried about demand growth in your existing markets, you may decide to diversify through conglomerate integration.

10.1 QUICK CHECK

For each of the following statements, say whether it is true or false.

a. A merger occurs when two or more organizations join together to form a new one.

b. A takeover occurs when one business gains control over another.

c. Vertical integration occurs between businesses at the same stage of the production process.

d. Horizontal integration may lead to internal economies of scale.

10.1 BUSINESS INSIGHT: CINEWORLD AND REGAL

In 2017 Cineworld agreed to buy US cinema chain Regal in a $3.6bn (£2.7bn) deal that was to create the world's second largest cinema group. The BBC reported in December 2017:

The new cinema giant will operate in 10 countries, and have 9,500 screens across the US and Europe.

The deal gave Cineworld access to North America, which has the largest box office market in the world. Cineworld currently has more than 2,000 screens across 221 sites and also owned the Picturehouse Cinemas chain. [. . .]

The deal is a big bet on the cinema sector, which is under threat from streaming sites such as Netflix, Amazon Prime and iTunes which allow viewers to watch films at home.

In the US this summer's takings at the box office were at their lowest level for more than two decades. But annual takings have been more than $11bn for the last two years.

And in the UK, cinema attendance is up around 8% so far this year with around 165 million tickets sold each year. The numbers are still a far cry from UK cinema-going's peak after World War Two which saw a record 1.63 billion cinema admissions in 1946.

Cineworld chief executive Mooky Greidinger said he expected to bring Regal's profit margins to nearer Cineworld's. Currently Cineworld has a 22% margin, while Regal has just short of a 20% profit margin. [. . .]

This year, Cineworld's audiences have been boosted by blockbusters *Dunkirk* and *Despicable Me 3*, with recent big releases including *Paddington 2* and *Justice League*. [. . .]

Cineworld has agreed to pay $23 a share for Regal, and is funding the deal mainly by asking investors to stump up £1.7bn by buying new shares through a procedure known as a rights issue.

The deal gave the combined group more than 9,500 screens and made it the world's second largest cinema chain by number of screens behind AMC Theatres, owned by China's Dalian Wanda Group. In December 2017, the *Financial Times* reported Greidinger as saying: 'Consolidation is an important move forward and the best practice we have successfully rolled out across Europe will be the key driver to continued success.'

Sources: BBC, https://www.bbc.co.uk/news/business-42234673; M. Ahmed and K. Martin (2017), 'Cineworld Clinches $3.6bn Reverse Takeover of Regal', *Financial Times* (5 December), https://www.ft.com/content/6cadfe02-d995-11e7-a039-c64b1c09b482

Question

Why do you think consolidation is important in the cinema sector?

10.2 BUSINESS INSIGHT: CHANGES IN SNACKING HABITS

The BBC reported on 18 December 2017 that the Hershey Company and Campbell Soup had recently spent billions of dollars to buy rival food businesses.

Hershey said its $1.6bn (£1.2bn) purchase of popcorn and Tyrrells crisps maker Amplify would help it turn into 'a snacking powerhouse'.

Meanwhile, Campbell Soup said it would splash $4.89bn on tortilla chip and pretzel crisps maker Snyder's-Lance. Both deals show how US firms are increasingly trying to cope with a shift in buying habits, with many people favouring smaller, more artisanal brands as well as food that is perceived to be healthier.

Amplify's popcorn brand Skinny Pop advertises itself as 'a tasty, guilt-free snack'. The firm also owns Otmega bars which are made with whey protein from grass-fed cows in New Zealand, and upmarket UK crisp brand Tyrrells. [. . .]

Snyder's-Lance also boasts of its health credentials saying its brands, which include Kettle Chips, offer 'healthy snack choices' that provide the 'perfect amount of portable fuel'. [. . .]

Crisps are the one snack which many see as 'an especially permissible indulgence' according to market research firm Mintel. It estimates that crisps and dips sales totalled $16.8bn last year in the US, up around 19% from 2011 when it last measured the sector.

Mintel said younger people aged between 18–34 were more adventurous and willing to buy a wider variety of crisps and dips than older customers.

Campbell Soup chief executive Denise Morrison said its purchase of Synder's-Lance would 'dramatically transform' the company. If Campbell Soup had already owned Synder's-Lance in 2017 then almost half of its sales for the financial year would have come from snacks, up from just under a third, the firm said. Similarly, Hershey chief executive Michele Buck said broadening its portfolio would enable it to 'capture more consumer snacking occasions'.

Source: https://www.bbc.co.uk/news/business-42396197

Question

Why did Campbell buy Snyder's-Lance?

Franchising

A business may also grow externally through franchising. This occurs when one business sells the right to other businesses to produce their product or provide their services. The seller of the franchise is called the franchisor; the buyer of the franchise is called the franchisee. The franchisee usually pays a fee to buy the franchise, and then a proportion of its sales revenue is paid to the franchisor. Selling a franchise enables a business to grow relatively fast because the funds for the expansion are mainly provided by the franchisee. Some advantages and drawbacks of both buying and selling franchises are listed in Table 10.2.

KEY CONCEPT

A **franchise** occurs when one business sells the right to use its name or sell its products to another business. The **franchisor** sells the franchise. The **franchisee** buys the franchise.

RESEARCH TASK

Research a franchise of your choice. Consider the terms and conditions of purchase of the franchise as well as market conditions. Recommend whether to buy the franchise.

MANAGEMENT TASK

You have built up a small but successful burritos business in the last five years called Beautiful Burritos. You are considering franchising the business and have received an offer from another business to buy a franchise to open abroad. Should you sell a franchise? Outline the factors you would need to consider.

Table 10.2 Benefits and disadvantages of buying and selling a franchise

Benefits of selling a franchise	Disadvantages of selling a franchise	Benefits of buying a franchise	Disadvantages of buying a franchise
Earn revenue from the original sale of the franchise and from the sales of the franchisee	Lose some control	Paying for an established name and reputation	Initial cost
Franchisees motivated because they retain most of profits	Do not keep all the profits	Can benefit from the experience of the franchisors	Loss of revenues to pay franchisor
Benefit from share ideas and experiences of different franchises	Risk to the brand if one franchisee performs badly	Can benefit from the experiences of other franchisees	May be at risk from actions of other franchisees

BUSINESS CASE QUESTIONS: NOW CAN YOU ANSWER . . .

What factors do you think influenced Sainsbury's strategic decision to buy HRG?

Taking over another business

To take over another company, a business needs to gain control of its shares. The bidding company will make a bid for the shares of the target company. The aim is to offer enough (but only just enough) to make the shareholders sell their shares. To do this it will usually be necessary to pay a premium, i.e. pay more than the current share price. This immediately generates an additional cost, which will need to be recovered somehow.

Problems of a takeover

Takeovers often seem attractive. They can be a quick way of increasing scale, of accessing technology, and of entering a market.

However, takeovers bring with them many potential problems.

- There is an initial cost of buying the shares at a premium, as discussed above; this expenditure will need to be recovered.
- There are often problems managing different cultures. The culture of a business refers to 'the way things are done around here'; it describes what, or who, is

regarded as important, how people behave, how they interact, and what they value. When you put two businesses together the differences in culture often cause problems—people think about issues in different ways, they prioritize things in different ways, they respond to issues in different ways. This can cause conflict and inefficiency.

- There can be internal diseconomies of scale. If a business gets too big there can be problems with managing such a large organization and with motivating and coordinating employees. In particular, large businesses often worry they will lose their entrepreneurial spirit and become too bureaucratic. This can lead to higher unit costs.

- In order to undertake a takeover, a business may need to borrow funds and this will incur interest costs.

External vs. internal growth

External growth can bring about rapid growth and therefore can bring many challenges. By comparison, internal growth tends to be slower and more managed, with managers determining how fast they want the business to grow.

A relatively high proportion of takeovers prove to be unsuccessful; the combined companies do not perform better financially than the individual ones did. However, managers still continue to think that their deal is going to be different.

MANAGEMENT TASK

Your investors want significant growth in the next few years. You believe this needs to be done via external rather than internal growth. Explain why.

10.3 BUSINESS INSIGHT: ROYAL BANK OF SCOTLAND

In 2008 the Royal Bank of Scotland (RBS) was on the edge of financial crisis. To help save the banking system, the government intervened and took ownership of the bank. The Financial Services Authority (FSA) investigated RBS to understand the causes of its downfall.

The report concluded that 'multiple poor decisions' were at the heart of its problems. The bank needed a bailout that eventually amounted to £45bn.

RBS chairman Sir Philip Hampton said:

Taxpayers should never have had to rescue RBS. The FSA are right to have given the British public its assessment of events and factors that led to RBS requiring government assistance. The FSA's views are an important contribution to the debate on how banks should be managed and regulated in the future.

The problems included 'underlying deficiencies in RBS management, governance and culture which made it prone to make poor decisions'.

The executive summary points out that

> Individual poor decisions can result from flawed analysis and judgment in particular circumstances: many of the decisions that RBS made appear poor only with the benefit of hindsight.
>
> But a pattern of decisions that may reasonably be considered poor, at the time or with hindsight, suggests the probability of underlying deficiencies in: a bank's management capabilities and style; governance arrangements; checks and balances; mechanisms for oversight and challenge; and in its culture, particularly its attitude to the balance between risk and growth.

Among other problems this had led to the takeover of ABN Amro. RBS paid far too much for the company because it did not do enough research into what it was worth. The strategy was put forward by the Chief Executive Fred Goodwin and no-one challenged him. He had been right in the past and it was assumed he would be right again.

Source: www.fca.org.uk/publication/corporate/fsa-rbs.pdf

Questions

1. What problems with management might have led to the disastrous bid by the Royal Bank of Scotland for ABN Amro?

2. What systems and processes could you put in place to make sure a business was well managed at the top?

RESEARCH TASK

Research a recent takeover. Analyse the case for and against the takeover.

10.4 BUSINESS INSIGHT: TESCO AND BOOKER

In December 2017 the UK's government competition regulator, the Competition and Markets Authority (CMA), reported on its examination of the merger between Tesco, a retailer, and Booker, a wholesaler. The question was whether there was a competition issue because Booker supplies shops—such as Premier, Londis, and Budgens—that compete with Tesco. The CMA report said:

> Booker does not own the shops it supplies and these retailers are free to set their prices and decide which products to stock. So, although these shops compete with Tesco, Booker cannot directly determine how they compete. [. . .] the CMA also examined whether the merged company could raise prices or reduce service quality at either the wholesale or retail levels. It found existing strong competition in wholesale and retail. [. . .] The CMA surveyed hundreds of retailers which showed that most shops use more than one wholesaler and frequently switch. A quarter of symbol group retailers and a third of independent shops switched at least once a month.

In addition, almost half of symbol group retailers surveyed and more than a third of independent retailers said that if Booker were to raise prices after the merger with Tesco, they might stop buying from Booker altogether. And only around a fifth would continue buying the same volumes from Booker, alongside their other wholesalers.

The chair of the CMA investigation said:

Millions of people use their local supermarket or convenience store to buy their groceries or essentials, so it is vital that they have enough choice to secure the best deal for them. Having examined the evidence in depth, we are satisfied this will remain the case following the merger.

Source: https://www.gov.uk/government/news/tescobooker-merger-cleared-after-in-depth-review

Question

1. Should the regulators have been concerned about the Tesco takeover of Booker's?

2. On what grounds would you, as a regulator, stop a takeover or merger?

BUSINESS CASE QUESTION: CAN YOU NOW ANSWER . . .

Why do you think Sainsbury's decided to take over Home Retail Group rather than use that money to invest in its own internal growth?

10.2 QUICK CHECK

For each of the following statements, say whether it is true or false.

a. External growth is often faster than internal growth.

b. Takeovers can lead to internal diseconomies of scale.

c. Horizontal integration can increase the four-firm concentration ratio.

d. Vertical integration can reduce input costs.

Growth and profit

Growth may lead to lower profits in the short run as a business expands its resources. Growth may require more stores, more staff, more equipment, and more marketing. This increases costs. It may take time for the revenue to grow to justify this investment. Many businesses including Ocado, Twitter, and Facebook took years before they made a profit. Managers must be sure they that are able to finance the short term and are confident that the long term returns will be sufficiently high over time. The danger is if the business faces financial problems during growth and is unable to keep trading; this is called 'over trading'.

10.5 BUSINESS INSIGHT: PURPLEBRICKS

Losses at the online estate agency Purplebricks increased in 2018 after the business expanded overseas, as reported by the BBC in July 2018:

> The company reported a pre-tax loss of £26.1m for the year to April, up from a loss of £6m the year before.
> Purplebricks launched its business in the US last September after it expanded into Australia in 2016, and has since moved into the Canadian market.

The company's presence in places such as Australia and the US are much earlier in their evolution, but its managing director said the company was very well positioned for growth. He said that the company had gained market share, increased its revenues, and grown customer engagement in these countries.
www.bbc.co.uk/news/business-44721667

Question
Explain how a company can be growing its revenue and yet have falling profits.

Stages of growth

Larry Greiner's model of growth (Figure 10.4; details under 'Read more' in this chapter) shows some of the challenges as businesses get older and get bigger. Greiner highlights common crises that a growing business might encounter.

When businesses are new and small there is often no formal organizational structure. There are relatively few people and it is easy to share ideas. At this stage the organization may be very creative. However, as a business continues to grow, this informal approach may no longer work—new employees may need more direction and need managing.

Crisis 1

At some point there is a need for direction and leadership which may not come naturally to those who founded the business and who are perhaps very entrepreneurial.

At this stage the business may need to appoint outside managers to run the business rather than rely on those who set it up. A more formal approach to management is likely to be needed. For example, the managers may now formally define its missions, set out its objectives, and formally define roles. They typically create a functional organizational structure and introduce more accounting systems and budgets.

This provides direction and control, but there may be little delegation. As the business grows more complex and those closer to the issues within their departments gain more experience, they want to have more independence. This creates Crisis 2: a crisis of autonomy.

Figure 10.4 Greiner's model of growth

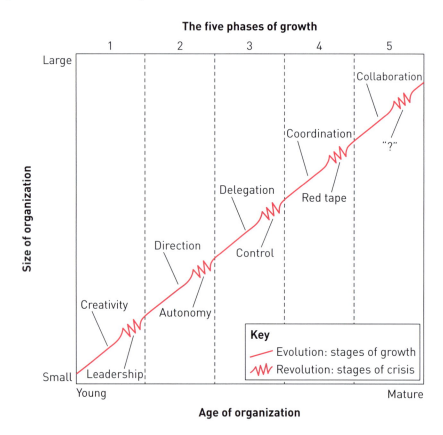

Crisis 2

At this stage the senior team may delegate more, enabling each unit to focus more on its specific demands (although this is often resisted by senior managers who are reluctant to let go). The delegation provides more autonomy. It involves greater de-centralization and creates profit centres.

This can lead to faster decision making but, at some point, top management may feel they are losing too much control and want to regain this. This leads to Crisis 3: a crisis of control.

Crisis 3

At this stage the senior management team has to establish controls over the different parts of the business such as more formal planning procedures, greater control over investment decisions, centralizing certain functions such as research and human resources, and using profit sharing schemes more widely to help provide a common focus to decision making. The danger of this approach is that there may become too many procedures for decisions to be made by the different business units, causing Crisis 4: a crisis of red tape.

Crisis 4

There may be too many systems and procedures getting in the way of competitiveness. This can lead to an attempt for greater personal collaboration between the managers of the different divisions and more focus on self-control rather than imposed control from head office.

Greater discussion and a shared approach replace some of the many rules. The focus is on teamwork across divisions, up-to-date information, and more communication between senior managers.

However, Greiner highlighted this might lead to a further crisis at some point in the future, although what it will be may vary; perhaps the impact on employees of working in such a demanding environment means that some time will have to be given to employees to reflect and revitalize themselves.

The growth of a business is, therefore, likely to be full of challenges.

BUSINESS CASE: CAN YOU NOW ANSWER . . .

What risks do you think come with Sainsbury's strategic move of growing by taking over Home Retail Group?

What actions can Sainsbury's managers take to reduce these risks?

READ MORE

You can find out more about Greiner's growth model here:

Greiner, L.E. (1972), 'Evolution and Revolution as Organizations Grow', *Harvard Business Review* Vol. 50, No. 4, pp. 37–46.

• •

SUMMARY

Managers often want to, or are told to, grow their business. They need to decide on the best way of doing this—for example, through internal or external growth—and how best to manage such growth.

KEY LEARNING POINTS

- Growth is a common business objective.
- Growth may be internal or external.
- External growth can be via merger, takeover, or franchising.
- Growth can bring benefits such as internal economies of scale, but also challenges such as the difficulties of managing more people.
- In the UK, takeovers and mergers may be monitored by the Competition and Markets Authority if there are competition issues.
- Different forms of takeover include horizontal, vertical, and conglomerate.

BUSINESS CASE EXTENSION QUESTIONS

1. Research the performance of Sainsbury's since the deal with Argos was announced. Analyse how well the company has been doing and the extent to which benefits appear to have resulted from the takeover.

2. Research a recent takeover. Analyse the reasons for the takeover. Discuss the possible consequences for different groups involved in the takeover, such as investors, employees, and customers.

3. It is often claimed that takeovers are not successful financially. Undertake your own research into the financial success of takeovers and summarize your findings.

QUICK QUESTIONS

1. What is an SME?
2. Why might managers want a business to grow?
3. What is the difference between a takeover and a merger?
4. What is the difference between vertical and horizontal integration?
5. What are typical reasons behind conglomerate mergers and takeovers?
6. What are the common advantages and potential disadvantages of selling a franchise?
7. What are the common advantages and potential disadvantages of buying a franchise?
8. What are the common challenges of growth?
9. What is the difference between external and internal growth?
10. Why do mergers and takeovers often fail?

Analysing the macro-economic environment

WHY DO I NEED TO KNOW ABOUT THE MACRO-ECONOMIC ENVIRONMENT?

You are the managing director of a low-price (discount) supermarket chain. Your business model relies on low costs, allowing you to undercut your competitors with price and still make a profit. Your business model is based on low profit margins and high volumes. You describe your business as 'lean' and you are constantly looking for ways of becoming more efficient. In the last three years, you have increased your market share from 3 to 5 per cent.

However, the macro-economic environment has not been helping profits recently. In the last few months the pound has fallen in value. Concerns over the UK's relationship with the European Union have led to less confidence in the UK economy and less demand for pounds from abroad. This fall in the value of the currency has increased your costs, and your profit margins have all but disappeared.

This shows how changes in the external economic environment can affect the performance of a business. In this chapter, we analyse some of the key features in the macro-economic environment and how they may affect a business.

BY THE END OF THIS CHAPTER YOU WILL BE ABLE TO . . .

- explain what is meant by gross domestic product and national income growth
- explain what is meant by inflation
- explain the meaning and significance of the interest rate
- explain what is meant by unemployment
- analyse the importance of the external environment
- analyse the effect of inflation on a business
- analyse the effect of unemployment on a business
- explain the effect of a change in interest rate on business
- explain the effect of a change in exchange rates on business

BUSINESS CASE: MARKS & SPENCER

Marks & Spencer is a leading retailer of food, clothing, and home products. This is an extract from its annual report:

Our Customer Insight Unit (CIU) gathers feedback through a number of different channels, including store exit surveys, online surveys and reviews, till surveys, the Customer Contact Centre and focus groups, to build a comprehensive picture of what our customers want from M&S. This year, we carried out over 700,000 customer interviews, either in person or through online surveys. Within the CIU, we have created an anonymized data analytics team to ensure we have a single accurate view of our customers. Through anonymized data analysis, we can better understand how our customers are shopping with us by examining purchasing behaviours and patterns both in our stores and online. By understanding how our customers choose to spend their money and time at M&S, we can ensure we are always working to deliver the products and shopping experience they want.

Our Consumer Barometer gives us a regular snapshot of how consumers are feeling about their household finances and the economy in general. Every month we talk to 70,000 M&S customers across our key customer groups, as well as those who don't shop with us regularly, to take the nation's pulse. We overlay this insight with external market data, such as weather patterns, travel time to our stores, local footfall data and the competitor environment, to build a solid understanding of our customers and our position in the overall retail landscape.

By understanding these groups in detail, we can build our strategies from the customer upwards rather than from the boardroom downwards.

WHAT CUSTOMERS ARE TELLING US

After holding up reasonably well over Christmas, consumer confidence in general dipped in the early months of 2017. People started to feel a little less certain about the wider economic outlook due to concern around issues such as rising inflation, the falling pound and uncertainty as a result of the UK's decision to leave the European Union.

When asked about their future spending intentions, all consumers—rather than M&S customers in particular—said they were likely to trim back their discretionary spending in the months ahead due to these economic concerns. They also said they were more likely than before to put their money into experiences and events, such as trips to the cinema, gym membership or meals out, rather than into buying consumer goods on the high street.

HOW WE USE OUR INSIGHTS

The information we gather gives us a crucial insight into the context in which we're trading. Our insights mean nothing unless we act on them. We share the information with all our business units and use the results to help us inform our business decisions.

From product development and design, to the content we put on our website, to our online delivery proposition—they are all guided by what our customers tell us.

Source: annualreport.marksandspencer.com/M&S_AR2017_Market&CustomerInsights.pdf

This chapter will help you answer the following questions.

1. How do you think the economy affects the costs of Marks & Spencer and the demand for its products?

2. How might economic change affect Marks & Spencer's strategy?

Introduction to the macro-economic environment

Businesses operate within an external environment. Within this environment, macro-economic factors can affect the costs and demand of a business, as illustrated in Figure 11.1. Managers must understand these factors because of their impact on their success. They must plan for changes in the macro-economic environment and adjust their strategy accordingly.

These macro-economic factors include

- gross domestic product
- the inflation rate
- the interest rate

Figure 11.1 The macro-economic environment

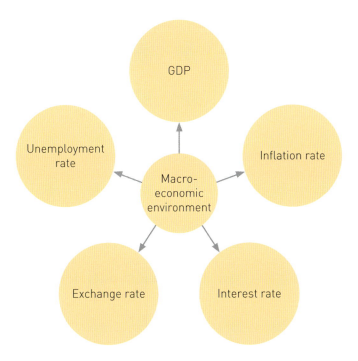

- the unemployment rate
- the exchange rate

Gross domestic product (GDP)

Why does gross domestic product matter?

Gross domestic product (GDP) measures the national income of a country over a year. It is an important measure of economic activity. If GDP is growing fast, then for many products this will mean demand is likely to grow, and managers will want to have the resources in place to meet this demand. Higher incomes will affect some products, such as luxuries, more than others—for example, with more income, consumers may be more willing to buy a new car or go abroad on holiday. These products would be called income elastic products, meaning they are sensitive to changes in income (as discussed in Chapter 3: any percentage change in income leads to a greater percentage increase in the quantity demanded)—see Table 11.1. By comparison, demand for products that consumers might consider necessities, such as sugar, is less likely to be closely linked to income changes; these are more likely to be income inelastic products. Demand for some products will actually be inversely related to income changes; these are called inferior products. For example, with a fall in income more people may go on holiday in the UK rather than abroad (this is known as having a 'staycation').

Managers will, therefore, want to estimate the income elasticities of their products and plan accordingly for what might happen given forecasted changes in income. For example, if the economy is expected to grow quickly the manager of a supermarket may focus on stocking more of the upmarket brands and less of the discount items. Of course, for most businesses these days it is not just UK GDP changes that matter—it is changes in GDP in the various countries where it might sell. Many UK businesses have relatively big export sales and therefore are affected by income changes around the world.

Table 11.1 Income elasticity and different types of product

Product	Income elasticity	Explanation
Necessity	Demand is income inelastic; income elasticity is positive	Any percentage change in GDP leads to a smaller percentage change in quantity demanded
Luxury	Demand is income elastic; income elasticity is positive	Any percentage change in GDP leads to a bigger percentage change in quantity demanded
Inferior	Income elasticity is negative	Any change in GDP leads to a change in quantity demanded in the opposite direction

GDP forecasts

GDP forecasts are important because of the potential impact of income changes on sales. If the relevant economies are expected to grow fast, this means most managers will be optimistic about sales and this will encourage investment. By comparison, slow growth is likely to lead to less investment as businesses are typically less optimistic about business growth.

Any expected change in sales will obviously have implications for staffing, the inventory held, investment, and budgeting.

KEY CONCEPT

Gross domestic product (GDP) measures the national income of a country over a year.

ANALYSING THE BUSINESS DATA

The Resolution Foundation predicted in 2017 that the UK was to experience its longest fall in living standards since records began in the 1950s. It predicted real disposable incomes would fall for 19 successive quarters. The Resolution Foundation's main focus was on the GDP growth downgrade that had occurred in the budget of that year, which it said put the economy on course to be £42bn smaller in 2022 than previously expected. The independent Office for Budget Responsibility (OBR) cut its growth forecast sharply for 2017, from 2 per cent to 1.5 per cent, with growth for the subsequent five years forecast to come in well under 2 per cent.

In the previous few years the growth rate of the economy had been slow (see Figure 11.2). This means that the economy was growing at a slower rate; however, it was still growing.

Figure 11.2 UK GDP growth rate, 2008–17

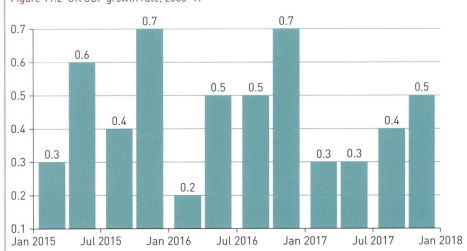

Sources: https://www.resolutionfoundation.org/media/press-releases/britain-on-course-for-longest-fall-in-living-standards-since-records-began-over-60-years-ago/; tradingeconomics.com/united-kingdom/gdp-growth

In 2009 the GDP grew at a negative rate. This means the economy got smaller. For example, if GDP grows at –2 per cent this means the economy is 2 per cent smaller by the end of the year than at the start.

Questions

1. With reference to the data, what do you think is the trend growth rate of the UK economy?

2. How might managers use this information?

ANALYSING THE BUSINESS DATA

Figure 11.3 shows a GDP projection that is based on data produced by the Office for National Statistics. The black line shows what actually happened. The future projections have a range of outcomes. The darker shaded area shows the most likely outcome. The lighter the shading the less likely the outcome, but it is possible that it would still be in this range.

Question

1. How might the projections of income shown in Figure 11.3 be used by managers?

2. How might these projections affect planning in the different functional areas of a business?

Figure 11.3 GDP projection from Bank of England Inflation Report, August 2017

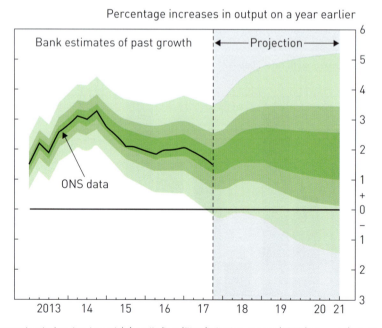

Source: www.bankofengland.co.uk/-/media/boe/files/inflation-report/2018/february/inflation-report-february-2018.pdf?la=en&hash=555ED88EF574D368B81BF703480C1987EEBBA883

READ MORE

Coyle, D. (2015), *GDP: A Brief but Affectionate History*, Princeton, NJ: Princeton University Press.

   This book focuses on the history of measuring GDP, what it is, how it is measured, and the strengths and weaknesses of it as a measure. It show how even small changes in GDP can affect the outcome of major elections, and it questions the value of this measure in the twenty-first century.

11.1 DOING THE BUSINESS MATHS

An index shows how much an item has changed relative to a base (or starting point). The base in Figure 11.4 was 2010 and this is set at a value of 100. Any change relative to this base will show much productivity has changed since 2010. For example, if UK productivity was 108 in G7 countries this means it is 8 per cent more than the base in 2010. (G7 countries are a group of seven industrialized countries: Canada, France, Germany, Italy, Japan, the United Kingdom, and the United States.)

Figure 11.4 UK productivity slowdown compared (output per hour)

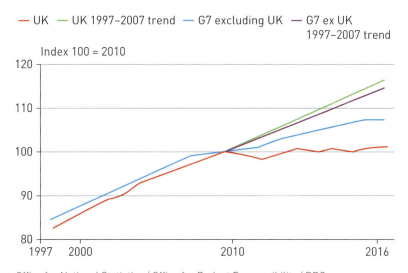

Source: Office for National Statistics / Office for Budget Responsibility / BBC

Year	GDP Index (base 2016)
2016	100
2017	120
2018	90
2019	130

Questions

1. How much has GDP changed between 2016 and 2017?
2. How much has GDP changed between 2016 and 2018?
3. How much has GDP changed between 2016 and 2019?
4. How much has GDP changed between 2018 and 2019?

11.1 BUSINESS INSIGHT: NATIONAL PRODUCTIVITY INVESTMENT FUND

Governments are usually eager for their economies to grow. This is because it means its citizens are generally better off and therefore are more likely to elect them again! If they are not growing, governments want to know why and what they can do about it. The UK economy has been growing slowly in recent years. One of the key issues holding back incomes in the UK is the slow pace of productivity growth, which is predicted to be down by an average of 0.7 per cent a year up to 2023.

In 2017 the UK chancellor, Phillip Hammond, tried to address the productivity problem by increasing the National Productivity Investment Fund (NPIF). This was launched in 2016 to provide additional investment in housing, infrastructure, and research and development. The 2017 budget increased the size of the NPIF from £23bn to £31bn. The Government also increased the Research and Development (R&D) Expenditure Credit, which is effectively tax relief for companies doing R&D.

Source: www.gov.uk/government/publications/autumn-statement-2016-documents/autumn-statement-2016

Question
How do you think improving productivity increases a country's income?

MANAGEMENT TASK

You are worried about the productivity of your office staff in your insurance business. Outline the steps you might take to improve productivity.

11.2 DOING THE BUSINESS MATHS

Remember that fast growth is a lot easier if the starting point is relatively low. If you earn £7 an hour and then start to earn £14, this is a 100 per cent increase in earnings even though in absolute terms it is a £7 difference; if you were earning £700 an hour you would need an increase of £700 for this to be 100 per cent. The UK is a large economy already, and therefore fast growth would require very significant increases in income. China has been growing very fast in recent years, but the bigger it gets as an economy the more difficult this gets.

Complete the table.

	Country A	Country B	Country C
Year 1 GDP (£bn)	50	500	5,000
Year 2 GDP (£bn)	60	550	5,250
Absolute change (£bn)	10	50	250
% change			

In the table, the absolute change in national income is greater for country B than country A. However, this is a smaller percentage change as national income was much bigger to start with. Country C has a much bigger absolute change than B or A; again, this is a smaller percentage change because it is a much bigger economy.

11.1 QUICK CHECK

For each of the following statements, say whether it is true or false.

a. If GDP increases, demand for necessities will fall.

b. If GDP increases, demand for inferior goods will fall.

c. GDP measures the number of goods produced in an economy in a year.

d. If GDP increases, demand for luxury goods will fall.

Inflation

Inflation occurs when there is a sustained increase in the general prices of goods and services. For example, if inflation is 2 per cent this mean that prices, in general, are increasing by 2 per cent over the year. Inflation will affect a business in many ways; for example, it may affect costs, wage demands, and the ability for a business to increase its prices.

Measuring inflation

Every month, the UK's Office for National Statistics (ONS) collects around 180,000 separate prices of about 700 items covering everything from food and drink to clothes, furniture, and train fares.

This 'basket of goods' is used to calculate the Consumer Price Index (CPI). The ONS publishes an updated rate every month. This is the inflation measure used in the UK government's inflation reports.

The index is a weighted index. This means that changes in the prices of some things have more impact than others on the final outcome (they have a greater weight). The weighting depends on the relative importance of a product in the overall a shopping basket, i.e. what proportion of the spending is on this product.

Table 11.2 Example of the calculation of the Consumer Price Index

Item	Weighting out of 100	Index last year	Index this year	Weighted index
A	10	100	105	$10 \times 105 = 1{,}050$
B	50	100	102	$50 \times 102 = 5{,}100$
C	20	100	102	$20 \times 102 = 2{,}040$
D	15	100	110	$15 \times 110 = 1{,}650$
E	5	100	120	$5 \times 120 = 600$
	Total = 100			Total = 10,440
				Weighted index = 10,440 ÷ sum of weights = 10,440 ÷ 100 = 104.4

Table 11.2 shows an example of the calculations used in preparing the CPI. Taking account of the relative importance of items in the typical shopping basket by assigning a weight to each item, the weighted index is 104.4. This means inflation for the year is 4.4 per cent.

Although some products have experienced much higher inflation, e.g. the price of D has increased by 10% and E by 20%, these are not especially significant items in the basket. The key item, B (which accounts for 50% of spending and so has a high weight), increased by only 2% in price. Taking account of the relative importance of items, the overall effect is a 4.4% increase in the general price level.

11.3 DOING THE BUSINESS MATHS

Calculate the rate of inflation using the table.

Item	Weighting out of 100	Index last year	Index this year	Weighted index
A	20	100	106	
B	30	100	107	
C	10	100	101	
D	25	100	110	
E	15	100	130	
	Total = 100			

KEY CONCEPT

The **Consumer Price Index** is a weighted index which measures inflation over a given period in the UK.

Causes of inflation

Inflation may be caused by too much demand in the economy relative to the available supply. The total demand for final goods and services is called aggregate demand. If this is growing faster than the total supply in the economy (which is called aggregate supply) this pulls up prices. Alternatively, rising prices may be caused by costs rising, perhaps due to rising import costs or higher wages not linked to any productivity gains. Higher costs push up prices in the economy.

KEY CONCEPTS

Aggregate demand is the total demand for final goods and services in an economy.
Aggregate supply is the total supply of final goods and services in an economy.

The aggregate supply curve is generally upward-sloping; to produce more and use more scarce resources, higher prices are needed. At full employment, the economy is operating at its potential given its existing resources. The supply curve is vertical because no more can be produced even if prices increase. At this level of output, the economy is operating at its capacity.

An increase in aggregate demand will pull up prices and output; businesses will produce more but will need higher prices to cover the higher resource costs needed to increase output. At full employment, more demand will simply pull up prices because output cannot increase.

An increase in costs means that higher prices are needed to produce any output, and this shifts the aggregate supply upwards. This increase prices in the economy, leading to inflation.

11.4 DOING THE BUSINESS MATHS

If prices are growing (i.e. the growth rate is positive) there is inflation.

Year	Price change
1	+2%
2	+3%
3	+1%
4	−2%
5	0%

Questions

1. What is happening to inflation between years 2 and 3?
2. What is happening to prices between years 2 and 3?
3. What is happening to prices between years 3 and 4?

Table 11.3 The effect of inflation on prices

	Year 1	Year 2	Year 3	Year 4
Inflation	2%	5%	1%	−2%
Effect on prices	Increase by 2%	Increase on last year by another 5%	Increase compared to last year (but only by 1%)	Decrease compared to last year by 2%

Why does inflation matter?

Inflation may mean that the input costs of a business are increasing and that employees may demand higher rewards to compensate for the higher prices that result from inflation, as shown in Table 11.3; this would further increase costs. Faced with higher costs, managers must decide if they can pass these on to customers in the form of higher prices or whether they need to absorb these via lower profit margins.

Views about inflation in the future will also affect consumer spending. If consumers think prices will increase significantly in the future they may spend now. If consumers think prices may fall (this is called deflation) they may save now and cut back on spending, hoping to benefit from lower prices later. Notice how important expectations are; the spending of consumers and businesses is influenced by what they think is going to happen in the future.

What also matters is how much people's incomes are going up compared to inflation. Real income measures the purchasing power of someone's income—it considers what happens to someone's income in relation to prices. Real income increases if purchasing power increases; income rises faster than prices. Real income decreases if prices are increasing faster than incomes.

Understanding what inflation is likely to be is critical to budgeting—managers must anticipate what costs might be, and how much it might be realistic to increase prices by.

KEY CONCEPTS

Inflation occurs when there is a sustained increase in the general prices of goods and services. **Deflation** occurs when there is a fall in the general price level. **Real income** shows nominal income adjusted for inflation to show its purchasing power.

11.5 DOING THE BUSINESS MATHS

It is important to take inflation into account to appreciate what is happening in real terms. If your income increases 2% but when you come to spend this additional money you find that prices have generally increased by 3%, this means that in real terms you are worse off.

Now complete the table showing the effect of inflation on real income.

	Year 1	Year 2	Year 3
Change in income	5%	5%	5%
Change in prices	2%	5%	7%
Effect: does real income increase or decrease?			

MANAGEMENT TASK

You are the manager of a hotel, faced with rising prices of inputs. Discuss the actions you could take to improve the profitability of your hotel.

11.2 QUICK CHECK

For each of the following statements, say whether it is true or false.

a. Inflation measures the standard of living.

b. A fall in inflation means prices are falling.

c. Inflation is measured by a weighted index.

d. If nominal wages increase faster than inflation, real wages increase.

ANALYSING THE BUSINESS DATA

Figure 11.5 UK inflation rate 2008–17, based on the Consumer Price Index

Source: Office for National Statistics; BBC, www.bbc.co.uk/news/business-42320052

Questions

1. In 2008 inflation reached over 5 per cent. What does this mean is happening to prices?

2. In 2015 inflation was 0 per cent. What does this mean is happening to prices?

Inflation forecasting

The Bank of England produces a quarterly Inflation Report which includes forecasts of inflation, as shown in Figure 11.6. Given that this is a forecast, the bank cannot be absolutely sure what the rate will be and so produces a set of outcomes with differing levels of confidence. The lighter shading covers a wider range of possible outcomes, meaning that the bank is more confident that the actual result will lie within this range. The darker shading shows the range where the bank think inflation is likely to be, but it cannot be as confident of this because it is a smaller range.

Note that the range widens the further ahead we are looking; this is because there is greater uncertainty and so a wider range of possible outcomes must be shown.

Figure 11.6 Inflation projection produced by the Bank of England, based on the Consumer Price Index

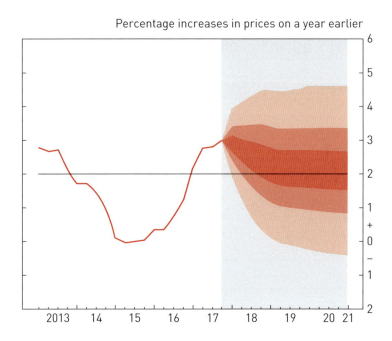

Percentage increases in prices on a year earlier

Source: www.bankofengland.co.uk/inflation-report/2018/

11.3 QUICK CHECK

For each of the following statements, say whether it is true or false.

a. Inflation may occur if demand is too low.

b. Inflation may be caused by higher costs.

c. Inflation is a measure of economic growth.

d. Deflation occurs when inflation is negative.

RESEARCH TASK

Research inflation rates in the UK compared to another country.

Analyse the possible impact of the differences in inflation rates on businesses in these countries.

MANAGEMENT TASK

You are the manager of a UK food delivery business. UK inflation next year is forecast to increase to 3 per cent. Outline how might this affect your business.

11.2 BUSINESS INSIGHT: SLOW WAGE GROWTH IN THE UK

According to a recent study by the Institute of Fiscal Studies, average UK earnings in 2022 may be less than in 2008. Since 2014, growth in earnings has been very slow and this is predicted to continue in the next few years. Although employment in the UK increased between 2007 and 2017, real earnings fell, as shown in Figure 11.7. Lord Adair Turner, the

Figure 11.7 UK wage growth compared to inflation, 2006–17

Source: Office for National Statistics; BBC, http://www.bbc.co.uk/news/business-42096806

former head of the UK's Low Pay Commission, said that this meant the capitalist system was no longer delivering on its promise to deliver higher earnings for people (discussed further in Chapter 7, Business insight 7.1).

Questions

a. Comment on the impact of the changes in earnings and prices on real earnings.

b. Why do you think earnings were not keeping pace with inflation in 2017?

c. What might be the implications for business of an increase in real earnings?

Controlling inflation

The Monetary Policy Committee (MPC) is responsible in the UK for controlling inflation and keeping it at a certain level; it had a target of 2 per cent in mid-2018. To achieve its target, the MPC sets interest rates, which will be discussed in the next section. The rate set by the MPC, known as the 'base rate', determines the rate at which it will lend to banks. Changes to the interest rate affect the cost of borrowing and therefore spending; this affects demand and the likelihood of demand, which in turn affect inflation.

Interest rates

The interest rate is the cost of borrowing money and the reward for saving. For example, if the interest rate is 3 per cent this means it costs 3 per cent to borrow money, or that individuals or businesses will receive a 3 per cent return on saving.

What is the impact on business of an increase in interest rates?

An increase in interest rates will increase the cost of borrowing. This will particularly affect the demand for goods and services that people tend to buy on credit or borrow money to purchase. For example, houses are often bought with a mortgage and involve large sums of money, so demand for housing is likely to be very sensitive to interest rate changes.

Similarly, when buying a car many people will borrow to finance the purchase, and so changes in the interest rate are likely to have a noticeable impact on demand. Given that most people in the UK have some form of borrowing, whether it be a mortgage, credit cards, or an overdraft, a change in interest rates will affect their disposable income and their spending. Higher interest rates will reduce disposable income and spending on goods and services generally. This would reduce demand and therefore reduce the upward pressure on prices.

KEY CONCEPT

The **interest rate** is the cost of borrowing money and the reward for saving.

The impact of interest rate changes will depend on the extent to which businesses and households have debt. At the moment, for example, around a third of UK households have a mortgage on their home and so many people will be affected by interest rate changes. However, most of these loans are on a fixed rate, so any change in interest rates would not have an immediate effect. Higher interest rates would take effect here when the original loan came to an end and the contract had to be renegotiated. The other main form of borrowing by households is consumer credit or student loans; again, these are generally on fixed rates so, again, a change in interest rates would take time to have any effect.

When will the Bank of England change interest rates?

Being able to anticipate when the Bank of England is going to change interest rates would be valuable to managers. They could then estimate the impact on spending in their sector and their own borrowing costs. The Governor of the Bank of England will make statements about the economy and this may indicate the likelihood of changes in the future. The decision about whether to change the interest rate and, if so, how much to change it by is made by the Monetary Policy Committee. This group meets monthly to review the situation. When they meet they are looking ahead to what inflation might be in the coming months. They are also trying to estimate the effect of any change in interest rates, how long this would take to work its way through the economy, and what other changes to the economy might take place in the meantime. This means the job of the Monetary Policy Committee is a difficult one because of the likely time lag before any change takes effect and the many changes that could occur in the economy in that time. It also means that anticipating when changes are going to occur is not easy for business.

Gearing

The impact of any change in interest rates on the costs of a business is likely to be linked to how much borrowing it has. This is measured by its gearing ratio.

The long-terms funds raised by a business are known as its 'capital employed'. The sources of these funds include

- retained profits—profits kept by the business rather than paid out to shareholders as dividends;
- issued share capital—companies raise funds by selling shares;
- long-term borrowing—with a loan, a business borrows money and agrees to repay over a fixed period with interest.

Capital employed is made up of retained profit plus issued share capital plus loans.

Gearing measures loans as a proportion of capital employed. There are different ways of calculating this, such as:

(long term borrowing ÷ capital employed) × 100

High gearing occurs if a high proportion of capital employed is borrowed. This may mean the business faces relatively high interest payments. The risk of borrowing is that no matter what the profits of the business are—even if profits fall—interest payments have to be paid. By comparison, if profits are lower managers might suggest that dividends are lowered rather than becoming committed to interest payments.

11.6 DOING THE BUSINESS MATHS

Complete the table. Comment on the absolute level of borrowing and the gearing of each business relative to the others.

	Business A	Business B	Business C
Long-term loans	£10m	£20m	£20m
Capital employed	£50m	£200m	£25m
Gearing %			

MANAGEMENT TASK

You are the manager of a family business. You need to raise £10 million. Should you try and borrow from a bank or try to raise money from selling shares? Justify your view.

11.3 BUSINESS INSIGHT: CARILLION

Carillion is a construction and services business. It had many government contracts such as providing food at schools, providing homes for the armed forces, and big public sector projects such as redeveloping Battersea Power station.

In 2018 it went into liquidation. This means the court appointed officials to raise money to repay creditors. Carillion had been predicted to have accumulated a debt of around £1bn by 2017 (see Figure 11.8). In the event, Carillion's debt was over £1.5bn by the time of liquidation.

Over a third of Carillion's business was with the government. The government has been keen to award contracts to the lowest bidder, and some say this meant that Carillion bid for contracts at such low prices that it was not able to make a profit. Its managers wanted the business to grow fast, so they borrowed to finance its expansion and win new contracts. This increased its costs.

Source: BBC, http://www.bbc.co.uk/news/business-42666275

Questions

1. Why would Carillion's managers want fast growth?
2. Why would they have borrowed to grow?
3. Why does debt add risk to growth?

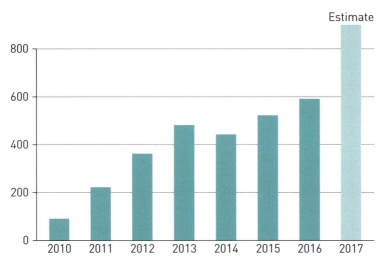

Figure 11.8 Carillion's debt, 2010–17

Source: Carillion/BBC, http://www.bbc.co.uk/news/business-42666275

11.7 DOING THE BUSINESS MATHS

Diageo is a global leader in alcohol products with world famous brands such as Johnnie Walker, Bells, J&B, Captain Morgan, Smirnoff, and Guinness. The table shows extracts from its accounts.

Table 11.4 Extracts from Diageo's accounts

Year	Long-term liabilities (£m)	Capital employed (£m)	Gearing = (long-term liabilities ÷ capital employed) × 100
2014	11,039	17,862	
2015	12,269	20,040	
2016	13,719	22,249	
2017	11,594	21,907	

Questions

1. Calculate the gearing for the business to complete the table.
2. Comment on your findings.
3. What do you think would determine if Diageo's gearing was too high or too low?

Unemployment

Unemployment is measured by the number of people who are out of work but who are actively seeking employment and are able to accept a job at a given time. The unemployment rate measures unemployment as a percentage of the workforce. Managers may be interested in the unemployment rate because it may be an indication of demand in the economy. It will also affect how easy it is likely to be to recruit staff and the likelihood of a demand for higher wages.

Measuring unemployment

Unemployment can be measured in different ways, including the following.

- **The claimant count:** this measures the number of individuals who are actually claiming unemployment-related benefits at any moment. This is a relatively straightforward figure to gather, but it may be misleading because governments can change the conditions under which people can claim such benefits. It is therefore open to abuse by governments because, to reduce unemployment figures, they can simply make claiming more difficult!

- **The Labour Force Survey (LFS):** this measure of unemployment is based on interviews with people to count those who want to work, but who are not employed. This is now the official way of measuring unemployment in the UK.

Types of unemployment

There are many types of unemployment—some people are simply between jobs, some work in seasonal industries, some are unemployed because their industry is in decline, but another cause may be the lack of demand in the economy.

Unemployment may be caused by a lack of demand; it is also likely to lead to less demand because people who are unemployed are likely to have less spending power.

Unemployment will also be of interest because it will influence the supply of labour. With more people unemployed, it may be easier to recruit and there may be less upward pressure on wages (because people will not want to price themselves out of work). High levels of unemployment may mean that more people actively approach your business for work and that you need to do less to recruit the people you need. However, what really matters is where the unemployment is occurring, and what skills and experience those unemployed actually have. Unemployment may be relatively high in the UK as a whole, but that does not necessarily mean that it is high in your area or for the type of job where you need staff.

It may be the case that a business is not recruiting but is having to make redundancies. Redundancies occur when employees lose their jobs because of a lack of demand; these jobs no longer exist. This is different from dismissal, which occurs when people lose their jobs because they are not competent to do them. Making redundancies is, of course, not easy on a personal level, but on a practical level it can be difficult as well. For example, when deciding who needs to be made redundant this must be done in a way which meets several legal requirements and which is not based on the ability of the individuals—they are not losing their jobs because of their capability but because the demand for their work is reduced or has disappeared. One way commonly used to select those to make redundant is called 'last in first out'; this means that those who joined most recently are the first to be asked to leave. More redundancies would add to the number unemployed.

KEY CONCEPTS

Unemployment is measured by the number of people who are out of work but who are actively seeking employment and are able to accept a job. The **unemployment rate** measures unemployment as a percentage of the workforce.

ANALYSING THE DATA

	GDP growth 2018 %	Consumer prices 2018 %	Unemployment rate 2018 %
United States	2.8	2.5	3.8
China	6.6	2.3	3.9
Japan	1.3	1.1	2.5
Britain	1.4	2.5	4.2
France	2.0	1.8	9.2
Greece	1.8	1.2	20.1
Venezuela	−16	12,615.2	7.3
Poland	4.2	1.7	6.1
Denmark	1.8	1.1	4.0

Source: adapted from www.economist.com/economic-and-financial-indicators/2018/06/28/output-prices-and-jobs

Questions

Discuss the significance of the data above for UK and local businesses.

Exchange rate

What is the exchange rate?

The exchange rate is the price of one currency in terms of another: for example, the price of a pound in terms of US dollars or euros. There will be many different exchange rates because the pound is traded against many different currencies.

Influences on the exchange rate

The demand for a currency may increase for a number of reasons such as higher domestic interest rates, a belief among speculators that it will increase further in the future (so they are buying now), or increased demand for UK goods and services (perhaps because of higher overseas incomes). This means that at the existing exchange rate there is excess demand. The exchange rate will increase, reducing the quantity demanded and increasing the quantity supplied until a new equilibrium is reached.

The supply of a currency may increase for a number of reasons, such as higher interest rates overseas leading to an outflow of the currency, a belief among speculators that it will decrease further in the future (so they are selling now), or increased demand for overseas products (perhaps because of higher UK incomes). This means that at the existing exchange rate there is excess supply. The exchange rate will decrease, increasing the quantity demanded and decreasing the quantity supplied until a new equilibrium is reached.

Change in currency market conditions	Effect on value of currency	Effect on quantity of currency traded
Increased demand	Increases	Increases
Decreased demand	Decreases	Decreases
Increased supply	Decreases	Increases
Decreased supply	Increases	Decreases

Why does the exchange rate matter?

The exchange rate is important because it influences the price of a product abroad and because it affects the purchasing power of a pound in other countries. Many businesses have overseas customers and so the price of their products abroad matters to their sales. Also, many business buy supplies in directly from abroad or they use supplies which themselves involve overseas elements, so that somewhere in the supply chain products or services are bought in from abroad. This means the purchasing power of the pound abroad will affect the costs of inputs.

The exchange rate is a particular concern for managers because it is out of their control. The exchange rate may increase or decrease in value, and managers have to plan for and react to this; they cannot directly do anything to make the exchange rate rise or fall.

KEY CONCEPT

The **exchange rate** is the price of one currency in terms of another.

11.6 QUICK CHECK

For each of the following statements, say whether it is true or false.
The exchange rate measures

a. the standard of living.

b. the cost of living.

c. the value of one currency in terms of another.

d. the level of national income.

What is the impact of the pound rising in value?

If the pound rises in value it is becoming more expensive in terms of foreign currency. This means that UK products would be more expensive abroad and sales are likely to fall. The amount they fall will depend on how sensitive demand is to price. Managers may try to respond to this by finding ways to cut costs; this would enable them to lower the UK price and therefore keep the prices abroad the same. However, cutting costs is not necessarily easy and may have a knock-on effect in terms of quality. A strong pound is, therefore, likely to be unfavourable for exporters.

However, a strong pound means that managers who are looking to buy products from abroad will not need to spend as much in pounds. One pound will buy more foreign currency, and so fewer pounds are needed for any given amount of spending in terms of foreign currency. This means that a strong pound is generally favourable for importers. As a result, costs should be lower and this can feed through into higher profit margins, and/or it may lead to lower prices.

MANAGEMENT TASK

How might a rise in the value of your currency against others affect your business?

What is the impact of a lower exchange rate?

If the exchange rate falls, this means the pound is weaker and has less purchasing power. The effect of this is to make UK exports cheaper, and this should increase sales (although the effect may take some time to work through, as buyers abroad may be contracted to domestic businesses already so cannot easily switch).

The price of imports will increase, all other factors unchanged, because more pounds will be needed to pay the price in foreign currency. This increases costs, which can reduce profit margins or lead to higher prices. Faced with this, managers will look to find lower-price suppliers—perhaps domestically—and/or find ways of reducing other costs. In 2017, many UK supermarkets were hit by the effect of a weak (low) pound which made their imported products more expensive; given the state of the economy, they did not feel they could pass on this increase, so their profit margins were squeezed.

11.8 DOING THE BUSINESS MATHS

Complete the table.

	Time period 1	Time period 2	Time period 3
Exchange rate	£1 = $1	£1 = $2	£1 = $0.90
Price of £100 UK item in US$			
Comment		The pound is worth more in dollars than last period. All other things being equal, this makes UK goods more expensive in dollars. UK exports are likely to suffer.	The pound is worth less in dollars than in period 1. All other things being equal, this makes UK goods less expensive in dollars. UK exports are likely to increase.
Price of US $45 good when bought in pounds			
Comment		The pound is worth more in dollars than last period. All other things being equal, this makes US goods cheaper in pounds, i.e. more competitive. UK imports from the US are likely to increase, and UK costs from US products are lower.	The pound is worth less in dollars than in period 1. All other things being equal, this makes US goods more expensive in pounds, i.e. less competitive. UK imports cost more.

Question

What can managers do about exchange rate changes?

Managers need to consider possible exchange rate changes and their impact on demand and costs. To avoid the impact of changes in the exchange rate, they might try to agree contracts that lock them into prices for a given period. For example, they might use a contract to fix the price they pay for supplies from abroad and set the price in pounds if they can negotiate this deal.

Managers may also hedge against currency changes. A foreign exchange hedge (also called a FOREX hedge) is a method used by companies to eliminate or 'hedge' the risk of foreign exchange rate movements.

KEY CONCEPT

A **foreign exchange hedge** (also called a **FOREX hedge**) is a method used by companies to eliminate or 'hedge' the risk of foreign exchange rate movements.

Hedging against currency changes

Imagine you want to buy products in from the US in six months' time. The exchange rate today is £1:$1.50 and the items you buy are priced at $150; this means at today's exchange rate, the price would be £100. If, however, the pound weakened in the future, making the exchange rate £1:$1, the price would increase to £150.

What you could do is agree now to buy currency in sixth months' time at a price of, say, £1:$1.50. That way you know you will be paying £100 per item in the future for the $150 items.

If the actual future exchange rate turns out to be £1:$1 you will have made a good deal, because you have saved money (as you would have needed £150 to buy the items from the US). However, if the actual exchange rate turns out to be £1:$2 then you could have bought these products for £75; you have paid more than you would have had to without the advance agreement, but you gained yourself the peace of mind of knowing in advance what you would be paying.

Of course, to be able to fix this price with someone you need to find someone who has a different view of how the exchange rate will change. You want to fix it at £1:$1.50 thinking you may do better than the actual rate in the future; for someone to sell at this rate, they think the market rate will be e.g. £1:$2, so they can give you $1.50 for every pound you want when they are getting $2 on the actual market and making 50 cents profit each time.

The exchange rate is a particularly significant risk because of the volatility that can occur in these markets. The exchange rate changes very regularly, and this increases the risk of trading abroad.

RESEARCH TASK

Research the changes that have occurred in the pound exchange rate against one other currency in the last five years. Can you explain the changes in the value? Select a business that would have been affected by these changes and analyse the possible impact of the currency movements.

11.7 QUICK CHECK

For each of the following statements, say whether it is true or false.

a. A strong pound means that the pound has fallen in value against other currencies.

b. A strong pound means that the pound has risen in value against other currencies.

c. A strong pound increases the price of exports in terms of foreign currencies, other factors unchanged.

d. A strong pound increases the UK price of exports, other factors unchanged.

BUSINESS CASE QUESTIONS: CAN YOU NOW ANSWER . . .

1. How do you think the economy affects the costs of Marks & Spencer and the demand for its products?

2. How might economic change affect Marks & Spencer's strategy?

Summary table of macro-economic factors

Macro-economic factor	. . . will affect
GDP	Purchasing power; demand
Inflation rate	Costs of inputs; demands for wages; investment planning; pricing
Interest rates	Costs of borrowing; reward for saving; costs; demand
Unemployment rate	• Purchasing power of those out of work, and therefore demand • The supply of labour: creates more available supply, which may bring wages down
Exchange rate	• Cost of imported inputs, which affects costs • Price of imported competitor products, which affects demand • Export prices abroad changing with exchange rates, which affects demand

RESEARCH TASK

Research the current position of the UK economy in terms of the following variables:

- GDP growth
- inflation
- unemployment rate
- trade position

- the interest rate
- the exchange rate

Discuss the possible effects of these variables on a UK-based business.

• •

SUMMARY

Businesses operate within the macro-economic environment. Many elements of this environment, such as inflation, GDP, unemployment, and exchange rates, can impact on the costs and revenues of a business. Managers need to understand these macro-economic factors and how they can affect their business. Changes in this environment can affect all aspects of managing a business, such as staffing decisions, inventory levels, choosing what products to develop, marketing strategies, capacity utilization levels, and financial planning.

KEY LEARNING POINTS

- GDP is the gross domestic product, which is a measure of national income in a country over a year.
- Inflation measures an increase in the general price level.
- Deflation is a decrease in the general price level.
- An interest rate is the cost of borrowing and a reward for saving.
- Higher interest rates are likely to encourage saving and discourage borrowing.
- Unemployment measures the number of people who are able and willing to accept a job at the given real wage, but who are not currently employed.

BUSINESS CASE EXTENSION QUESTIONS

1. Visit the Marks & Spencer website. Can you find examples of each of the strategies in the Ansoff matrix discussed in Chapter 10?
2. Which of Marks & Spencer's product categories are most likely to be income elastic and which are likely to be relatively income inelastic, do you think? Explain your answers.
3. Which of the Marks & Spencer's product categories are most likely to be price elastic and which are likely to be relatively price inelastic, do you think? Explain your answers.

4. Look at the most recent annual report for Marks & Spencer plc. Analyse the micro- and macro-economic factors that are identified in its business environment.

5. Look at the most recent annual report for a competitor of Marks & Spencer. Analyse the micro- and macro-economic factors that are identified in its business environment. Compare and contrast your findings with your results for Marks & Spencer.

QUICK QUESTIONS

1. Why can economic growth can be important for business?
2. What is the difference between inflation and deflation?
3. How can inflation affect a business?
4. How can changes in interest rates affect the profits of a business?
5. How can changes in exchange rates affect the profits of a business?
6. How can changes in unemployment affect a business?
7. Why does gearing matter?
8. What is the Consumer Price Index?
9. What is hedging?
10. What is the difference between nominal and real income?

Government macro-economic policy and business

WHY DO I NEED TO KNOW ABOUT MACRO-ECONOMIC POLICY?

You have been considering investing in new production facilities. You have estimated the likely revenues and costs in order to calculate the possible profits and decide whether it would be worthwhile. You have considered the funds required to finance this expansion and the return you will make on this investment. You have compared this with the cost of borrowing and have just decided it is viable to go ahead with this project.

Just as you were about to press the green button to go ahead, you get the news that Bank of England has increased the base rate (discussed in Chapter 11). A quick call to your own bank and you discover you will now have to pay more for your loan. These additional costs now mean the returns from the investment will not be high enough to satisfy your investors. The deal is off.

Changes in the economic environment can have an effect on business decisions. Managers must understand this environment and how the government may change its economic policy to achieve its objectives. It should then try to plan accordingly. In this chapter, we consider how government economic policy can affect managers' decisions.

BY THE END OF THIS CHAPTER YOU WILL BE ABLE TO . . .

- explain what is meant by fiscal policy
- explain what is meant by a budget
- analyse why government fiscal policy is important to business
- explain what is meant by monetary policy
- analyse the effects of monetary policy changes on business
- explain what is meant by supply side policies
- explain what is meant by an exchange rate policy

BUSINESS CASE

In 2017 the UK government announced its Plan for Britain. This was partly in response to Brexit—the government wanted to show it was planning for what might happen when the UK left the European Union. In the Foreword, Prime Minister Theresa May wrote that it was 'a plan to shape a new future for the kind of country we will be when we have left. It is a plan to build a stronger, fairer Britain that works for everyone, not just the privileged few'. May went on to write:

> It will help to deliver a stronger economy and a fairer society—where wealth and opportunity are spread across every community in our United Kingdom, not just the most prosperous places in London and the South East. It will help our young people to develop the skills they need to do the high-paid, high-skilled jobs of the future. And it will back Britain for the long term: creating the conditions where successful businesses can emerge and grow, and backing them to invest in the long-term future of Britain.
>
> Underpinning this strategy is a new approach to government, not just stepping back and leaving business to get on with the job, but stepping up to a new, active role that backs business and ensures more people in all corners of the country share in the benefits of its success. This active government will build on Britain's strategic strengths and tackle our underlying weaknesses, like low productivity. This is vital because if we want to increase our overall prosperity, if we want more people to share in that prosperity, if we want higher real wages, and if we want more opportunities for young people to get on—we have to raise our productivity.
>
> Through this new approach we will move beyond short-term thinking to focus on the big decisions that will deliver long-term, sustainable success.

The Introduction, written by Greg Clark (Secretary of State for Business, Energy and Industrial Strategy), said:

> British excellence in key technologies, professions, research disciplines and institutions provides us with crucial competitive advantages. But we cannot take them for granted. If other countries invest more in research and development, and we do not, then we cannot expect to keep, let alone extend, our technological lead in key sectors—or the world-beating performance of our universities. The same goes for our record as Europe's leading destination for inward investment or our position as a centre of international finance. Our competitors are not standing still. They are upgrading infrastructure networks and reforming systems of governance. Therefore we too must strive for improvement.
>
> In industrial sectors—from automotive and aerospace to financial and professional services and the creative industries—the UK has built a global reputation. But the competition for new investment is fierce and unending. The conditions that have allowed UK investment destinations to succeed include the availability of supportive research programmes, relevant skills in local labour markets and capable supply chains. However, for continuing success, these foundations must be maintained and strengthened.

The second challenge is to ensure that every place meets its potential by working to **close the gap** between our best performing companies, industries, places and people and those which are less productive. [. . .]

For all the progress of more people going to university than ever before, too many people do not have the education and skills they need to be able to command a good wage. We have more university graduates than the OECD average, but also more people with low levels of literacy and numeracy.

We must address these long 'tails' of underperformance if we are to build a strong economy and ensure sustainable growth in living standards.

The third challenge is to **make the UK one of the most competitive places in the world to start or to grow a business**. A fatal flaw of 1970s-style industrial strategies was the dominant focus on existing industries and the companies within them—and then mostly the biggest firms. Too often they became strategies of incumbency.

It is worth noting that many of the most important companies in the world today did not even exist 25 years ago. Unlike in the past, industrial strategy must be about creating the right conditions for new and growing enterprise to thrive, not protecting the position of incumbents.

Source: beisgovuk.citizenspace.com/strategy/industrial-strategy/supporting_documents/buildingourindustrialstrategygreenpaper.pdf

BUSINESS CASE QUESTIONS

This chapter will help you answer the following questions.

1. What does the UK government set out as its macro objectives?
2. What challenges does the UK economy face?
3. What does the UK government think it can do to help business and the economy?
4. Do you think the UK government should get involved in industrial strategy?

Government objectives and policies

Governments will have micro and macro objectives. Micro objectives refer to specific markets. For example, the government may want to reduce the consumption of tobacco and sugar. It may want to make the banking sector more financially stable and more competitive. The macro-economic objectives usually include economic growth, stable prices, low unemployment, and a healthy trade position.

To achieve these objectives a government will use a range of policies (Figure 12.1). These policies are aimed at the levels of demand and supply in the economy. Sometimes a particular policy may help achieve more than one objective—for example, boosting demand may help increase income in the economy and reduce unemployment. However, policies aimed at one objective may adversely affect another; more spending may pull up prices, for example.

Figure 12.1 Types of government policy

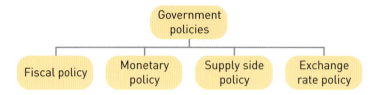

Government fiscal policy

The fiscal policy of a government refers to its spending plans and its taxation and benefits system. The UK government's fiscal policy is administered by the Treasury, which is led by the Chancellor of the Exchequer. Each year the Chancellor announces the government's spending plans and taxation and benefits policy in a budget statement. The budget sets out the expenditure plan of the government and the ways in which it expects to raise money. In the budget statement the government will announce new policies. Managers will want to analyse the effects of any budget statement because of its direct impact on their businesses and its impact on their customers.

The government's budget position

The budget position of a government refers to the difference between its spending and its revenue from taxation over a given period. If the revenue is greater than the spending over a given period, there is a surplus. This is rare. If the spending is greater than the revenue over a given period, there is a budget deficit (Figure 12.2). This is common!

Figure 12.2 A budget deficit

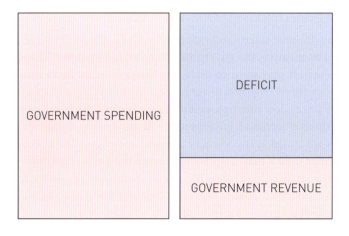

KEY CONCEPT

The **budget position** of a government refers to the difference between its spending and its revenue from taxation over a given period.

Government spending takes many forms. It includes

- local government spending by councils—for example, on local services and facilities;
- central government spending—for example, on defence and the National Health Service.

Public sector spending can also be analysed in terms of how much goes on operating (day-to-day) expenditure and how much goes on capital expenditure (which is investment for the future).

ANALYSING THE BUSINESS DATA

1. Can you suggest why the budget figures change from the spring to autumn budgets?
2. What might explain the forecasted changes in the spring and autumn budget positions in the coming years?

Figure 12.3 Government deficit 2015–23; forecasts made in 2017

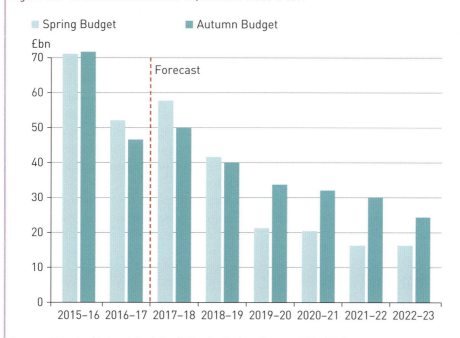

Source: Office for National Statistics/Office for Budget Responsibility/BBC

ANALYSING THE BUSINESS DATA

Figure 12.4 UK public sector spending, 2018–19

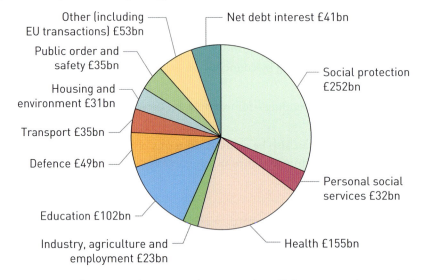

Other (including EU transactions) £53bn

Net debt interest £41bn

Public order and safety £35bn

Social protection £252bn

Housing and environment £31bn

Transport £35bn

Defence £49bn

Personal social services £32bn

Education £102bn

Industry, agriculture and employment £23bn

Health £155bn

Source: www.gov.uk/government/publications/autumn-budget-2017-documents/autumn-budget-2017

Looking at Figure 12.4, what are the three biggest areas of UK government (public sector) spending in 2018–19?

Do you think more should be spent in these areas? What might be the consequences of this?

The UK government spends hundreds of billions of pounds each year on goods and services. This means that the government is a major consumer within the economy and therefore is very important to many businesses. Cutbacks in education spending, for example, would affect businesses that supply furniture for schools and colleges, general supplies such as photocopying paper, recruitment agencies, teacher training colleges, textbooks publishers, and so on.

Equally, increases in government spending will create new opportunities for sales—greater spending on defence, for example, creates demand for new military equipment.

The multiplier

When considering the effect of changes in government spending, it is important to examine not only the direct impact on supplies but also the trickle-down effect of the demand throughout the supply chain. If demand increases for new hospitals, this creates demand for construction businesses; these companies then demand construction materials, which also creates demand for logistics businesses to move material around. Meanwhile, there will be more employees, or higher earnings for employees in these businesses. These employees will be spending their money on goods and services, and this will stimulate a whole range of other sectors. Any change in government spending therefore has a multiplied effect. The term 'the multiplier' refers to how much greater the overall effect of a change in government spending is on the overall income of the economy.

KEY CONCEPT

The **multiplier** measures how much national income increases relative to an initial change in demand, e.g. caused by a change in government spending.

The size of the multiplier depends on how much income is used for further spending at any stage. This depends on what is called the marginal propensity to consume (mpc).

The mpc measures how much of each extra pound is spent on consumption. For example, if the mpc is 0.5 this means 50 pence out of each pound is spent on consumption. If the government spends £100 million on a project, this becomes the income of those doing the work (e.g. those renovating the government building); if the mpc is 0.5, then £50 million will be spent on further consumption, e.g. the business buying materials and employees spending their earnings. The people who earn this £50 million will also spend some of it on other goods and services. If the mpc is still 0.5 they would spend $0.5 \times £50$ million $= £25$ million. The process would continue, so the initial £100 million of spending leads to

£100m + £50m + £25m + . . .

—and these rounds of spending continue.

Imagine that the mpc was higher at 0.8. This would mean that more of any income was spent at each stage and this would lead to a bigger multiplier effect. If an initial £100 million was spent this would lead to

£100m + £80m + £64m + . . .

The bigger the mpc the bigger the multiplier, because more is spent at each stage of spending.

KEY CONCEPT

The **marginal propensity to consume** measures the extra spending on consumption out of each extra pound.

12.1 **QUICK CHECK**

For each of the following statements, say whether it is true or false.

a. An increase in government spending may lead to a bigger increase in income due to the multiplier.

b. The marginal propensity to consume measures total consumption spending relative to total income.

c. The multiplier will be bigger if the marginal propensity to consume increases.

Taxation

The government raises funds from taxes. There are various forms of tax in the UK.

- **Direct taxes** are taxes placed directly on earnings. For example, UK income earners pay income tax; UK businesses pay tax on their profits.

- **Indirect taxes** are taxes paid when a household or business buys a product. For example, consumers will pay Value Added Tax (VAT) on many products. The producer is responsible for paying this to the government but tries to pass the cost on to the buyers.

Direct taxes will affect the income and wealth of consumers and other businesses. This will affect their ability and willingness to buy products.

Indirect taxes will directly affect a business, as they will have to charge them to consumers; this will affect their sales. The scale of the impact depends on how sensitive demand is to price.

ANALYSING THE BUSINESS DATA

Figure 12.5 UK public sector current receipts, 2018–19

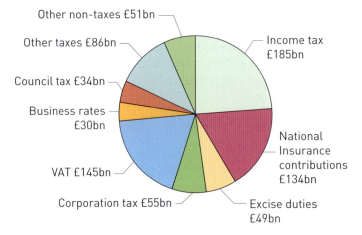

Source: Office for Budget Responsibility; www.gov.uk/government/publications/autumn-budget-2017-documents/autumn-budget-2017

Questions

1. What were the three largest sources of tax revenue in the UK in 2018–19?

2. What do you think would be the impact on business if the government tried to rise more money through corporation tax? What about if it increased the income tax rate?

The uses of tax

Taxes will be used by the government in various ways:

- to raise revenue to finance its spending;
- to change consumers' and firms' behaviour, e.g. to make some products (such as cigarettes) more expensive and less desirable;
- to make foreign products less competitive;
- to redistribute income.

Business and tax

From the perspective of a business, tax can affect both its demand and its costs. Higher income tax, for example, may reduce consumers' spending power and so reduce demand.

Meanwhile, higher taxes on foreign products may increase costs, and higher taxes payable by employees may lead to more demands for higher wages.

Paying benefits

The government will pay benefits to some groups in society: for example, to those who are pensioners or who are unemployed. Benefits help to protect certain groups and to redistribute income to increase the earnings of low-income groups. In 2013 the UK began to introduce the Universal Credit scheme. This brought together many different benefits. The aim was to simplify the system and ensure that no-one is better off not working than they would be if they were in employment.

12.1 BUSINESS INSIGHT: THE TREASURY

The following is an extract from the 'About' page of the UK Treasury website.

Responsibilities
We are responsible for:

- public spending: including departmental spending, public sector pay and pension, annually managed expenditure (AME) and welfare policy, and capital investment
- financial services policy: including banking and financial services regulation, financial stability, and ensuring competitiveness in the City

- strategic oversight of the UK tax system: including direct, indirect, business, property, personal tax, and corporation tax
- the delivery of infrastructure projects across the public sector and facilitating private sector investment into UK infrastructure
- ensuring the economy is growing sustainably

Priorities

Our priorities are:

- achieving strong and sustainable growth
- reducing the deficit and rebalancing the economy
- spending taxpayers' money responsibly
- creating a simpler, fairer tax system
- creating stronger and safer banks
- making corporate taxes more competitive
- making it easier for people to access and use financial services
- improving regulation of the financial sector to protect customers and the economy

Objectives

Our objectives are:

1. Place the public finances on a sustainable footing
2. Ensure the stability of the macro-economic environment and financial system, enabling strong, sustainable and balanced growth
3. Increase employment and productivity, and ensure strong growth and competitiveness across all regions of the UK

Source: www.gov.uk/government/organisations/hm-treasury

Question

Explain why Treasury decisions are so important to businesses.

12.2 QUICK CHECK

For each of the following statements, say whether it is true or false.

a. Fiscal policy involves the use of interest rates.

b. Lower taxation rates are likely to increase demand in the economy.

c. An increase in government spending may be used to reduce unemployment.

d. An increase in government spending may cause inflation.

BUSINESS CASE QUESTIONS: CAN YOU NOW ANSWER . . .

1. What does the UK government set out as its macro-economic objectives?
2. What challenges does the UK economy face?
3. What does the UK government think it can do to help business and the economy?

12.1 DOING THE BUSINESS MATHS

When analysing the effect of direct taxes such as income tax and corporation tax (on profits) you need to consider the rate of tax, e.g. 20%, and the tax thresholds, i.e. at what level of earnings different tax rates have to be paid. For example, the rule might be that you can earn £20,000 tax-free and then start paying 20% on earnings above that, or that you could only earn £5,000 before starting to pay tax.

In the UK income tax system, as you earn more you enter into higher tax bands, with the higher rate of tax paid on the earnings within that band. This is known as a progressive taxation system.

Example of a progressive tax system

Income	Tax rate for income in this income band
<£20,000	0%
£20,000 to <£40,000	20%
£40,000 to <£60,000	40%
£60,000+	60%

If someone earns £50,000 in this system:
   The first £20,000 has no tax to be paid
   The next £20,000 is taxed at 20% = £4,000
   The next £10,000 is taxed at 60% = £6,000 at 40% = £4,000
   Total tax paid is £8,000

Question
In the same system, how much tax would someone earning £80,000 pay?

The income tax paid and the benefits available to the unemployed will affect the incentive to work. Higher income tax rates or lower bands at which different rates take effect may reduce the incentive to work, affecting the size of the labour force.

KEY CONCEPT

In a **progressive tax system**, the average rate of tax increases with more income.

MANAGEMENT TASK

You run a chain of restaurants. You are expecting an increase in VAT. How do you think this might affect your business? Outline the actions you might take if it does happen.

12.2 BUSINESS INSIGHT: TAXES AND THE DEMAND FOR CARS

Taxes can be used by the government to encourage more environmentally friendly behaviour. For example, taxes on environmentally unfriendly goods and services can make consumers and businesses more aware of the full social cost of what they are consuming or providing. Diesel vehicles produce most of the nitrogen oxide gases coming from roadside sources. The UK government announced a new tax on diesel fuel to encourage households to switch from diesel cars towards cars that use more environmentally friendly fuel. This has contributed to the decline in new cars sales in the UK since 2016: sales of diesel cars fell by almost 20%. The BBC reported in January 2018 that in the UK the previous year, 'In total, there were about 2.5 million new cars registered, according to the industry body the Society of Motor Manufacturers and Traders' (see Figure 12.6). This was down 5.7% from 2016. Diesel fuel sales were hit by higher taxes as the government

Figure 12.6 UK car sales, 2007–17

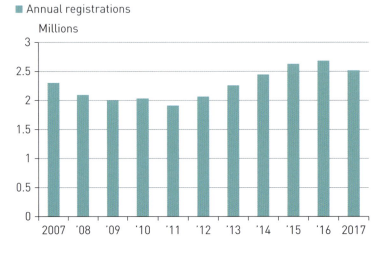

Source: The Society of Motor Manufacturers and Traders (SMMT); BBC, www.bbc.co.uk/news/business-42571828

made owning a diesel car more expensive. Consumers were worried that government policy would punish diesel owners even more in the future. Pollution fears hit demand.

Demand for electric cars is growing fast given that they are environmentally friendly. However, out of 2.5 million vehicles sold in the UK in 2017, only 13,500 were battery electric.

Source: www.bbc.co.uk/news/business-42571828

Questions

1. Apart from taxes, what other factors do you think might affect the demand for cars?

2. How sensitive do you think demand for diesel cars is to increases in indirect taxes? Explain your answer.

Deficit and debt

The deficit is the difference between government spending and revenue each year. The debt is the total amount owed by the government. Every time the government has a deficit it adds to the total debt. If, for example, the deficit was £10 billion, this increases the national debt by £10 billion. If the deficit is increasing year on year, this means the debt is increasing at an increasing rate. If the deficit falls from one year to the next, but still exists, this means the debt increases, but by less than before. The debt will only fall if the government manages to have a budget surplus during the year.

12.2 DOING THE BUSINESS MATHS

Complete the table.

Year	Budget position	Debt position
1	n/a	£100bn
2	Deficit £10bn	
3	Deficit £20bn	
4	Deficit £5bn	
5	Surplus £10bn	

Questions

1. If the deficit is decreasing but still exists, what will happen to the total debt?

2. How can the government reduce its total debt?

Government policy and business

A problem in recent years in the UK has been the scale of the government's deficit. If the government is borrowing every year at relatively high levels, this increases the total debt. This debt has to be 'serviced', i.e. paid for. To do this the government must pay interest. These interest payments are using up money that could otherwise be used by the government for, say, education or health.

Different political parties and economists take different views on the deficit in the UK. Some have argued that the interest payments are far too great and that the government must reduce its deficit. This has involved pursuing an 'austerity programme' aimed at controlling or even reducing spending where possible and looking for ways of increasing revenue. The aim of austerity is for the government to 'stop spending beyond its means' to reduce the interest payments. However, others argue the impact of such a programme can be too severe: for example, cutbacks in health and education or reductions in spending on welfare payments can have too negative an effect on society. They also argue that more spending may be required in some instances, for example in the infrastructure of the economy to provide the investment needed to promote economic growth. The outcome of these policy debates will affect the spending by government and its taxation policies; this will affect demand in the economy.

12.3 QUICK CHECK

For each of the following statements, say whether it is true or false.

a.   A budget deficit occurs when government spending is less than government revenue.

b.   A budget deficit increases government debt.

c.   The budget deficit is usually smaller than the government debt.

d.   An austerity programme will increase the budget deficit.

MANAGEMENT TASK

The newly elected government has a policy of significantly reducing the deficit within the next five years. Outline how this might affect your house-building business.

12.3 BUSINESS INSIGHT: THE GOVERNMENT AND THE RAILWAYS

In 2018 the Labour Party confirmed it wanted to bring the railways back under government control. This may well be popular with the electorate, many of whom feel that price increases in recent years have been too great. However, in reality most of the rail industry is already government controlled. In 2001 Railtrack, which was the privatized owner of the actual railway network, went into administration and was replaced by the government with Network Rail. Network Rail is a not-for-profit organization whose budgets are set by the government. The parts of the system that are still privatized are the companies that own the trains and the companies that run the trains. It is the companies running the trains through franchises that the Labour Party want to control again.

The aim would be a better-integrated transport system serving passengers more effectively and with lower prices. However, some question whether government officials should try and run the train system and believe there would be a lack of investment. If the train companies are part of the government, they may have to fight to funds with other departments such as education and health. Even now, the government has to subsidize the industry by over £3bn. Some question whether it could realistically keep prices low and at the same time provide a good service.

Source: www.bbc.co.uk/news/business-43158919

Question

Do you think the trains would be better run by the government?

What can businesses do to influence government policy?

An individual business is not usually in a position to influence government policy unless it is particularly large. A major employer, for example, may be able to exert some influence on government policy, perhaps because of the possible effect on jobs. However, what businesses can do is join together to try and promote their views and interests. For example, the Confederation of British Industry (CBI) is a leading voice for UK business trying to influence policy makers. There are also industry associations, such as the Society of Motor Manufacturers, which represent the interests of their particular industry.

Of course, what matters is not just whether the government intervenes but how it intervenes. Some would argue that the role of the government is to focus on creating a competitive landscape where businesses can function effectively and where there is an incentive to innovate. This would argue for relatively little intervention and a reliance on making market forces work more effectively. Others would argue for a more interventionist approach where the role of government is to regulate more heavily in order to control more directly the provision of certain goods and services. There are ongoing debates between politicians on where and how to intervene.

MANAGEMENT TASK

You have been asked to advise the government on policies it can introduce (or remove) to help business startups.

Outline three actions the government could take to help more businesses start up and be successful in the UK.

YOU, THE MANAGER

Here is an extract from the 'About us' page of the website of the Confederation of British Industry.

> With over 50 years of experience, we are the UK's most effective and influential business organisation.
>
> We provide our members with the influence, insight and access they need to plan ahead with confidence and grow. We represent their views as we work with policy-makers to deliver a healthy environment for businesses to succeed, create jobs and ultimately, drive economic growth and prosperity.
>
> It is our purpose to help business create a more prosperous society.
>
> The CBI speaks on behalf of 190,000 businesses of all sizes and sectors. Together they employ nearly 7 million people, about one third of the private sector-employed workforce.
>
> With 13 offices around the UK as well as representation in Brussels, Washington, Beijing and Delhi, the CBI communicates the British business voice around the world.
>
> Source: www.cbi.org.uk/about/about-us/

Questions

1. If you were leading the CBI, what would you say were the key issues for business that you would lobby the UK government about?

2. How can business create a more prosperous society?

MANAGEMENT TASK

You are the chairman of the Society of UK Solar Panel Producers. You would like the government to support your industry more, on the basis that this is environmentally friendly energy. You are due to present to government officials in the next few days. How will you justify subsidies to your industry?

12.4 BUSINESS INSIGHT: TAX CUTS IN THE USA

In 2017 the US government introduced some of the most significant changes in the tax system for three decades, as reported by the BBC in December of that year:

> Republicans said that the tax cuts for corporations, small businesses and individuals would boost economic growth. Democrats, who all voted against it, say it is designed to benefit the ultra-rich at the expense of the national deficit. [. . .] Corporate taxes will be set at 21%, instead of the current rate of 35%. The bill will also lower individual tax rates, albeit temporarily.

Other key elements include:

* Less inheritance tax
* An expanded child tax credit
* Lower taxes on overseas profits

Source: www.bbc.co.uk/news/world-us-canada-42421821

Questions

1. Why do you think the US government made these changes to the tax system?
2. What do you think are the advantages and disadvantages of these changes?

What is meant by monetary policy?

Monetary policy is the government's attempts to control the money supply in an economy using interest rates or intervention in the banking system. In the UK, monetary policy is determined by the Bank of England.

KEY CONCEPT

Monetary policy is the government's attempts to control the money supply in an economy using interest rates or intervention in the banking system.

What determines the actions the Bank of England will take?

The Bank of England is set an inflation target by the government. At the time of writing, this is a target of 2%. The Bank of England will then intervene in the economy to achieve this objective. Its main tool is the interest rate. If inflation is 1% higher or lower than the target (e.g. below 1% or above 3%) the Governor of the Bank of England is required to write an open letter to the government to explain why this has happened and what it intends to do to bring in back in line with the target.

Generally, when spending is high—i.e. when demand for goods and services exceeds supply—inflation tends to rise. Prices are pulled upwards. When demand is lower than supply, inflation tends to fall.

To meet its inflation target, the Monetary Policy Committee (MPC) at the Bank of England changes the interest rate it charges (known as the bank rate or the base rate). This is the rate of interest that the Bank of England pays on reserves held with it by commercial banks. Generally, banks will pass on any changes on to their customers. If the high street banks such as Barclays and HSBC earn 2% on their reserves at the Bank of England they can pay their savers, say, 1.75% and still make a profit. If they earn 2.5% they can pay their savers 2.25%. If they earn just 1% at the Bank of England they will pay their own savers, say, 0.75%. Similarly, if the banks have to borrow from the Bank of England at 2% they will charge their borrowers a bit more to ensure they are still profitable, e.g. 2.25%. If the banks have to pay only 1% to the Bank of England they can charge their borrowers, say, 1.25%. The high street interest rates for households (e.g. on credit cards and overdrafts) and businesses (e.g. on business loans) tend, therefore, to follow any changes in the base rate.

So, if inflation looks set to go above its target the Bank of England would probably increase interest rates. By increasing the interest rate the Bank of England hopes to make it more expensive to borrow, and this should deter borrowing and encourage saving. People and businesses will want to save to earn higher returns; they will be less likely to borrow because it is more expensive. This should reduce demand and reduce inflation.

On the other hand, if inflation looks likely to fall below target the Bank of England would cut interest rates to increase spending in the economy and help inflation to rise.

A decrease in aggregate demand will reduce prices. At full employment, less demand will simply bring down prices but below full employment it will reduce output as well. This relationship is illustrated in Figure 12.7.

MANAGEMENT TASK

Your business rents villas in Spain. You think the Monetary Policy Committee will increase the base rate soon. Outline how this might affect your business.

Figure 12.7 The effect of a change in aggregate demand

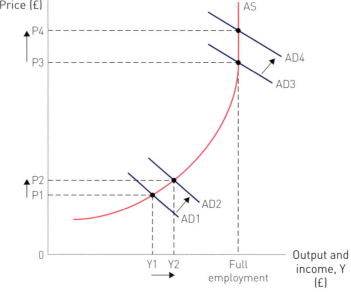

12.5 BUSINESS INSIGHT: INCREASING INTEREST RATES IN THE USA

In 2017 the US central bank—called the Federal Reserve or 'the Fed'—raised interest rates three times. The Fed said the move reflected the underlying strength of the US economy. As the BBC reported in December 2017:

> Officials also boosted their economic forecasts, projecting 2.5% growth in GDP in 2017 and 2018, due in part to planned tax cuts. The Fed said it anticipates three further increases in rates next year [. . .]. The decision to raise interest rates, raising the cost of borrowing, takes the Fed further away from the ultra-low rates it put in place during the financial crisis to boost economic activity. [. . .] The Fed is targeting a range of 1.25% to 1.5% for its benchmark rate. But a majority of officials said they expect interest rates above 2% will be appropriate next year.

Source: https://www.bbc.co.uk/news/business-42344170

Question
Why might the Federal Reserve have increased the base rate?

12.6 BUSINESS INSIGHT: 'SLACK' IN THE ECONOMY

In November 2017 the Bank of England increased the base rate by 0.25% to 0.5%. It did this because it was worried about the rate of inflation and wanted to bring it down. It said:

> The decision to leave the European Union is having a noticeable impact on the economic outlook. The overshoot of inflation throughout the forecast predominantly reflects the effects on import prices of the referendum-related fall in sterling. Uncertainties associated with Brexit are weighing on domestic activity, which has slowed even as global growth has risen significantly. And Brexit-related constraints on investment and labour supply appear to be reinforcing the marked slowdown that has been increasingly evident in recent years in the rate at which the economy can grow without generating inflationary pressures.
>
> Monetary policy cannot prevent either the necessary real adjustment as the United Kingdom moves towards its new international trading arrangements or the weaker real income growth that is likely to accompany that adjustment over the next few years. It can, however, support the economy during the adjustment process. The MPC's remit specifies that, in such exceptional circumstances, the Committee must balance any trade-off between the speed at which it intends to return inflation sustainably to the target and the support that monetary policy provides to jobs and activity.
>
> The steady erosion of slack has reduced the degree to which it is appropriate for the MPC to accommodate an extended period of inflation above the target. Unemployment has fallen to a 42-year low and the MPC judges that the level of remaining slack is limited. The global economy is growing strongly, domestic financial

conditions are highly accommodative and consumer confidence has remained re-silient. In line with the framework set out at the time of the referendum, the MPC now judges it appropriate to tighten modestly the stance of monetary policy in order to return inflation sustainably to the target. Accordingly, the Committee voted by 7–2 to raise Bank Rate by 0.25 percentage points, to 0.5%. Monetary policy con-tinues to provide significant support to jobs and activity in the current exceptional circumstances. All members agree that any future increases in Bank Rate would be expected to be at a gradual pace and to a limited extent.

Source: www.bankofengland.co.uk/monetary-policy-summary-and-minutes/2017/november-2017

Questions

1. Why does the amount of 'slack' in the economy affect inflation?

2. Why do you think a weaker pound is likely to lead to more inflation?

3. Why has the Monetary Policy Committee increased interest rates in the UK?

Quantitative easing

In recent years the UK economy has grown sluggishly and the Bank of England has used low interest rates to stimulate demand. However, even when the base rate was as low as 0.5% this did not seem to stimulate the economy sufficiently. The Bank of England then introduced quantitative easing.

Quantitative easing occurs when a central bank such as the Bank of England creates new money electronically and uses this to make large purchases of assets. These purchases are made from the private sector, for example from pension funds, high-street banks and non-financial firms. Most of these assets are government bonds (also known as gilts). Government bonds are IOUs sold by the Government to raise money. The market for government bonds is large, so it is possible to buy large quantities of them easily and quickly. The purchases are of such a scale that they push up the price of assets, lowering the yields (the return) on them. This en-courages those selling these assets to use the money they received from the sale to buy assets with a higher yield instead, such as company shares and bonds.

KEY CONCEPT

Quantitative easing occurs when a central bank such as the Bank of England creates new money electronically and uses this to make large purchases of assets.

As more of these other assets are bought, their prices rise because of the increased demand. This brings down yields in general. The companies that have issued these bonds or shares benefit from cheaper borrowing because of these lower yields, encouraging them to invest more and increasing their spending.

The Bank of England may also buy a smaller amount of private debt such as corporate bonds (IOUs). This is aimed at making it easier for companies to raise money in capital markets to invest in their business. Again, this should increase demand in the economy.

Those selling assets to the Bank of England have more money in their bank accounts as a result. Commercial banks can use these new funds to finance new loans, encouraging more spending and investment.

Quantitative easing should, therefore, increase the amount of lending and spending in the economy and boost demand.

If, however, inflation looks like it is becoming too high, the Bank of England can sell the assets it has purchased through quantitative easing to reduce the amount of money and spending in the economy.

Buying and selling assets is, therefore, another monetary policy instrument alongside interest rates used to affect demand in the economy and inflation rates.

12.3 DOING THE BUSINESS MATHS

A bond is an IOU; it is sold by the government or businesses to raise finance. Typically a bond will have a coupon. This is an amount it will pay each year and a redemption date which is when the IOU will be repaid.

For example, a bond may have a face value of £100, a coupon of £10 a year and a redemption date of 2025. This would mean that if you bought the bond you would receive £10 a year and then be paid £100 in 2025.

When calculating the return (or yield) on the bond you received, you could consider the price paid, the coupon and final redemption. To keep the calculations simpler we will imagine the bond does not actually have a redemption date, so that the return is entirely the coupon.

If you paid £100 for the bond and receive £10 a year this is a 10% return.

Imagine that 10% was a much higher return than was available for other assets. For example, imagine that the return elsewhere was typically 5%. Investors will want to buy the bonds to benefit from the high return of these bonds. With this high demand, the price of the bonds will increase. As the price increases the £10 becomes a lower percentage, i.e. the £10 becomes a smaller percentage of a higher price.

Imagine again that the bond has a price of £100 and pays a £10 coupon per year. This is a 10% annual return. If this is lower than is available elsewhere, investors will want to sell their bonds and invest in alternative forms of assets. This will lead to a fall in the bond price until the return on bonds is equal to the returns available elsewhere.

Given a fixed coupon, the higher the bond price the lower the return on bonds. The lower the bond price the higher the return on bonds.

Complete the table.

Price of bond (£)	Annual coupon (£)	Return (%)
100	10	
120	10	
200	10	
80	10	
50	10	

Exchange rate policy

The exchange rate of a country can change with changes in supply and demand conditions in the foreign currency markets. This changes the prices of UK products overseas and the price of foreign products in pounds. A government may intervene in the currency markets to influence the price of the currency. It may do this to stabilize the price. This will help businesses with their planning. It may intervene to affect the competitiveness of exports or the price of imports (and therefore costs and inflationary pressures).

The exchange rate may be affected by various factors.

- Changes in the interest rate by the Bank of England will have an effect. A higher domestic interest rate is likely to attract money from abroad as investors seek these higher returns by saving in the UK. This increases the demand for the currency and the value of the pound in terms of foreign currency.

- Buying and selling currency will also have an effect. If the government buys pounds using its foreign currency reserves, this increases the demand for the pound on the currency markets and increases its value. If the government wants the currency to fall in value it sells pounds on the currency markets; this increases supply and brings its value down.

12.4 DOING THE BUSINESS MATHS

Figure 12.8 An increase in the supply of a currency

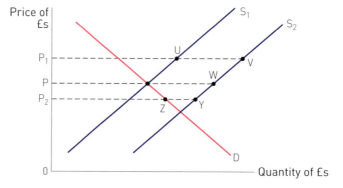

Looking at Figure 12.8, imagine

- that the supply of a currency has increased from S1 to S2;
- that the government wants to keep the value of the currency at P.

Question

Which of the following is the action needed by the government to keep the exchange rate at this value?

a) Sell UV of its currency.

b) Buy XW of its currency.

c) Sell ZY of its currency.

d) Buy UX of its currency.

Supply side policies

Supply side policies are government policies aimed at making markets work more effectively to increase the quantity and quality of resources available in the economy. They are aimed at increasing the aggregate supply on an economy. The government may intervene in various ways.

- It may intervene in financial markets to make funds more easily available for businesses to fund investment.
- It may aim to develop the infrastructure of the economy to help your business to compete more effectively. This may include either directly investing in, or supporting investment in, elements of the country's infrastructure such as transport systems or communications systems. These may be huge projects that have greater social benefits than private benefits and therefore require government involvement.
- It may try to ensure that markets work fairly and competitively. For example, it may want to prevent large businesses dominating and forcing out smaller rivals, or it may aim to prevent corruption to enable businesses to compete on an equal basis.
- It may try to help businesses to be more innovative: for example, by encouraging research and development spending.
- It may intervene to make the labour market work better: for example, by improving the incentives for people to look for work and investing in skills, or by increasing employability by developing people's skills and their ability to relocate.
- It may help businesses to start up and help you to do business by reducing the administrative procedures necessary to do so.

Figure 12.9 shows the effect of successful supply side policies. If the economy is originally at full capacity with a maximum supply of Y1, the output will be Y1 and the price P1. With supply side policies the government aims to shift the aggregate

Figure 12.9 Effect of successful supply side policies

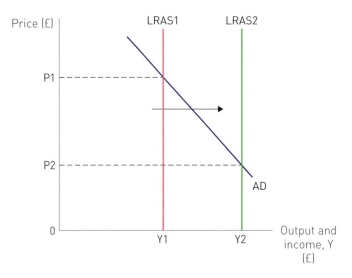

supply in the economy. This would increase output, e.g. to Y2, and could help bring down prices to P2 (or reduce inflation).

MANAGEMENT TASK

You believe that the government needs to invest more in faster broadband in the UK to help business. Summarize your arguments on why more investment in broadband would be a good investment for the government.

12.7 BUSINESS INSIGHT: INFRASTRUCTURE

Here is an extract from the Foreword of a document entitled 'Analysis of the National Infrastructure and Construction Pipeline', which was published by the UK Infrastructure and Projects Authority in 2017.

Infrastructure has the power to increase our living standards, drive economic growth and boost productivity. This government is building an economy that is fit for the future by investing for the long-term. We have put infrastructure at the heart of our economic plan and it is a central pillar of the Industrial Strategy. The UK is at the forefront of infrastructure delivery around the world. [. . .]

The 2017 update to the National Infrastructure and Construction Pipeline sets out details of over £460 billion of planned infrastructure investment across the public and private sectors. Looking across the next ten years, we project total public and private investment in infrastructure to be around £600 billion.

For our investment to be realised we need delivery of complex infrastructure projects on time and on budget. This requires long-term decision making, significant capital investment and a renewed focus on our priorities. We have already taken steps to improve our delivery framework. The creation of the National Infrastructure Commission and the Infrastructure and Projects Authority (IPA) were significant steps towards ensuring we make the right long-term investment decisions and then deliver those investments as effectively as possible.

Andrew Jones MP, Exchequer Secretary to the Treasury

Source: https://assets.publishing.service.gov.uk/government/uploads/system/uploads/attachment_data/file/665332/Analysis_of_National_Infrastructure_and_Construction_Pipeline_2017.pdf

Question

How might investment in infrastructure help British businesses to be more competitive?

MANAGEMENT TASK

You have been asked to advise the government on its supply side policies. Recommend two key supply side measures you think the government should adopt.

12.8 BUSINESS INSIGHT: CORRUPTION INDEX

Table 12.1 shows an extract of data from 2016 produced by transparency.org for an index of corruption. Over two-thirds of the 176 countries and territories in that year's index fell below the midpoint of the scale of 0 (highly corrupt) to 100 (very clean). The global average score was 43, indicating endemic corruption in a country's public sector.

Table 12.1 Corruption perception index 2016

2016 Rank	Country	2016 Score	Region
1	Denmark	90	Europe and Central Asia
1	New Zealand	90	Asia Pacific
3	Finland	89	Europe and Central Asia
4	Sweden	88	Europe and Central Asia
5	Switzerland	86	Europe and Central Asia
6	Norway	85	Europe and Central Asia
7	Singapore	84	Asia Pacific
8	Netherlands	83	Europe and Central Asia
9	Canada	82	Americas
10	Germany	81	Europe and Central Asia
10	Luxembourg	81	Europe and Central Asia

(Continue...)

2016 Rank	Country	2016 Score	Region
10	United Kingdom	81	Europe and Central Asia
13	Australia	79	Asia Pacific
14	Iceland	78	Europe and Central Asia

Visit www.transparency.orq/cpi for more information

Source: https://www.transparency.org/news/feature/corruption

Question

a) How might corruption affect aggregate supply in an economy?

b) How might corruption affect a business?

12.9 BUSINESS INSIGHT: EASE OF DOING BUSINESS

Supply side policies can affect the ease of setting up and doing business in a country. For example, how long does it take to register a business? How easy is it to get energy or telecommunications to get connected? How easy it is to enforce any contracts that you make? The data in Table 12.2, as presented by doingbusiness.org, ranks countries on the ease of doing business in them.

Here is doingbusiness.org's explanation of how the rankings are determined.

Economies are ranked on their ease of doing business, from 1–190. A high ease of doing business ranking means the regulatory environment is more conducive to the starting and operation of a local firm. The rankings are determined by sorting

Table 12.2 The seven top-ranked countries for ease of doing business, 2017.

Economy	Ease of doing business rank	Starting a business	Dealing with construction permits	Getting electricity	Registering property
New Zealand	1	1	3	37	1
Singapore	2	6	16	12	19
Denmark	3	34	1	16	11
Korea, Rep.	4	9	28	2	39
Hong Kong SAR, China	5	3	5	4	55
United States	6	49	36	49	37
United Kingdom	7	14	14	9	47

(Continue...)

Economy	Getting credit	Protecting minority investors	Paying taxes	Trading across borders	Enforcing contracts
New Zealand	1	2	9	56	21
Singapore	29	4	7	42	2
Denmark	42	33	8	1	32
Korea, Rep.	55	20	24	33	1
Hong Kong SAR, China	29	9	3	31	28
United States	2	42	36	36	16
United Kingdom	28	10	23	28	31

Source: http://www.doingbusiness.org/rankings

the aggregate distance to frontier scores on 10 topics, each consisting of several indicators, giving equal weight to each topic. The rankings for all economies are benchmarked to June 2017.

Source: http://www.doingbusiness.org/rankings

Question

How might the ease of doing business affect an economy?

12.10 BUSINESS INSIGHT: BROADBAND SPEED IN THE UK

The BBC reported in December 2017 that the UK government had announced recently that homes and businesses would have a legal right to demand faster broadband speed of at least 10 megabits per second (Mbps) by 2020. The report goes on:

BT, which is responsible for the infrastructure, had previously offered to carry out improvements according to its own timetable. But the company said it accepted the government's decision. [. . .] The government believes the regulatory Universal Service Obligation offers 'certainty'. Under the plan, broadband providers will face a legal requirement to provide this minimum standard to anyone requesting it, subject to a cost threshold. The UK lags behind many countries in terms of speed and reliability. [. . .]

Regulator Ofcom said that 4% of UK premises, or about 1.1 million, could not access broadband speeds of at least 10 Mbps [see Figure 12.10]. It said poor connections were a particular concern for small businesses, with almost 230,000 unable

Figure 12.10 UK download speeds by local authority, in Mbps

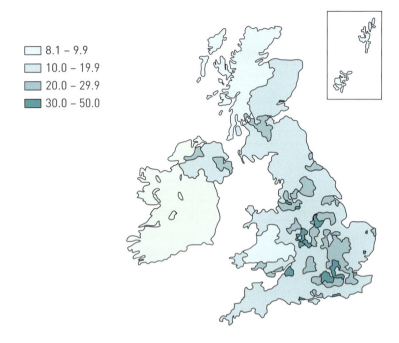

8.1 – 9.9
10.0 – 19.9
20.0 – 29.9
30.0 – 50.0

Source: Ofcom Connected Nation 2016; BBC, www.bbc.co.uk/news/business-42423047

to get a decent service. Ofcom defines superfast broadband as a download speed of 30 Mbps or more.

Question

Why is a good broadband system important for business?

BUSINESS CASE QUESTIONS: CAN YOU NOW ANSWER . . .

Do you think the UK government should get involved in industrial strategy?

What determines how the government intervenes?

How the government intervenes will depend on what it regards as the priority at any given moment. An underlying focus of the UK government for many years, for example, has been to achieve stable prices; unemployment by comparison has been less of an issue in recent years due to relatively high levels of employment. This means that interest rates have been regarded as a key policy instrument to try and control demand. The government has also been eager to reduce its borrowing, which means that aggressive use of government spending to stimulate growth has not been used.

The nature of government intervention will also depend on the government's view of how the economy works or does not work. Classical economists believe that markets work well and that the economy will settle at its maximum output (known as its potential output) given its resources. If, for example, the economy was below the potential there would be unemployment, wages would fall, and then more people would be employed, helping to get the economy back to its potential output. In this situation the focus of the government would be on supply side economics to improve the potential of the economy.

Other economists, known as Keynesian (after the work of John Maynard Keynes), believe that the economy can get stuck below its maximum capacity and could take a very long time to return to its potential. For example, if demand falls there will be unemployment but Keynes argued wages might be slow to fall; employees may be reluctant to accept pay cuts and/or may have negotiated contracts for a year ahead. In this situation the government may want to actively intervene on the demand side to increase aggregate demand. Keynesian economists are associated with increased government spending and lower tax rates when needed to increase demand and pull the economy back to its potential. Keynesian views came back into favour after the 2008 global recession. At this time some economists argued that governments should pursue austerity measures to control their deficit; others, such as Paul Krugman, argued that governments should adopt a Keynesian approach and spend to stimulate demand.

READ MORE

You can discover more about the neo- classical views of the economy if you read Milton Friedman's defence of markets:

Friedman, M. (1962), *Capitalism and Freedom*, Chicago: University of Chicago Press.
John Maynard Keynes' most famous work is

Keynes, J.M. (1936), *The General Theory of Employment, Interest and Money*, London: Macmillan.
You can follow Paul Krugman's work on his *New York Times* blog:
www.nytimes.com/2018/06/29/opinion/

• •

SUMMARY

Governments have several macro-economic objectives; typically these include stable prices, low rates of unemployment, economic growth, and a healthy trade position. To achieve these aims the government uses policies such as fiscal policy, monetary policy,

Table 12.3 Government policies and how they might be used to achieve macro-economic objectives

Policy	Objective			
	Reducing un-employment	Increasing economic growth	Reducing inflation	Improving trade position
Fiscal policy: government spending and taxation changes	Increase government spending or reduce tax rates to boost demand; lower benefits for the unemployed to encourage people to accept a job	Lower corporation taxes to encourage investment	Reduce government spending and raise tax rates to dampen demand	Tax foreign products to reduce demand for them; reduce government spending and raise taxes to reduce demand for all products including imports
Monetary policy: interest rate changes and quantitative easing	Lower interest rates to encourage spending and boost demand	Lower interest rates to encourage investment	Raise interest rates to reduce borrowing and spending and dampen demand	Raise interest rates to dampen demand including demand for imports
Supply side policies to make market work more efficiently and improve the quantity and quality of resources	Improve labour market: provide more information about availability of jobs; lower relocation costs; improve skills	Make finance more easily available for investment	Increase aggregate supply to bring down prices	Improve supply conditions to make UK firms more competitive internationally
Exchange rate policy: use of interest rates and government buying and selling of currency	Lower exchange rates to make exports more competitive in foreign currency	Lower exchange rates to make exports more competitive	Increase exchange rates to reduce import costs in pounds	Allowing weaker currency in the short term may make exports more competitive and switch demand away from more expensive imports

Table 12.4 Government policies and how they impact on business

Policy	Impact on demand	Impact on costs
Fiscal policy: government spending and taxation changes	Increased government spending or reduced tax rates boost demand	Lower corporation taxes encourage investment and reduce costs
Monetary policy: interest rate changes and quantitative easing	Lower interest rates encourage spending and boost demand	Lower interest rates reduce costs
Supply side policies to make market work more efficiently and improve the quantity and quality of resources	Improved labour market with more information about availability of jobs, lower relocation costs, and better skills, leads to more employment and demand	More supply may reduce costs
Exchange rate policy: use of interest rates and government buying and selling of currency	Lower exchange rates make exports more competitive in foreign currency and so increase demand	Higher exchange rate may reduce import costs

supply side policy, and exchange rate policy (Table 12.3). This involves pulling various 'levers' such as taxation rates and interest rates to influence the decisions of groups such as businesses and households.

These policy changes will change the economic environment of business by influencing supply and demand in many markets such as the goods and services market, the labour market, the currency market, and the money market (Table 12.4). Governments may also try to influence the exchange rate—for example it may want to keep it stable to make investment easier to plan. It may also use supply side policies to increase the quantity and quality of resources available in the economy; this will affect the costs and productivity of businesses.

KEY LEARNING POINTS

- A budget deficit occurs when government spending over a period is greater than its revenue.
- A budget surplus occurs when government spending over a period is less than its revenue.
- Fiscal policy attempts to influence the economy through changes in government spending and the tax and benefits system.
- Monetary policy attempts to influence the economy through interest rates and changes to the money supply (e.g. through quantitative easing).

- Supply side policies attempt to influence the quantity and quality of the supply of resources in the economy.
- Exchange rate policy aims to change the value of the currency to affect import and export prices.

BUSINESS CASE EXTENSION QUESTIONS

1. Analyse the key elements of UK government macro-economic policy. Discuss the effects of these policies on UK business.

2. Compare and contrast UK government macro-economic policy with that of another national government of your choice.

3. Assess the effectiveness of UK government policy in terms of meeting its macro-economic objectives.

4. Analyse the key factors that are affecting the global competitiveness of UK businesses at the moment.

QUICK QUESTIONS

1. What is meant by a government budget deficit?
2. What is meant by a government budget surplus?
3. What is the relationship between a government's deficit and its debt?
4. Why might a government worry about its debt?
5. How does the Bank of England use monetary policy to intervene in the economy?
6. How does the government use fiscal policy to intervene in the economy?
7. How does the government use supply side policies to intervene in the economy?
8. How does the government intervene to influence the exchange rate?
9. What factors might influence the ease of doing business in a country?
10. What is meant by a government bond?

Global business

WHY DO I NEED TO KNOW ABOUT GLOBAL BUSINESS?

You are the managing director of a business that produces luxury sports cars. China has been one of your biggest markets in recent years. The rapid growth of incomes in that economy has led to a major increase in demand for Western products. You were one of the first to spot the opportunity and after many challenges along the way you have managed to build the network and relationships needed to access this market.

Over 30 per cent of your sales now come from China and the brand seems to go from strength to strength. Your recent investment in a new model of your car was based on its expected sales in China. So far, so good. But today, after many rumours, the Chinese government announced it was introducing a high tax on imported sports cars. This is very bad news. You plan to contact the UK government to try to get it to retaliate. You want the UK government to force the Chinese to change their mind.

BY THE END OF THIS CHAPTER YOU WILL BE ABLE TO . . .

- explain how trade can benefit a business
- explain the possible problems trade can cause a business
- analyse how, and why, a government may protect an industry
- analyse the impact of protectionism on business

BUSINESS CASE

Burgers have traditionally been seen as fast food—basic and cheap. However, market tastes are changing and the growth sector of the burger industry is the 'better burger'. Customers are now willing to wait longer and pay more for what is perceived to be better-quality burgers. A BBC article on this phenomenon mentions Five Guys as an example of a 'better burger' business that has grown fast and is now expanding rapidly overseas. However, it is not always easy to offer exactly the same products around the world, not least because of different rules regarding ingredients that can used. Companies want the brand to be consistent, but that may require some experimentation with different ingredients around the world. Five Guys opened its first restaurant outside the US in 2014. It is a family business started by Jerry and Janie Murrell (husband and wife) and their five sons in 1986 when the boys were given the advice to 'Start a business or go to college'. It is now one of the biggest providers of 'better burgers'. The Five Guys website says the company's philosophy is simple: 'To perfect and serve. That's the principle that has brought us so far. It's the promise we make every day to our customers who count on us to keep delivering the food and experience they love.'

Under the 'Freshness' tab on the Five Guys website, the family say:

> We don't have freezers on-site because we don't use frozen ingredients. At Five Guys, everything's cooked fresh from scratch. That's the way we like people to serve food to us, so why would we serve our customers any other way?
>
> Sure, we're great believers in keeping life simple. But if the simplicity of freezing food means compromising on its quality and flavour, then we're just not going to do it. For us, fresh and delicious go hand-in-hand. And what could be simpler than that?
>
> So our potatoes are hand-cut daily. We always tell you where they come from too, with posters on our walls. And our beef . . . is grain-finished for the last 120 days to give it the marbled texture perfect for mince.
>
> We don't use automated cooking timers, because great cooking is all about knowing instinctively when food is perfectly cooked—based on sight, aroma and texture. What's more, we prep all our food daily only to ensure maximum freshness. This is good food the way it deserves to be cooked—no corners cut, no cheaper alternatives, all about flavour.
>
> It's your meal. So it's our belief that you should get exactly what you want. With burgers, hotdogs, sandwiches and a multitude of toppings, you've got more than 250,000 possible topping combinations to choose from (not-to-mention the 1,000 mix-in milkshake combinations).
>
> That said, lots of our customers relish the prospect of their regular favourite meal each time they visit. Whatever tickles your own personal taste buds. Total freedom!

This type of burger restaurant tends to be two or three times as expensive as McDonald's or Burger King but still cheaper than more traditional restaurants.

As the BBC reported, 'Five Guys is currently in nine countries and expects to expand to 28 over the next five years. [. . .] [Five Guys CEO Paul] Reynish says it was demands from visitors to the US desperate to experience the burgers in their home countries that drove their decision to expand.'

Another US success story in Shake Shack. Unlike Five Guys, Shake Shack expanded before it even had a chain in America. It started as a temporary stand in a park in New York. It was founded by Danny Meyer and just after he opened its second restaurant he was approached by Kuwaiti firm Alshaya, which was interested in opening a franchise. Shake Shack agreed to a licensing deal whereby it had a one-off fee and a percentage of sales. It still uses this model for all its overseas restaurants.

According to the company website:

In 2004, a permanent kiosk opened in the park: Shake Shack was born. This modern day 'roadside' burger stand serves up the most delicious burgers, hot dogs, frozen custard, shakes, beer, wine and more. An instant neighbourhood fixture, Shake Shack welcomed people from all over the city, country and world who gathered together to enjoy fresh, simple, high-quality versions of the classics in a majestic setting. The rest, as they say, is burger history.

However, there is growing competition in this 'better burger' market. The market research company Mintel says that this means it's becoming harder for firms to attract customers.

Sources:
www.bbc.co.uk/news/business-40170738
www.shakeshack.com
www.fiveguys.com

BUSINESS CASE QUESTIONS

1. Why do you think Five Guys wanted to expand overseas?

2. What problems might Five Guys face when expanding overseas?

3. Do you think it is better to open your own restaurants or to use licensing as Shake Shack does?

Global business

We live in a global economy. As consumers, when we go shopping we are choosing from products either produced abroad or using supplies and materials from abroad. Spanish oranges, French wine, German cars, Italian ham, Swiss cheese, Chinese t-shirts . . . our lives are full of foreign products. What we wear, what we listen to, what we eat or watch, are often internationally linked. The UK in particular is a very open economy. This means that it is very open to trade. We import large quantities of goods and services (i.e. we buy them from abroad) and we also export high quantities of goods and services (i.e. we sell them abroad).

Global trade is, therefore, very important to UK consumers. And also to UK businesses. Trade enables you as a manager to find the supplies you want and have a wider choice of providers. This should lead to better quality inputs supplied at lower prices. The number of international players in the UK Premier League in football highlight the benefits of having access to the best resources available around the world.

Trade also provides export markets for UK businesses. This should allow you to find more customers and enable you to generate revenue and benefit from economies of scale. Companies such as Jaguar and Burberry have clearly benefited from selling overseas, enabling them to achieve much higher sales than they could if they just focused on the UK. Your business may be able to do the same. The UK has a population of 65 million. China has a population of around 1.3 billion. The world's population is around 7.6 billion. Just think of all those potential customers around the world! And by selling in different countries it is possible to benefit from more favourable conditions—for example, economies overseas may be growing faster than in the UK—and so you can spread risk by not just being dependent on the UK market.

BUSINESS CASE QUESTION: NOW CAN YOU ANSWER . . .

Why do you think Five Guys wanted to expand overseas?

Entering overseas markets

As mentioned in the previous section, entering an overseas market can provide opportunities for more sales and help the business to grow. However, trading abroad can be complex. There are likely to be differences in the business environment abroad compared to the UK, such as differences in the laws that affect business and the state of the economy. There are also likely to be variations in social norms which can make decisions—such as how to promote your products—more challenging. A significant issue is simply that you as a manager will not know how business is done as well as you know how things are done in your existing markets. You won't have the contacts and you won't know the best way of doing things or what others are doing to the same extent. There is, therefore, a considerable degree of risk in becoming involved in international business. This is why most businesses that do engage in international trade actually still tend to trade within regions that are relatively close by. For example, most of the UK's trade is with European countries. This may well be because managers are more familiar with these countries and tend to be culturally more similar to their inhabitants than to those in regions further away.

Typically, a business will start getting involved in international business by exporting. This means it sells some of its products abroad. This may be in response to enquiries from foreign buyers. There are other options too.

- You may license your idea to an overseas operator. If you sell the franchise to a local business, you will limit your risk. Typically you would charge an initial fee to the business that buys the franchise (the franchisee) and then a percentage of revenue. This arrangement may carry both advantages and disadvantages (see Table 13.1). The more successful the overseas operator, the more revenue you own. However, the downside to franchising is that the franchisee gets the majority of the earnings. It can also be difficult to control quality and ensure there is consistency across the brand.

- You might link up with a local business in a partnership or joint venture. This uses the knowledge and experience of businesses already operating in the overseas market.

Table 13.1 Selling a franchise

Advantages of selling a franchise	Disadvantages of selling a franchise
Raise revenue from sale	Do not retain all profits
Earn revenue from turnover of franchisee	Loss of control
Growth financed partly by franchisee	May be difficult to control quality

- You might take over a local provider. This again makes use of the expertise and links of an existing overseas-based producer. However, it requires much higher levels of investment and risk than simply selling some products abroad.

The riskiest way of entering an overseas market is to set up your own business. This has the highest level of investment but does mean that you have full control of the operations.

The decision on how to enter an overseas market will depend on the level of commitment you want to make; this will in turn will depend on your view of the likely returns.

13.1 BUSINESS INSIGHT: PRODUCTION OF THE MINI IN CHINA

Electric Mini cars are to be built in China as well as in Oxford, where Minis are produced at the moment. The production in China is part of a venture undertaken by BMW, which owns the Mini brand, with the Chinese manufacturer Great Wall Motors.

The cars produced will be for sale in China. The Chinese government has a target that by 2025, 20 per cent of cars sold should be electric. The joint venture involves two plants assembling the cars, and an engine plant.

In 2017, BMW sold 560,000 cars in China—more than twice the number sold in its next two largest markets, the US and Germany, combined.

Source: BBC, www.bbc.co.uk/news/business-43166956

Question
Why do you think BMW decided to enter a joint venture with Great Wall Motors rather than produce on its own?

BUSINESS CASE: CAN YOU NOW ANSWER . . .

Do you think it is better to open your own restaurants or to use licensing as Shake Shack does?

MANAGEMENT TASK

You are a cosmetics manufacturer. You are trying to decide which overseas market to target with your new perfume. What would you need to know to decide?

RESEARCH TASK

Research a business that is entering an overseas market or withdrawing from it. Analyse the reasons for the decision.

Managing global supply chains

More open markets provide access to new customers but also new suppliers. You can select the best suppliers from all over the world; you can benefit from the resources and specialist skills of many different regions. Aspects of production can be outsourced to producers elsewhere who can produce at a better quality or a lower price.

Take apart an iPhone and you will find components from many different suppliers all over the world. You may well employ staff globally and have employees in your UK operations from many different countries. Your operations process is very likely, therefore, to have a global element to it.

13.2 BUSINESS INSIGHT: APPLE'S SUPPLIERS

The graphic in Figure 13.1 highlights some of the many supplies involved in the production of an iPhone. Apple focuses on the design and branding. It then uses specialist suppliers around the world to produce the product itself. The suppliers' profit margins are much smaller than Apple's.

Source: BBC, www.bbc.co.uk/news/business-42909989

Questions

1. Why does Apple use suppliers from all over the world?
2. The profit margin of Apple suppliers is far lower than Apple's profit margin. Why do you think this is?

Managing a supply chain involves managing all the different elements of the process, from the raw materials to the finished product. This will involve you choosing the suppliers, organizing the contracts and service agreements, and ensuring appropriate standards are met. It can also involve monitoring the behaviour of suppliers to ensure that they meet your agreed ethical standards and that you know exactly where they get their supplies from. In the food industry, for example, it is increasingly important that a business can identify exactly what goes into all of its products, where it is sourced from and how it is produced. The danger of not doing this was shown by the horsemeat scandal in the UK in 2012 and 2013, when it was found that some meat being sold as beef was actually horsemeat, as described in Business insight 13.3.

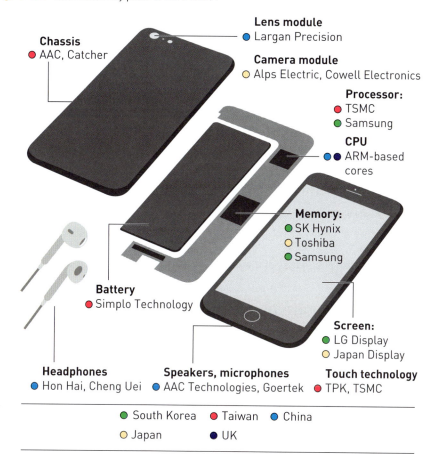

Figure 13.1 Who makes key parts of the iPhone?

Chassis
● AAC, Catcher

Lens module
● Largan Precision

Camera module
○ Alps Electric, Cowell Electronics

Processor:
● TSMC
● Samsung

CPU
●● ARM-based cores

Memory:
● SK Hynix
○ Toshiba
● Samsung

Battery
● Simplo Technology

Screen:
● LG Display
○ Japan Display

Headphones
● Hon Hai, Cheng Uei

Speakers, microphones
● AAC Technologies, Goertek

Touch technology
● TPK, TSMC

● South Korea   ● Taiwan   ● China
○ Japan   ● UK

KEY CONCEPT

A **supply chain** is comprised of all the businesses and individual contributors involved in creating a product, from raw materials to finished merchandise.

13.3 BUSINESS INSIGHT: THE FOOD SUPPLY CHAIN

Two men have recently been jailed for their roles in a conspiracy to sell 30 tonnes of horsemeat as beef. Horsemeat was added to batches of beef which were all labelled as 'pure beef'. This was not the only incidence of tampering with beef at the time. The effect of the revelations about horsemeat hit consumers' confidence badly—people stopped trusting that the food they were being sold was what they were told it was.

In 2012, beef was selling at around €3 (£2.60) a kilogram at wholesale prices. Horsemeat sold for around €2 (£1.75) a kilogram.

Tesco, the UK's largest supermarket chain, ran apology adverts in newspapers for selling beefburgers that contained horse meat. It ran a two-page national press campaign with the headline 'What burgers have taught us'. The ad campaign said that the problems that have arisen with meat are 'about more than burgers and bolognese'. 'It's about some of the ways we get meat to your dinner table. It's about the whole food industry', it added.

The advertisement was designed to show that Tesco was serious about the horsemeat issue and was listening to the public. It ended with the line: 'We know that our supply chain is too complicated. So we're making it simpler . . . Seriously. This is it. We are changing.'

However, ensuring that every product's ingredients are exactly what they say they are all the way down the supply chain is not easy, especially when supermarkets typically stock 35,000–40,000 different food products.

Source: https://www.bbc.co.uk/news/uk-england-london-40775328

Question
What do you think the challenges of managing a food supply chain might be?

13.4 BUSINESS INSIGHT: OUTSOURCING AT MCDONALD'S

The McDonald's system—which involves outsourcing 100 per cent of its supplies—has expanded to more than 100 countries and more than 35,000 restaurants serving more than 68 million customers a day. McDonald's has also set the food industry standards for food quality, safety, and assured supply. Customers know they will get the same consistent food and service wherever they are in the world.

As explained in an article published in 2016 on the supplychain247.com site, McDonald's achieves this success with a 100 per cent outsourced supply chain. The founder, Ray Kroc, decided to use an outsourced model for suppliers from the very start of McDonald's. The decision was simple. First, he did not have the finances to build his own vertical supply chain. But he had also seen as a salesman how some other companies forced their franchised restaurants to buy goods from the business even when they were not good enough.

McDonald's supply chain model is aimed at creating long-term wealth and competitive advantage for everyone involved by controlling costs, and producing quality and innovative products that improve sales. The result is improved customer value, a strong brand, and a better business performance. McDonald's aims to 'grow the profits pie' and share it out.

Suppliers that help McDonald's succeed build their own businesses. Both McDonald's and its suppliers aim to create value together rather than simply exchanging value, which is what happens in conventional transaction-based relationships where buyer and seller fight over profit margins.

As the supplychain247.com article explains:

Kroc's 'System' philosophy is often described as a three-legged stool. One of the legs is McDonald's employees, a second leg is the owner/operators that run the restaurants and the third leg is McDonald's supplier partners.

The stool is only as strong as all three legs. This means that franchisees, suppliers and company employees each support the weight of McDonald's equally. Kroc believed that if the restaurant owner/operators and suppliers were successful, success would come to him as well. Simply put, McDonald's, its owner/operators and their suppliers have a vested interest in helping each other succeed.

Source: www.supplychain247.com/article/mcdonalds_secret_sauce_for_supply_chain_success

Questions

1. Why does an outsourced model help McDonald's?

2. What is the difference between the McDonald's approach and the typical value-exchanging relationship between most businesses and their suppliers?

The benefits of trade to your business

A key underlying principle of international trade is called 'comparative advantage'. This is based on the opportunity cost of producing any given product. According to the law of comparative advantage, producers in a country should specialize in the production of products where they have a low opportunity cost and buy in from abroad products where they have a relatively high opportunity cost. That is, you should specialize in producing items where you have a comparative advantage and avoid producing products where you have a comparative disadvantage. Basically you can focus on what you are good at and buy in the resources or components where you are not so good.

KEY CONCEPT

Comparative advantage occurs when a country has a lower opportunity cost in the production of a product than other countries.

Whether you have a comparative advantage compared to businesses abroad will depend, in part, on the conditions in your region or country. The UK is always going to struggle to have an advantage in the production of bananas, for example, because it does not have the climate. To produce bananas will require high levels of resources and a high opportunity cost. Businesses in the UK will also struggle to compete in low-price labour-intensive industries because labour costs in the UK are relatively high compared to, say, Vietnam, thanks to the minimum wage, the employment laws, and the cost of living. However, the UK does have access to a relatively skilled labour force which may help it to be more competitive in the higher-value-added areas such as research and design. There are sectors such as banking, music, and film-making where the UK has built up the experience and infrastructure to have an advantage. Of course, the precise comparative advantage of a business does depend on its particular circumstances, but the environment in which it operates will play a significant factor.

By using specialists overseas you can buy in goods and services where you have a relative disadvantage for a lower price than you could produce them for yourself. This saves you money and allows you to use your resources efficiently. The same is true for a country as a whole. If its resources are used in sectors where it has a comparative advantage, it can buy in other goods and services where it has a disadvantage and do so more cheaply than it can produce them itself. A country can also export the products it does produce to those who are not so efficient at producing these. This means that trading can be a win–win situation for everyone. Producers can sell their products for a profit, and consumers and businesses abroad can buy them in for less than they would pay if they were produced domestically.

Free trade between countries should therefore have two benefits:

- enabling producers and consumers to benefit from cheaper products from abroad;
- providing producers and consumers with a greater variety of products than would be produced if a country did not allow trade.

Of course, having open borders for trade is not just about goods and services; it can also mean allowing people to move between countries. This can allow a business to have access to a wider pool of labour. This can in some cases provide a cheaper labour force than is available domestically. It can also provide access to talent that may not exist locally.

COMPARATIVE ADVANTAGE

Imagine there are two countries producing goods A and B. They put half of all their resources in to the production of each and are not trading.

	Good A	Good B
Country 1	1	3
Country 2	2	4
Total world output	**3**	**7**

The opportunity of cost of producing A and B is calculated for each country (i.e. how much of the other product is sacrificed to produce an extra A or B).

	Opportunity cost of producing 1 A	Opportunity cost of producing 1 B
Country 1	3 B	⅓ A
Country 2	2 B	½ A

The countries then decide to specialize in the producing the product where they have a lower opportunity cost.

Country 2 will produce As because it has the lower opportunity cost here (2 is less than 3).

Country 1 will produce Bs because it has the lower opportunity cost here ($\frac{1}{3}$ is less than $\frac{1}{2}$).

This means the countries put all their resources into one product, doubling the amount of resources in the industry. We assume this doubles the output in the world.

	Good A	Good B
Country 1	0	8
Country 2	4	0
Total world output	**4**	**8**

By specializing, it is possible to use resources more effectively and thus increase the total amount produced in the world. In fact the gains from trade may be even greater because by specializing in one area, production may increase even more.

Trade can also benefit each country as it can get access to products for less than it could produce them for itself.

For example, the opportunity cost of making 1A is 3B in country 1 and 2 in country 2. If the second country specializes and sells 1A for the cost of 2.5B, then it will make a profit and country 1 will be buying them for less than it would cost to produce it itself. Both countries win.

13.1 DOING THE BUSINESS MATHS

	Good A	Good B
Country 1	3	6
Country 2	4	6

Questions

1. Which country has a comparative advantage in the production of good A? Which has a comparative advantage in the production of good B?

2. What are the possible terms of trade which would be beneficial for both countries?

UK trade

The European Union (EU) countries have been hugely important trade partners for the UK for many years. Countries that belong to the EU have relatively open markets in terms of goods, services, and the movement of money and people. According to the Office for National Statistics the EU has accounted for nearly 50 per cent of goods exports from the UK, and the goods imported from the EU have been worth more than imports from the rest of the world combined in recent years. Motor vehicles and parts is the largest product group by value of exports. The next-largest product group exported to the EU is chemicals and chemical products. Financial services contributed the most to services exported to the EU. The UK has a surplus in services (i.e. the value of its service exports is greater than the value of its service imports over a year) but a deficit in goods (i.e. value of its goods exports is less than the value of its goods imports over a year).

Trade relationships are usually stronger with countries with large economies. China and the US are large economies and are important UK trading partners, despite their distance from the UK. However, distance is important. The value of the UK's trading relationship with Ireland is higher than the value of UK trade with Italy or Spain. Ireland is the UK's neighbour, even though the total size of its economy is much smaller than Italy's or Spain's.

13.1 QUICK CHECK

For each of the following statements, say whether it is true or false.

a. Comparative advantage occurs when a country has a lower opportunity cost in the production of an item.

b. Free trade occurs when there are no barriers to trade.

c. According to comparative advantage if the opportunity cost of 1A is 2B in country X and 3B in country Y then country X has a comparative advantage.

d. Free trade can be mutually beneficial.

READ MORE

Alan Rugman's work suggests that most trade by multinationals is within certain trading areas, such as Europe or America, rather than between these trading zones. You can read more about International business strategy in

Rugman, A., and Nguyen, Q. (2013), 'International Business Theory for International Economists'. In Beugelsdijk, S., Brakman, S., Van Ees, H., and Garretsen, H. (eds.), *Firms in the International Economy: Firm Heterogeneity Meets International Business*, Boston, MA: MIT Press, pp. 23–54.

Rugman, A., Verbeke, A., and Nguyen, Q. (2011), 'Fifty Years of International Business Theory and Beyond', *Management International Review* Vol. 51, No. 6, pp. 755–86.

The exchange rate and your business

The price of a country's currency in terms of other currency (i.e. the exchange rate) often adds to the complexity of trading abroad compared to trading locally. Changes in the exchange rate change the purchasing power of your currency abroad and the price of your products in foreign currency. Changes in the exchange rate can happen frequently and are out the control of the business. They can affect costs and demand and so can have a big impact on competitiveness and profitability.

If the pound increases in value this means that it costs more in other currencies. For example, imagine that the exchange rate changes from £1:$1.20 to £1:$1.50. This means that buyers in the US would have to pay more dollars to buy the same number of pounds. All other things being equal, this will reduce the quantity of UK exports to the US (see Table 13.2); the extent of the fall would depend on how much the currency increased in value and how sensitive demand in the US was to changes in the price of UK products.

However, the stronger pound means that £1 buys $1.50, not $1, so for UK businesses it is cheaper to buy items in the US. This means the quantity of imports from the US is likely to increase. This leads to cheaper US products competing in UK markets and cheaper US components to be used in UK production.

13.2 DOING THE BUSINESS MATHS

Complete the table.

Change in demand and supply of the currency	Possible cause of change	Impact on the exchange rate (increase or decrease)
Increase in demand		
Decrease in demand		
Increase in supply		
Decrease in supply		

Table 13.2 The effects of changes in the value of the currency on imports and exports

	Impact on exports	Impact on imports
Increase in the value of the pound	Makes UK exports more expensive in terms of foreign currency; other things being equal, exports decrease	Makes foreign products cheaper in pounds; other things being equal, imports increase
Decrease in the value of the pound	Makes UK exports cheaper in terms of foreign currency; other things being equal, exports increase	Makes foreign products more expensive in pounds; other things being equal, imports decrease

Meanwhile a weaker pound means it has depreciated in value; for example, its value may decrease from £1:$1.20 to £1:$1. This means that, other things being equal, exports to the US would be cheaper in dollars and exports would increase. However, when UK businesses buy from abroad the pound buys fewer dollars and so more pounds would have to be spent to buy the same value of products. Imports become more expensive in pounds and imports are likely to fall. The lower pound also means that foreign goods increase in price in pounds; this makes imports less competitive against domestic products.

There are, of course, many currencies and thus many different exchange rates, such as the pound to the dollar (US), the yen (Japan), the euro (Eurozone member countries), and the krone (Denmark). The value of the pound against these currencies will be constantly changing (sometimes quite suddenly) and may change in different directions against different currencies.

MANAGEMENT TASK

You think the value of the pound will increase against the dollar, which could affect your exports to the US. Should you keep the price of your products the same in dollars?

ANALYSING THE DATA

Country	Currency units per $1	Currency units per $1, previous year
China	6.60	6.81
Japan	110	112
Russia	62.9	59
Venezuela	95,850	10.2

Data as at June 27th 2018

Source: www.economist.com/economic-and-financial-indicators/2018/06/28/trade-exchange-rates-budget-balances-and-interest-rates

Questions

1. Explain the currency changes shown in the table.
2. Discuss the significance of these changes for businesses.

KEY CONCEPT

If the pound **appreciates** in value it is 'stronger': for example, if its value rises from £1:$1.20 to £1:$1.50. If the pound **depreciates** it is 'weaker' and loses value.

KEY CONCEPT

An **exchange rate** is the price of one currency in terms of another.

ANALYSING THE BUSINESS DATA

Figure 13.2 The value of the pound (GBP) against the dollar (USD)

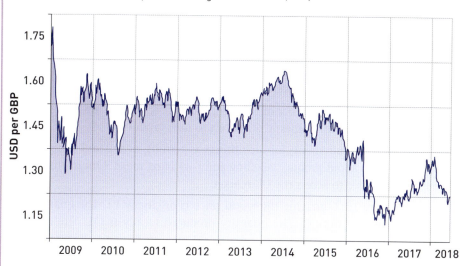

Questions

The chart in Figure 13.2 shows how the value of the pound has changed against the US dollar.

1. Explain, using supply and demand analysis, the possible causes of these changes.

2. Explain how these changes might have affected the costs and demand of a UK business.

3. What is the value of one pound against the US dollar now? What changes in currency supply and demand conditions are having an impact on the value of the pound at the moment? What is causing these changes?

13.2 QUICK CHECK

For each of the following statements, say whether it is true or false.

a. If the value of an exchange rate changes from £1:$1 to £1:$2, the pound has appreciated.

b. A strong pound is worth more in foreign currency than a weak pound.

c. If a country's exchange rate increases, this makes its goods more expensive in foreign currency, all other factors unchanged.

d. If a country's exchange rate increases, this makes its goods more expensive in domestic currency, all other factors unchanged.

BUSINESS CASE QUESTION: CAN YOU NOW ANSWER . . .

What problems might Five Guys face when expanding overseas?

What is protectionism?

While there may be considerable benefits to you as a business of having access to overseas markets this does not mean that trade will necessarily be straightforward. It is not unusual for governments to place barriers in the way of trade and introduce what are known as 'protectionist' measures. Protectionism may take the form of tariffs, quotas, or administrative requirements.

- Tariffs add a tax to imported products. This increases their price and makes them less competitive. For domestic producers, a tariff raises the world price and allows them to sell products which were previously uncompetitive with foreign imports.

- Quotas limit the total number of foreign products. This forces up the price and again allows inefficient domestic producers to now produce.

- Administrative requirements for such things as permits, health and safety regulations, and rules about product labelling and packaging make it more difficult for foreign businesses to access the UK market.

Looking at Figure 13.3, imagine the world price is originally P1. The quantity demanded in the world is Q2. The quantity produced locally is Q1. The quantity imported is Q2Q1. The tariff increases the world price to P2. This allows domestic producers who were too inefficent to compete at the previous price to now sell their output. Domestic producers Q1Q3 can now supply at the higher price and the domestic customers are paying more. Given the higher price, the quantity demanded is lower so customers buy less at a higher price. Total imports fall to Q4Q3 and the government collects tax on these.

Figure 13.3 The effect of a quota

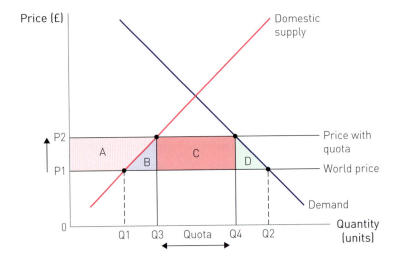

KEY CONCEPTS

A **tariff** is a tax on foreign products. A **quota** limits the number of foreign products that can be sold in a country.

13.3 QUICK CHECK

Figure 13.4 shows a tariff imposed on the world price of a good.

a. How much does domestic output increase?

b. How much does the quantity demanded increase?

c. What is the new level of imports?

d. How much revenue does the government collect?

Figure 13.4 The introduction of a tariff

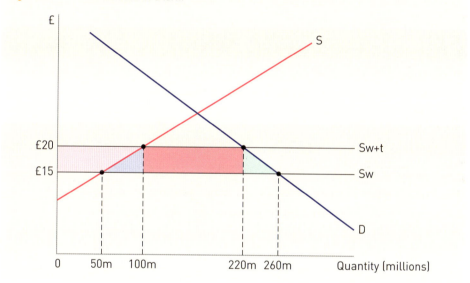

Why do some countries restrict trade?

These barriers limit the access that foreign products have to domestic markets. The aim of protectionism is to protect certain industries from foreign competition. If you are a manager of a business within a protected industry you may well welcome this support from your government because it gives you more monopoly power over the market. However, if you are a business or consumer in other sectors you may not—the reason being that protectionism tends to increase prices and reduce choice. It may also lead to retaliation, making it difficult for you to export in the future.

There are a number of typical reasons for a government to protect an industry.

- The government may wish to protect jobs in a particular industry which is suffering from overseas competition. This may help win votes. However, it is potentially subsidizing inefficient domestic producers and forcing consumers to buy products that are more expensive and of less good quality.

- The government may want to protect industries that are still developing, in order to help them become more established and gain from economies of scale; this is called the infant industry argument.

- The government may decided to protect selected industries that are regarded as essential to a country, e.g. a government may want to protect its farmers for the food supplies or its defence industries for security.

- There may be political reasons. A government may impose sanctions on foreign governments—they may place a complete ban (an embargo) on trade to try and reduce the country's income from exports in order to force political change. For example, sanctions have been used against Iran and North Korea in an effort to change their government's policy on nuclear weapons (see Business insight 13.5).

KEY CONCEPT

Protectionism occurs when a government introduces measures to support domestic businesses, and makes it difficult for overseas businesses to compete.

13.4 QUICK CHECK

For each of the following statements, say whether it is true or false.

a. A tariff limits the quantity of foreign products allowed into a country.

b. Protectionism tends to reduce the prices of goods domestically.

c. Protectionism puts pressure on domestic businesses to be efficient.

13.5 BUSINESS INSIGHT: SANCTIONS AGAINST NORTH KOREA

In 2017 North Korea continued with its nuclear development programme. In an attempt to stop this, several governments took political actions including trade sanctions against the North Korean government. Individuals and organizations linked to North Korea had their assets frozen and were prevented from trading. Businesses on the blacklist include banks, coal and minerals traders, and transport firms. The aim of these actions by governments such as Japan and South Korea was to impose peaceful pressure on the North Korean government.

Source: https://www.bbc.co.uk/news/world-asia-43601040

Question

To what extent do you think UK businesses would be affected by sanctions against North Korea?

What is the impact on a business facing protectionist measures?

If producers face protectionist measures that are introduced in its export markets this will reduce its exports sales, which could affect profits. Protectionism may force a business to look for new markets to export to, or that business may try to boost domestic sales. In some cases managers may look to find ways around the measures, such as relocating to operate within the other region. In 2108, for example, Harley Davidson responded to European Union tariffs on US motorbikes by announcing it would relocate some of its production to Europe because Europe was so important to sales.

On the supply side, protectionism will restrict the ability of a business to access resources. UK businesses have been able to benefit from the free flow of labour from within the European Union. After Brexit this flow will be restricted, which could create labour shortages in some sectors.

The impact of protectionism on your business will depend largely on three factors:

- what type of protectionism has been introduced;
- how long it is introduced for;
- what actions you take—e.g. do you use this an opportunity to improve competitiveness?

13.6 BUSINESS INSIGHT: BOMBARDIER

According to the BBC in an article published in December 2017, the US Department of Commerce had recently ruled against the aerospace business Bombardier in its dispute with rival US business Boeing. A tariff of 80 per cent was imposed on the import of Bombardier's C-Series jet to the US for allegedly selling the planes below the costs of production to win orders and market share. The US argued that Bombardier was being subsidized unfairly by the UK governments to keep the business and jobs going. The 80 per cent tariff is on top of an earlier tariff of 220 per cent which related to subsidies that Bombardier got from Canada and the UK.

There have been warnings that the import tariffs could threaten Bombardier jobs in Belfast. About 1,000 jobs are linked to the C-Series, the wings of which are made at a purpose-built £520m factory in the city.

The programme is not just important to Bombardier jobs in Belfast, but also to 15 smaller aerospace firms in Northern Ireland—and dozens more across the UK—which make components for the wings.

The US Department of Commerce rulings, which could more than triple the cost of a C-Series aircraft sold into the US, could jeopardize a major order placed last year from US airline Delta.

Source: BBC, www.bbc.co.uk/news/business-42434537

Question
Is the US justified in imposing these tariffs on Bombardier, do you think?

RESEARCH TASK

Research a recent trade dispute between countries. Analyse the reasons for this dispute and the possible consequences of it.

Why do countries join trade agreements?

To try and overcome protectionist measures, countries may join together in different forms of trade agreement. These usually allow for free trade (i.e. no protectionism) between member countries on some or all products. In some cases, this free trade will extend to the freedom to move money between countries and for employees to work easily in different countries. The agreement might also include common approaches to trade with non-member countries. One such agreement is in the European Union, which is an economic and political union of countries. This is a customs union where goods, services, money, and people can travel relatively freely throughout most of the continent. All EU citizens have the right and freedom to choose in which EU country they want to study, work, or retire. Every member country must treat EU citizens in exactly the same way as its own citizens for employment, social security, and tax purposes. Members of the European Union have the same protectionist measures against non-members.

KEY CONCEPT

A **customs union** occurs when there is freedom of movement of products between member countries, and all members have the same protectionist measures against non-members.

Brexit

In 2016 the UK voted to leave the European Union (EU). This was known as Brexit (British exit). There were various motivations for this, including a desire by some to have more control over UK borders and not have freedom of movement of EU citizens, a desire to have laws determined by the UK parliament and not European institutions, and the wish to allow the UK to make its own trade deals with non-EU members rather than have to follow EU rules on this.

As part of the European Union, the UK participated in free movement of goods, services, money, and people between member countries; however, it had to impose commonly agreed protectionist measures against non-member countries—it could not have its own trade agreements. For some UK businesses, this meant that the trading agreements were not necessarily as favourable as they might have been if the UK made its own trade deals.

Brexit would give the UK government the freedom to decide what, if any, protectionist measures it wanted in relation to any other country. It was also free to negotiate deals with any government it wished. Despite the decision to leave the EU, many British businesses were keen to keep access to European markets without barriers—they wanted 'frictionless trade'; but the European Union did not necessarily want to allow a country to leave and still benefit from free trade. The challenge facing the UK government was to negotiate a deal that kept as many of the benefits of free trade while having the freedom to create its own deals elsewhere.

The full effect of Brexit is not yet known at the time of writing, as the terms of leaving have not been finalized, but the decision to leave has caused uncertainty for business. Unsure of what post-Brexit would look like or the long-term consequences of it, UK managers have had to make plans for what could happen. Some businesses have looked to relocate to continental Europe to be based within the European Union, for example, while others have delayed investment decisions until it was clearer what would happen.

The uncertainty of Brexit has also affected the UK currency. Investors were reluctant to hold pounds because the future value for the currency was not predictable and because there was less investment into the UK. The lower value of the pound meant that buying products from abroad was more expensive in pounds, increasing costs.

READ MORE

You can find more data about UK trade on the website of the Office for National Statistics: www.ons.gov.uk/businessindustryandtrade/internationaltrade

13.7 BUSINESS INSIGHT: JLR AND THE SINGLE MARKET

In 2018 the precise terms of the UK's departure for the European Union were still being negotiated. In July of that year, as reported by the BBC, Jaguar Land Rover (JLR)

> warned that a 'bad' Brexit deal would threaten £80bn worth of investment plans for the UK and may force it to close factories. The UK's biggest carmaker, owned by India's Tata Motors, said its 'heart and soul is in the UK'. But without frictionless trade JLR said its UK investment plans would be in jeopardy.

The chief executive of JLR said that barriers to trade with the European Union would cost the business more than £1.2bn profit each year.

JLR had already announced that it would cut production at its plant in Halewood, Merseyside, where it builds three Range Rover models. It also said it would shift production of the Land Rover Discovery SUV to Slovakia, which could lead to job cuts.

A company spokesperson said that Jaguar Land Rover needed free and full access to the single market beyond the two year transition phase post-2019 in order to remain competitive.

JLR made more than 600,000 cars in 2017, 20 per cent of which were sold to mainland Europe. It spent £5.67bn with UK suppliers of parts during its previous financial year, and £5.37bn with businesses based in the EU.

Source: BBC, www.bbc.co.uk/news/business-44719656

Questions

1. Why do you think Jaguar Land Rover is reconsidering its investment decisions?
2. What do you think the impact of less investment by Jaguar Land Rover would be on UK-based businesses?

• •

SUMMARY

Trade creates many potential opportunities for UK businesses. It opens up new markets around the globe with far more potential buyers than exist in the UK. At the same time, it provides UK businesses access to more suppliers than are available locally. This should lead to lower-cost and better-quality inputs and more sales. However, this does require UK businesses to be globally competitive; if they are not, they will lose sales to global businesses that are abroad and in their domestic markets.

In terms of increasing demand, accessing markets will not always be easy due to differences in the political, economic, social, and technological environments; operating in one country or region can be very different from operating in another. Businesses will want to consider the degree of commitment to a region and how best to enter it.

In terms of supply, businesses will often have global supply chains to benefit from lower costs and better skills abroad. Managing global supply chains can be a complex operation, not least dealing with exchange rate changes.

Some governments will use protectionist measures to protect domestic industries. This generally increases prices and supports inefficient producers. It can be politically popular, at least in the short run, but often leads to retaliation and provokes opposition as it reduces choice and enables inefficient businesses to survive.

KEY LEARNING POINTS

- Trade creates opportunities for businesses both in sales and in sourcing materials.
- Trade is based on the principle of comparative advantage, where countries with lower opportunity costs in the production of a product can specialize in it and export it.
- International business brings with it particular challenges, such as exchange rate fluctuations.
- Governments sometimes protect domestic industries from foreign competition.
- Protectionism takes various forms, such as tariffs and quotas.
- Protectionism can help selected industries but may raise prices and reduce choice generally in an economy.

BUSINESS CASE EXTENSION QUESTIONS

1. Analyse the factors that influence the demand for burgers in a country.

2. Using five forces analysis, assess the competitive forces in the burger industry in a country of your choice.

3. Outline the terms and conditions of buying a Five Guys franchise. Analyse what else you would want to know before deciding whether to invest in a franchise or not.

4. Research the success of franchising as a business model.

QUICK QUESTIONS

1. What is meant by comparative advantages?
2. What are the potential benefits of free trade?
3. What is protectionism?
4. What is a tariff?
5. What is a quota?
6. Why might a government protect an industry?
7. What is meant by an exchange rate?
8. How might a low exchange rate affect a country's businesses?
9. What is meant by a global supply chain?
10. What is the European Union?

Answers to questions

CHAPTER 1

1.1 QUICK CHECK

a. true
b. true
c. false; owners do not need to be managers within the business

1.2 QUICK CHECK

a. micro
b. macro
c. micro
d. macro
e. macro
f. micro

1.3 QUICK CHECK

a. false; resources are limited
b. false; they do not reflect reality fully—they are simplifications—but they attempt to predict results
c. false; these are outputs
d. false; owned by shareholders

CHAPTER 2

2.1 QUICK CHECK

a. true
b. true
c. false; it needs to be specific
d. false; it needs to be specific
e. false; it needs to be time-specific

2.2 QUICK CHECK

a. false; costs may increase by more
b. not necessarily; maximum profit occurs when there is the biggest positive difference between revenue and costs
c. not necessarily; depends on the size of the initial investment
d. false; profits are maximized when marginal revenue equals marginal cost
e. false; maximum revenue occurs when marginal revenue is zero

2.3 QUICK CHECK

a. true
b. true
c. true
d. false; total revenue minus total costs

2.1 DOING THE BUSINESS MATHS

1. At which output is revenue maximized?
   50 units

2. At which output are costs the lowest?
   10 units

3. At which output is profit maximized?
   40 units

Output (units)	Total revenue (£)	Total costs (£)	Profit (£)
10	100	20	80
20	150	100	50
30	300	120	180
40	600	220	380
50	1,000	700	300

2.2 DOING THE BUSINESS MATHS

What is the overall effect on profits of allocating over 2 or 5 years?
No effect; in both cases the total cost over the period is £40,000

What is the impact on profits in (a) Year 1 and (b) Year 5 of the two different methods?
Life span of two years: in year 1 cost is £20,000; in year 5 cost is £0.
Life span of 5 years: in year 1 cost is £8,000; in Year 5 cost is £8,000.

So profits would be £12,000 higher in year 1 and £8,000 lower in year 5 if it is assumed that the life span is 5 and not 2 years.

Year	Annual cost (£000) Expected life span of 2 years	Annual cost (£000) Expected life span of 5 years
1	20,000	8,000
2	20,000	8,000
3	0	8,000
4	0	8,000
5	0	8,000

2.3 DOING THE BUSINESS MATHS

How many units should be produced? Why? Three, as this maximizes profit.

Units	Marginal revenue (£)	Marginal cost (£)	Produce or not?	Impact on profits
1	10	5	Yes	Profits increase
2	10	7	Yes	Profits increase
3	10	10	Yes	Profits stay same
4	10	13	No	Profits decrease
5	10	17	No	Profits decrease

CHAPTER 3

3.1 QUICK CHECK

a. false; quantity demanded will change but by proportionally less than the change in price
b. false; a price rise increases revenue if demand is price inelastic
c. true

3.2 QUICK CHECK

a. true
b. more elastic: it means the per cent change in quantity demanded is 3 times the per cent change in price, rather than 0.3 times
c. true
d. false; demand is perfectly price inelastic

3.1 **DOING THE BUSINESS MATHS**

Change in quantity demanded (units)	Change in price (£)	% change in quantity demanded	% change in price	Price elasticity of demand
50 to 40	£2.00 to £2.20	−20%	10%	−2
50 to 75	£2.00 to £1.80	50%	−10%	−5
200 to 195	£20.00 to £21.00	−2.5%	5%	−0.5
100 to 100	£50.00 to £60.00	0%	20%	0

3.2 **DOING THE BUSINESS MATHS**

Complete the following table

Change in quantity demanded (units)	Change in income (£000)	% change in quantity demanded	% change in income	Income elasticity	Normal or inferior? Elastic or inelastic?
20 to 30	10 to 11	50%	10%	+5	Normal; elastic
50 to 45	40 to 44	−10%	10%	−1	Unitary; inferior
3 to 2	100 to 98	−33.3%	−2%	16.6	Normal; elastic
80 to 60	50 to 60	−25%	20%	−1.25	Inferior; elastic

4.4 QUICK CHECK

a. true

b. false; extra total costs

c. true; marginal cost pulls up average cost

d. true

4.5 QUICK CHECK

a. false; normal profit

b. false; abnormal profit

c. true

4.6 QUICK CHECK

a. false; when unit costs fall

b. true

c. true

d. true

4.1 DOING THE BUSINESS MATHS

Questions

1. A business buys 200 units of materials at £5 each on credit. It sells 40 of them for £9 each in cash. The labour cost per unit is £2 paid in cash.

   As a result of these transactions what is:

   a. the level of profits? = revenue £360 – costs £280 = £80

   b. the cash position of the business? = inflow – outflow = £360 – £80 = £280

   c. the stock level of the business? = 160 units

2. A business buys 200 units of materials at £5 each in cash. It sells 40 of them for £9 each on credit. The labour cost per unit is £2 paid in cash.

   As a result of these transactions what is:

   a. the level of profits? = revenue – costs = £360 – £280 = £80

   b. the cash position of the business? = inflow – outflow = £0 – (£1,000 + £80) = –£1,080

   c. the stock level of the business? = 160 units

4.2 DOING THE BUSINESS MATHS

	Business A (£m)	Business B (£m)	Business C (£m)
Revenue	100	100	100
Costs	60	60	60
Profit (to an accountant)	40	40	40
Estimated opportunity cost	30	70	40
Profit (to an economist)	10	–30	0

4.3 DOING THE BUSINESS MATHS

1. What is the level of fixed costs when output is 300 units? £100

2. What is the level of variable costs when output is 500 units? £1,000

4.4 DOING THE BUSINESS MATHS

Output (units)	Revenue (£)	Variable costs (£)	Contribution (£)	Fixed costs (£)	Profit/loss (£)
10,000	200,000	150,000	50,000	150,000	−100,000
20,000	400,000	300,000	100,000	150,000	−50,000
30,000	600,000	450,000	150,000	150,000	0
40,000	800,000	600,000	200,000	150,000	50,000
50,000	1,000,000	750,000	250,000	150,000	100,000

4.5 DOING THE BUSINESS MATHS

Units (000)	Price (£)	Variable cost per unit (£)	Contribution (£)	Fixed costs (£)	Profit or loss (£)
10	10	6	40,000	120,000	−80,000
20	10	6	80,000	120,000	−40,000
30	10	6	120,000	120,000	0
40	10	6	160,000	120,000	40,000
50	10	6	200,000	120,000	80,000

4.6 DOING THE BUSINESS MATHS

Imagine the selling price is now £15, the variable cost per unit is still £8, and fixed costs are still £20,000. What is the break-even output now that the price is higher?

Break-even = 20,000 ÷ (15 − 8) = 2857.1 = 2,858 units

Imagine the selling price remains at £15, the variable cost per unit is reduced to £5, and fixed costs are still £20,000. What is the break-even output now that the variable cost per unit is lower?

Break-even = 20,000 ÷ (15 − 5) = 2,000 units

Lower variable cost per unit means a higher contribution per unit, which means a lower break-even level of output.

4.7 DOING THE BUSINESS MATHS

Number of employees	Wage bill if each employee paid £300 a week	Output per week	Labour productivity per week	Labour cost per unit (£)
20	£6,000	20,000	1,000	£0.30
20	£6,000	40,000	2,000	£0.15
20	£6,000	80,000	4,000	£0.75
20	£6,000	120,000	6,000	£0.05

4.8 DOING THE BUSINESS MATHS

Number of employees	Output = total product (units)	Marginal product	Average product
2	20	n/a	10
3	40	20	13.3
4	90	50	22.5
5	120	30	24
6	140	20	23.3
7	150	10	21.4

4.9 DOING THE BUSINESS MATHS

Output (units)	Total cost (£)	Average cost (£) = total cost ÷ output	Marginal cost	Relationship between marginal cost and average cost (e.g. higher or lower and impact on average)
1	10	10	n/a	
2	18	9	8	Marginal lower than previous average, so brings it down
3	27	9	9	Marginal same as previous average, so average stays the same
4	36	9	9	Marginal same as previous average, so average stays the same
5	50	10	14	Marginal above previous average, so average increases
6	66	11	16	Marginal above previous average, so average increases
7	84	12	18	Marginal above previous average, so average increases

4.10 DOING THE BUSINESS MATHS

Units	Total cost (£)	Average cost per unit (£)
100	200,000	2,000
200	220,000	1,100
300	250,000	833.3
400	280,000	700
500	300,000	600
600	350,000	583.3
700	470,000	671.4
800	600,000	750

CHAPTER 5

5.1 QUICK CHECK

a. false; price change causes a movement along a demand curve
b. true
c. false; there is excess supply
d. true
e. true
f. false; price will tend to rise

5.2 QUICK CHECK

a. decrease in supply
b. increase in demand
c. decrease in demand
d. increase in supply

5.3 QUICK CHECK

a. false; increases both equilibrium price and quantity
b. false; reduces both equilibrium price and quantity
c. false; decreases equilibrium price and increases quantity
d. false; increases both equilibrium price and quantity

5.1 DOING THE BUSINESS MATHS

Price (£)	Quantity supplied (units)	Quantity demanded (units)	Market outcome (units)	Impact on price
10	320	50	270 excess supply	fall
9	250	80	180 excess supply	fall
8	180	120	60 excess supply	fall
7	150	150	equilibrium	no change
6	90	200	110 excess demand	increase
5	20	250	230 excess demand	increase
4	15	300	285 excess demand	increase

CHAPTER 6

6.1 QUICK CHECK

a. true
b. true
c. true

6.2 QUICK CHECK

a. true
b. false; it will lead to a movement along the supply of labour
c. true
d. true

6.3 QUICK CHECK

a. true
b. false; excess demand
c. true
d. true

6.4 QUICK CHECK

a. false; it may be that they have different jobs; discrimination would occur if the pay was different for men and women doing the same job
b. true; if more is produced then, all other things unchanged, the value of employees' output increases and therefore so does the demand for labour
c. false; the wage will be above equilibrium and therefore the quantity supplied will be greater than the quantity demanded; there will be excess supply

d. true; the low wage reduces the quantity supplied and increases the quantity demanded, leading to excess demand for labour

6.1 DOING THE BUSINESS MATHS

Number of employees	Extra cost of employing employee (£)	Value of marginal product (£)	Employ or not? (Yes or no)
1	10	90	Yes
2	20	60	Yes
3	30	30	Yes
4	50	10	No
5	70	5	No

6.2 DOING THE BUSINESS MATHS

In terms of shifts in supply of and demand for labour what might cause:

a) an increase in the equilibrium wage and quantity of labour? An increase in demand for labour

b) an increase in the equilibrium wage and a decrease in the quantity of labour? A decrease in supply of labour

c) a decrease in the equilibrium wage and quantity of labour? A fall in demand for labour

d) a decrease in the equilibrium wage and an increase in the quantity of labour? An increase in supply of labour

6.3 DOING THE BUSINESS MATHS

Number of employees	Wage bill if each employee paid £600 a week	Output per week (units)	Labour productivity per week	Labour cost per unit (£)
50	30,000	50,000	1,000	0.6
50	30,000	60,000	1,200	0.5
50	30,000	100,000	2,000	0.3
50	30,000	200,000	4,000	0.15

CHAPTER 7

7.1 QUICK CHECK

a. true
b. false; non-diminishable and non-excludable
c. false; would be under-provided
d. true

7.2 QUICK CHECK

a. false; it will want to subsidize those products
b. true
c. false; used to stabilize price
d. false; this is privatization

7.1 DOING THE BUSINESS MATHS

Imagine the government is operating a buffer stock system to keep the price of a product at £10.

Market price (£)	Quantity demanded (units)	Quantity supplied (units)	Excess demand or supply (units)	Government action: buy or sell?
8	200	40	Excess demand 160	Sell
9	150	70	Excess demand 80	Sell
10	100	100	Equilibrium	Do nothing
11	80	120	Excess supply 40	Buy
12	50	150	Excess supply 100	Buy

7.2 DOING THE BUSINESS MATHS

1. What would be the equilibrium output in a free market? 30 units

2. What about if businesses took full account of the external costs of their actions? 20 units

Output	Marginal benefit (£)	Private marginal costs (£)	Social marginal costs (£)
10	50	5	15
20	40	25	40
30	30	30	50
40	20	40	70
50	10	50	85

CHAPTER 8

8.1 QUICK CHECK

a. false; a business could gain a bigger share of a smaller market and actually be selling less than before
b. false; it means the market share of the largest 5 firms combined is 20%
c. true
d. false; it depends on whether your sales are increasing and, if so, how fast

8.2 QUICK CHECK

a. true
b. false; similar products
c. false; easy entry and exit
d. true

8.3 QUICK CHECK

a. true
b. true
c. false; strong brand loyalty would be a barrier

8.4 QUICK CHECK

a. false; single seller
b. false; downward sloping
c. true
d. true

8.5 QUICK CHECK

a. false; relatively few firms dominate
b. false; the five firm concentration ratio will be high as a few firms dominate the industry
c. true
d. true

8.6 QUICK CHECK

a. true
b. false; price maker
c. true
d. true

8.7 QUICK CHECK

a. true

b. true

c. false; marginal revenues

d. true

8.1 DOING THE BUSINESS MATHS

a. Calculating market growth

Original market size (£)	New market size (£)	Market growth (%)
10,000	12,000	20%
60,000	62,000	3.3%
500,000	500,000	0%
500,000	490,000	−2%

b. Calculating market share

Sales of one business (£)	Total market size (£)	Market share (%)
10,000	120,000	8.33%
60,000	620,000	9.68%

8.2 DOING THE BUSINESS MATHS

Price (£)	Quantity (units)	Total revenue (£)	Marginal revenue (£)	Marginal cost (£)	Would a profit maximizer produce this unit or not?
20	4	80	n/a	n/a	n/a
19	5	95	15	3	Yes
17	6	102	7	7	Yes
15	7	105	3	10	No
13	8	104	−1	12	No
11	9	99	−5	17	No
9	10	90	−9	20	No

CHAPTER 9

9.1 QUICK CHECK

a. false; long term

b. false; high risk

c. true

d. false; senior managers

9.2 QUICK CHECK

a. true

b. true

c. false; existing products in new markets

d. false; existing products in existing markets

9.3 QUICK CHECK

a. true
b. false
c. true
d. false
e. true

9.4 QUICK CHECK

a. true
b. false
c. true

d. true
e. true
f. false

9.5 QUICK CHECK

a. true
b. false; number of votes is usually related to number of shares owned
c. false; elected by shareholders
d. false; managers run the business; shareholders own the business

9.1 DOING THE BUSINESS MATHS

Item	Index (where industry average is 100)	Strength or weakness? Why?
Labour productivity	80	Weakness; less productive
Absenteeism	120	Weakness; higher absenteeism
Gearing	300	Weakness; high borrowing so higher risk
Unit costs	130	Weakness; higher unit costs
Research and development spending	65	Weakness, assuming firm wants to be innovative, as there is less investment in this area
% of repeat sales	110	Strength; higher repeat business

CHAPTER 10

10.1 QUICK CHECK

a. true
b. true
c. false; at different stages of the production process
d. true

10.2 QUICK CHECK

a. true
b. true
c. true
d. true

10.1 DOING THE BUSINESS MATHS

At which level of output does the business stop benefiting from internal economies of scale? 5,000 units

Output (units)	Total cost (£)	Unit cost (£) = total cost ÷ output
2,000	30,000	15
3,000	42,000	14
4,000	48,000	12
5,000	50,000	10
6,000	60,000	10
7,000	77,000	11

CHAPTER 11

11.1 QUICK CHECK

a. false; demand likely to increase, albeit not in proportion with the income increase

b. true

c. false; measures income, not number of goods

d. false; demand for luxury goods likely to increase more than proportionately with income

11.2 QUICK CHECK

a. false; it measures the cost of living

b. false; it means that prices are growing more slowly

c. true

d. true

11.3 QUICK CHECK

a. false; inflation is likely to occur if demand is very low.

b. true

c. false; it measures changes in prices

d. true

11.4 QUICK CHECK

a. true

b. true

c. false; it is measured by loans plus issues share capital plus retained profit

d. true

11.5 QUICK CHECK

a. true

b. true

c. false; it is likely to increase unemployment as there is less demand

d. true

11.6 QUICK CHECK

a. false; it measures the value of one currency in terms of another

b. false; it measures the value of one currency in terms of another

c. true

d. false; it measures the value of one currency in terms of another

11.7 QUICK CHECK

a. false; it has increased

b. true

c. true

d. false; increases price in foreign currencies

11.1 DOING THE BUSINESS MATHS

1. How much has GDP changed between 2016 and 2017? 20%

2. How much has GDP changed between 2016 and 2018? −10%

3. How much has GDP changed between 2016 and 2019? 30%

4. How much has GDP changed between 2018 and 2019? $(40 \div 90) \times 100 = 44.4\%$

11.2 DOING THE BUSINESS MATHS

	Country A	Country B	Country C
Year 1 GDP (£bn)	50	500	5,000
Year 2 GDP (£bn)	60	550	5,250
Absolute change (£bn)	10	50	250
% change	20%	10%	5%

11.3 DOING THE BUSINESS MATHS

Weighted index = 11,040 ÷ 100 = 110.4

Item	Weighting out of 100	Index last year	Index this year	Weighted index
A	20	100	106	2,120
B	30	100	107	3,210
C	10	100	101	1,010
D	25	100	110	2,750
E	15	100	130	1,950
	Total = 100			11,040

11.4 DOING THE BUSINESS MATHS

1. What is happening to inflation between years 1 and 2? Increasing by 3%

2. What is happening to prices between years 2 and 3? Increasing by 1%

3. What is happening to prices between years 3 and 4? Falling by 2%

11.6 DOING THE BUSINESS MATHS

	Business A	Business B	Business C
Long-term loans	£10m	£20m	£20m
Capital employed	£50m	£200m	£25m
Gearing %	20%	10%	80%

11.5 DOING THE BUSINESS MATHS

	Year 1	Year 2	Year 3
Change in income	5%	5%	5%
Change in prices	2%	5%	7%
Effect: does real income increase or decrease?	Increase	No change	Decrease

11.7 DOING THE BUSINESS MATHS

Gearing is falling. To decide whether it is high or low we could consider interest rates and profits.

Year	Long-term liabilities (£m)	Capital employed (£m)	Gearing = (long-term liabilities ÷ capital employed) × 100
2014	11,039	17,862	62%
2015	12,269	20,040	61%
2016	13,719	22,249	62%
2017	11,594	21,907	53%

11.8 DOING THE BUSINESS MATHS

	Time period 1	Time period 2	Time period 3
Exchange rate	£1 = $1	£1 = $2	£1 = $0.90
Price of £100 UK item in US$	$100.00	$200.00	$90.00
Comment		The pound is worth more in dollars than last period. All other things being equal, this makes UK goods more expensive in dollars. UK exports are likely to suffer.	The pound is worth less in dollars than in period 1. All other things being equal, this makes UK goods less expensive in dollars. UK exports are likely to increase.
Price of US $45 good when bought in pounds	£45.00	£22.50	£50.00
Comment		The pound is worth more in dollars than last period. All other things being equal, this makes US goods cheaper in pounds, i.e. more competitive. UK imports from the US are likely to increase, and UK costs from US products are lower.	The pound is worth less in dollars than in period 1. All other things being equal, this makes US goods more expensive in pounds, i.e. less competitive. UK imports cost more.

CHAPTER 12

12.1 QUICK CHECK

a. true
b. false; it measures the extra spending out of an extra pound
c. true

12.2 QUICK CHECK

a. false; this is monetary policy
b. true
c. true
d. true

12.3 QUICK CHECK

a. false; this is a surplus
b. true
c. true; the debt is the total of all the deficits
d. false; will involve cutbacks

12.1 DOING THE BUSINESS MATHS

Income	Tax rate for income in this income band
<£20,000	0%
£20,000 to <£40,000	20%
£40,000 to <£60,000	40%
£60,000+	60%

Question
• How much tax would someone earning £80,000 pay?

Income	Tax rate	Tax payable (£)
<£20,000	0%	0
£20,000 to <£40,000	20%	£4,000
£40,000 to <£60,000	40%	£8,000
£60,000 to £80,000	60%	£12,000
Total tax payable		£24,000

12.2 DOING THE BUSINESS MATHS

Year	Budget position	Debt position
1	n/a	£100bn
2	Deficit £10bn	£110bn
3	Deficit £20bn	£130bn
4	Deficit £5bn	£135bn
5	Surplus £10bn	£125bn

12.3 DOING THE BUSINESS MATHS

Price of bond (£)	Annual coupon (£)	Return (%)
100	10	10%
120	10	8.3%
200	10	5%
80	10	12.5%
50	10	20%

12.4 DOING THE BUSINESS MATHS

Figure 12.8 An increase in the supply of a currency

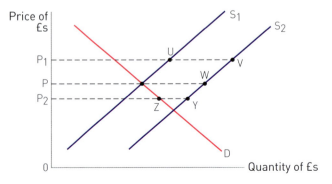

Imagine:
- that the supply of a currency has increased from S1 to S2;
- that the government wants to keep the value of the currency at P.

Which of the following is the action needed by the government to keep the exchange rate at this value?

a.   Sell UV of its currency – No

b.   Buy XW of its currency – Yes

c.   Sell ZY of its currency – No

d.   Buy UX of its currency – No

CHAPTER 13

13.1 QUICK CHECK

a.   true

b.   true

c.   true

d.   true

13.2 QUICK CHECK

a.   true

b.   true

c.   true

d.   false; in itself, an exchange rate increase does not affect price in domestic currency

13.3 QUICK CHECK

a.   domestic output increases from 50m to 100m

b.   quantity demanded decreases from 260m to 220m

c.   new level of imports = 220 – 100 = 120m

d.   revenue the government collects on each unit = £5; number of units = 120m; government revenue = £5 × 120m = £600m

13.4 QUICK CHECK

a.   true

b.   false; with less coming in, higher prices are paid for domestic products

c.   false; they can be inefficient because they are protected

13.5 QUICK CHECK

a.   false; it is a tax, not a limit on the quantity

b.   false; likely to increase the price

c.   false; it allows inefficient businesses to survive

13.1 DOING THE BUSINESS MATHS

	Good A	Good B
Country 1	3	6
Country 2	4	6

Questions

1.   Which country has a comparative advantage in the production of good A? Which has a comparative advantage in the production of good B?

For Country 1:

the opportunity cost of 1A is 6 ÷ 3 = 2B;

the opportunity cost of 1B is 3 ÷ 6 = 0.5A.

For Country 2:

the opportunity cost of 1A is 6 ÷ 4 = 1.5B;

the opportunity cost of 1B is 4 ÷ 6 = 0.66A.

Country 2 has the comparative advantage in production of A, and Country 1 has the comparative advantage in production of B.

2.   What are the possible terms of trade which would be beneficial for both countries?

They could trade at 1.5B < 1A < 2B.

13.2 DOING THE BUSINESS MATHS

Change in demand and supply of the currency	Possible cause of change	Impact on the exchange rate (increase or decrease)
Increase in demand	More demand from abroad for goods, e.g. foreign incomes rising	Increase
Decrease in demand	Foreign incomes falling	Decrease
Increase in supply	Increased domestic demand for foreign goods, e.g. increased domestic income	Decrease
Decrease in supply	Falling domestic income	Increase

Data sources

Listed below are some key sources for economic data which you might find valuable in your further studies.

Adam Smith Institute

www.adamsmith.org

The Adam Smith Institute is an independent, non-profit think tank. Its aims include promoting neoliberal and free market ideas through research, publishing, media commentary, and educational programmes.

Bank of England

www.bankofengland.co.uk

The role of the Bank of England is to promote the good of the people of the United Kingdom by maintaining monetary and financial stability.

Reports include the Inflation Report.

CIA World Factbook

www.cia.gov/library/publications/the-world-factbook/

The World Factbook provides information on the history, people, government, economy, energy, geography, communications, transportation, military, and transnational issues for 267 world entities.

Reports include overviews of each country's economy.

Confederation of British Industry (CBI)

www.cbi.org.uk

The CBI represents 190,000 businesses of all sizes and sectors. Together these businesses employ nearly 7 million people, about one-third of the private-sector-employed workforce. The CBI aims to influence government policy, share information, and help businesses to network.

Freakonomics

freakonomics.com

A collection of interviews and insights into a wide range of current issues.

Gapminder

www.gapminder.org/answers/how-did-babies-per-woman-change-in-the-world/

The website created by Professor Hans Rosling.

Gapminder is an independent Swedish foundation. It produces free resources aimed at making the world understandable based on reliable statistics and promoting a fact-based worldview. Gapminder collaborates with universities, the UN, public agencies, and non-governmental organizations.

Full of fascinating data and presentations.

HM Treasury

www.gov.uk/government/organisations/hm-treasury/about

HM Treasury is the government's economic and finance ministry, maintaining control over public spending, setting the direction of the UK's economic policy, and working to achieve strong and sustainable economic growth.

Institute for Fiscal Studies

www.ifs.org.uk

The goal of the Institute for Fiscal Studies is to promote effective economic and social policies by better understanding how policies affect individuals, families, businesses, and the government's finances.

International Monetary Fund

www.imf.org

The International Monetary Fund is an organization of 189 countries working to foster global monetary cooperation, secure financial stability, facilitate international trade, promote high employment and sustainable economic growth, and reduce poverty around the world.

Its primary purpose is to ensure the stability of the international monetary system—the system of exchange rates and international payments that enables countries (and their citizens) to transact with each other. The Fund's mandate was updated in 2012 to include all macro-economic and financial sector issues that bear on global stability.

Tim Harford

www.ft.com/tim-harford

Tim Harford is economics leader writer for the *Financial Times* and writes the 'Undercover Economist' columns published on Saturdays.

Harford's book, *The Undercover Economist*, is a *Business Week* bestseller and a *Sunday Times* bestseller, and was number one on Amazon.co.uk.

John Kay

www.ft.com/john-kay

John Kay has been writing a column on economics and business since 1995. He is currently a visiting professor at the London School of Economics. He also had a career in the policy world which established the Institute for Fiscal Studies as

one of the most respected think tanks, and a business career. His columns are well worth reading.

Paul Krugman

You can follow the writings of economist Paul Krugman at www.nytimes.com/2018/06/29/opinion/friday-night-music-chvrches-self-indulgent-not-a-column.html.

Office for National Statistics

www.ons.gov.uk

The UK's largest independent producer of official statistics and the national statistical institute of the UK.

Office for Budget Responsibility

www.obr.uk

The Office for Budget Responsibility was created in 2010 to provide independent and authoritative analysis of the UK's public finances. It is one of a growing number of official independent fiscal watchdogs around the world.

It produces the Economic and Fiscal Outlook.

The Organisation for Economic Co-operation and Development

www.oecd.org/

The mission of the Organisation for Economic Co-operation and Development (OECD) is to promote policies that will improve the economic and social well-being of people around the world. The OECD provides a forum in which governments can work together to share experiences and seek solutions to common problems. It works with governments to understand what drives economic, social, and environmental change. It measures productivity and global flows of trade and investment.

The Society of Professional Economists (SPE)

spe.org.uk

The Society of Professional Economists (SPE) is an organization serving business economists in the UK.

The Society exists to help all those who use economics in a business environment—whether in industry, commerce, finance, consultancy, or public service. Its activities aim to advance the use of economic analysis as a tool to support business decision-making and to enhance the standing of the professional economist working outside academia. It provides a forum for its members to discuss and debate economic issues and helps them keep in touch with practical and theoretical developments within the discipline.

Trading Economics

tradingeconomics.com

Trading Economics provides its users with accurate information for 196 countries including historical data for more than 20 million economic indicators, exchange rates, stock market indexes, government bond yields, and commodity prices.

World Bank

data.worldbank.org

The World Bank's website provides access to a huge amount of global development data which you can sort and filter as you wish.

Index